Unequal Democracies

While economic inequality has risen in every affluent democracy in North America and Western Europe, the last three decades have also been characterized by falling or stagnating levels of state-led economic redistribution. Why have democratically accountable governments not done more to distribute top-income shares to citizens with low and middle incomes? *Unequal Democracies* offers answers to this question, bringing together contributions that focus on voters and their demands for redistribution with contributions on elites and unequal representation that is biased against less-affluent citizens. While large and growing bodies of research have developed around each of these perspectives, this volume brings them into rare dialogue. The chapters also incorporate analyses that center exclusively on the United States and those that examine a broader set of advanced democracies to explore the uniqueness of the American case and its contribution to comparative perspectives. This book is also available as Open Access on Cambridge Core.

Noam Lupu is Associate Professor of Political Science at Vanderbilt University. He is the author of *Party Brands in Crisis* (2016) and the coeditor of *Campaigns and Voters in Developing Democracies* (2019). He has received numerous awards for his publications and three Emerging Scholar awards from the American Political Science Association.

Jonas Pontusson is a research-active Emeritus Professor at the University of Geneva. Before moving to Geneva in 2010, he taught at Cornell University and Princeton University. He has published extensively in the domains of comparative political economy and comparative welfare states, focusing on labor markets, trade unions, partisan politics, and income inequality and redistribution. From 2017 to 2023, he directed a research program funded by the European Research Council on political inequality and the politics of inequality in advanced industrial states.

SSRC Anxieties of Democracy

Editors

John A. Ferejohn, *New York University*
Ira Katznelson, *Columbia University*
Deborah J. Yashar, *Princeton University*

With liberal democracies afflicted by doubt and disquiet, this series probes sources of current apprehensions and explores how such regimes might thrive. What array of pressures most stresses democratic ideas and institutions? Which responses might strengthen these regimes and help them flourish?

Embedded in the Social Science Research Council's program on "Anxieties of Democracy program," the series focuses on how representative institutions – including elections, legislatures, political parties, the press and mass media, interest groups, social movements, and policy organizations – orient participation, learning, and accountability.

The volumes in the series further ask how particular policy challenges shape the character of democratic institutions and collective actors, and affect their capacity to address large problems in the public interest. These challenges include, but are not limited to: (1) designing democratic institutions to perform successfully under conditions of social and political polarization; (2) managing and orienting contemporary capitalism and alleviating hierarchies of inequality; (3) addressing questions of membership, including population movements and differentiated citizenship; (4) choosing policies to balance national security and civil liberty; (5) exploring the effects of global climate on citizens and the human impact on the environment; (6) managing the development of media and information technologies to ensure they enhance, rather than degrade, robust pluralism and civil political engagement.

Other Books in the Series

Can America Govern Itself? Frances E. Lee and Nolan McCarty

Social Media and Democracy: The State of the Field, Prospects for Reform Nathaniel Persily and Joshua A. Tucker

The Disinformation Age: Politics, Technology, and Disruptive Communication in the United States W. Lance Bennett and Steven Livingston

Who Gets What? The New Politics of Insecurity Frances Rosenbluth and Margaret Weir

Contested Representation: Challenges, Shortcomings and Reforms Edited by Claudia Landwehr, Thomas Saalfield, and Armin Schäfer

When the People Rule: Popular Sovereignty in Theory and Practice Edited by Ewa Atanassow, Thomas Bartscherer and David A. Bateman

Sponsored by the Social Science Research Council

The Social Science Research Council (SSRC) is an independent, international, nonprofit organization driven by its mission to mobilize social science for the public good. Founded in 1923, the SSRC fosters innovative research, nurtures new generations of social scientists, deepens how inquiry is practiced within and across disciplines, and amplifies necessary knowledge on important public issues.

The SSRC is guided by the belief that justice, prosperity, and democracy all require better understanding of complex social, cultural, economic, and political processes. We work with practitioners, policymakers, and academic researchers in the social sciences, related professions, and the humanities and natural sciences. We build interdisciplinary and international networks, working with partners around the world to link research to practice and policy, strengthen individual and institutional capacities for learning, and enhance public access to information.

Unequal Democracies

Public Policy, Responsiveness, and Redistribution in an Era of Rising Economic Inequality

Edited by

NOAM LUPU
Vanderbilt University

JONAS PONTUSSON
University of Geneva

CAMBRIDGE
UNIVERSITY PRESS

CAMBRIDGE
UNIVERSITY PRESS

Shaftesbury Road, Cambridge CB2 8EA, United Kingdom

One Liberty Plaza, 20th Floor, New York, NY 10006, USA

477 Williamstown Road, Port Melbourne, VIC 3207, Australia

314–321, 3rd Floor, Plot 3, Splendor Forum, Jasola District Centre, New Delhi – 110025, India

103 Penang Road, #05–06/07, Visioncrest Commercial, Singapore 238467

Cambridge University Press is part of Cambridge University Press & Assessment, a department of the University of Cambridge.

We share the University's mission to contribute to society through the pursuit of education, learning and research at the highest international levels of excellence.

www.cambridge.org
Information on this title: www.cambridge.org/9781009428644

DOI: 10.1017/9781009428682

First published 2024

A catalogue record for this publication is available from the British Library

Library of Congress Cataloging-in-Publication Data
Names: Lupu, Noam, editor. | Pontusson, Jonas, editor.
Title: Unequal democracies : public policy, responsiveness, and redistribution in an era of rising economic inequality / edited by Noam Lupu, Jonas Pontusson.
Description: Cambridge, United Kingdom ; New York. NY : Cambridge University Press, 2024. | Series: SSRC anxieties of democracy | Includes bibliographical references and index.
Identifiers: LCCN 2023029220 (print) | LCCN 2023029221 (ebook) | ISBN 9781009428644 (hardback) | ISBN 9781009428682 (ebook)
Subjects: LCSH: Democracy – Economic aspects – United States. | Democracy – Economic aspects – Europe. | Income distribution – Political aspects – United States. | Income distribution – Political aspects – Europe. | Representative government and representation – United States. | Representative government and representation – Europe.
Classification: LCC JK271 .U5325 2024 (print) | LCC JK271 (ebook) | DDC 320.473–dc23/eng/20230907
LC record available at https://lccn.loc.gov/2023029220
LC ebook record available at https://lccn.loc.gov/2023029221

ISBN 978-1-009-42864-4 Hardback
ISBN 978-1-009-42863-7 Paperback

Additional resources for this publication at www.cambridge.org/9781009428644

Cambridge University Press & Assessment has no responsibility for the persistence or accuracy of URLs for external or third-party internet websites referred to in this publication and does not guarantee that any content on such websites is, or will remain, accurate or appropriate.

Contents

Additional resources for this publication at www.cambridge.org/9781009428644

Figures

Tables

Contributors

Macarena Ares is Assistant Professor in the Political Science Department of the University of Barcelona and part of the WelfarePriorities project at the University of Zurich. Her research focuses on social class politics, distributive conflict over welfare policies, and corruption voting.

Larry M. Bartels is University Distinguished Professor of Political Science and Law and May Werthan Shayne Chair of Public Policy and Social Science at Vanderbilt University. His books include *Unequal Democracy: The Political Economy of the New Gilded Age* (2nd ed.), *Democracy for Realists: Why Elections Do Not Produce Responsive Government* (with Christopher H. Achen), and *Democracy Erodes from the Top: Leaders, Citizens, and the Challenge of Populism in Europe*.

Michael Becher is Assistant Professor in the School of Global and Public Affairs at IE University in Madrid. His research on political economy and comparative politics focuses on issues related to accountability, (unequal) representation, and the design of political institutions. His work has been published in the *American Journal of Political Science*, the *American Political Science Review*, and the *Journal of Politics*, among others.

Nicholas Carnes is Professor of Public Policy and Sociology in the Sanford School of Public Policy at Duke University. He is the author of *White-Collar Government* and *The Cash Ceiling*.

Charlotte Cavaillé is Assistant Professor at the Ford School of Public Policy at the University of Michigan. She received a Ph.D. in government and social policy from Harvard University. Her research examines the dynamics of popular attitudes toward redistributive social policies at a time of rising inequality, fiscal stress, and high levels of immigration.

Katherine J. Cramer is Natalie C. Holton Chair of Letters & Science and Virginia Sapiro Professor of Political Science at the University of Wisconsin–Madison, and Visiting Professor at the Center for Constructive Communication at the Massachusetts Institute of Technology Media Lab. She is the author of *The Politics of Resentment: Rural Consciousness in Wisconsin and the Rise of Scott Walker.*

Marta Curto-Grau is General Director of Economic Analysis in the Catalan government. She holds a Ph.D. in economics from the University of Barcelona and has written about economic history, public economics, and political economy. She was a postdoctoral scholar at Heidelberg University and a Marie Curie Fellow.

Mads Andreas Elkjær is a postdoctoral research fellow in the Department of Politics and International Relations at the University of Oxford and at Nuffield College. His research interests include political representation, inequality, and redistribution, and more broadly comparative politics and political economy.

Lea Elsässer is a postdoctoral researcher at the University of Münster and the University of Duisburg-Essen, Germany. From 2013 to 2017, she was a doctoral researcher at the Max-Planck Institute for the Study of Societies in Cologne, Germany. Her work focuses on representational inequality along class lines.

Aina Gallego is Associate Professor of Political Science at the University of Barcelona and a research associate at the Barcelona Institute for International Studies. She has worked on inequalities in political participation, attitudes toward corruption, and the characteristics of political elites, among other topics.

Jacob S. Hacker is Stanley Resor Professor of Political Science at Yale University. An expert on American politics and policy, he is the author or coauthor of more than a half-dozen books, numerous journal articles, and a wide range of popular writings. He is a member of the American Academy of Arts and Science, a Robert A. Dahl Fellow of the American Academy of Political and Social Science, and a recipient of the Robert Ball Award of the National Academy of Social Insurance.

Silja Häusermann is Professor of Political Science at the University of Zurich in Switzerland. She studies welfare state politics and party system change in advanced capitalist democracies. She directs the European Research Council (ERC) project "WelfarePriorities" and is the codirector of Equality of Opportunity, the University of Zurich Research Priority Programme.

Svenja Hense is a postdoctoral researcher at Goethe University Frankfurt, where she works in the ERC-funded project Polarization and Its Discontent. Before joining the team in Frankfurt, she was a research associate at the University of Osnabrück and the University of Münster.

Timothy Hicks is Associate Professor of Public Policy at University College London. He is a political scientist who studies "developed democracies" and is currently engaged in research projects relating to the politics of economic inequality, the politics of austerity, and political economy and the media.

Torben Iversen is Professor of Political Economy in the Government Department at Harvard University. His research interests lie at the intersection of comparative political economy, electoral politics, and applied formal theory. He is the coauthor of five books, including (with David Soskice) *Democracy and Prosperity: Reinventing Capitalism through a Turbulent Century*.

Alan M. Jacobs is Professor of Political Science at the University of British Columbia, working in the fields of comparative political economy, political behavior, and qualitative and multimethod causal inference. His research interests include the relationship between economic inequality and democratic accountability, the politics of public goods provision, and models of causal inference.

Noam Lupu is Associate Professor of Political Science and Associate Director of LAPOP Lab at Vanderbilt University. He is the author of *Party Brands in Crisis* and coeditor of *Campaigns and Voting in Developing Democracies* (with Virginia Oliveros and Luis Schiumerini).

Ruben Mathisen is a Ph.D. candidate in the Department of Comparative Politics at the University of Bergen. His research focuses on political inequality, in particular the policy influence of affluent citizens and its consequences in established democracies.

J. Scott Matthews is Associate Professor in the Department of Political Science at Memorial University. He specializes in the study of voting and public opinion in established democracies, with a focus on the impact of political information on policy attitudes and evaluations of government performance.

Mikael Persson is Professor of Political Science at the University of Gothenburg. His research revolves around political representation, political behavior, and public opinion.

Yvette Peters is Professor of Comparative Politics at the University of Bergen in Norway. She is Principal Investigator of The Politics of Inequality, a Trond Mohn Foundation Starting Grant. She has received the Gordon Smith and Vincent Wright Memorial Prize and the François Mény Prize. Her latest book is *Political Participation, Diffused Governance, and the Transformation of Democracy*.

Paul Pierson is John Gross Professor of Political Science at the University of California, Berkeley, where he serves as Director of the Berkeley Center for the Study of American Democracy and as Co-Director of the multiuniversity

Consortium on American Political Economy. His research focuses on American political economy and public policy.

Jonas Pontusson is a research-active Emeritus Professor at the University of Geneva. Before moving to Geneva in 2010, he taught at Cornell University and Princeton University. He has published extensively in the domains of comparative political economy and comparative welfare states, focusing on labor markets, trade unions, partisan politics, and income inequality and redistribution. From 2017 to 2023, he directed a research program funded by the European Research Council on political inequality and the politics of inequality in advanced industrial states.

Wouter Schakel is a postdoctoral fellow in the Departments of Political Science and Sociology at the University of Amsterdam. His research focuses on the political economy of democratic representation and has appeared in *Socio-Economic Review*, the *European Journal of Political Research*, *West European Politics*, and *Politics & Society*.

Daniel Stegmueller is Associate Professor in the Department of Political Science at Duke University. His research interests include the genesis of political preferences, the political economy of inequality and representation, and the role of religion in politics. He is a coauthor, with David Rueda, of *Who Wants What? Redistribution Preferences in Comparative Perspective*.

Sam Zacher is a Ph.D. candidate in political science at Yale University, studying the politics of redistribution and the climate crisis. He is the coeditor of *The Trouble* magazine on climate-left politics.

Acknowledgments

Our work on this volume has been supported by the ERC (grant no. 741538) as well as by Vanderbilt University and the University of Geneva. The idea was hatched while Noam was a visiting researcher at Jonas' ERC-funded Unequal Democracies program, at the University of Geneva, in the Spring of 2020. We intended to bring potential contributors together for a conference, but the pandemic forced us instead to opt for an online seminar, which ran every other week from January to June 2021. Despite our initial reservations about the format, the seminar was consistently well attended and the discussion lively and stimulating, convincing us to move forward with plans for a volume.

We are most grateful to the chapter authors for the time and effort they put into this project. We learned a great deal from their contributions and from our discussions with them. We are also grateful for their patience when we, as editors, have missed deadlines that we set for them and for ourselves. We also thank Brian Burgoon and two anonymous reviewers for providing detailed comments and suggestions, and Guilherme Fasolin and Martín Gou for editorial assistance. Last but not least, we thank the editors of the *Anxieties of Democracy* series – John Ferejohn, Ira Katznelson, and Deborah Yashar – and the staff at Cambridge University Press – Rachel Blaifeder and Jadyn Fauconier-Herry in particular – for their encouragement and support.

The Political Puzzle of Rising Inequality[*]

Noam Lupu and Jonas Pontusson

Many theories in political economy posit that government redistribution ought to be a function of the income distribution. The number of citizens who stand to gain from redistribution increases with inequality, so it seems intuitive to suppose that electoral competition would translate this into more redistributive policy. When the market earnings of the affluent increase relative to the market earnings of the less affluent, democratically elected governments ought to compensate low- and middle-income citizens by increasing redistribution. Put formally, the pivotal median income earner will prefer more redistribution as the upper half of the income distribution becomes dispersed and his/her distance from the mean increases (Meltzer and Richard 1981).

And yet cross-national comparisons do not seem consistent with this basic intuition. Instead, government policy actually tends to be less redistributive in more unequal countries (see, e.g., Iversen and Soskice 2009), in what Lindert (2004) famously calls the *Robin Hood paradox*.[1] Defenders of the theory retort that broad inequality measures, such as the Gini coefficient, do not necessarily capture variation in the median–mean distance at the heart of the model, or that its implications should really be tested by looking at over-time changes within countries rather the cross-national variation.[2]

In response, scholars studying how inequality affects citizens' preferences for redistribution and how governments respond to those preferences (including

[*] For their comments and advice, we are grateful to the contributors to this volume and the anonymous reviewers. We are also grateful to Marc Morgan, Jérémie Poltier, and Jan Rosset for assistance with the data presented in this chapter.

[1] In Lindert's (2004) felicitous formulation, Robin Hood comes out of the woods to steal from the rich and give to the poor only when he is least needed.

[2] For the 1979–2000 period, Kenworthy and Pontusson (2005) find a positive correlation between market inequality and redistribution among working-age households in nine out of ten OECD countries, with the United States as the outstanding exception.

several contributors to this volume) frame their work in terms of change over time. Income inequality, they argue, especially at the top of the income distribution (Piketty 2014), has risen sharply in advanced capitalist societies in recent decades, and elected governments have failed to compensate low- and middle-income earners for this development. The puzzle, then, is why rising income inequality has failed to translate into either increased demand for redistribution among the public or greater supply of redistributive policies from elected governments.

This chapter begins by taking a closer look at this conventional framing and arguing that it needs to be qualified in two important ways. The first concerns temporality. Income inequality rose sharply in the fifteen years before the financial crisis of 2007 to 2008 in advanced democracies. But there has been no uniform trend of rising inequality in the period since the crisis. The conventional claim that inequality has risen consistently in these countries for the last three decades is somewhat misleading.

The second qualification concerns the effects of government policy on inequality. Although the puzzle of rising inequality is typically framed in terms of governments failing to compensate citizens for a market-driven phenomenon, the data suggest that this trend is partly also a function of policy decisions. Governments across the ideological spectrum reduced the generosity of welfare states during the precrisis period. Tax and transfer systems not only failed to respond to the exogenous forces expanding market inequality, but they themselves became less redistributive and drove inequality higher. In addition, changes to the social structure and labor market meant that existing welfare-state benefits, such as unemployment insurance, also became less redistributive. In other words, the puzzle of rising inequality lies not only in the failures of democratically elected governments to respond to market forces but also in the political choices of those governments to abandon redistributive policies or to ignore societal changes that were rendering welfare states less redistributive.

The conventional story of a steady rise in income inequality generated by market forces and a political failure to offset these forces must be qualified, but it remains the case that advanced capitalist societies are, with few exceptions, more unequal today and their tax and transfer systems are less redistributive than they were in the early 1990s.

Two streams of recent research, developed along separate tracks, shed some light on the political puzzle of rising inequality. The first focuses on elites and the policymaking process yielding unequal representation of voter preferences. Voters may demand redistribution, but it could be that policymakers do not listen. They may fail to perceive the changing winds of public opinion. Or they may just not be all that responsive to the preferences of most voters, acting only upon the priorities and preferences of the very wealthy, especially when it comes to economic issues. This could be because the affluent fund political campaigns and lobbying, because less-affluent citizens are less likely to vote, or because elected representatives are typically themselves affluent, among other possibilities.

A second approach to explaining the political puzzle posed by the trend of rising inequality focuses instead on voters' preferences for redistribution. If canonical theories are wrong about the effects of rising inequality on redistribution, then one explanation could be that they wrongly assume that rising inequality will make voters demand more redistribution. This could be because voters lack information about or misperceive rising inequality, because the media offers biased assessments of such economic conditions, or because they prioritize other policy dimensions (such as immigration) or other political considerations (such as partisanship). Alternatively, it could be that voters do respond to rising inequality with stronger preferences for redistribution, but they fail to translate those preferences into votes or mobilize around the issue in ways that might influence policymaking.

This volume seeks to bring these two research agendas into conversation in an effort to better understand what it is about the political process that has led to rising inequality. Doing so allows us to address some of the shortcomings of prior work but also to highlight the unresolved tensions between different arguments as well as their persistent limitations.

One shortcoming of prior research in this field is the isolated way in which research about the United States is typically conducted. Studies of preferences for redistribution have become commonplace among scholars of comparative political economy, and many of these studies use cross-national datasets that are strictly European. At the same time, studies of unequal representation were pioneered by students of the United States, and comparative scholars have only very recently begun to catch up. And yet the puzzle of rising inequality applies as much in Europe as it does in the United States, as we show in this chapter.

If we are going to make strides toward resolving this puzzle, it seems fruitful to bring the United States into comparative perspective. Do the explanations for this puzzle offered by scholars of US politics generalize to other contexts as well? If they do not, this may suggest that other factors are actually more important. Conversely, comparative explanations could benefit from paying more attention to the factors emphasized in American politics. While the United States is certainly different from other affluent democracies in a variety of ways, we do not think it is so unique that it cannot be fruitfully compared. Or, if it is unique, we think social scientists should seek to theorize what it is about the United States that makes it exceptional. Both endeavors require bringing scholars of American politics into direct dialogue with scholars of comparative politics.

The chapters in this volume grapple with finding answers to the political puzzle of rising inequality. They do so by focusing either on the voter side of demand for redistribution or on the elite side of representation and the policymaking process. Many focus either on the US case or on some comparison across European cases. But they do so by clearly engaging with theories from across these arbitrary divides, offering a more nuanced and more generalizable set of findings to push forward this important research agenda. Together, they suggest important directions for future research and raise new questions and disagreements about everything from methodological choices to broader interpretations of the implications of their findings.

CHANGES IN INCOME INEQUALITY AND REDISTRIBUTION

Research on unequal representation and the politics of redistribution often begins by noting that income inequality has risen sharply across advanced democracies and proceeds to ask why governments have done so little to offset that trend. This conventional framing serves useful heuristic purposes but also misses important nuances.

The Luxembourg Income Study (LIS), the European Union Statistics on Income and Living Conditions (EU-SILC), and the World Inequality Database (WID) allow us to track the evolution of income inequality and redistribution over time. For reasons of data availability and simplicity, our descriptive analysis covers the period from 1995 to 2019 and is restricted to twelve countries: the United States, Australia, and the UK (commonly characterized as liberal market economies or liberal welfare states); the four Nordic countries (Denmark, Finland, Norway, and Sweden); and five continental European countries (Belgium, France, Germany, the Netherlands, and Switzerland). The European countries in this sample commonly serve as explicit or implicit comparative reference points in the literature that explores the politics of inequality in the United States. These countries are more egalitarian than the United States and they are often assumed to have done more than the United States to counteract rising inequality.

LIS and EU-SILC provide survey-based measures of household income that allow us to compute various measures of the distribution of household income before and after taxes and transfers as well as the redistributive effects of taxes and transfers. Combining information from labor-force surveys with administrative tax data, the WID adjusts for the fact that people at the very top of the income distribution are underrepresented in surveys. WID data represent an advance on LIS/EU-SILC data in that they provide a more accurate picture of top-end inequality. At the same time, the WID only provides measures of pretax income and disposable personal income, with public pensions and unemployment benefits included in pretax income, and does not readily enable us to distinguish between economically active and retired individuals.[3] As a

---

[3] The most obvious reason for focusing on the working-age population is to make cross-national comparison more straightforward. In countries that provide generous public pensions, people have limited incentive to save for their retirement and elderly households typically earn very little market income. Including retirees in our measures in these countries would make redistribution

result, measures of redistribution based on WID data are effectively restricted to redistribution through taxes and cash transfers other than public pensions and unemployment benefits.[4]

Rather than choosing one or the other data source, we take advantage of the strengths of each by looking at top-10-percent income shares for the population as a whole based on WID data alongside Gini coefficients for the working-age population based on LIS/EU-SILC data.[5] Following conventional practice, we measure redistribution among working-age households as the percentage change between the Gini coefficient for market income and the Gini coefficient for disposable income, or, in other words, the percentage reduction of Gini coefficient brought about by taxes and government transfers. Based on WID data, we also report on redistribution as the percentage reduction in the top-10-percent income share of total (personal) income brought about by taxes and targeted social assistance.

Figure 1.1 provides an overview of what happened to overall inequality of disposable income, measured by the Gini coefficient, and top-end inequality of disposable income, measured by the share of the richest 10 percent, between 1995 and the late 2010s. Both panels show that disposable income inequality has risen in recent decades; taken together, they indicate that rising income inequality cannot be attributed to rising top-income shares alone. Averaging across countries, the Gini coefficient for working-age disposable income increased by 10.6 percent while the top-10-percent share increased by 7.2 percent. It is also interesting to note that Gini coefficients rose sharply in all the Nordic countries and that the United States does not stand out as having a particularly inegalitarian trajectory. Disposable income inequality among working-age households increased more in Germany and the Nordic countries than it did in the United States over this period. Of course, we are measuring changes in inequality relative to their

appear to be very high relative to countries with less generous pension systems. From a dynamic perspective, changes in the market income of elderly households also reflect changes in public pension provisions as much as (or more than) market dynamics, rendering the question of how tax-transfer systems respond to market income inequality much less tractable.

[4] WID data pertain to the income of individuals, with survey-based household income split equally among adults in the household. Note that the WID also includes measures of the national income distribution consistent with national accounts, distributing government spending on health as a lump sum to all individuals and spending on education proportional to income. The national income data series also attributes undistributed corporate profits to individuals. See Caranza, Morgan, and Nolan (2022) for further discussion of the differences between LIS/EU-SILC and WID data.

[5] Working-age households are defined as those headed by someone under sixty-five years old. The estimates of Gini coefficients for the working-age population are based on LIS or EU-SILC data for years when one or the other are available and the average of the two when both are available (the two data series are closely correlated). Due to lack of data on personal income, our estimates of top-10-percent income shares for the United States are based on national income (see footnote 4).

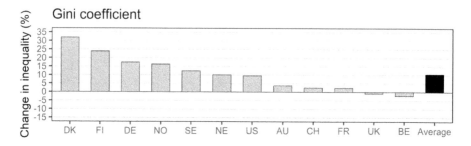

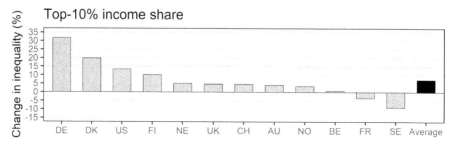

FIGURE 1.1 Income inequality growth, 1995–2018/2019

Note: Bars plot the percentage change in disposable income Gini coefficients and top-10-percent income shares between 1995 and 2018 (Gini coefficients) or 2019 (top-10-percent shares).

Sources: EU-SILC, LIS, and WID.

starting levels, and inequality was much higher in the United States than in the Nordic countries in the mid-1990s. The Nordic countries remain less unequal than the United States, but they have to some extent converged on the United States in this respect.

Most observers suppose that the trends displayed in Figure 1.1 result entirely from rising market inequality and then ask why governments have not responded. But as Tables 1.1–1.4 show, this misses two important elements of the story: the role of policy changes to tax and transfer systems in reducing redistribution, and the differences in these trends before and after the financial crisis.

Table 1.1 shows how inequality and redistribution among working-age households changed from 1995 to 2007.[6] For each country, the columns show initial levels of inequality (measured by the Gini coefficient), percentage changes in inequality, and absolute changes in the redistributive effect of taxes and transfers over this precrisis period. The key observation that emerges from this table is that disposable income inequality increased more than market

---

[6] We use 2007 as a cutoff because this was the peak year for top-10-percent income shares in the majority of the countries included in our analysis.

TABLE 1.1 *Inequality and redistribution among working-age households, 1995–2007*

| Country | Starting levels | | Change (%) | | |
	Market income	Disposable income	Market income	Disposable income	Change in redistributive effect
Finland	0.434	0.222	−5.5	+19.4	**−13.5**
Germany	0.391	0.252	+10.7	+17.5	**−3.9**
Denmark	0.378	0.210	+0.3	+13.3	**−7.2**
Netherlands	0.402	0.248	+3.0	+9.3	**−3.8**
Norway	0.351	0.233	+7.7	+7.3	+0.2
Australia	0.417	0.294	+1.9	+7.1	**−3.6**
Switzerland	0.336	0.278	+1.5	+4.0	**−2.0**
United States	0.437	0.345	+1.4	+3.8	**−1.9**
Sweden	0.428	0.241	−14.3	+3.7	**−11.8**
France	0.424	0.290	+0.2	+2.1	**−1.3**
Belgium	0.401	0.262	+3.2	−0.4	+2.3
UK	0.467	0.324	−5.6	−1.9	**−2.7**
Average	0.406	0.267	+0.1	+7.1	**−4.1**

Notes: Values indicate the starting levels and changes in market and disposable income inequality measured as the Gini coefficients for working-age households. Bolded values represent regressive changes to redistributive policy.
Sources: EU-SILC and LIS.

income inequality in ten out of twelve countries. This pattern represents a regressive turn in redistributive policy. Market income inequality actually fell in three countries over this period. In two of these (Sweden and Finland), disposable income inequality nonetheless increased significantly and in a third (the UK), disposable income inequality declined by only 1.9 percent, while market income inequality declined by 5.6 percent. Belgium stands out as the only country in which the tax-transfer system clearly became more redistributive between 1995 and 2007.

Table 1.2 repeats the exercise for top-10-percent income shares. Here we observe a universal trend of increasing market income inequality, albeit with a very wide range of cross-national variation (from Belgium at 2.5 percent to Germany at a whopping 31.8 percent). In France and Sweden, increases in tax progressivity and targeted social assistance effectively cancelled out the impact of rising market income inequality on disposable income inequality measured this way. In five other countries (Australia, Denmark, Germany, Norway, and the United States), redistribution also increased, but not enough to offset the effects of rising market inequality. In the remaining five countries (Belgium, Finland, the Netherlands, Switzerland, and the UK), changes in redistribution reinforced the rise of

TABLE I.2 *Top-10-percent income shares and redistribution, 1995–2007*

| Country | Starting levels | | Change (%) | | |
	Market income	Disposable income	Market income	Disposable income	Change in redistributive effect
Germany	28.0	24.4	+31.8	+23.4	+5.6
Norway	27.5	22.6	+22.9	+15.9	+4.7
UK	34.5	27.7	+12.5	+14.8	**−1.7**
Switzerland	29.8	28.1	+12.8	+13.9	**−0.9**
Netherlands	27.6	23.4	+12.3	+13.3	**−0.7**
Finland	29.9	24.6	+10.7	+12.1	**−1.1**
Belgium	32.5	23.9	+2.5	+10.4	**−6.4**
United States	39.9	34.4	+10.3	+7.9	+1.9
Denmark	28.5	25.1	+7.7	+4.4	+2.3
Australia	28.2	23.9	+11.7	+1.3	+7.9
Sweden	31.5	27.8	+4.8	+0.4	+3.7
France	32.0	28.6	+4.8	0.0	+3.0
Average	30.8	26.5	+12.2	+9.8	+1.8

Notes: Values indicate the starting levels and changes in market and disposable income inequality measured as the top-10-percent income share. Bolded values represent regressive changes to redistributive policy.
Source: WID.

top-10-percent income shares. Regardless of whether we look at Gini coefficients or top-income shares, governments across these countries either failed to respond to market inequality or adopted policies that reduced redistribution.

Tables 1.3 and 1.4 show that these trends changed markedly in the wake of the financial crisis. Averaging across countries, market income inequality among working-age households increased more from 2007 to 2018 than it had from 1995 to 2007. But disposable income inequality among working-age households increased much less in this postcrisis period. Confronted with rising market income inequality, measured by the Gini coefficient, tax-transfer systems in this period became less redistributive in Denmark, Finland, Norway, Sweden, and the United States. In other countries (Germany, the Netherlands, and the UK), market inequality declined but tax-transfer systems also became less redistributive. Finally, progressive turns of redistributive policy offset rising market income inequality in France, Switzerland, and Belgium and reinforced declining market inequality in Australia. In the postcrisis period, inequality measured by Gini coefficients has been rising less sharply, and some governments do seem to have compensated for market forces.

TABLE I.3 *Inequality and redistribution among working-age households, 2007–2018*

| Country | Starting levels | | Change (%) | | |
	Market income	Disposable income	Market income	Disposable income	Change in redistributive effect
Denmark	0.433	0.296	+7.1	+16.4	**−5.4**
Norway	0.378	0.250	+3.2	+8.4	**−3.2**
Sweden	0.367	0.250	+2.7	+8.4	**−3.8**
United States	0.443	0.358	+5.0	+5.6	**−0.5**
Finland	0.410	0.265	+2.4	+3.8	**−0.8**
UK	0.441	0.318	−0.7	+0.9	**−1.2**
Netherlands	0.414	0.271	−4.1	+0.7	**−3.3**
France	0.425	0.296	+2.1	+0.3	+1.2
Germany	0.433	0.296	−5.3	0.0	**−3.8**
Switzerland	0.341	0.289	+3.5	−1.4	+4.0
Belgium	0.414	0.261	+0.5	−1.9	+1.5
Australia	0.425	0.315	−1.7	−3.2	+1.2
Average	0.410	0.292	+1.3	+3.2	**−1.2**

Notes: Values indicate the starting levels and changes in market and disposable income inequality measured as the Gini coefficients for working-age households. Bolded values represent regressive changes to redistributive policy.
Sources: EU-SILC and LIS.

In all these countries, top-10-percent shares of market income fell sharply during the financial crisis. As shown in Table 1.4, they were still lower at the end of the 2010s than they had been in 2007 in most countries. Measured by their impact on top-10-percent shares, taxes and targeted social assistance have become more redistributive in Belgium, Sweden, Finland, the Netherlands, and the UK, while they have become less redistributive in Denmark, France, Germany, and the United States, and have remained essentially unchanged in Australia, Norway, and Switzerland since 2007. Measured in this way, it becomes less clear that we can characterize the postcrisis era as a period of rising inequality, although some governments have continued to reduce the redistributive effects of taxes and targeted social assistance.

Tables 1.1–1.4 display a lot of cross-national variation as well as differences between the precrisis period and the postcrisis period. As such, they call into question the conventional notion that market forces favor the rich while democratic politics favor low- and middle-income citizens (an idea encapsulated by the title of Esping-Andersen's 1985 book, *Politics against Markets*). Measured before taxes and income transfers, top-income shares indeed rose sharply in most countries in the precrisis period, but the same is

TABLE 1.4 *Top-10-percent income shares and redistribution, 2007–2019*

Country	Starting levels		Change (%)		
	Market income	Disposable income	Market income	Disposable income	Change in redistributive effect
Denmark	30.7	26.2	+8.1	+14.9	**−5.3**
Germany	36.9	30.1	+1.6	+8.3	**−5.4**
United States	44.0	37.1	+3.9	+5.1	**−1.0**
Australia	29.9	24.6	+3.5	+2.9	+0.5
Finland	33.1	28.7	0.0	−1.7	+1.5
France	34.1	28.6	−5.0	−3.5	**−1.3**
Netherlands	31.0	26.5	−5.2	−7.2	+1.8
Switzerland	33.6	32.0	−8.3	−8.1	**−0.2**
Belgium	33.3	29.7	−0.9	−8.8	+7.1
UK	38.8	31.8	−7.7	−8.8	+0.9
Sweden	33.0	27.9	−7.6	−10.0	+2.3
Norway	33.8	26.2	−10.6	−10.7	0.0
Average	34.5	29.1	−2.4	−2.3	+0.1

Notes: Values indicate the starting levels and changes in market and disposable income inequality measured as the top-10-percent income share. Bolded values represent regressive changes to redistributive policy.
Source: WID.

not true for overall income inequality among working-age households. In the years since the financial crisis, even these market top-income shares have not risen consistently.[7]

We can get a sense of political dynamics by treating each row in Tables 1.1–1.4 as a separate observation and looking at the redistributive effects of government policy. This yields twenty-one cases – a majority – in which changes to the distributive effects of taxes and transfers contributed to rising disposable income inequality and another six cases in which reductions in market income inequality did not fully pass through as reductions in disposable income inequality.[8] By contrast, we only observe thirteen cases in which increases

---

[7] Market forces are of course also embedded in politically created institutions, including collective-bargaining systems, employment regulation, and minimum wage legislation, and they respond to public policies. Piketty and Saez (2014) argue persuasively that reductions in top marginal tax rates in the 1990s boosted top-income shares by stimulating demand for corporate compensation.

[8] It is important to keep in mind that changes in the redistributive effects of tax and transfers are not necessarily the results of policy changes pertaining to the progressivity of taxes or the generosity of welfare benefits. For instance, many studies show that unemployment insurance has a strong redistributive effect for the simple reason that low-income households are more exposed to unemployment than high-income households (e.g., Pontusson and Weisstanner 2018). In all countries,

in market income inequality were fully offset by taxes and transfers or declines in market inequality did fully pass through. The remaining ten cases are cases of partial offsets or very little change in disposable as well as market income inequality. In most countries across both the pre- and postcrisis eras, governments appear to be allowing income inequality to rise.

The inequality and redistribution estimates presented in Tables 1.1–1.4 convey an overall picture partly at odds with the findings presented by Elkjær and Iversen in their contribution to this volume. According to their analyses, taxes and transfers have compensated low- and middle-income citizens for rising market income inequality more than our estimates suggest. There are several differences between their measures and ours. Most obviously, their analysis includes more countries over a longer period of time than our analysis here. A second difference has to do with the way we deal with retirees. While our inequality estimates are based on excluding households headed by people above the age of 64, Elkjær and Iversen deal with this issue by excluding households without any labor income. Lastly, Elkjær and Iversen's estimates of income transfers take in-kind benefits into account. While this seems valuable, how we attribute government spending on education, health, childcare, and elderly care to income deciles involves making many assumptions about who consumes these services.[9] Our (more conventional) estimates remain, we think, informative about trends in inequality and redistribution since the early 1990s.

There is also a noteworthy conceptual difference between our approaches. While our analysis focuses on the impact of taxes and transfers on the distribution of income, Elkjær and Iversen focus on transfer rates, measured as (a) the percentage of market income of the upper income group that is transferred to low- and middle-income groups through the tax-transfer system, and (b) transferred income as a percentage of the disposable income of low- and middle-income groups. Transfer rates are useful metrics for some applications, but as measures of redistributive effects, they leave something to be desired.

Consider two societies, each consisting of a low-income household and a high-income household that jointly earn the same total income. In one society, a more egalitarian one, the low-income household earns 150 and the high-income household earns 250 before taxes and transfers; in the other, a less egalitarian society, the low-income household earns 100 and the high-income household earns 300 before taxes and transfers. Now suppose that the

people in fixed-term and part-time employment have more limited access to unemployment benefits than permanent full-time employees. Under these conditions, expanding part-time and fixed-term employment and/or concentrating unemployment among part-time and fixed-term employees reduces the redistributive effects of unemployment insurance at constant benefit generosity.

[9] See Verbist, Förster, and Vaalavuo (2012) for a detailed discussion of the assumptions and empirical estimates behind this approach to allocating spending on services to income deciles.

government transfers 10 percent of the high-income household's income to the low-income household in both cases. Measured as a proportion of the high-income household's pretransfer income, the transfer rate is the same in the two cases (10 percent). Measured as a proportion of the low-income household's posttransfer income, the transfer rate is higher in the society with a more unequal distribution of pretransfer income (23 percent compared to 14 percent). Yet the low-income household's posttransfer share of total income is lower in the more inegalitarian case (33 percent compared to 44 percent), and the low-income household is worse off in absolute terms as well (with a posttransfer income of 130 instead of 175). The transfer from rich to poor would have to be increased for the inegalitarian society to achieve the same distribution of disposable income as the egalitarian one. Put differently, an increase in the high-income household's share of pretransfer income without an increase in the transfer rate should be considered a political victory for the rich.

The question of whether income transfers from the rich have increased enough to offset rising top-end inequality of market income is an empirical one. While Elkjær and Iversen unambiguously answer this question in the affirmative, our analysis yields a more nuanced answer. In the precrisis period, top-10-percent market income shares increased across all twelve countries included our analysis, and top-10-percent disposable income shares increased significantly in ten countries. In several countries, the transfer rate from the rich increased, but not enough to offset rising top-end inequality. It should also be noted that seven of the thirteen country-period cases in which increases in market income inequality were fully offset by taxes and transfers or declines in market inequality fully passed through pertain to top-10-percent income shares in the 2010s. Still, the estimates in Tables 1.1–1.4 suggest that market and/or political dynamics have, in general, become more favorable to the rich over time.

POLITICAL INEQUALITY AND REPRESENTATION

If overall policy outputs have become less redistributive in recent decades, they have also become more closely aligned with the preferences of affluent citizens. In just about every democracy, surveys show that more-affluent respondents are less likely to support government redistribution than less-affluent respondents. Affluent citizens have not necessarily become more politically influential, but they appear to have gotten their way in the domain of redistributive policy.

A crucial assumption in theories of political economy is that democratic governments respond to the preferences of the majority. Because politicians and political parties want to be reelected, governments are expected to respond to citizen demands for redistribution by delivering more redistribution. Why, then, are affluent citizens in advanced democracies getting their way when it comes to redistribution?

A growing body of research shows that at least part of the story may lie with political inequalities in the process of representation itself (see Burgoon et al. 2022).[10] Scholars of representation typically distinguish between two aspects of the representative process (see Achen 1978; Miller and Stokes 1963): whether elections produce representative bodies that reflect the preferences of citizens (through descriptive representation or opinion congruence) and whether those bodies produce legislation that responds to the wishes of citizens. Recent studies have documented income- or class-based inequalities on both scores. Across many electoral democracies, elected representatives' own political preferences and positions seem to reflect more closely the preferences of more-affluent citizens than they do the preferences of less-affluent citizens (e.g., Bernauer et al. 2015; Giger et al. 2012; Lupu and Warner 2017, 2022a). Of course, even if legislators themselves largely agree with more-affluent citizens, we might expect electoral incentives to induce them to still respond to the demands of a majority of citizens – assuming they have some information about citizens' preferences (see Butler 2014).

And yet, a number of studies, inspired by pioneering work on the United States by Gilens (2012), have found that policy outcomes in a number of affluent democracies appear to respond unequally to different income or class groups (Bartels 2017; Elkjær 2020; Elsässer, Hense, and Schäfer 2021; Lupu and Tirado Castro 2023; Mathisen 2023; Persson 2021; Rosset et al. 2013; Rosset and Stecker 2019; Schakel 2021; Wagner 2021). The chapter in this volume by Mathisen, Schakel, Hense, Elsässer, Persson, and Pontusson uses survey data from four Northern European countries – Germany, the Netherlands, Norway, and Sweden – to compare mass preferences to actual policy outcomes following the Gilens (2012) research design. Having confirmed that governments in all four countries are on average more responsive to the preferences of high-income citizens than to those of middle- and low-income citizens, they proceed to test whether government partisanship affects the degree of unequal representation.

Parties appear to cater to the preferences of their core constituencies, such that Left and Right parties in advanced democracies end up pursuing very different levels of social spending and redistribution. To the extent that Left parties cater to less-affluent core constituencies and Right parties to more-affluent ones, we might expect unequal responsiveness to depend in part on the

---

[10] The policymaking process itself is another possible structural or elite-level explanation, and might include the institutional rules that shape policymaking, the role of interest groups, or a general status-quo bias in policymaking. External constraints like globalization or European integration might also help to explain why governments underprovide redistribution in some contexts. Given the wide variation on these dimensions across advanced democracies, it seems to us that these are less likely explanations for the generalized pattern of declining redistribution.

partisanship of the national government – particularly in Northern European parliamentary systems. Moreover, this might be especially true prior to the moderation of many Social Democratic parties in the 1990s. What Mathisen and coauthors find is that unequal responsiveness does appear to be less pronounced when Left-leaning governments are in power in Germany, the Netherlands, and Sweden. Norway seems to be a puzzling case, although that may have to do with differences in responsiveness across types of policies. At the same time, Left-leaning governments in all four countries are still much more responsive to the affluent than they are to the poor. Moreover, Mathisen and coauthors go on to offer tentative evidence that the partisan filter has shifted over time. Whereas Left-leaning governments had been more equally responsive on economic and welfare issues prior to 1998, since then they and Right-leaning governments have converged in their pro-affluent bias. On other policy domains, Left- and Right-leaning governments were equally biased before 1998, but Left-leaning governments have become more equally responsive since then. Mathisen and coauthors speculate that this suggests Left-leaning governments may be trying to use noneconomic policy responsiveness to compensate their core constituencies for their lack of responsiveness on economic issues.

Studies showing unequal responsiveness to voter preferences have their share of skeptics, notably Elkjær and Iversen (2020, 2023). As discussed earlier, Elkjær and Iversen's contribution to this volume presents data and analysis suggesting that governments have actually done much to compensate low- and especially middle-income citizens for rising inequality in market earnings, just as canonical theories of redistribution would expect. They argue that we should focus on the (objective) *interests* of citizens rather than their stated (subjective) *preferences*, a conceptual question also taken up by Bartels in his chapter and Hacker, Pierson, and Zacher in theirs. According to Elkjær and Iversen, then, if we look at certain distributional outcomes rather than stated preferences, there is no general puzzle to be explained.

In his chapter, Bartels reviews the body of work on unequal representation from both a conceptual and a methodological perspective. Bartels notes a host of complications involved both in how empirical scholars define representation and in how they measure unequal representation. Drawing on Dahl (2006), he argues that there are good normative reasons to care about the relative political influence of different groups, although he highlights the numerous inferential difficulties in attributing influence. Despite these challenges, he argues convincingly that we should do the best we can with the available data and suggests, in particular, that analyses should account for the indirect influence citizens can have on policymaking via political parties and interest groups.

Political parties become a centerpiece of the analysis by Hacker, Pierson, and Zacher in their chapter on the United States. Like Elkjær and Iversen, they focus on interests rather than preferences, in particular on what they call the place-based economic interests of the knowledge economy: the interests of American residents of metro areas thriving in the new economic model and those of residents of the nonmetro areas largely being left behind. They identify a puzzling feature of contemporary American politics, one that contrasts the arguments made in comparative political economy about how the knowledge economy is reshaping political competition (see Ansell and Gingrich 2022; Iversen and Soskice 2019). Republicans increasingly represent nonmetro residents but continue to pursue policies that benefit the urban affluent and large corporations based in metro areas. Democrats, meanwhile, increasingly represent city dwellers, but continue to pursue policies that disproportionately benefit the rural residents who are more and more reliably Republican. Why are both parties failing to represent the interests of their electoral bases?

Hacker, Pierson, and Zacher argue that the answer has to do with features of the American political system that they refer to as filters, features that determine whether interests become reflected in national political competition. The particular filters they focus on include the nonmetro skew of American political institutions like the Electoral College and the Senate, the polarized and nationalized character of party coalitions that create incentives to cater policy toward interest groups rather than voters, and the local character of many important policy areas that inhibits national interventions. Unequal representation in the United States is a product of the territorial distribution of inequality and the ways territorial interests get filtered out of getting represented in national politics by features of the American political system. Not all policies and not all policy areas get reflected in national politics, either because they are not all equally important to voters or because the political context filters them out. These features make the United States unique in some respects, but Hacker, Pierson, and Zacher's chapter highlights the filtered nature of representation and invites us, like Bartels, to consider what those institutional filters might be in other contexts as well.

The role of interest groups is the focus of Becher and Stegmueller's contribution, largely concerned with the money interest groups pour into American politics. If these groups influence policymaking and disproportionately reflect the preferences of the affluent, then they may sway government policies away from the less-affluent's demands for redistribution. In previous work, Becher and Stegmueller (2021) showed that the presence of labor unions can enhance political equality. Here, they consider whether the reverse might also obtain: namely, that the activities of monied interests increase political inequality.

Empirical researchers studying US policymaking have largely concluded that lobbying and financial contributions to political candidates appear not to influence legislative outcomes, suggesting that we should not look to interest groups to explain political inequality. But Becher and Stegmueller note that interest groups can influence different political processes: they can influence who gets elected through their role in supporting campaigns, and they can influence policy outcomes through lobbying. Moreover, they demonstrate formally that these roles are in fact complements, and that interest groups can make strategic decisions about where to invest their resources. The upshot of this theoretical framework is that it highlights that even studies that can identify the causal effect of an interest group on legislative behavior may underestimate it – something Becher and Stegmueller also demonstrate with simulations. As a result, they argue, we should not rule out the possibility that the role of monied interests in both the selection of candidates and the legislative process may be partly responsible for unequal policy responsiveness.

Two contributions to this volume, one by Curto-Grau and Gallego and the other by Carnes and Lupu, take up the issue of candidate selection. Political scientists have become increasingly interested in the personal characteristics of politicians in recent years (Carnes and Lupu 2023b). On the one hand, descriptive representation by politicians who share voters' ascriptive characteristics may itself be normatively important (Mansbridge 2003). On the other hand, there is growing evidence that those characteristics inform what those legislators do once they take office, with consequences for the kinds of policies that make it through the legislative process (e.g., Carnes 2013; Carnes and Lupu 2015). In their chapter, Curto-Grau and Gallego convincingly show that Spanish mayors with university degrees pursue more fiscally conservative policies than those with lower levels of educational attainment. At the same time, they find no differences between these mayors in terms of their performance. The implication for understanding unequal representation is that if politicians are themselves more affluent than the people they represent – a pattern Carnes and Lupu demonstrate in their chapter – then policy outcomes may skew in favor of their personal preferences, which are more closely aligned to the preferences of the affluent. The fact that less-affluent citizens are descriptively underrepresented in politics may help to explain why governments have failed to address rising inequality.

Why, then, are less-affluent citizens descriptively underrepresented? This is the question Carnes and Lupu set out to consider in their contribution to this volume, focusing specifically on politicians with working-class backgrounds. Using data on the personal characteristics of national legislators across the OECD, they consider whether country-level factors might help to explain why working-class people do not run for public office. They find that economic factors – wealth, inequality, and unionization – do matter, but they only go so far in explaining variation. One reason for this is that all countries wildly underrepresent working-class people, so it may make more sense to look for factors that are common to all advanced democracies than to try to explain variation at the margin. At the same time, Carnes and Lupu show considerable variation within countries across parties – and they suggest that examining this variation, the differing roles party gatekeepers play, may be a more fruitful way forward.

One important issue this final analysis raises is whether elite-centered explanations about unequal representation can account for the temporal changes in governments' attention to economic inequality. As we showed at the outset, inequality has risen in nearly every advanced democracy during the last three decades, although that growth is not uniform or unidirectional. If governments are about as unresponsive to the preferences of less-affluent citizens today as they were three or four decades ago, if interest groups are about as influential now as then, and if less-affluent people were just as descriptively underrepresented then as they are today, then can these explanations help us understand why elites took more measures to address inequality in the past than they have in recent decades? There may be reasons to think so, but it will be important for future elite-centered research on representation to address these temporal changes directly, as Mathisen and his coauthors begin to do in this volume.

A final explanation for the representation gap is that it reflects disproportionalities in political participation. Analyzing survey data from twenty-nine European democracies, Mathisen and Peters show that less-affluent citizens are not only less likely to vote in elections, but they are also substantially less likely to engage in other political activities, including signing petitions, contacting politicians, and working in civic organizations. All of these forms of participation serve to communicate public preferences to elected representatives, and if less-affluent citizens are doing less communicating, then a potential explanation for government inaction in the face of rising inequality is that representatives are simply more likely to hear from more-affluent citizens. Even if less-affluent citizens would prefer more redistribution, those preferences are not getting communicated to governments effectively or consistently.

The fact that less-affluent citizens participate less in politics is well known (Gallego 2010, 2015; Schlozman et al. 2012), but it is typically associated with the fact that less-affluent citizens have fewer of the resources – time, money, and skills – needed to participate. What Mathisen and Peters show in their chapter is that while these resources certainly matter, part of the participation gap – at least with regard to voting and a couple of other activities – can also be explained by the fact that less-affluent citizens are also less likely to trust their political system. If less-affluent citizens were as satisfied with their governments as are more-affluent citizens, these participation gaps would decline significantly. This suggests, as in Cramer's chapter, that trust in government is a crucial moderator of mass demand for redistribution, but also that there may be a counterintuitive vicious cycle in which the less governments respond to rising inequality, the less citizens either demand redistribution or communicate those preferences to elected officials.

VOTERS AND DEMAND FOR REDISTRIBUTION

Focusing on representation alone may not provide us with a full understanding of why governments in advanced democracies have allowed inequality to rise in recent decades. Another straightforward possibility, anticipated by Mathisen and Peters' chapter, is that voters have not responded to rising inequality by

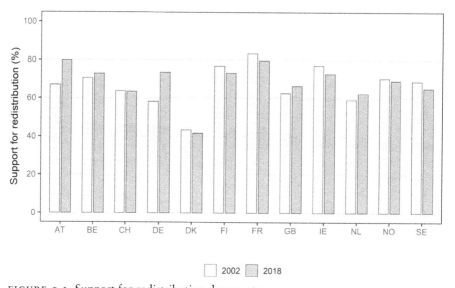

FIGURE 1.2 Support for redistribution, by country
Note: Bars plot the proportion of respondents who say they agree or strongly agree with
the statement, "the government should take measures to reduce income differences."
Source: ESS.

demanding more redistribution, as canonical theories might have expected.
According to Kenworthy and McCall (2007), inequality of individual earnings and household income increased across a number of advanced democracies from 1980 to 2000, yet the percentage of survey respondents who agreed
with proposition that, "it is the responsibility of the government to reduce
the differences in income between people high incomes and people with low
incomes," hardly changed at all in any of these countries.

Figure 1.2 shows the proportion of respondents to the European Social
Survey (ESS) who agreed or strongly agreed with a similar statement in the
countries we examined earlier in 2002 and 2018. Although a couple of cases
exhibit more substantial increases in support for redistribution over this period,
the overall message from these data is that support for redistribution hardly
changed at all over the first two decades of the twenty-first century. Equally
noteworthy, survey data do not seem to lend much, if any, support for the intuitive idea that rising inequality has rendered low- and middle-income citizens
more supportive of redistribution while it has reduced support for redistribution among affluent citizens. Analyzing ESS data for the period 2006–2012,
Gonthier (2017) finds that the redistribution preferences of different income
groups have moved in tandem, to the extent they have moved at all.

The apparent stability of demand for redistribution in the face of rising
inequality has motivated many scholars to explore subjective perceptions

of inequality (e.g., Gimpelson and Treisman 2018; Osberg and Smeeding 2006; Page and Goldstein 2016). The common expectation that democratically elected governments should respond to rising inequality by undertaking redistributive measures rests on two propositions: (1) that government policy responds to the preferences of the majority of voters and (2) that low- and middle-income voters recognize that they stand to gain more from redistribution as inequality rises. The latter proposition in turn assumes that voters know where they are in the income distribution, that they understand what the income distribution looks like, and that they perceive changes in the income distribution. Research on perceptions of inequality teaches us that these assumptions do not necessarily hold. Specifically, two persistent biases might explain the stability of demand for redistribution in the face of rising inequality: people tend to underestimate the extent of inequality in their country (Trump and White 2018) and people tend to think they are closer to the median than they actually are.

Still, while studies of perceptions of inequality offer important insights, research also consistently finds that support for redistribution falls with relative income. It is difficult to see how this persistent finding would come about if people were completely confused about their place in the income distribution. And research on perceptions has yet to address the fact that redistribution has declined over time. Did citizens use to perceive inequality and their own positions more accurately than they do today? And, if so, what would explain these changes? Finally, rising inequality should be relevant to individuals even if they do not perceive it. Most obviously, rising inequality translates into slower income growth for low-income households and more rapid income growth for high-income households. As long as individuals perceive and care about changes in their own income, they ought to be responsive to changes in inequality.

Another strand of work tackles the puzzle of stable redistribution with methodological critiques of our measures of public opinion (see the review by Dallinger 2022). The standard survey item is broad and vague, arguably capturing normative dispositions rather than support for any specific redistributive policies. Some respondents are bound to interpret the statement with reference to the status quo, that is, to register their agreement with the statement that "government should do *more* to reduce income differences" as compared to what it is currently doing. Also, as illustrated by Figure 1.2, the question elicits very high levels of support for redistribution in most advanced democracies, creating an obvious concern about ceiling effects. With 60 to 70 percent of survey respondents supporting redistribution already in the early 2000s, it is perhaps not so surprising that it does not increase much further in the subsequent two decades.

Cavaillé's contribution to this volume makes a related critique building on her prior work (Cavaillé and Trump 2015): namely, that the standard measure fails to distinguish between support for redistribution from the rich ("redistribution from") and support for redistribution to the poor ("redistribution to"). Analyzing 2008 ESS data, Cavaillé and Trump (2015) demonstrate that the individual-level determinants of attitudes on the two dimensions of support for redistribution are strikingly different. In marked contrast to the stability of overall support for redistribution shown in Figure 1.2, Pontusson et al. (2018) document a broad-based public opinion shift in favor of flat-rate or low-income-targeted pension and unemployment benefits (away from earnings-differentiated benefits) across eleven West-European countries from 2008 to 2019. Also noteworthy, Rosset and Pontusson (2021) as well as Limberg (2020) present evidence suggesting that the financial crisis of 2007–2008 and the ensuing recession boosted public support for progressive income taxation in many countries.[11]

Though it does not feature prominently in this volume, the question of how changes in inequality affect specific policy preferences among different income groups represents an important research agenda for scholars interested in the comparative politics of inequality and redistribution. But pursuing this question requires recognizing, as we have already seen, that changes in inequality are not simply a story of ever-rising inequality. It also means that we may need to pay more attention to the structure of inequality than to levels of inequality. Following the logic set out in Lupu and Pontusson (2011) as well as Meltzer and Richard (1981), we might expect pivotal middle-income voters to respond to rising top-end inequality (measured by top income shares or the 90–50 ratio) by demanding more compensatory redistribution, but it is less obvious that they would respond to rising bottom-end inequality (the 50–10 ratio) in this manner.

Still, voters seem to contradict these kinds of theoretical expectations. As Matthews, Hicks, and Jacobs show in their chapter, low- and middle-income voters are more likely to vote for incumbent parties when the incomes of the rich grow fast while their propensity to vote for incumbents does not respond to average income growth in Western Europe (Hicks, Jacobs, and Matthews 2016) as well as the United States (Bartels 2016). Not only do low- and middle-income voters fail to punish incumbents who preside over unfavorable shifts in the distribution of income, they actually seem to reward these incumbents.

Matthews, Hicks, and Jacobs argue convincingly that the tone of economic news provides a key mechanism linking rising top-income shares to

---

[11] While Limberg (2020) analyzes ISSP data for 1999 and 2009, Rosset, Pontusson and Poltier (2023) as well as Pontusson et al. (2018) rely on a 2019 survey that replicated policy-specific questions asked in ESS 2008. The fact that policy-specific measures are more prone to change than the overall support for redistribution dovetails with experimental results reported by Condon and Wichowsky (2020): priming subjects to compare themselves to the rich, these authors do not find any significant treatment effects on overall support for redistribution, but they do find significant effects on support for specific social spending programs, most notably unemployment compensation.

the electoral behavior of low- and middle-income citizens. According to their analysis, the tone of economic news is more positive when incomes at the top of the income distribution grow more rapidly, and that positive tone prompts average voters to support incumbents. An extensive literature attributes the pro-rich bias of news coverage to the interests and ideological dispositions of news media owners and executives, but Matthews, Hicks, and Jacobs instead argue that journalists of all stripes are preoccupied with economic aggregates – unemployment and GDP growth as well as stock prices – that are correlated with income growth at the top.

One interpretation of Matthews, Hicks, and Jacobs' findings is that citizens might care about the distribution of income as well as economic performance, but the latter concern dominates the former, and news media reinforce this dominance. Or, alternatively, that economic performance weighs particularly heavily in the voting decisions of critical swing voters (Kayser and Wlezien 2011). If news media paid more attention to distributive issues, politicians would have to pay more attention to the distributive preferences of low- and middle-income citizens. The question this raises is whether mainstream news coverage of the economy has changed in ways that might explain why voters no longer seem to punish incumbents that preside over disproportionate income growth at the top. Although Matthews, Hicks, and Jacobs' empirics indicate that the ideological orientation of media outlets does not condition the positive effect of top-income growth on the tone of their reporting, it may be that mainstream media of all stripes have become increasingly focused on those economic aggregates that are closely correlated with top-income growth – most obviously, stock prices – at the expense of other aggregates, such as the rate of unemployment. Alternatively, media outlets may give greater coverage to market-oriented or corporate policy views (Guardino 2019). It is noteworthy that support for redistribution tends to be lower in countries with more concentrated media ownership (Niemanns 2023).

While Matthews, Hicks, and Jacobs invoke economic news coverage to explain government neglect of distributive issues, Cavaillé's chapter engages with the extensive literature on how fairness considerations shape citizens' attitudes toward inequality and redistribution. The main strand of the fairness literature proceeds from the observation that people consider income differences to be fair to the extent that they reflect differences in individual effort, while they consider income differences to be unfair to the extent that they derive from luck or privilege, let alone government favors (e.g., Alesina and Guiliano 2011; Bénabou and Tirole 2006; Scheve and Stasavage 2016). As Cavaillé points out, this fairness norm, which she refers to as the proportionality norm, is broadly shared across all advanced capitalist societies: people do not disagree about the norm itself, but they disagree about the extent to which the income differences that they observe around them are proportional to effort. The balance between those who think that education systems and labor markets generate fair outcomes and those who do not think so in turn varies across countries.

Cavaillé's key contribution is to argue that support for redistribution also involves a second fairness norm, the reciprocity norm, which prescribes that all members of a group should contribute collective efforts and that freeriding should be punished. Again, the norm itself is broadly shared, but citizenries differ in their assessments of whether the primary beneficiaries of social insurance schemes and other redistributive policies – in the first instance, the poor – deserve to be supported. Documenting that fairness assessments according to the reciprocity norm are orthogonal to fairness assessments according to the proportionality norm, and that both kinds of assessments are stable over time, Cavaillé identifies three country types among liberal democracies: (1) income differences are considered fair and the poor are deemed to be undeserving in the UK and the United States, (2) income differences are considered unfair, but the poor undeserving in Southern Europe, and (3) income differences are considered fair and the poor deemed to be deserving in the Nordic countries. (The fourth combination, unfair income differences and deserving poor, is represented in Cavaillé's analysis by some former communist countries.)

How does taking fairness considerations into account help us explain the apparent lack of government efforts to reverse rising inequality? It stands to reason that citizens who think income differences are proportional to effort are less likely to demand compensatory redistribution when inequality rises. To the extent that inequality has grown most rapidly in countries where many citizens believe that income differences are proportional to effort, this provides an obvious solution to the puzzle that motivates much of the literature on the politics of inequality and, in particular, the Nordic puzzle identified by our descriptive discussion. Fairness assessments pertaining to the reciprocity norm might in turn be invoked to explain reforms that have reduced the redistributive effects of tax-transfer systems, but this line of reasoning would seem to suppose that fairness assessments, as distinct from fairness norms, are more malleable than Cavaillé's discussion suggests.[12] Most importantly, Cavaillé's contribution to this volume invites us to explore cross-national differences in how public opinion responds to changes in bottom- and top-end inequality.

The question of whether the poor are deserving of redistribution is also closely bound up with the extent to which poverty is concentrated among immigrants and racial/ethnic minorities (see Alesina and Glaeser 2004). Our volume does not engage with the extensive comparative literature on the effects of immigration on demand for redistribution in Europe (e.g., Burgoon 2014; Finseeras 2008), but it includes a chapter by Cramer on how race and economic concerns are intertwined in the thinking of white Americans living in rural areas. Cramer's distinctive research strategy involves listening to local talk radio shows addressing the murder of George Floyd on May 25, 2020

---

[12] Changes in public beliefs about the sources of poverty (1976–2014) and assessments of the fairness of income differences (1987–2009) are documented and analyzed from a comparative perspective by Giger and Lascombes (2019) and Marquis and Rosset (2021). See also Limberg (2020).

and the ensuing protests against racial injustice. Her careful reconstruction of these conversations uncovers an interactive process through which right-wing talk-show hosts and their listeners deflect from race relations to focus on the neglect of "hard-working Americans" by urban political elites identified with the Democratic Party. In right-wing talk-show discourse, racism is first and foremost a trope used by Democrats to advance their political goals. The hosts and callers deflect from racism by emphasizing law and order and free markets, expressing a kind of parochial patriotism and nostalgia that defines "real Americans" as white, rural, and Christian.

What these narratives reveal to Cramer is how aversion to redistribution becomes intertwined with racism. In right-wing talk-show discourse, Democrats are portrayed as using accusations of racism to garner support for redistribution and expanding the federal government as part of a political project to undermine American capitalism. Rather than Republicans deflecting from uncomfortable conversations about systemic racism in the United States, their portrayal equates accusations of racism and redistribution as profoundly un-American. Even in the left-wing talk shows that Cramer analyzes, rural whites clearly see themselves as the true victims of neglect by policymakers in Washington. For them, economic policies are a zero-sum game in which people of color seem to be benefiting and they seem to be losing out, undermining the kind of multiracial class-based coalition that might support redistribution in the United States. There is a fundamental lack of trust in the government among rural whites that shapes how citizens' policy preferences respond to rising inequality (Cramer 2016; see also the chapter in this volume by Hacker, Pierson, and Zacher).

The chapter by Ares and Häusermann also relates to trust in government by exploring perceptions of political representation by social class. Focusing on perceptions of representation by political parties in the broad domain of welfare-state politics, Ares and Häusermann proceed from the observation that "social policy conflict today revolves as much around prioritizing particular social policy fields as around contesting levels of benefits, redistribution and taxation in general." Their empirical analysis is based on an original survey in eight West-European countries that asked respondents to prioritize benefit improvements across different social programs and then asked them to assess the priorities of their preferred party and one other party in the same manner. They show that working-class respondents perceive themselves to be less well represented by political parties, including their preferred political party, than middle-class and especially upper-middle-class respondents (see also Rennwald and Pontusson 2022).

Ares and Häusermann's analysis focuses on perceptions of political inequality rather than economic inequality, but it highlights the relationship between the two. Citizens who perceive themselves as poorly represented by political parties are less likely to trust government. And if trust in government is an important determinant of support for government redistribution (see Goubin and Kumlin 2022; Macdonald 2020), then class gaps in perceptions of unequal representation might explain why low-income and working-class citizens have not responded to rising income inequality by demanding more redistribution. Whereas Mathisen and coauthors speculate that Left-leaning governments may be trying to use noneconomic policy responsiveness to compensate their core constituencies for their lack of responsiveness on economic issues, Ares and Häusermann show that those core constituents may not be convinced.

LOOKING AHEAD

The remainder of the volume proceeds in three parts. We begin with four chapters that debate how to think about representation and the degree to which the recent past in advanced democracies offers evidence of unequal representation. The next two parts mirror the two types of explanations of the political puzzle of rising inequality: those that focus on elites and the process of representation and those that focus on voters and demand for redistribution. Although each chapter engages in specific scholarly debates, they also offer answers to our central motivating question: why governments in advanced electoral democracies have largely allowed economic inequality to rise during the last three decades.

Together, these chapters offer some plausible political explanations for the puzzle of rising inequality in advanced democracies, but they also leave some possibilities unexplored. None of the chapters in this volume, for instance, take up the possibility that rising immigration has undermined support for redistribution or that elites misperceive the preferences of citizens. There are also many possible explanations for the puzzle of rising inequality that have nothing to do with voters or the process of representation like the role of interest groups in policymaking or external constraints on governments, on which the chapters in this volume say little. Our goal, of course, is not to give a holistic treatment of every possible explanation, but to focus on those that seem especially plausible and to invite more direct engagement between those that focus on voters and those that focus on elites.

Even within this subset of explanations, the contributions to this volume leave some questions unaddressed. Most glaring is the heterogeneity, across both space and time, in rising inequality across advanced democracies that we illustrated earlier. Although each of the chapters in this volume offers a compelling way to explain the overall puzzle of inequality, it would be harder to deploy them to explain that variation. Why, for instance, did the Nordic countries become much less redistributive at the same time that France became more progressive? It is not clear that arguments about fairness norms, media coverage, or descriptive representation (to name just a few) can explain these differences. Why did some countries respond to the financial crisis by reversing course and becoming more redistributive? Again, we are not convinced that the arguments in this volume shed much light. There is still much work to be done to understand this variation.

One debated dimension of this heterogeneity is the comparability of the United States with other advanced democracies. By inviting scholars of American and comparative political economy to contribute to this volume, we evinced our conviction that it would be fruitful to consider the United States as one case among many and that treating the United States as an exception hinders more than it helps out understanding of political economy. As we noted previously, at least since the mid-1990s, the US experience of rising inequality has not been particularly exceptional as compared to other affluent democracies. At the same time, there are differences between the United States and its counterparts, differences that some chapters in this volume emphasize. Still, we think it is more productive to theorize about these differences, as with other cross-country variation, than to consider them in isolation. We hope that this volume encourages such an approach.

The studies in this volume also define inequality in a variety of ways, each of which draws on different conceptions about relevant social groups. Cavaillé, Elkjær and Iversen, and Mathisen and coauthors compare income groups; Curto-Grau and Gallego study education groups, while Mathisen and Peters examine both income and education; and Ares and Häusermann and Carnes and Lupu focus on occupational categories. Political economy has for years been dominated by theories that focused on income groups, so it is important that the analysis of social class is making a return. But our discipline has yet to grapple with the concept of social class and how to measure it in consistent or standardized ways.

Our volume focuses on these class- and income-based inequalities, and why and when governments tolerate them. But as Bartels usefully points out in his chapter, there are surely also racial, ethnic, and other political inequities that may be more pronounced and possibly more consequential than the ones we are concerned with here. There may also be reasons to think that economic inequality and political inequality are not entirely independent. The wealthy may be able to exert disproportionate influence on policymakers where economic resources are distributed unequally (Erikson 2015; Rosset et al. 2013). In their cross-national analysis, Lupu and Warner (2022b) indeed find that economic inequality is related to inequalities in opinion congruence between citizens and representatives. Ares and Häusermann's chapter in this volume also highlights the possibility that political inequalities, if they disempower and disengage certain groups of voters, can lead to policies that exacerbate economic inequality. We hope scholars take up studying these complex relationships and that this volume's efforts to explain the political puzzle of rising economic inequality might help to inform those efforts as well.

PART I

GOVERNMENT RESPONSIVENESS

2

Unequal Responsiveness and Government Partisanship in Northwest Europe[*]

Ruben Mathisen, Wouter Schakel, Svenja Hense,
Lea Elsässer, Mikael Persson, and Jonas Pontusson

Income and class biases in political representation have attracted the attention of many political scientists in recent years. More than any other scholarly work, Martin Gilens' (2012) study of unequal policy responsiveness in the United States has stimulated research and debate on this topic. Sorting survey respondents by relative income and estimating the probability of policy change based on some 1,800 survey items asking about support for specific reform proposals, Gilens finds that the preferences of high-income citizens predict policy change, but the preferences of low-income and even middle-income citizens have no influence on policy outcomes when they diverge significantly from the preferences of high-income citizens. These findings have sparked lively debates among scholars working on American politics. One debate focuses on the frequency and extent of divergence in preferences between income groups.[1] Simply put, do low- and middle-income citizens lose out to

[*] Replication data for this chapter are available at Harvard Dataverse, https://doi.org/10.7910/DVN/3YL7XU. Earlier versions of the paper were presented at workshops of the Unequal Democracies project at the University of Geneva, financed by ERC Advanced Grant 741538, and in the Unequal Democracies online seminar run by Noam Lupu and Jonas Pontusson in Spring 2021. We thank workshop and seminar participants for useful criticisms and suggestions. In particular, we are indebted to Larry Bartels, Brian Burgoon, Silja Häusermann, Noam Lupu, and Armin Schäfer for detailed feedback. The Dutch data that we analyze were collected with the financial support of the Netherlands Organisation for Scientific Research (grant no. 406-15-089), the Swedish data were collected with the support of the Swedish Research Council for Health, Working Life and Welfare (grant no. 2017:00873), and access to Norwegian data was made possible by the Norwegian Centre for Research Data. Pontusson's work on this paper was funded by the aforementioned ERC Advanced Grant, Mathisen's work was funded by the Meltzer Foundation and Schakel's work was funded by the Netherlands Organisation for Scientific Research (grant no. 453-14-017).
[1] Important contributions to this debate include Bashir (2015), Bowman (2020), Branham, Soroka and Wlezien (2017), Enns (2015), Gilens (2009, 2015a), and Soroka and Wlezien (2008).

affluent citizens all the time or only occasionally? And, perhaps more importantly, do they lose out on issues that truly matter to them or (mostly) on issues that are not so salient? A second debate concerns the causal mechanisms behind the income biases in policy responsiveness identified by Gilens and other scholars (e.g., Bartels 2016, Ellis 2017, Hayes 2013, and Rigby and Wright 2011, 2013).

This chapter seeks to contribute to the debate about the reasons for unequal responsiveness by bringing data from European countries to bear and, in particular, by exploring whether policymaking under Left-leaning governments is less biased than policymaking under Right-leaning governments. Less directly, our empirical analysis also speaks to the debate about the meaning of unequal representation by exploring policy responsiveness and partisan conditioning of policy responsiveness across different policy domains.

It is tempting to suppose that the income biases identified by Gilens and others represent a uniquely American phenomenon. Indeed, many explanations for unequal responsiveness advanced by students of American politics imply that we should observe much more equal policy responsiveness in countries with lower income inequality, stronger unions, lower income inequality in voter turnout, and less costly, publicly subsidized election campaigns. However, recent studies replicating Gilens' research design find that policy responsiveness is also biased in favor of affluent citizens in Germany (Elsässer, Hense, and Schäfer 2021), the Netherlands (Schakel 2021), Norway (Mathisen 2023), and Sweden (Persson 2023). In what follows, we summarize the main findings of these studies and reanalyze the data on which they are based.[2] While the original studies largely focused on overall differences in political influence between low-income and high-income citizens, our reanalysis focuses on differences between middle-income and high-income citizens and the conditioning effects of government partisanship. By focusing on responsiveness to the preferences of high-income citizens relative to middle-income citizens, we respond to a common critique of the literature on unequal responsiveness, viz., that it shows that the affluent are better represented than the poor – a finding that is arguably unsurprising and entirely consistent with the median voter theorem (cf. Elkjær and Klitgaard 2021).

Gilens (2012: Ch. 7) finds that responsiveness is equally skewed in favor of affluent citizens regardless of whether Democrats or Republicans control Congress and the White House, but most studies of unequal responsiveness in the United States support the intuitive hypothesis that the Democrats represent low- and middle-income citizens better than Republicans (Becher, Stegmueller, and Käppner 2018; Ellis 2017; Lax, Phillips, and Zelizer 2019;

---

[2] Gilens' approach to the study of policy responsiveness has also been replicated for Spain (Lupu and Tirado Castro 2023) and Switzerland (Wagner 2021), but these cases are not relevant for our present purposes. While democratization makes Spain a special case (as Lupu and Tirado Castro emphasize), the partisan composition of government does not vary in the Swiss case.

Rhodes and Schaffner 2017). In comparative politics, there is a large literature examining the effects of government party affiliation on social spending, welfare-state generosity, redistribution, and other policy outcomes on which citizens' preferences are polarized by income.[3] Much of this literature follows Garrett (1998) in positing that governing Left and Right parties alike seek to maximize their reelection chances by boosting macroeconomic performance and also cater to the policy preferences of their core constituencies, with core constituencies of Left parties identified as risk-exposed wage-earners with relatively low earnings and the core constituencies of Right parties identified as occupational strata characterized by lower exposure to labor market risks and higher earnings.

This stylized differentiation of Left and Right parties and their core constituencies would lead us to expect that Left-leaning governments are more responsive to the policy preferences of low- and middle-income citizens, and less responsive to the preferences of high-income citizens than Right-leaning governments. However, more recent literature (e.g., Manwaring and Holloway 2022; Mudge 2018) suggests that the mainstream Left – Social Democratic (and Labour) parties – have undergone a profound transformation since the 1980s, moving toward the center and adopting policy priorities associated with the notion of a "Third Way." Key features of this trend have been a move away from redistributive tax and spending policies and a focus on social investment, a policy shift apparently designed to appeal to new middle strata and, in particular, "socio-cultural professionals" (Gingrich and Häusermann 2015). Against this background, we first analyze whether Left-leaning governments mitigate income biases in policy responsiveness across all issues included in our datasets. We then focus on economic and social policies with direct distributive implications and, finally, explore temporal change in the effects of government partisanship on unequal responsiveness in this policy domain.

To anticipate, our results confirm that government policies in the four countries that we analyze are more responsive to the preferences of high-income citizens than to the preferences of middle- and low-income citizens. We find that unequal responsiveness is less pronounced under Left-leaning governments in Germany, the Netherlands, and Sweden, but there is still bias in favor of the high-income citizens even under Left-leaning governments, at least in Germany and the Netherlands. The Norwegian case is a puzzling exception in that Left-leaning governments seem to favor the affluent more than Right-leaning governments. However, this inversion of partisan conditioning disappears when we restrict our analysis to economic and welfare

---

[3] Noteworthy contributions to this literature include Allan and Scruggs (2004), Iversen and Soskice (2006), Kwon and Pontusson (2010), and Huber and Stephens (2001). See also Schakel and Burgoon's (2022) analysis of party manifestos, connecting the literature on unequal representation to the literature on partisan effects.

issues. More tentatively, we also find some support for the proposition that partisan conditioning of unequal responsiveness on distributive issues has indeed diminished over time.

In what follows, we proceed directly to empirics, leaving theoretical issues for later discussion. The first section presents the data we analyze and addresses methodological issues. The second section looks at patterns of unequal responsiveness across our four countries and presents the results of estimating different regression models with support for policy change at the 10th, 50th, and 90th income percentiles as predictors of policy adoption. In the third section, we introduce government partisanship as a variable that conditions policy responsiveness to the preferences of different income groups. In the fourth section, we restrict the analysis to economic and welfare issues and, in the fifth section, we explore changes in partisan conditioning over time. The final section summarizes our empirical findings and discusses their implications for the debate on mechanisms behind income bias in political representation.

DATA AND METHODOLOGY

For each of the four countries included in our analyses, authors of this paper created original datasets that matched public opinion with policy outcomes. In so doing, we followed the approach set out by Gilens (2012). To begin with, we identified questions in preexisting public opinion surveys that asked respondents to indicate whether they supported specific proposals for policy change. The selection of survey items was restricted to items that asked about policy changes that could be implemented at the national level and were worded in such a way that it was possible to determine whether the proposed change was implemented subsequent to the survey. For Sweden and Norway, the original datasets included questions about constitutional changes, but we have removed these questions from the analyses presented here. Note also that some questions in the original datasets and the merged dataset are phrased in terms of support for status-quo policy and that responses to such questions have been inverted to capture support for changing policy in a particular direction.[4]

The merged dataset contains nearly 2,000 observations (survey items), covering a wide range of issues, from raising the retirement age and cutting taxes to immigration reform, construction of nuclear power plants, and the introduction of same-sex marriage. As shown in Table 2.1, the items are unevenly distributed across countries and over time. In the pooled analyses presented later, we ensure that each country carries the same weight by weighting individual survey items by the inverse of the total number of items for each country. (The weights are adjusted when we analyze subsets of survey items.)

---

[4] For more detailed information about each of the original datasets, see Elsässer, Hense and Schäfer (2021), Schakel (2021), Mathisen (2023), and Persson (2023).

TABLE 2.1 *Survey items by country*

Country	N	Years	Sources
Germany	266	1998–2016	Commercial
Netherlands	291	1979–2012	Mostly public
Norway	557	1966–2014	Mostly commercial
Sweden	844	1960–2012	Public

The research projects on which we draw then harmonized the income of survey respondents in the manner proposed by Gilens (2012: 61–62), using percentile midpoints to generate estimates of the share of respondents at the 10th, 50th, and 90th percentiles who support policy change (henceforth P10, P50, and P90). An obvious and important limitation, to which we shall return, is that we do not have any information about the salience of proposed policy changes for respondents.

The dependent variable in our regression models is a dummy variable that takes the value of one if the policy change in question was enacted within a given time period after the survey and otherwise the value of zero. Like Gilens, we estimate the probability of a policy change in the direction preferred by respondents at different positions in the income distribution and do not take into account how much policy changed. For example, we treat all increases or decreases in unemployment benefits as equivalent, irrespective of their magnitude (unless the magnitude was specified in the survey question).

Using information from legislative records, government budgets, and newspaper articles, we coded survey items as adopted or not adopted within two and four years of the survey in which they appeared. The main results presented here are based on two-year windows for adoption, with results based on four-year windows (Gilens' default) presented in the online appendix (Tables 2.A2 and 2.A8–9). We prefer two-year windows because they provide a more precise measure of government partisanship, but the results for four-year windows turn out to be very similar.[5]

Our preferred measure of government partisanship is the combined share of cabinet portfolios held by left-wing parties (Social Democratic and Green parties), as reported on an annual basis by Armingeon, Engler, Leemann, and Weisstanner (2023). For each survey item, we calculate the average share of

---

[5] Note also that our "adoption windows" include the year in which the survey item was fielded for Germany and Sweden and the remainder of the year in which the survey item was fielded for the Netherlands and Norway (in addition to the following two or four years). In all four countries, more than three quarters of the policy changes that were adopted within four years were in fact adopted within the first two years following the survey being fielded. Based on the original Swedish dataset, Persson (2023) explores policy responsiveness over more extended periods of time (up to ten years) and finds that the income bias in responsiveness increases with time.

TABLE 2.2 *Average values of independent and dependent variables by country*

	Germany	Netherlands	Norway	Sweden
Policy change	0.57 (0.50)	0.20 (0.40)	0.21 (0.41)	0.13 (0.34)
(two years)				
P10 support	0.55 (0.22)	0.48 (0.22)	0.48 (0.23)	0.55 (0.21)
P50 support	0.56 (0.21)	0.48 (0.22)	0.47 (0.23)	0.53 (0.22)
P90 support	0.57 (0.19)	0.48 (0.21)	0.46 (0.23)	0.48 (0.21)
P90–P10 support	0.02 (0.15)	−0.01 (0.15)	−0.02 (0.12)	−0.07 (0.13)
P90–P50 support	0.01 (0.10)	−0.00 (0.11)	−0.01 (0.09)	−0.05 (0.12)
P50–P10 support	0.01 (0.08)	0.00 (0.08)	−0.01 (0.07)	−0.02 (0.07)
Left cabinet share	0.45 (0.36)	0.26 (0.14)	0.57 (0.32)	0.59 (0.43)

Note: Standard deviations in parentheses.

cabinet portfolios held by left-wing parties in the year of the survey and in the two or four subsequent years. As reported in the online appendix (Table 2.A11), we obtain substantively equivalent results if we instead measure government partisanship with a dummy for the office of prime minister being held by a Social Democrat and restrict the analysis to survey items with two-year windows in which there was no change of prime minister.

Table 2.2 reports average values for our partisanship variable as well as support for policy change at P10, P50, and P90 and the frequency of policy change by country. For now, suffice it to note that, over the time period(s) covered by our analyses, Left parties have participated in government more frequently and more extensively in Norway and Sweden than in Germany and, especially, the Netherlands.

We explore how government partisanship affects responsiveness to low-income, middle-income, and high-income citizens by interacting our measure of government party affiliation with measures of P10, P50, and P90 support for policy change. To avoid the complications associated with interpreting interaction effects estimated with logistic regression models (e.g., Gomila 2021), we present results based on estimating linear probability models, with heteroskedasticity-consistent standard errors, throughout the paper.[6]

It is important to keep in mind that the public opinion data that form the basis for our analyses refer to policy changes that were discussed in a particular country at a particular point in time. The issues captured by our data and the overall balance across policy areas differ within countries over time as well as between countries. A further complication has to do with the sources of the survey data. As indicated in Table 2.1, the German dataset relies exclusively on commercial surveys, while the Swedish dataset relies exclusively on publicly funded surveys designed by academic researchers and the Dutch

---

[6] We obtain very similar results when we estimate logistic regression models (available upon request).

and Norwegian datasets combine both types of surveys. According to our data, policy change is much more common in Germany than in Sweden (see Table 2.2), but this may well be because the survey sources are different in the two countries, commercial surveys being more likely to ask about policy changes currently being discussed by policymakers. Based on these data, we cannot say with any certainty that status-quo bias is stronger in Sweden than in Germany. More generally, cross-national differences in policy responsiveness must be interpreted with caution. However, our primary interest pertains to patterns of unequal responsiveness within countries – how government partisanship conditions responsiveness to P10, P50, and P90 – and, for this purpose, cross-country differences in the questions asked in surveys would seem to be less relevant. Moreover, cross-national and temporal variation in survey items becomes less of a concern when we focus on economic and welfare policies. The issues pertaining to this policy domain are quite similar across our four cases and have not changed so much since the 1980s.

UNEQUAL POLICY RESPONSIVENESS

We begin our empirical analysis by looking at overall policy responsiveness to the preferences of P10, P50, and P90 in our four countries. In so doing, we replicate the results of the underlying country studies and establish the baseline for our subsequent analysis of how government partisanship conditions income biases in policy responsiveness. As indicated at the outset, we focus more explicitly on the political representation of middle-income citizens relative to high-income citizens than in our previous work.

Figure 2.1 shows the bivariate coefficients that we obtain when we regress policy adoption within a two-year window on our measures of support for policy changes at P10, P50, and P90 in separate models. For comparison, we include equivalent estimates based on Gilens' data for the United States.[7] We also show the results that we obtain when we pool data for the four European countries. (Confidence intervals in this and all subsequent figures are displayed at the 95 percent level.)

While overall responsiveness to public opinion varies across countries, unequal responsiveness appears to be a common feature of liberal democracies. In Germany, the Netherlands, and Sweden, the likelihood of policy change increases significantly with P90 support for policy change, but this is not the case for P50 support, let alone P10 support. The coefficients for P50 and P10 support almost clear the 95 percent significance threshold for the Netherlands, but they are indistinguishable from zero for Germany and Sweden. Among the four European countries, Norway stands out as the only country where support for policy change at any point in the income distribution increases the

---

[7] Downloaded from www.russellsage.org/datasets/economic-inequality-and-political-representation, the US data cover the period 1981–2002.

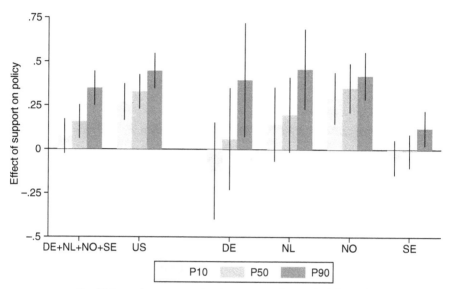

FIGURE 2.1 Coefficients for support by income on the probability of policy change (bivariate linear probability models with two-year windows)
Note: See Table 2.A1 in the online appendix for full regression results.

likelihood of adopting policy changes, though the effect becomes stronger as we move up the income ladder. In this respect, Norway resembles the United States. As measured here, income biases in unequal responsiveness are more pronounced in Germany, the Netherlands, and Sweden than in the United States. Pooling our European data, the size of the coefficient for P50 preferences is about half the size of the coefficient for P90 preferences and the size of the coefficient for P10 preferences is about one quarter of the size of the coefficient for P90 preferences.

As commonly noted in the literature on this topic, the policy preferences of low-, middle-, and high-income citizens are correlated, and this renders the results presented in Figure 2.1 dubious. The effect of support for policy change among low- and middle-income citizens that we observe in the Norwegian and United States data may actually be the effect of support for policy change among high-income citizens (or vice versa). To get around this problem, Table 2.3 shows the average marginal effects we obtain when we replicate the pooled model shown in Figure 2.1 with two subsets of our data: first, a subset consisting of proposed policy changes on which P10 and P90 support diverges by at least 10 percentage points and, secondly, a subset consisting of proposed changes on which P50 and P90 support diverges by at least 10 points. Averaging across our four European countries, we find no responsiveness at all to the preferences of P10 or P50 when the analysis is restricted to survey items on which they clearly disagree with P90.

TABLE 2.3 *Average marginal effects of support for policy change when preferences diverge by at least 10 percentage points (two-year windows)*

	P10 vs. P90		P50 vs. P90	
	P10	P90	P50	P90
Support for policy	−0.061	0.563**	−0.090	0.539**
Change	(0.083)	(0.083)	(0.110)	(0.114)
Country dummies	Yes	Yes	Yes	Yes
Constant	0.604**	0.261**	0.605**	0.259**
	(0.058)	(0.062)	(0.078)	(0.084)
N	959	959	740	740
Adjusted R^2	0.168	0.217	0.144	0.182

Note: $^+p < 0.1$, $p < 0.05$, $^{**}p < 0.01$.

As noted by Bartels in this volume, analyses of subsets of data like those presented in Table 2.3 reduce the correlation between group preferences, but are still limited in that they include only one group at a time. The statistical relationships uncovered in these models might well be spurious. One way of considering multiple income groups' preferences simultaneously is simply to include them in the same multivariate models. We report results from such models in Table 2.A3 in the online appendix. When P10 or P50 is paired with P90, the coefficient for the lower income group is negative and statistically significant. When P10 is paired with P50 and when all three groups are included, the coefficient for P10 is again negative and statistically significant.

Low-income citizens appear to be "perversely represented" in the sense that their support for policy change reduces the probability of policy change. As suggested by Gilens (2012: 253–258), it seems very likely that this effect is a statistical artifact, due to the inclusion of predictors with correlated measurement error (see also Achen 1985). Following Schakel, Burgoon, and Hakhverdian (2020), we address this problem by estimating models that regress policy adoption on the difference in support for policy change between two positions in the income distribution, while controlling for support for policy change at the median income. We go beyond Schakel, Burgoon, and Hakhverdian (2020) by estimating such models not only for the gap between P90 and P10 support for policy change, but also for the gap between P90 and P50 support for policy change and the gap between P50 and P10 support for policy change. The average marginal effects that we obtain by estimating such models provide a measure of the responsiveness to the preferences of one income group relative to another income group. While Table 2.4 reports on marginal effects, Figure 2.2 displays the predicted probabilities of observing a policy change for different values of the preference gap between P90

TABLE 2.4 *Average marginal effects of preference gaps on policy adoption, controlling for P50 support (two-year windows)*

	Pooled	Germany	Netherlands	Norway	Sweden
P90–P10 support	0.666**	0.954**	0.653**	0.492**	0.432**
P90–P50 support	0.910**	1.529**	1.133**	0.691**	0.432**
P50–P10 support	0.676**	1.422**	0.357	0.477*	0.356*

Notes: $^+$ < 0.1, * $p < 0.05$, ** $p < 0.01$, see Tables 2.A4–6 in the online appendix for full regression results.

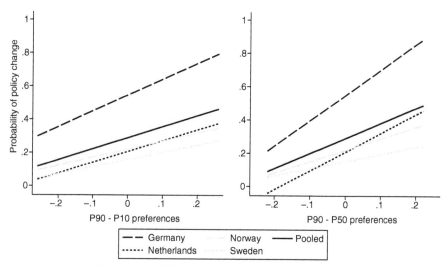

FIGURE 2.2 Predicted probabilities of policy change at different preference gaps between P90 and P10 or P50 (two-year windows)

and P10 (left panel) and the preference gap between P90 and P50 (right panel) for each country individually and for the four countries combined. (To make the figure clearer, we show only the 95 percent confidence interval for the pooled results.)

To clarify, the preference-gap variables shown in Table 2.4 and Figure 2.2 take on higher values when P90 is more in favor of a policy change than P50 or P10. A positive effect of this variable indicates a bias in favor of the affluent, as policy change becomes more likely when high-income citizens are more supportive of policy change relative to low- or middle-income citizens. An obvious complication is that the middle of the scale includes any scenario in which preferences are the same at different positions in the income distribution, regardless of whether the two income groups favor or oppose policy change. This complication is at least partially resolved by controlling for the level of P50 support for policy change.[8]

For all four countries, Table 2.4 and Figure 2.2 indicate that policymaking is more responsive to the preferences of high-income citizens than to the preferences of middle-income citizens and, less surprisingly, to the preferences of low-income citizens. The bias in favor of the high-income citizens relative to the middle is only slightly less pronounced than the bias in favor of the high-income citizens relative to low-income citizens in the Swedish case and it is more pronounced than the bias in favor of high-income citizens relative to low-income citizens in the Dutch case. In Germany and Norway, these two biases are essentially the same. While we observe a significant bias in favor of middle-income citizens relative to low-income citizens in Germany, this bias is quite small in Norway and Sweden and non-existent in the Netherlands. Overall, the basic patterns are strikingly similar across the four countries, despite cross-country differences in the samples of survey items on which these results are based.

Finally, Figure 2.3 summarizes the results that we obtain when we try to capture different "coalition scenarios" with the pooled dataset, again following Gilens (2012: 83–85). The two panels in this figure are based on estimating separately the average marginal effects of P90, P50, and P10 support for policy changes (i.e., bivariate models) for two different subsets of survey items. The results in the left-hand panel are based on the subset of survey items where P90 and P50 support differs by less than 8 percentage points and P10 support differs by more than 10 percentage points from that of the other income groups. Conversely, the right-hand panel is based on a subset of survey items where P50 and P10 support differs by less than 8 points and P90 support differs by more than 10 points. The alternative theoretical accounts of redistributive politics proposed by Iversen and Soskice (2006) and Lupu and Pontusson (2011) both suggest that P50 and P10 preferences will prevail over P90 preferences when they are closely aligned. While P50 preferences seem to be well represented when they are asymmetrically aligned with P90 preferences, P50 preferences do not seem to affect the likelihood of policy change when they are

---

[8] As shown in the online appendix (Tables 2.A4-A6), the coefficients for P50 support are invariably positive and mostly clear the 95 percent threshold for statistical significance. To account for overlapping preferences, we have also estimated models including both P90–P50 and P50–P10 gaps while still controlling for P50 support for policy change. Based on these models, Figure 2.A1 in the online appendix plots estimates of the influence of the P50 alongside estimates of P50 – (P50–P10) and P50 + (P90–P50). Figure 2.A1 suggests that the net influence of P10 preferences is negative in Germany and Sweden and positive but very small in Norway and the United States. In the Netherlands, policy appears to be more responsive to P10 preferences than P50 preferences. Policy responsiveness to P50 is particularly weak in Sweden, but even in the other three countries, responsiveness to P90 preferences is several times greater than responsiveness to P50 preferences (about 2.5 times greater in Norway and five times greater in Germany).

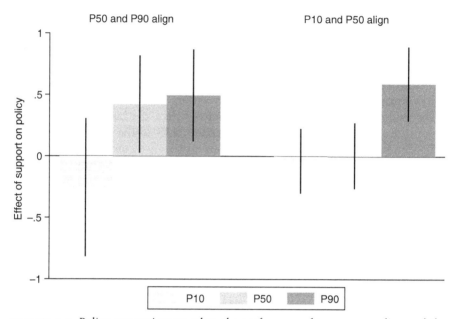

FIGURE 2.3 Policy responsiveness when the preferences of two groups align and the
third group diverges (two-year windows)
Notes: See Table 2.A7 in the online appendix for full results. N = 115 for the left-hand
panel, N = 426 for the right-hand panel.

instead asymmetrically aligned with P10 preferences. We hasten to add that
this analysis is based on rather small samples and that the results shown in
Figure 2.3 are sensitive to the thresholds that we use to identify different coalition scenarios.[9]

PARTISAN CONDITIONING OF POLICY
RESPONSIVENESS BY INCOME

We now turn to the question of how government partisanship affects policy
responsiveness. We address this question by adding measures of government
partisanship to models that identify the effects of preference gaps between
income groups while controlling for P50 support for policy change and interacting preference gaps with government partisanship. A negative interaction
effect indicates that the pro-affluent bias in policy responsiveness becomes

---

[9] Gilens (2012) uses 5 percentage points as the criterion for characterizing two income groups
as being closely aligned. This would leave us with only seventy-eight instances of P90 and P50
being closely aligned against P10 and would substantially reduce the average marginal effects of
P90 and P50 support alike.

smaller as the presence of Left parties in government increases.[10] As we have seen (Table 2.4), preference gaps between P90 and P50 or P10 are consistently better predictors of policy adoption than preference gaps between P50 and P10 and the effects of the P90–P50 gap are quite similar to the effects of the P90–P10 gap. In light of these findings, and the pivotal role that most theories of democratic politics assign to middle-income citizens, we focus on partisan conditioning of the effects of preference gaps that involve the affluent and, especially, the gap between the preferences of high-income and middle-income citizens. In other words, the question we ask is the following: do Left (or Left-leaning) governments cater less to the high-income citizens relative to low- and middle-income citizens than non-Left (Right-leaning) governments?

Reported in Tables 2.5 and 2.6, our main results are based on measuring government partisanship as the average share of cabinet portfolios held by Social Democratic and Green parties in the year that a particular survey item was fielded and the two subsequent years.[11] As noted at the outset, Norway stands out as an exceptional case in Tables 2.5 and 2.6. In the other three countries, the effect of P90 being more supportive of policy change than P10 and P50 is positive and significant when the interaction term equals zero (indicating an absence of Left parties in government) and the coefficient of the interaction term itself is negative. It is important to note here that our Swedish sample of survey items is nearly three times as large as our German and Dutch samples, explaining why coefficients of similar magnitude for Sweden clear statistical significance thresholds while the German coefficients do not. When we pool the three countries, the coefficients for the interaction terms clear the 95 percent threshold. According to these results, pro-affluent bias in policy responsiveness is significantly less pronounced when Left parties are in power in Germany, the Netherlands, and Sweden. In Norway, by contrast, the interaction terms are positive (and significant with 95 percent confidence), suggesting that pro-affluent bias in policy responsiveness only occurs when Left parties are in power.

---

[10] The following analysis might be biased if surveys systematically ask about different policy changes when Left parties and Right parties are in power. Based on the proportions survey items that pertain to different issue domains (as operationalized by Kriesi et al 2006), this does not appear to be the case.

[11] See Tables 2.A8–9 in the online appendix for results with four-year windows for coding policy adoption and cabinet shares averaged over five years. Our partisanship measure becomes less precise as we extend the length of the window for coding policy adoption, more often encompassing two or even three different governments. Nonetheless, the results with four-year windows are similar to the results presented in Tables 2.5 and 2.6. We also obtain similar results when we measure government partisanship by a dummy for the prime minister being from a Left party and restrict the analysis to survey items for which this dummy has the same value over the two-year window for coding policy adoption (see Tables 2.A10–11). Lastly, note that the 50–10 preferences gap is not significantly moderated by the participation of Left parties in government (Table 2.A12).

TABLE 2.5 *Linear probability models interacting the P90–P10 preference gap with Left government (two-year windows)*

	Pooled	Pooled (w/o NO)	Germany	Netherlands	Sweden	Norway
P90–P10 gap	0.791**	0.898**	1.235**	1.058**	0.742**	−0.125
	(0.122)	(0.134)	(0.297)	(0.317)	(0.138)	(0.303)
Left government	−0.025	−0.041	−0.049	−0.079	−0.065+	0.024
	(0.031)	(0.038)	(0.094)	(0.165)	(0.034)	(0.052)
P90–P10 × Left	−0.253	−0.441*	−0.483	−1.547	−0.547**	1.015*
government	(0.190)	(0.214)	(0.509)	(1.047)	(0.186)	(0.449)
P50 support	0.220**	0.170**	0.223	0.284**	0.026	0.353**
	(0.049)	(0.062)	(0.156)	(0.108)	(0.049)	(0.071)
Country dummies	Yes	Yes	No	No	No	No
Constant	0.445**	0.484**	0.451**	0.097	0.185**	0.037
	(0.043)	(0.050)	(0.101)	(0.074)	(0.038)	(0.042)
N	1958	1401	266	291	844	557
Adjusted R^2	0.190	0.222	0.071	0.061	0.034	0.063

Notes: $^+p < 0.1$, $^*p < 0.05$, $^{**}p < 0.01$.

TABLE 2.6 *Linear probability models interacting the P90–P50 preference gap with Left government (two-year windows)*

	Pooled	Pooled (w/o NO)	Germany	Netherlands	Sweden	Norway
P90–P50 gap	1.160**	1.316**	2.058**	1.500**	0.937**	−0.225
	(0.157)	(0.173)	(0.530)	(0.419)	(0.170)	(0.409)
Left government	−0.024	−0.040	−0.024	−0.141	−0.069*	0.025
	(0.032)	(0.038)	(0.090)	(0.165)	(0.032)	(0.052)
P90–P50 × Left	−0.510*	−0.800**	−0.951	−1.332	−0.859**	1.648*
government	(0.231)	(0.250)	(0.837)	(1.462)	(0.211)	(0.651)
P50	0.299**	0.257**	0.364*	0.406**	0.063	0.399**
	(0.050)	(0.065)	(0.166)	(0.114)	(0.051)	(0.070)
Country dummies	Yes	Yes	No	No	No	No
Constant	0.406**	0.440**	0.366**	0.054	0.163**	0.013
	(0.044)	(0.051)	(0.105)	(0.074)	(0.036)	(0.041)
N	1958	1401	266	291	844	557
Adjusted R^2	0.190	0.224	0.067	0.087	0.038	0.066

Notes: $^+p < 0.1$, $^* p < 0.05$, $^{**}p < 0.01$.

Based on the results in Table 2.6, Figure 2.4 displays predicted probabilities of policy adoption at different values of the P90–P50 gap under two partisan scenarios: no Left parties in government (left-hand panel) and Left parties

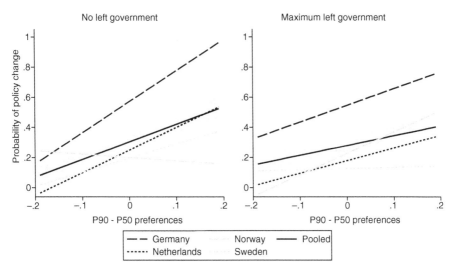

FIGURE 2.4 Predicted probabilities of policy change conditional on the P90–P50 preference gap and government partisanship (two-year windows)

holding all cabinet seats (right-hand panel).[12] The Norwegian case again stands out as exceptional in this figure. Importantly, Figure 2.4 also illustrates that the Left government diminishes but does not eliminate pro-affluent bias in Germany and the Netherlands. Sweden appears to be the only case in which policy is equally responsive to high-income and middle-income citizens when Left parties control the government.

GOVERNMENT PARTISANSHIP AND REDISTRIBUTIVE POLICY RESPONSIVENESS BY INCOME

The Norwegian puzzle invites further discussion of how party politics is related to income biases in political responsiveness. As noted in the introduction, our theoretical expectations regarding the impact of government partisanship apply most clearly to issues involving economic and social policies with direct distributive implications. It is much less evident that citizens' preferences are polarized by income on the many and varied "noneconomic" (or "nonmaterial") issues that divide Left and Right parties and, if there is polarization by income, it may well be the inverse of the polarization that we observe with issues pertaining to economic policy (in particular, fighting unemployment, taxation, and social spending). Indeed, an extensive literature on new cleavages in electoral politics argues that mainstream Left parties have sought to offset

[12] For the Netherlands, the second scenario is simulated based on Left parties holding 50 percent of cabinet portfolios, as this is the maximum value for the period under investigation.

the decline of the traditional working class by aligning their programs with the preferences of "new middle strata" – relatively affluent and primarily urban voters – on environmental issues as well as immigration and a host of cultural issues encompassed by the notion of "cosmopolitanism" while seeking to retain the support of low-income voters by maintaining their commitment to redistribution of income (e.g., Gingrich and Häusermann 2015; Kitschelt 1994; Kriesi et al. 2006). This general characterization holds for Dutch, German, and Swedish Social Democrats as well as Norwegian Social Democrats, but one might plausibly assume that the urban–rural divide is a more prominent feature of Norwegian politics – perhaps a more prominent feature of Norwegian income inequality as well – and that this has rendered the Norwegian Social Democrats, and other progressive parties with an urban base, less responsive to low-income citizens than their Dutch, German, and Swedish counterparts (Bjørklund 1992; Rokkan 1966).

A detailed analysis of the issues on which Norwegian governments headed by Social Democrats have gone against the preferences of low- and middle-income citizens lies beyond the scope of this paper. We must also set aside the question of whether or not the strength of the populist Progress Party (with a vote share ranging between 14.6 percent and 22.9 percent since 2000), and its participation in government between 2014 and 2020, might have rendered Right-leaning governments more responsive to low-income citizens. What we can do to shed some light on "Norwegian exceptionalism" and, more generally, to further enhance our understanding of partisan conditioning of unequal responsiveness is to replicate the preceding analysis for a subset of survey items that pertain to economic and welfare issues. Needless to say, this involves a significant reduction in the total number of data points at our disposal and some loss of statistical power.

In assigning survey items to policy domains, we rely on the typology proposed by Kriesi et al. (2006). The category "economic issues" thus encompasses policy questions pertaining on macroeconomic management, government regulation of the economy as well as government interventions (industrial policy), taxes, and government spending on income transfer programs as well as public services. Pooling data across the four countries, this definition of economic and welfare issues yields a sample of 681 survey items (as compared to 1,958 items for the preceding analysis).

To begin with, Table 2.7 shows the results of estimating our baseline models with preference gaps as the main independent variables (controlling for P50 support), without interacting preference gaps with government partisanship. For Germany and Sweden, these results are quite similar to the results for all survey items (shown in Table 2.4). In both of these cases, P90 preferences dominate P50 and P10 preferences. In the German case, P50 preferences also dominate P10 preferences. Although the coefficients for preference gaps are also positive for the Netherlands and Norway, none of the Norwegian coefficients clear conventional thresholds for statistical significance, suggesting

TABLE 2.7 *Average marginal effects of preference gaps on policy adoption, controlling for P50 support, economic, and welfare issues only (two-year windows)*

	Pooled	Germany	Netherlands	Norway	Sweden
P90–P10 support	0.577**	1.010**	0.339	0.157	0.482*
P90–P50 support	0.787**	1.563**	0.671*	0.338	0.440*
P50–P10 support	0.506*	1.422**	0.154	−0.268	0.021

Notes: *p < 0.05, **p < 0.01. See Tables 2.A13–15 in the online appendix for full regression results.

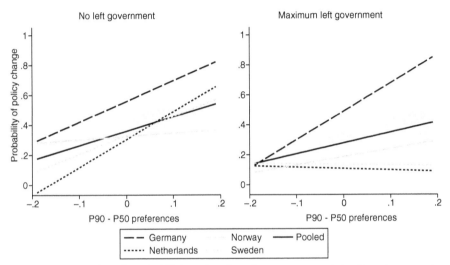

FIGURE 2.5 Predicted probabilities of policy change, economic/welfare issues only, conditional on the P90–P50 preference gap and government partisanship (two-year windows)
Note: See Table 2.A16 in the online appendix for full regression results (and Table 2.A17 for results using the P90–P10 preference gap instead).

that there is no systematic bias in favor of the affluent on economic issues. In the Dutch case, P90 preferences dominate P50 preferences more clearly than P10 preferences.

Turning to the conditioning effects of government partisanship, we again interact our partisanship variable (Left parties' share of cabinet portfolios) with the P90–P50 preference gap. The results are summarized in Figure 2.5. The first thing to note is that Norway no longer stands out as an exceptional case when we restrict the analysis to economic and welfare issues. For the Netherlands and Sweden alike, Left participation in government significantly reduces pro-affluent bias in this policy domain. We do not observe such an effect for Norway, but it is no longer the case that Left participation increases unequal responsiveness. We also do not observe any significant reduction of unequal responsiveness in the German case. In short, the conventional partisan hypothesis seems to hold for the Netherlands and Sweden, but not for Germany and Norway.

CHANGES IN POLICY RESPONSIVENESS BY INCOME AND PARTISAN CONDITIONING

Our German data begin in 1998, at a time when many Social Democratic parties, including the German one, had already embraced more market-friendly, less-redistributive "Third Way" policies, but our data for the other three countries extend farther back in time (to the early 1980s for the Netherlands and to the 1960s for Norway and Sweden). To explore whether the reorientation of Social Democratic parties in the 1990s entailed a decline in policy responsiveness to the preferences of low- and middle-income citizens under Left government participation, we conduct separate analyses for the period before 1998 and for the period from 1998 onwards, separating economic and welfare issues from other issues. For the P90–P50 preference gap, Figure 2.6 shows predicted probabilities of policy under the minimum Left government scenarios based on pooling survey items for all countries, that is, for three countries (the Netherlands, Norway, and Sweden) for 1960–1997 and for all four countries for 1998–2016.[13]

Our analysis of temporal change features only pooled results for two reasons. To begin with, it goes without saying that the number of observations in country-specific analyses becomes very small when we restrict them to economic and welfare policies in one or the other subperiod.[14] Secondly, irrespective of the loss of statistical power, country-specific analyses restricted to one of these subperiods often end up comparing one or two Left-leaning governments with an equally small number of Right-leaning governments and they are arguably "contaminated" by the idiosyncratic experiences of one of these governments. We would not want to generalize about long-term changes in partisan conditioning of unequal responsiveness based on which parties happened to be in government during the Great Recession of 2008–2010.[15] Pooling data across our four countries serves to minimize the effects of such

---

[13] We obtain very similar results interacting the P90–P10 preference gap with government partisanship for separate time periods: see Figure 2.A2 in the online appendix.

[14] For 1960–1997, the number of economic/welfare items in our dataset ranges between 63 (for the Netherlands) and 112 (for Norway). For 1998–2016, the number ranges between 49 (for Norway) and 167 (for Sweden).

[15] Over the three years 2008–2010, the Norwegian Social Democrats held the office of prime minister while the Dutch Labor Party was a junior coalition partner and the Swedish Social Democrats were in opposition. The German Social Democrats exited the government after the election in September 2009.

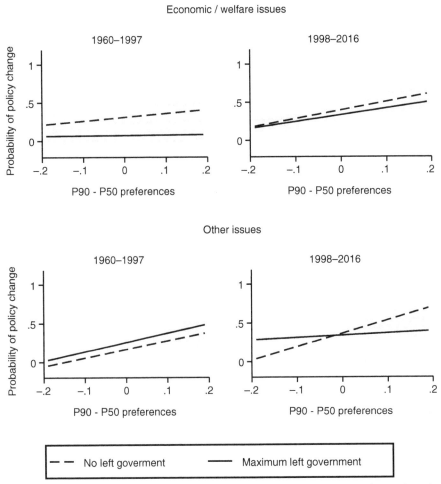

FIGURE 2.6 Predicted probabilities of policy change by time period, conditional on the P90–P50 preference gap and government partisanship (two-year windows)
Note: See Table 2.A18 in the online appendix for full regression results.

events and seems to be justified in light of the common patterns of unequal responsiveness and partisan conditioning that we have already observed.

Pooling data from all four countries, we find that Left-leaning governments were distinctly different from Right-leaning governments in the domain of economic and welfare policies prior to 1998. While the policy choices of Right-leaning governments responded primarily to the preferences of affluent citizens, Left-leaning governments were equally responsive to the preferences of low- and middle-income citizens in this policy domain. By contrast, Left-leaning and Right-leaning governments were equally biased in favor of the preferences of affluent citizens in other policy domains. Crucially for our present purposes, we no longer observe any partisan conditioning of policy responsiveness on economic and welfare issues in the post-1998 period. The pro-affluent bias of Right-leaning governments appears to have been more pronounced than in the earlier period and, at the same time, Left-leaning governments are no longer distinct from Right-leaning governments in the post-1998 period. Outside the domain of economic and welfare policies, we find that Left-leaning and Right-leaning governments were equally biased in favor of the preferences of affluent citizens in the pre-1998 period and that the pro-affluent bias of Left-leaning governments has diminished while the pro-affluent bias of Right-leaning governments has become more pronounced.

We hasten to note that the differentiation between Left-leaning and Right-leaning governments on "other issues" in the post-1998 period fails to meet standard criteria for statistical significance. The 95 percent confidence intervals overlap in two of the other panels of Figure 2.6 as well. The main take-away from the analysis summarized in Figure 2.6 is that we observe a significant effect of interacting preference gaps with government partisanship only for economic and welfare issues and only for the period prior to 1998.

RETHINKING UNEQUAL RESPONSIVENESS

Our main empirical findings can be summarized as follows. First, we find that middle-income as well as low-income citizens in Northwest Europe are consistently underrepresented compared to high-income citizens when representation is measured as responsiveness of policy outputs to stated preferences across the full range of issues captured by public opinion surveys. Second, we find that unequal responsiveness is moderated by government partisanship, such that the pro-affluent bias is less pronounced (but not zero) when Left parties are in government. The second observation comes with more qualifications than the first: it does not hold for one of our four countries (Norway) when pooling all issues, and when we separate policy domains and time periods, it applies mostly to economic and welfare issues before 1998 (possibly to noneconomic issues after 1998).

In closing, let us briefly reflect on the implications of these findings for the debates about the meaning of unequal responsiveness, as measured by Gilens (2012), and the reasons why governments appear to be most responsive to the preferences of high-income citizens than to the preferences of low- and middle-income citizens. To begin with, it is truly striking that income biases in policy responsiveness, measured in this manner, are at least as pronounced in "social Europe" as in "liberal America" (Pontusson 2005). How do we reconcile this observation with the fact that tax-transfer systems are significantly more redistributive in Germany, the Netherlands, Norway, and Sweden than in the United States?

As documented by Brooks and Manza (2007), American citizens are, in general, less supportive of progressive taxation and redistributive social programs than Dutch, Germans, Norwegian, and Swedish citizens. This contrast holds across the income distribution and may well be more pronounced in the upper half of the income distribution. Support for redistribution among high-income citizens provides a partial explanation for the coexistence of unequal responsiveness and redistribution, but the origins of redistributive politics in Northwest Europe can hardly be explained by reference to the preferences of high-income citizens.

More plausibly, support for redistribution among high-income citizens in Northwest Europe represents an adaptation to policy developments generated by the political mobilization of low- and middle-income citizens in the wake of democratization and the Second World War. In making this argument, we think it is important to recognize that the status quo informs the policy agenda of policymakers and the questions that public opinion surveys ask as well as the way that citizens respond to these questions. And the status quo is, of course, an expression of past policy decisions. Though we lack the data necessary to test this proposition in a systematic fashion, it seems likely that policy responsiveness on economic and welfare issues, by Left-leaning and Right-leaning governments alike, was significantly more equal in Northwest Europe than in the United States in the postwar era.

Our finding that Germany, the Netherlands, and Sweden are comparable to the United States in terms of income biases in policy responsiveness in the period since the 1980s fits with the observation that German, Dutch, and Swedish governments undertook reforms that reduced the redistributive effects of taxation and government spending in the 1990s and 2000s (see Pontusson and Weisstanner, 2018, as well as the introductory chapter to this volume). For our present purposes, the key point is that the starting point of these developments was very different from the status quo in the United States. Consistent with this argument, perusing lists of proposed policy changes makes it quite clear that antiredistributive policy proposals are more common and more radical in Gilens' US dataset than in our European datasets.[16]

Left parties and their trade-union allies played a key agenda-setting role in Northwest Europe in the 1960s and 1970s, when redistribution became a prominent feature of tax-transfer systems in these countries. Again, our analysis yields suggestive evidence that Left-leaning governments in Northwest Europe were more responsive to low- and middle-income citizens than to the high-income citizens in the economic and welfare policy domain prior to the

---

[16] Examples include privatizing Social Security, Bush's trillion-plus dollar tax cuts and curtailing government employees' right to strike. Even proposed changes in the direction of *more* redistribution – such as raising the minimum wage from $4 to $5 an hour in the late 1990's – reflect the low levels of redistribution at the time. See Witko et al (2021) on agenda-setting as crucial dimension of unequal representation in US politics.

mid-1990s. In this respect, our findings are consistent with the long-standing literature on partisan politics as factor behind cross-national variation in the development of the welfare state.

On the other hand, these findings represent something of a challenge for the conventional view that mainstream Left parties in Northwest Europe have sought to offset the decline of the working-class constituency by appealing to middle-class voters based on new ("post-materialist") issues while retaining the support of working-class voters based on their continued commitment to redistribution. This interpretation of the reorientation of mainstream Left parties would lead us to expect that mainstream Left parties remain "pro-poor" in the domain of economic and welfare policy while they have become more "pro-affluent" in other policy domains. Generalizing across our four countries, we find instead that mainstream Left parties, like mainstream parties of the Center-Right, have historically been biased in favor of affluent citizens outside the domain of redistributive politics and that post-1998 Left governments are first and foremost distinguished from earlier Left governments by their lack of responsiveness to low- and middle-income citizens in the domain of redistributive politics.

Setting government partisanship aside, what are the implications of our empirical findings for the debate about the causal mechanisms behind income and class biases in political representation? The "Americanist" literature identifies four plausible (and complementary) explanations for the income biases identified by Gilens (2012) and others.[17] Perhaps most prominently, and most obviously, this literature posits that the costs of election campaigns and politicians' reliance on private sources of campaign funding – what Gilens (2015a: 222) refers to as the "outsize role of money in American politics" – constitute a key reason why policy outputs disproportionately correspond to the preferences of affluent citizens. A second line of argumentation in the US literature invokes the income gradient in political participation – in the first instance, in electoral turnout – to explain unequal policy responsiveness. Yet another line of argument focuses on lobbying by corporations and organized interest groups, positing either that the policy preferences of affluent citizens coincide with corporate interests to a greater extent than the policy preferences of low- and middle-income citizens or that affluent citizens are better organized and thus better represented through "extra-electoral" politics. Finally, Carnes (2013) has pioneered a line of inquiry that focuses on the social and occupational backgrounds of elected representatives as the key source of unequal policy responsiveness in the United States.

As commonly noted by "Europeanists," the fact that we also observe unequal responsiveness of a consistent and pervasive nature in countries like Germany and Sweden raises questions about the relevance of campaign

---

[17] In addition to contributions cited already, see Hacker and Pierson (2010) and Gilens and Page (2014).

finance. Surely, money matters to parties and politicians in these countries as well, but election campaigns are much less expensive and, for the most part, financed by public subsidies. The point here is not to deny that campaign finance might be an important factor in the US case, but rather to point out that other factors must be taken into account in order to explain the ubiquity of unequal responsiveness across countries. The same arguably holds for electoral participation as an explanation of unequal responsiveness. In all four of the countries analyzed in this chapter, we observe unequal turnout by income, but aggregate turnout is higher than in the United States and the income gradient is flatter. And yet overall policy responsiveness does not appear to be markedly more equal.[18]

The argument about unequal responsiveness via the interest-group channel is more difficult to evaluate comparatively, but it seems reasonably clear that corporations and business associations wield less unilateral influence over elected representatives and unelected policymakers in countries with centralized policy consultations and, in particular, tripartite bodies that provide for negotiations over policy implementation as well as policy formulation between representatives of unions, employers, and governments. Our four countries all exemplify this model of "corporatist intermediation." Especially in Norway and Sweden, unions have historically played, and continue to play, an important role as counterweights to the political influence of business actors (organized or not). Again, it is puzzling that we do not observe more equal policy responsiveness under these circumstances.

Of the various arguments invoked to explain unequal responsiveness in the United States, the argument about descriptive misrepresentation by income and social class seems most easily applied to Northwest Europe. Elected representatives in Germany, the Netherlands, Norway, and Sweden are less likely to be multimillionaires than their American counterparts, but they come overwhelmingly from the ranks of university-educated professionals and tend to belong to the top two or three deciles of the income distribution (see Carnes and Lupu's contribution to this volume). A growing number of studies show that occupational background and associated life circumstances and social networks influence the policy preferences and priorities of elected officials across a wide range of different national contexts (Alexiadou 2022; Carnes and Lupu 2015; Hemingway 2020; O'Grady 2019; Persson 2021; Curto-Grau and Gallego in this volume). In a related vein, recent studies find that elected representatives tend to be more accurate in their perceptions of the preferences of affluent citizens than in the perceptions of the preferences of poor citizens (Pereira 2021; Sevenans et al. 2020). Arguably, this line of argumentation is particularly relevant for understanding the reorientation of mainstream Left

---

[18] Note, however, that Peters and Ensink (2015) find that aggregate voter turnout conditions the responsiveness of social spending to the preferences of poor and affluent citizens across twenty-five European countries. See also Mathisen and Peters' contribution to this volume.

parties, as the social backgrounds of candidates for public office fielded by these parties at the national level have become more like those of candidates fielded by other mainstream parties over the last two or three decades.

Beyond these four possible mechanisms, a number of alternatives ought to be considered. In addition to factors pertaining to the behavior of citizens and political elites, the unequal policy responsiveness that we observe across many countries might plausibly be attributed to the systemic power of capital. Following Block (1977), the argument would be that governing parties are not responding to any specific demands placed on them by citizens or interest groups, but rather seeking to maximize their chances of reelection by incentivizing capital owners (private individuals) to invest and thereby improve macroeconomic performance. A crucial additional step in the argument would be that the policy preferences of high-income citizens tend to be more closely aligned with the interests of capital owners than the preferences of low- and middle-income citizens. For our present purposes, suffice it to note that this line of argument would seem to imply that unequal responsiveness should be most pronounced with regard to policy issues that bear directly on the interests of capital owners (and conflicts of interest between capital and labor). In other words, we should observe greater pro-affluent bias in the domain of economic and welfare policies than in other policy domains. Our analysis does not yield any evidence in support of this expectation.

Articulated by Persson (2023), another argument that might explain the ubiquity of unequal responsiveness concerns status-quo bias. Simply put, this argument posits that low-income citizens are less satisfied with the status-quo than high-income citizens and, as a result, more likely to support policy changes in general. To the extent that this is true, and given the way that we measure policy outcomes, status-quo bias produces policy outcomes that look as if policymakers were responding disproportionately to the demands of affluent citizens. Analyzing the Swedish dataset on which we draw for this paper, Persson (2023) shows that income groups have had very similar preferences with regard to policy changes that have been adopted, but low-income citizens have been much more supportive of policy changes that have not been adopted than affluent citizens (with middle-income support very much in the middle). As shown in Table 2.2, however, we observe little or no difference between income groups in their average support for policy changes in Germany, the Netherlands, and Norway.[19]

Related to status-quo bias, there is an alternative interpretation of the evidence for unequal policy responsiveness presented earlier that we ought to engage with in a more systematic way than scholars working in this domain have done so far. Observing that policy change happens more often when it

---

[19] In the Netherlands, P90 and P10 have the same average support for policy change; in Norway, P90 is 2 percentage points less in favor of policy change than P10; while in Germany, P90 is actually 2 percentage points *more* in favor of policy change than P10.

is supported by affluent citizens and that support by citizens in the lower half of the income distribution has little, if any, effect on the probability of policy adoption, it is commonplace to conclude that politicians listen to affluent citizens more than they listen to low- and middle-income citizens. But perhaps it is the other way around. Perhaps it is the case that affluent citizens listen more to politicians than low- and middle-income citizens do. We know that income and education are closely correlated and many studies demonstrate that more educated citizens are more interested in and knowledgeable about politics (e.g., Schlozman, Verba, and Brady 2012). Arguably, this means that affluent citizens are more likely to take their cues from policymakers (or debate among "insiders") in deciding whether they favor or oppose specific policy proposals. More specifically, it seems quite plausible to suppose that more "sophisticated" citizens are more likely to rule out policy options that are unrealistic in the sense that they are unlikely to be entertained by policymakers.[20]

Our empirical findings concerning partisan conditioning of unequal responsiveness raise questions about the reverse-causality line of argument. For the period prior to 1998, our results indicate that Left governments were more responsive to the preferences of low- and middle-income preferences in the domain of economic and welfare policies, but they were more responsive to high-income preferences in other policy domains. Simply put, why should the affluent (well-educated) adapt their preferences to elite discourses under some governments but not others and in some policy domains but not others? And why did low-income citizens apparently take cues from Left governments prior to the 1990s, but not thereafter? When all is said and done, the evidence on partisan conditioning presented in this paper suggests that unequal policy responsiveness to the preferences of different income groups does capture something important about the distribution of political influence in Northwest Europe as well as the United States. Yet much research remains to be done in order to explain the ubiquity of unequal policy responsiveness as well as variation in responsiveness across time, policy domains, and countries.

---

[20] In their study of Swedish parliamentarians and voters, Esaiasson and Holmberg (1996) show that the opinions of citizens and political representatives covary over time: trends in opinion changes are very similar among voters and representatives, but changes appear to be driven by the elites rather than the citizens. See also Lenz (2012) and Joosten (2022).

3

Democracy, Class Interests, and Redistribution

What Do the Data Say?

Mads Andreas Elkjær and Torben Iversen

A long line of work on advanced capitalist democracies argues that the need for governments to assemble majority electoral coalitions accords the middle class a strong say over government policies and virtually ensures that it will share in the prosperity that modern capitalism enables (e.g., Baldwin 1990; Esping-Andersen 1990; Iversen and Soskice 2006; Korpi and Palme 1998; Meltzer and Richard 1981; Rothstein 1998). Such sharing takes many forms, but the two main vehicles are investments in skills and the welfare state (Huber and Stephens 2001; Iversen and Stephens 2008). Recent work, however, including several contributions to this volume, call the conventional wisdom into doubt. One line of research argues that policies are strongly biased toward the preferences of the rich, as revealed in public opinion surveys (e.g., Bartels 2008, 2017; Gilens 2005, 2012; Gilens and Page 2014); another argues that the structural power of increasingly footloose capital undermines the capacity of the state to tax and redistribute rendering democratic governments increasingly incapable of responding to majority preferences (e.g., Piketty 2014; Rodrik 1997, 2011; Streeck 2011, 2016). This chapter is a critical reassessment of these and related arguments using macro evidence on government taxation and spending. Without probing preferences directly, we ask which classes gain and lose from government policies, and whether such "revealed power" has changed over time. We base our estimates on LIS data amended by data on in-kind government spending and we complement this evidence with data from the new World Inequality Database (WID). In a separate paper, we have examined evidence on preferences based on ISSP data (Elkjær and Iversen 2020).

Broadly consistent with the older literature, we find that government policies and outcomes in most cases are responsive to the economic interests of the middle class, and we show that middle-class power over fiscal policies has remained remarkably stable over time, even though market inequality has risen sharply and despite a large recent literature on the "hollowing-out of the middle." The rich are as large net contributors to the welfare state today as they were in the past, and it does not appear that the democratic state is increasingly constrained by global capital. In most cases, the middle class, measured by posttax income, has kept up with the advancement of the economy as a whole. The partial exception is the United States where middle-income growth has lagged average growth, although in absolute terms posttax incomes rose at a comparable rate to Europe.

Perhaps surprisingly, these conclusions appear to also apply to the bottom end of the income distribution. Growth in the posttax incomes of the bottom income quintile largely follows average incomes, although here the United States is an even greater outlier with bottom-end inequality rising sharply. We find that the bottom benefits from center-left governments, but the capacity of the bottom to keep up with the middle seems to be mainly driven by demand for insurance and public goods in the middle class.[1] In this sense, the poor are highly vulnerable, even under democracy, since they depend on the middle class defining its interests as being bound up with those of the poor. There are reasons to think this may be less true today than in the past.

Our comparison of the LIS data, which is based on equivalized household income, and the WID data, which is based on individualized income, reveals the important role of the family in shaping distributive outcomes. There is much redistribution going on within the household because members share consumption (notably living space, food, and consumer durables), but lower marriage rates and rising divorce rates have created many more single-adult households, which affect both distributive outcomes and distributive politics. Interestingly, this trend has produced very different outcomes in Europe and the United States, and it seems to be bound up in part with the role of race in US politics.

As Lupu and Pontusson note in their introduction, our overall findings appear at odds with theirs. We agree that one reason is that our data are for a longer period and for a larger sample of countries. It also matters that we include in-kind transfers in our analysis, while they do not. Lupu and Pontusson note that the distribution of these transfers depends on assumptions that cannot be fully validated with current data. Yet excluding in-kind transfers implicitly assumes that they are proportional to after-tax income, which is almost certainly not the case, so that is not a solution. Still, if we do exclude in-kind transfers, it does not much affect the trends we document over time (our focus) since the magnitude and composition of in-kind transfers do not

---

[1] For this reason, the balance of benefits between the middle and the bottom cannot easily be used to gauge the relative power of the two classes. For example, rising bottom-end inequality may lead to more demand for insurance, and transfers, even if the political power of the poor declines. By contrast, the rich are always net contributors to the welfare state, so for this class changes in contribution rates are a sure sign of changes in class power.

change much. We should also note that our results are substantively identical whether we exclude students and retirees from the analysis or exclude people without factor income. Finally, while we agree that transfer rates are not the only test of models of redistributive politics, a remarkable implication of our results is that the evolution of transfer rates – which we use as a signal of political power – produces largely constant relative post-fisc incomes over time for the middle and bottom. This is not an accounting relationship, as Lupu and Pontusson's hypothetical example in the introduction illustrates, and it is consistent with rising inequality in the top half.

The rest of the chapter is organized into three sections. The first is a critical assessment of the state of the literature, comparing recent arguments about the subversion of democracy to more long-standing theories of the pivotal role of the middle class. We offer definitions of class interests over government tax-and-spend policies, and we hypothesize different patterns of spending priorities depending on class power. We then turn to the empirics, showing evidence from eighteen advanced democracies going back to the 1970s, with a focus on how different classes have fared over time according to both LIS and WID data. The last section concludes.

THEORETICAL PERSPECTIVES

The Subversion of Democracy Debate

In recent decades, a deep pessimism about advanced democracy and its capacity to serve the needs of ordinary people has taken hold. It is not hard to find reasons to be concerned: rightwing populism, rising inequality, declining growth, and a concentration of wealth that leaves the impression that the system increasingly works only for the rich and powerful. There is worrying evidence to back up such pessimism. Work by Bartels (2008), Gilens (2005, 2012), and Gilens and Page (2014) on the US, as well as recent work testing and extending their approach to other advanced democracies (e.g., Bartels 2017; Elsässer, Hense, and Schäfer 2018; Peters and Ensink 2015; contributions to this volume) find that the affluent dominate democratic politics to the point where other income classes do not matter. This is of obvious normative concern, and it also challenges standard models of democracy, which accord a strong role to the middle class.

Yet, the interpretation of the public opinion evidence is contested (see e.g., Elkjær and Klitgaard 2021). Subgroup preferences are highly correlated over time (Page and Shapiro 1992; Soroka and Wlezien 2008), and the middle class emerges as far more politically influential when preferred levels of spending are used instead of preferred changes in spending (Elkjær and Iversen 2020). Nor do public opinion data capture the role of political parties. Voters may be generally uninformed about politics, which shows up as noisy survey responses and ill-considered policy positions, but they may know enough to vote for parties that are broadly representative of their interests, using either ideological cues (as originally argued by Downs 1957) or retrospective economic evaluations (Fiorina 1981; Kitschelt 2000; Munger and Hinich 1994). Political parties may thus act as "trustees" for their constituencies and advance their long-term interests in government; what Mansbridge (2003) calls "promissory representation." Most plausibly, effective representation requires parties to pay attention to both interests and preferences, as argued long ago by Pitkin (1967). For this reason, evidence on expressed preferences as well as interests is salient for assessing power and influence.

In his contribution to this volume, Bartels criticizes some of this and our other earlier work, arguing that we assign undue importance to bivariate associations of policies and preferences. In reality, though, we follow a line of scholarship dating back to at least Nagel (1975), who distinguished between the 'influence' an actor exerts on an outcome and the "benefit" they receive from their own and others' influence. The latter, Nagel (1975: 156–7) argued, can be measured as the correlation between preferences and the outcome. In practical terms and considering the strong model dependency of published results (Elkjær and Klitgaard 2021), we also think it's ill-advised to ignore the bivariate associations. In the face of even minor model misspecifications, the high levels of multicollinearity that are inherent in multivariate models of preferences and political outcomes might thus greatly exacerbate statistical bias (see Winship and Western 2016). Finally, and perhaps most importantly, Bartels' critique has no bearing on our substantive conclusions: when we use Bartels' preferred specification, the middle class still stands out as a pivotal player in redistributive politics (some of these results are presented in appendices to the original papers).

Even if governments respond to middle-class electorates, however, these responses may be increasingly constrained and inadequate. New work in comparative political economy highlights macro trends that appear to show that governments do not respond to rising inequality – a puzzle that is known as the Robin Hood paradox (following Lindert 2004). In addition, there is evidence that partisanship matters less for government policies than in the past (Huber and Stephens 2001; Kwon and Pontusson 2010). Such "convergence" could reflect that governments are increasingly hamstrung by footloose capital, as argued by Streeck (2011, 2016), Piketty (2014), and Rodrik (1997, 2011). Closely related, businesses and high-income earners may have the ability to shift their consumption, income, and effort to offset higher taxes, which places a binding constraint on how much governments can tax. Rising top-end incomes would incentivize the rich to engage in additional tax shifting. Another possibility is that big business and the rich exert political influence behind the scenes, outside the light of public discourse and open electoral contests (Hacker and Pierson 2010; Hertel-Fernandez 2018, 2019; Rahman and Thelen 2019).

On the other side of the debate are arguments about the geospatial embeddedness of advanced capitalism. As argued by economic geographers (e.g., Glaeser 2011; Storper 1997, 2013) and business scholars (e.g., Iammarino and McCann 2013; Rugman 2012), advanced production is rooted in local skill clusters, which tend to be concentrated in the successful cities, and these clusters are complemented by dense colocated social networks, which are very hard to uproot and move elsewhere (Iversen and Soskice 2019). In this perspective, trade and foreign investment tend to reinforce local specialization and raise the dependence of multinational capital on location cospecific assets, most importantly highly skilled labor, and the mostly tacit knowledge they represent. This makes sustained tax evasion through mobility or income shifting hard. Intense market competition, especially in globalized markets, also makes it hard for business to coordinate politically. From this perspective, globalization does not undermine the capacity of governments to respond to democratic demands and may in fact augment it.

Class Interests

In this chapter, we abstract from public opinion data and instead use an axiomatic approach where class interests are derived deductively and then compared to actual tax-and-spend policies over time.[2] This offers partial evidence on class power. As noted earlier, a fuller picture would also require attention to preferences. We have done so in a separate paper (Elkjær and Iversen 2020). The assumptions and mathematical derivations for our predictions are relegated to Appendix 3.A; here we focus on the key intuitions. The baseline model predicts patterns of taxation and spending, but our empirical approach does not presuppose any particular channel of influence, or whether voters are informed or not, or whether governments have high capacity or not. Deviations from the baseline predictions will instead alert us to potential violations of assumptions, which invite alternative interpretations.

As in much work before ours, we divide the adult population into three income classes: low (L), middle (M), and high (H). We assume that each class is only concerned with maximizing its own material welfare. Altruism, racial animosity, and moral reasoning are all ignored for the purpose of parsimony and clear predictions, but we will consider some of these alternative motivations in the discussion of the evidence.

Fiscal policies are characterized along three dimensions, which reflect the main material concerns of each class: (i) maximize net income; (ii) optimize social insurance, and (iii) optimize the provision of public goods. In the case of M, net income is maximized by taxing H and transferring the proceeds to M, subject to a standard cost of taxation, which is rising exponentially in the tax

---

[2] We have critically assessed the public opinion evidence in Elkjær (2020), Elkjær and Iversen (2020), and Elkjær and Klitgaard (2021).

rate because of multiplying work and investment disincentives, rising administrative costs of enforcing tax rules, etc. Optimal taxation of H will stop well short of confiscatory taxation for these reasons.[3] This approach follows a long "optimal taxation" tradition going back to Mirrlees (1971) and also employed by Meltzer and Richard (1981).

A somewhat different approach focuses not on what is the optimal tax rate, but instead on what is feasible. Known as the New Tax Responsiveness literature (Feldstein 1995, 1999; Gruber and Saez 2002; Saez, Slemrod, and Giertz 2012), the focus is on the capacity of businesses and high-income earners to shift their consumption, income, and effort to offset higher taxes, which places a binding constraint on how much governments can tax. Higher taxes essentially induce a substitution effect into lower-taxed income streams. An unambiguous implication of the New Tax Responsiveness literature is that rising top-end incomes incentivize the rich to engage in more tax shifting, and it therefore ties into the broader argument about inequality and class power used in this volume. In this formulation, for M to retain its political influence and keep up taxation of H during periods of rising top-end inequality, it must counter not only the "instrumental power" of the rich to shape the tax structure but also their "structural power" to evade taxation within any given tax structure. With rising top-end inequality governments must continuously find new ways to plug tax loopholes and dissuade tax evasion. In this version, the difference between a constant and a falling H transfer rate is the difference between a politically resilient nonrich majority and an ascending rich minority.

In a changing world, governments need to continuously update their tax regimes to address demands from the middle class. This is also true on the spending side. Demand has shifted away from traditional social consumption toward social investment (Garritzmann, Hausermann, and Palier 2022). It is precisely because the content of policies is changing all the time that a theory of class power cannot rely entirely on arguments about path dependence (Pierson 1996; 2000). The focus of our analysis is the capacity of the lower and (especially) the middle classes to continuously reinvent tax and spend policies to satisfy their material interests. Our argument is not about the stasis of policy, but about the resilience of class power.

We start by defining what we will refer to as *transfer rates* for each class:

$$\tau_{C_i} = C_i\text{'s transfer rate} = \frac{T_{C_i}}{y_{C_i}^{net}} = \frac{\text{net transfer to } C_i}{C_i\text{'s net income}},$$

---

[3] We also assume that tax and transfers cannot be regressive (in this example regressive policies would be to tax L and transfer to M). There are no instances of regressive net transfers in our data, and this may reflect democratically guaranteed rights of collective action, including protests, strikes, and so on. An abstract argument builds on Acemoglu and Robinson's (2006) model of democracy: For democracy to be feasible and stable, there needs to be a credible commitment to redistribution, and since advanced democracies are stable, the assumption must be satisfied.

where, C_i refers to each of the three classes, $i = \{L, M, H\}$. We measure transfer rates relative to net (after-tax and transfer) income because it is readily observable whereas we cannot observe market income in the counter-factual case of zero taxation. A positive number means that a group is a net beneficiary; a negative number that it is a net contributor.

In Appendix 3.A, we first show that if M is pivotal, optimal taxation implies a constant transfer rate from H:

(H1) $\tau_H^{M*} = constant,$

where the superscript indicates that this is M's preferred rate for H. If M chooses the optimal rate, there is no relationship between top-end inequality and redistribution.[4] The reason is that higher income of H always compensates M optimally through higher transfers, without changing the rate at which H is taxed. Note, however, that H will pay more into the public purse and M will consequently see transfers rise as a share of its *own* income, as H's relative income rises:

(H2) $\dfrac{\partial \tau_M^{M*}}{\partial \left(y_H^{net} / y_M^{net} \right)} > 0$ (M's transfer rate rises when H's income rises relative to M's)

This prediction stands in contrast to arguments that the rich enjoy increasing influence over policies as they become richer. If that was true, H's and M's transfer rates should fall as high-end inequality rises.

In the New Tax Responsiveness approach, the H-transfer rate is a direct measure of the power to tax high incomes, but unlike the optimal taxation approach, it does not make any predictions about how the transfer rate changes in response to top-end inequality. This will depend on the capacity of the rich to find ways to shift income to lower-taxed assets versus the capacity, administrative and political, of the state to close such opportunities. In this formulation, a constant H transfer rate is an expression of constant middle-class power, but the prediction of a constant transfer rate follows only from complementary arguments about democracy and the power to tax, which we reviewed earlier.

Social insurance follows a distinct logic. M may well want to spend money on social insurance, which we can think of as guarantees against the risk of losing income and falling into the L group. This could be because of unemployment, illness, or just bad luck (such as being in an industry or profession facing

---

[4] In the Meltzer-Richard model, with a proportional tax and lump-sum transfer, the optimal tax rate is rising in inequality because M gets an increasing share of the transfer when its income approximates L's. But when class interests between L and M are not bound together by assumption, M should pick the optional H transfer rate – irrespective of the relative incomes of L, M, and H. That's the simple idea captured by the formal model.

falling demand and wages). Those with high incomes tend to be less exposed to such risks (Moene and Wallerstein 2001; Rehm 2011), and they also tend to have better access to private insurance (Busemeyer and Iversen 2020). For *M*, on the other hand, insurance against labor market and other social risks is usually seen as a critically important motive for supporting public spending, and it has been documented to matter greatly in historical accounts (Baldwin's 1990; Esping-Andersen 1990; Mares 2003); it is implied by economic models (Barr 2001, 2012; Boadway and Keen 2000); and it has been shown to matter for government spending and demand for such spending (Iversen and Soskice 2001; Moene and Wallerstein 2001; Rehm 2011). This may be particularly true in an intergenerational perspective, where health insurance and old-age care help alleviate worries about older parents and where concerns about downward mobility of children give cause to support policies that ensure a decent living even for those at the bottom.

Because the demand for social insurance is proportional to risk *times* the loss if that risk is realized, bottom-end inequality should increase the transfer rate for *L* (see Appendix 3.A, eq. A6):

(H3) $\dfrac{\partial \tau_L^{M*}}{\partial \left(y_M^{net} / y_L^{net} \right)} > 0$ (*L*'s transfer rate rises when *M*'s income rises relative to *L*'s)

In the Lupu-Pontusson (2011) model, low-end inequality instead increases "social distance," which undermines the solidarity or affinity *M* feels with *L*. Since this is not a strictly material incentive, it is outside our model and both motives could matter. In the end, it is therefore an empirical matter.

Preferences for public goods should follow a very similar pattern because *L* (and *H*) share in spending on in-kind goods, such as infrastructure, primary and secondary schooling, policing, postal services, and so on, which are typically guaranteed as a citizen right. No person will be required to show proof of income to be admitted to, say, the local school or public library. If utility for such goods is concave, the demand function will look very similar to that for insurance, and for some in-kind services like hospitals, the distinction between insurance and public goods is blurred (see Busemeyer and Iversen 2020).

Our focus has been on the policy interests of *M* because of the centrality of the middle class in standard arguments about the welfare state. But we have implicitly assumed the interests of *L* and *H*, and they can be easily summarized: *L* would want to tax *M* and *H* at the maximum rate and transfer everything to *L*; *H* would want to cut taxes and transfers to zero, or perhaps a positive but low number that reflects its demand for public goods and social insurance that cannot be purchased in the private market (the private market is preferable for *H* because it involves no redistribution).

If *M* cannot govern alone, the outcome will reflect a coalition bargain, which can be conceived as a policy vector of taxes and transfers to and from each class based on the above set of interests. Because the interests of L and H are diametrically opposed, it stands to reason that LH coalitions are rare. For the two other feasible coalitions, an LM coalition is expected to benefit L more, and hurt H more, than an MH coalition. Depending on bargaining power within the coalition, which we approximate in the empirical analysis as the share of right cabinet seats minus the share of left cabinet seats, M can ordinarily ensure that it will emerge as a net beneficiary. Of course, this is also ultimately an empirical matter.

As is true for the pure M model, government partisanship only matters if the power of democratic governments is not subverted by money or by the structural power of capital. If H is powerful, despite not being a majority, it will be reflected in a lower (absolute) H transfer rate. We have already suggested that if "money talks" in politics, we should expect rising upper-end inequality to be associated with lower transfer rates to M and L. The same is true if rising incomes at the top lead to more tax shifting, which is not counter-balanced by government revisions of the tax code. The argument that mobile capital undermines redistribution is readily captured in the optimal taxation model as an increase in the efficiency costs of taxation (alpha in the formal representation in Appendix 3.A). If capital moves offshore in response to higher taxation, it reduces the optimal tax rate:

(H4) $\overline{\tau_M^H} = g(\text{capital mobility})$.

In the embedded capitalism interpretation, which implies that the state is strong, neither rising inequality nor increasing globalization of capital should affect the transfer rate to M.

EMPIRICS

Estimating Equation

We can put our hypotheses to a test using a simple encompassing regression model, where the transfer rate to M (measured either relative to H's or M's income) is the dependent variable:

$$\tau_{M,i,t} = a_i + \beta_1 \cdot \left(\frac{y_H}{y_M}\right)_{i,t} + \beta_2 \cdot \left(\frac{y_M}{y_L}\right)_{i,t}$$
$$+ \beta_3 \cdot Mobility_{i,t} + \beta_4 \cdot Gov\ partisanship_{i,t} + \varepsilon_{i,t},$$

where the first two terms measure the direct effects of relative income on the transfer rate to M; *Mobility* refers to widely used measures of the internationalization of capital; and *Government partisanship* captures the relative influence of Right versus Left parties in government (measured by cabinet shares). The relative income of M to L is included to test for social insurance motives for spending at the bottom.

Data

For the main part of the analysis, we use a new dataset that relies on household income data from the Luxembourg Income Study (LIS), supplemented by OECD and Eurostat data on spending on services and transfers, taxation of property, capital, and consumption. LIS provides a cross-national database of harmonized household income surveys going back to the 1970s. We restrict our sample to eighteen advanced democracies[5] for which data are recorded at more than one point in time between 1974 and 2016, and we confine the sample to households that have positive market and disposable incomes. Market income inequality and transfers are greatly exaggerated when including non-working households, the far majority of which are retirees. This is particularly true of countries with generous public pension benefits, where many do not save for their old age and will therefore appear as "poor" (Huber and Stephens 2001). Another sizable group is students, who we would not ordinarily think of as poor since they have high expected future income.

We measure market income as the sum of labor, cash, and capital income plus private transfers, and disposable income as total cash income minus income taxes and social contributions. Following LIS standards, market and disposable incomes are equivalized by the square root of the number of household members, and they are bottom- and top-coded at one percent of the mean equivalized income and ten times the median unequivalized income. We use market income to calculate inequality indices and divide households into deciles.

The LIS household income surveys account for cash transfers but not for in-kind services (public goods in the theoretical discussion). To include the value of services, we rely on estimates of the combined value of education, healthcare, social housing, elderly care, and early childhood education and care. The estimates are from the OECD/EU database on the distributional impact of in-kind services and are, to the best of our knowledge, the only available data (OECD 2011: Ch. 8). We also rely on an allocation key from this database to distribute the gross value of services to each income decile's disposable cash income.[6] The exact procedure we used is explained in Appendix 3.B.

Before estimating the transfer rate, we allocate the costs of transfers and services to the income deciles' disposable income. Transfers and services are financed by tax revenues that mainly come from taxation of income, capital, property, and consumption. The LIS data capture the income tax burden of each income decile. Business taxes are treated as neutral with respect to income classes and simply added to government revenues. The rest is financed by (i) property

---

[5] The eighteen countries are: Australia, Austria, Belgium, Canada, Denmark, Finland, Germany, Greece, Iceland, Ireland, Luxembourg, Netherlands, Norway, Spain, Sweden, Switzerland, United Kingdom, and the United States.

[6] For more information about these data, see Verbist, Förster, and Vaalavuo (2012). We are grateful to these authors for providing us with the estimates.

and wealth taxes, which are paid almost exclusively by those in the top few percentiles and therefore added to the tax burden of the top income decile, and (ii) consumption taxes, which we assume are paid in proportion to each income decile's consumption share. Further details are provided in Appendix 3.B.

The sum of disposable cash income and the net value of in-kind services is called the net "extended" income of each income decile. Subtracting market income from net extended income yields net transfers received. Following the theoretical expectations discussed earlier, the rate of transfers to M is net transfers received by the 5th income decile divided by the net extended income of the top income decile. To account for the value of insurance, we add (in some models) the transfer rate to L weighted by the sum of the unemployment and involuntary part-time employment rates (the mean weight is .1).[7] We also calculate transfer rates for all three groups expressed as a share of their own net extended income and use these as dependent variables in some models.

Variation in Transfer Rates

Figure 3.1 shows net transfers to M as a share of the net extended income of H (top panel) and M (bottom panel) with and without accounting for insurance (left and right panels). The gray lines are country-specific local polynomial smoothers and the black line describes the entire sample of countries and years.

The panels illustrate that there is considerable spatial variation in the rate of transfers to M. The highest average values are observed in Ireland, Luxembourg, and Sweden and the lowest in the Netherlands and Germany. The average transfer rate to M is .05, ranging from –.06 in the Netherlands in 1993 to .14 in Ireland in 2010 (top left panel). The negative values imply that the 5th income decile is a net contributor to spending in a few country years. That is the case in Germany in the 1990s, in Netherlands in the 1990s and 2000s, and in Australia in 1981.

Accounting for insurance increases the rate of transfers to M on average by .022 and makes the 5th income decile a net beneficiary of spending in Germany already in the mid-1990s and in the Netherlands in the mid-2000s (top right panel). However, we may significantly underestimate the value of insurance. The calculation is based on the twin assumptions that people are mildly risk-averse (RRA = 1) and that the risk of falling into the L group is equal to the rate of unemployment and underemployment.[8] If people are more risk-averse

---

[7] Nine values of involuntary part-time employment were imputed in Australia, the UK, and the United States based on trends of countries belonging to the liberal welfare state cluster.

[8] If a tax t on M when employed is spent to finance a transfer that goes to the unemployed, the (log) M welfare function can be defined as $W_M = (1 - p_M) \cdot \ln[(1 - t) \cdot y_M] + p_M \cdot \ln\left(\frac{t \cdot y_M}{n}\right)$, where n is the share of the population who are poor and p_M is the risk of becoming unemployed. In this case, the optional tax rate is equal to p_M ($t_M^* = p_M$), so the value of insurance to M is directly proportional to the risk of unemployment.

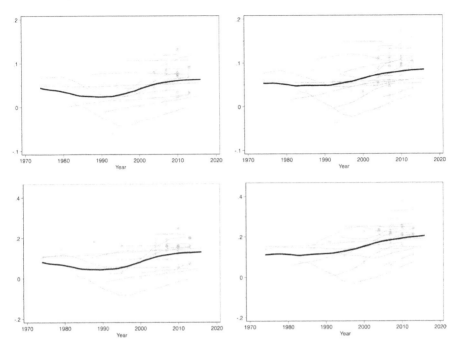

FIGURE 3.1 Net transfers to *M* as a share of the net extended income of *H* and *M*

Notes: N = 110. The figure shows net transfers to M as a share of the net extended income of H (top panel) and M (bottom panel) excluding and including the value of social insurance (left and right panels). The grey lines are country-specific local polynomial smoothers and the black line describes the entire sample of countries and years.

(as empirical estimates suggest), if there are risks of falling into the *L* group for other reasons (such as illness or divorce), or if concerns about downward intergenerational mobility matter, the value of insurance will increase. More accurately accounting for the value of insurance is an important task for future research. Our substantive results are robust to increasing the weight of *L*'s transfer rate all the way to 50 percent (models are reported in Table 3.C1 in Appendix 3.C).

The lower panels show that transfers and services account for a substantial part of *M*'s extended income. On average, 9.3 percent of *M*'s extended income comes from transfers and services, topping at 25 percent in Ireland in 2010. Adding the value of insurance increases the average to 16 percent, with a maximum of 44.1 percent in Spain in 2013.

Turning to the trends in the top panel of Figure 3.1, we see that during the last forty years, a period of sharply rising inequality, the rate of transfers to *M* has been remarkably stable if not slightly increasing. This is consistent with (H1) and suggests that *M*'s transfer rate is unrelated to the relative income of *H* to *M*. It serves as a first indication that increased inequality has not weakened the power of the middle class to tax and redistribute income from the rich. Given that the rate of transfers from *H* to *M* is stable, it follows

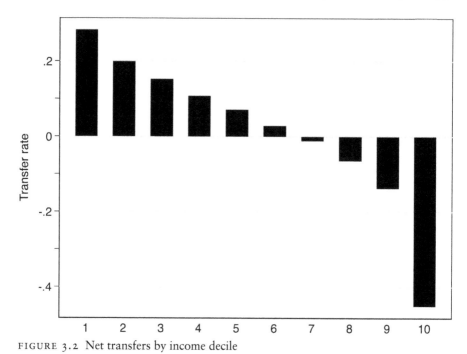

FIGURE 3.2 Net transfers by income decile

directly that net transfers to M have increased over time when expressed as a share of M's own extended income. This is shown in the bottom panels of Figure 3.1, and it corroborates (H2).[9]

In Figure 3.2, we show net transfer rates for all ten income deciles (net transfers for each decile as a share of the net income of H). We only show period averages (for 2010) because the rates are very stable over time, with only a slight increase in the transfer from the top decile to the other groups. What stands out is the overall redistributive effect of the tax and spending system (including transfers and public services) and the extent to which those in the top decile are net contributors. One might infer that the bottom end are the greatest beneficiaries, but it must again be kept in mind that if public spending serves insurance purposes, bottom-end transfers are also benefits for the middle. The overall picture that emerges is consistent with standard arguments about the redistributive effects of democracy, and there is no hint that the rich can skirt contributing to the system or that they are better able to do so today than fifty years ago.[10]

---

[9] In Table 3.C2 in Appendix 3.C, we show that net transfers to M as a share of M's net income are indeed positively related to top-end inequality. The effect is imprecisely estimated, however, and the significance levels differ across models.

[10] Of course, there may be differences in this respect between the rich and the very rich, which our top-coded data are not well suited to uncover.

What Drives Transfers to and from Different Classes?

To put the descriptive results to a stricter test, we regress in Table 3.1 the rate of transfers to M on market income inequality, capital mobility, and partisanship of the government (using the previous estimating equation). Capital mobility is measured by Chinn and Ito's (2006, 2008) capital account openness variable and we also include trade openness as a measure of globalization (it is the sum of imports and exports as a share of GDP).[11] Partisanship of the government is a twenty-year moving average of the share of government-controlled parliamentary seats held by Right parties minus the share of government-controlled seats held by Left parties (based on Armingeon et al. 2018).[12] In addition, we include controls for labor force participation rates, unemployment, and real GDP growth.

The results of Table 3.1 show that there is *no* association between top-end market income inequality and the rate of transfers to the middle class, providing further supportive evidence of (H1). In fact, the coefficients are positive, although they are always insignificant. The coefficients are also positive, and significant, for bottom-end inequality (the P50/P10 ratio). It is tempting to interpret this result from a Lupu-Pontusson (2011) perspective to imply that a greater economic "distance" to the poor causes more resources to be concentrated in the middle. Yet, we will see later that the P50/P10 ratio is also positively related to L's transfer rate (the skew has no effect). It appears that a middle class with a higher relative position in the income distribution has more political clout to redistribute to itself, which also brings L up in the process. Perhaps a higher P50/P10 ratio signals a more educated and politically efficacious middle class, but this is speculation – we do not know the mechanisms behind this effect. It stands up to a variety of controls, so it is not the result of any obvious omitted variable bias.

Capital mobility, whether measured by capital account openness or trade openness, has no impact on the rate of transfers to the middle class. The most obvious interpretation is that trade and foreign direct investment do not undermine, and may reinforce, specialized local knowledge clusters, which are not themselves mobile and therefore leave the state in a position to tax. Nothing in our data suggests that globalization has undermined the position of the middle class, which is consistent with (H4).

---

[11] We have imputed five values on Chinn and Ito's capital account openness variable. One for Switzerland in 1992 and four values for Luxembourg between 2004 and 2013. In all cases, we have imputed values equal to 1. The mean for Switzerland is 1 with a standard deviation of 0 and the mean of the EU countries included in our models between 2004 and 2013 is also 1, with a standard deviation of 0. Two values of trade openness have been linearly extrapolated: Germany from 2014 to 2015 and the United States from 2014 to 2016.

[12] Because the Comparative Political Data Set (Armingeon et al. 2018) contains data going back to 1960, the average partisanship of the government in the UK and United States in 1974 is only fifteen-year averages. Trade openness and control variables are also from this dataset.

TABLE 3.1 *Determinants of net transfers to M as a percentage of H's net income*

	(1)	(2)	(3)	(4)
	Transfer rate M (%)		Transfer rate M incl. insurance (%)	
P90/P50	0.84	2.62	0.26	1.99
	(3.33)	(4.16)	(3.29)	(4.07)
P50/P10	1.79*	1.34⁺	2.59*	2.23*
	(0.78)	(0.76)	(0.70)	(0.75)
Trade openness (ln)	2.40	0.71	1.82	0.61
	(1.93)	(2.79)	(1.93)	(2.80)
Capital market openness	1.16	2.04	0.22	1.03
	(2.21)	(2.10)	(1.93)	(2.03)
Government partisanship (right)	−4.31*	−3.67*	−4.58*	−4.07*
	(1.46)	(1.06)	(1.55)	(1.24)
Labor force participation	−0.23⁺	−0.14	−0.27*	−0.20
	(0.12)	(0.13)	(0.11)	(0.12)
Unemployment	−0.05	−0.02	0.15	0.16
	(0.14)	(0.12)	(0.11)	(0.10)
Real GDP growth	−0.21	−0.12	−0.20	−0.13
	(0.14)	(0.11)	(0.14)	(0.12)
Trend		−0.27		−0.22
		(0.19)		(0.20)
Trend²		0.01		0.00
		(0.00)		(0.00)
Constant	3.66	3.33	9.53	7.77
	(9.01)	(18.23)	(8.58)	(17.78)
R-squared	0.38	0.42	0.49	0.52
N	110	110	110	110

Notes: $^*p < 0.05$, $^+p < 0.1$. Standard errors clustered by country in parentheses. All models include country fixed effects.

Instead, distributive politics seems to depend strongly on partisanship. In model (1), the coefficient for partisanship of the government suggests that stronger Left party participation in government is associated with higher rates of transfers to the middle class. And the size of the effect is substantial. A one standard deviation increase in left (right) partisanship of the government is associated with a 0.74 percentage points increase (decrease) in the rate of transfers to M.

In model (2), we add a time trend to the specification to ensure that our results are not driven by temporal trends. The results are robust to this alternative specification. The time-trend variables themselves are also not indicating any significant decline in transfer rates over time, as would be

TABLE 3.2 *Determinants of net transfers to L and H as a percentage of own net income*

	(1)	(2)	(3)	(4)
	Transfer rate L (%)		Transfer rate H (%)	
P90/P50	–6.07	–13.69[+]	–20.00[+]	–15.50
	(5.03)	(7.67)	(10.17)	(14.29)
P50/P10	9.11[*]	9.47[*]	–2.56	–2.22
	(1.40)	(1.36)	(2.34)	(2.54)
Trade openness (ln)	5.06	3.03	14.92[*]	19.41[*]
	(3.68)	(3.36)	(6.57)	(8.02)
Capital market openness	7.44[+]	4.54	12.66	14.07
	(3.59)	(3.45)	(7.68)	(11.06)
Government partisanship (right)	–2.89[+]	–3.16[*]	14.07	13.34[+]
	(1.66)	(1.48)	(8.49)	(7.65)
Labor force participation	0.33[*]	0.15	0.28	0.32
	(0.14)	(0.16)	(0.36)	(0.47)
Unemployment	–0.21	–0.16	–0.48	–0.57
	(0.16)	(0.18)	(0.35)	(0.38)
Real GDP growth	–0.11	–0.07	0.38	0.20
	(0.17)	(0.22)	(0.46)	(0.57)
Trend		0.35[+]		0.08
		(0.19)		(0.77)
Trend^2		–0.00		–0.00
		(0.00)		(0.01)
Constant	5.48	38.13[+]	–85.02[*]	–115.50[*]
	(16.08)	(20.97)	(28.88)	(51.30)
R-squared	0.80	0.80	0.23	0.24
N	110	110	110	110

Notes: $^*p < 0.05$, $^+p < 0.1$. Robust standard errors in parentheses. All models include country fixed effects.

expected if governments were increasingly limited by capital mobility (in case these are not fully captured by the Chinn and Ito or the trade measures) or by new high-income veto players.

In models (3) and (4), we include insurance as part of the transfer rate to M. Overall, the results are very similar to those of models (1) and (2). Top-end inequality and capital mobility are not related to the transfer rate, while bottom-end inequality is. The effect size of partisanship remains stable. All in all, accounting for insurance increases the transfer rate to the middle class but the associations between the transfer rate, inequality, capital mobility, and government partisanship remain stable.

In Table 3.2, we show the results for the rate of transfers to L and to H, defined as the bottom and top deciles, respectively. For L, the results largely mirror those for *M*: there is little-to-no effect of top-end inequality, of capital openness, or of trade whereas left partisanship and bottom-end inequality increase transfers, as expected. For partisanship, a one standard deviation increase in right (left) partisanship decreases (increases) the transfer rate to *L* by 0.5 percentage points. For the P50/P10 ratio, a one standard deviation increase raises transfers to *L* substantially by 5.5 percent of *L*'s net income. It appears that as the distance between *L* and *M* increases, *M* becomes increasingly concerned about the risk of downward mobility and therefore supports more transfers to *L*. This result is consistent with (H3).

The results for *H* show that right partisanship improves top-end net income by reducing transfers away from *H* (although the effect is only marginally significant at the 0.1 level). So, apparently, does trade, which hints of a globalization effect. Capital market openness is, however, never significant. Perhaps most surprisingly, top-end inequality is associated with a rise in transfers from *H* to other groups (a negative sign means that *H* retains less of its income). The result is, however, only borderline significant in model (3), and it does not hold up when including the time trends in model (4), but there is clearly no support in our data for the notion that the rich have become politically more powerful as their market income has risen.

Overall, the results indicate that the power of the middle class is stable over time, despite the sharp rise in top-end inequality. The rich are becoming richer, but this wealth is not translated into greater influence over fiscal policy; the political power of capital and the rich over redistribution is only as great as their electoral strength (via Right parties).

A potential objection to this conclusion is that the rising incomes of *H* *before* taxes and transfers have come at the expense of *M* and *L*. This could reflect declining unionization, rising monopsony power in labor markets, rising monopoly power in product markets, skill-biased technological change, or a combination. There is ample evidence that the earnings distribution has widened, but how this affects the net income distribution, and relative welfare after accounting for public services, is not obvious. As the top earners gain, some of those gains are shared with the middle and the bottom. Iversen and Soskice (2019, ch. 1) suggest a simple test of this broader notion of power, which is to examine the position of the middle class in the overall income distribution over time. If a fall in earnings in the middle – what is sometimes referred to as a hollowing-out or polarization effect (Goos and Manning 2007) – outweighs middle-class power over government spending policies, it will show up as a decline in median-to-mean net incomes.

We test this possibility in Figure 3.3. The figure displays median-to-mean disposable income ratios for nineteen countries around 1985 and 2010 (i.e., the value of in-kind benefits and indirect taxes are not included in disposable income). This is the period with the sharpest rise in market income inequality, yet the figure shows that the median disposable income relative to the mean disposable income has been largely stable (the average change is not

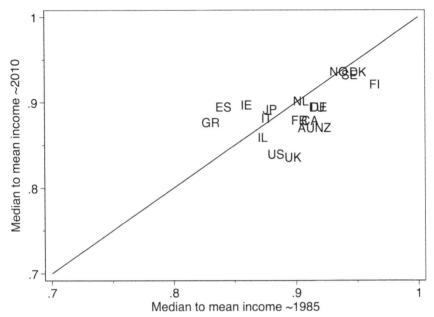

FIGURE 3.3 The median net income relative to mean net income, 1985–2010
Notes: The measures for AU, CA, DK, FI, FR, DE, IE, IL, IT, LU, NL, NO, ES, UK, and the US are the disposable income of the median relative to the mean (working households) from the LIS database (authors' calculations). For GR, JP, NZ, and SE, the measures are the disposable income of the median relative to the mean (working-age population) from the OECD income distribution database. The start and end points of the countries are AU: 1985–2010, CA: 1987–2010, DK: 1987–2010, DE: 1984–2010, ES: 1985–2010, FI: 1987–2010, FR: 1984–2010, GR: 1986–2010, IE: 1987–2010, IL: 1986–2010, IT:1986–2010, JP: 1985–2009, LU: 1985–2010, NL: 1983–2010, NO: 1986–2010, NZ: 1985–2009, SE: 1983–2010, UK: 1986–2010, US: 1986–2010.

significantly different from zero).[13] There is some modest variance around the 45-degree line: Spain, Greece, and Ireland have all seen increases of 4.4–6.5 percent, while Australia, Canada, Finland, New Zealand, the United Kingdom, and the United States have all experienced declines of 3.5–6.8 percent. It is not an accident that much of the literature proclaiming a declining middle class comes from the liberal market economies because this is where we observe some erosion.[14] Still, even in these cases, the relative drop (4.8 percent on average) is greatly outpaced by the rise in mean (and median) incomes (an average

[13] The average change in the median-to-mean net income ratio is -1.2 percent ranging from a decline of 6.8 percent in the UK to an increase of 6.5 percent in Spain.
[14] In the case of Finland, the likely culprit is the collapse of the Soviet Union, which had large and unanticipated economic effects; it may not reflect changes in underlying class power.

of 34 percent). It is also noteworthy that the relative income of the median falls within a narrow band of 0.83 to 0.93, with the Nordic countries somewhat higher and the UK and United States somewhat lower than the rest.

These findings may seem surprising against the evidence of a hollowing-out effect of skill-biased technological change, but those most affected by SBTC are clerical jobs and manual jobs in manufacturing, which are typically somewhat below the median. The middle class has generally been able to either acquire new skills to retain a foothold in the knowledge economy, or it has been able to rely on government transfers and generous provision of public services (and insurance) to defend its living standards. This should not be taken to mean that the political upheaval over rising inequality and fear of middle-class decline is not real. To the contrary, such upheaval is precisely the political expression of a middle class striving to defend its position.

Distribution of Macroeconomic Growth

Although Figure 3.3 shows that median household income has been fairly stable relative to the mean in most countries, it does not capture how overall macroeconomic growth has been distributed to income classes. A common way of doing so is to compare median equivalized household income growth with GDP per capita growth. Yet even though this approach is widely adopted by both scholars and political pundits, it has significant limitations.

First, disposable household income accounts for cash income, cash transfers, and direct taxes, but it does not account for indirect taxes, the value of in-kind benefits or public goods, or economic activity in other sectors than the household sector. Consequently, disposable household income is a far narrower concept than GDP, which is a measure of the overall economic output of a country. Second, to account for economies of scale, household income is usually equivalized by the square root of the number of household members, whereas GDP is measured per capita. This difference is important because changes in family structures will directly affect equivalized household income even if the underlying (personalized) income distribution is constant. Falling marriage rates and rising divorce rates have increased the number of single-member households and this has caused a relative decline in equivalized median disposable household income in many countries. Indeed, Nolan, Roser, and Thewissen (2018, 95) find that "[h]ousehold size is the most important factor on average across countries, accounting for 45 percent of the overall discrepancy [between median equivalized household income and GDP per capita]; it is also the most consistent factor in terms of the scale and direction of its effects, since average household size declined in most countries." For these reasons, it is problematic to assess the distribution of macroeconomic growth by comparing growth in median equivalized household income to GDP per capita growth. Instead, one needs estimates that are directly comparable and consistent with macroeconomic aggregates.

As part of the development of the WID, Piketty, Saez, and Zucman (2018) were the first to provide such estimates. Using a combination of survey, tax, and national accounts data for the United States, they distribute total national income (GDP minus capital depreciation plus net foreign income) to individuals across the income distribution. These distributional national accounts series are consistent with macroeconomic aggregates, which enables a direct examination of the distribution of economic growth to different groups. Thanks to the work of Blanchet, Chancel, and Gethin (2022), comparable estimates are now available for Europe.

The WID income measures differ in several respects from the LIS measures that we use to study the median-to-mean disposable income ratio earlier. First, and as discussed, disposable household income includes only cash income and transfers, and it subtracts only direct taxes. The WID measures are broader and account not only for cash income (including transfers) and direct income taxes, but also for in-kind transfers, public goods, and indirect taxes. Although the WID measures are broader than what individuals and households will be able to see on their bank accounts, it is widely seen as superior to the measure of cash disposable income as a measure of a household's standard of living (Garfinkel, Rainwater, and Smeeding 2006). Second, as in most other studies that rely on household income surveys to study redistribution, we sought to exclude students and retirees by restricting the LIS samples to households with positive market and disposable incomes. The WID data, by contrast, include all individuals twenty years or older. Third, whereas disposable household income is equivalized using an equivalence scale, the WID individualizes income using an equal-split approach that divides income equally between spouses. Sharing between spouses is a real form of redistribution and therefore important to account for, but the equal-split approach also makes the WID estimates dependent on changes in the structure of families, as we will discuss later.

Overall, however, the WID data are superior to household income surveys when it comes to assessing the distribution of macroeconomic growth over recent decades, and we therefore rely on these data in the following analysis. We have data for sixteen European countries as well as the United States in the period 1980 to 2019.

Figure 3.4 displays the real extended income growth of the bottom and middle-income quintiles compared to the mean income growth in each of the seventeen countries included in the sample.[15] The figure shows that both the bottom and middle-income quintiles have experienced significant income growth in a wide range of European countries since 1980, and in most cases, the middle has kept up quite well with the overall expansion of the economy; in Belgium and Spain, its income growth has even outpaced that of the

---

[15] As for the LIS data, we allocate in-kind transfers and public goods as an equal lump sum to all individuals, consistent with the OECD estimates cited above.

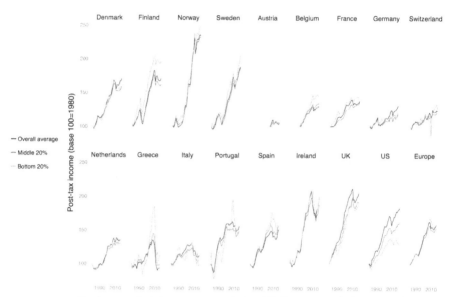

FIGURE 3.4 Real extended income growth in 17 Europe and the United States, 1980–2019

Notes: In Austria, Belgium, and Switzerland, the base 100 is 2004, 1991, and 1982. The graph for Europe includes all the European countries except Austria and Belgium and has base 100 in 1982.

Source: World Inequality Database (accessed on March 26, 2021).

mean. Rather surprisingly, in several countries, the bottom quintile has experienced stronger income growth than both the middle and the overall economy. By contrast, in Greece and Italy, income growth has been meager overall, and both L and M have experienced close to zero percent income growth. In Europe as a whole, the income growth of both L and M has kept up reasonably well with the overall economy (see the graph for the European average): their income growth is within five percentage points of the mean income growth of 59 percent. Because this pattern has been driven in large part by fiscal transfers and in-kind government spending, we see it as a sign of well-functioning democratic systems.

The United States is a major outlier, however. While the overall economy has expanded by 77 percent between 1980 and 2016, the bottom quintile has experienced an extended income growth of just 33 percent. Moreover, a significant part of L's income growth is due to increases in public goods provision. When we change the distribution of public goods from an equal lump sum to being proportional to disposable income (except for health), thereby assuming that public goods (other than those related to health) are neutral with respect to redistribution, bottom-end incomes have grown just 13 percent in real terms since 1980. With a real extended income growth of 56 percent, the middle has done better than the bottom and experienced income growth at comparable levels to the overall European average, but it is still significantly lagging the mean (as opposed to *L, M*'s income growth declines only slightly to 51 percent when we change the allocation of public goods). The United States is the only advanced democracy in which greater economic prosperity has been distributed so unequally. Comparing the LIS data to the WID data thus exposes the United States as a large outlier, while the results for other countries are very consistent across datasets. What explains this finding?

Part of the reason appears related to race and changes in family structure. The theoretical model assumes that redistributive politics is governed by class, but racism is a widely recognized dimension of American politics in general, and redistributive politics in particular (Alesina and Glaeser 2004; Cramer 2016; Gilens 2009). Even though racism has been a constant feature of American politics, it might affect our results dynamically for two reasons. First, rising poverty and risk of poverty have been concentrated among minorities, which has undermined the demand for insurance among the majority. Second, a declining marriage rate has been a source of inequality and the decline has been more pronounced among poor minorities. Single black mothers – Reagan's "welfare queens" – get little sympathy among the white majority. European countries have seen a similar decline in marriage rates, but the state has compensated for the implied rise in inequality through increased family allowances and other transfers. This conjecture finds direct support in the WID data because if each spouse is given his or her own labor income, instead of dividing income equally between spouses, the evolution of real extended income, for especially the bottom, pulls much closer to the mean income line (see Figure 3.C1 in Appendix 3.C). Still, redistribution within the household is real, and the puzzle remains of why the government has not compensated for lower within-household redistribution.

CONCLUSION

The rise in income inequality over the past four decades has created concerns that democracy is being undermined by the rich, by footloose capital, or both. These concerns have been backed by alarming recent evidence that public policies – especially those pertaining to taxes, social spending, and redistribution – are being dictated by the rich or by the rising structural power of capital. This chapter does not assuage the concern over rising inequality, but it does challenge the notion that democratic governments are no longer responsive to majority demands, and in particular to those of the middle classes.

Using macro evidence for transfer rates, we find consistently that policies are well aligned with the distributive interests of the middle class, and the transfer rate (including the value of services) to the middle class as a share of high incomes has remained constant or even slightly risen during a period when top-end inequality grew notably. This is not consistent with a view that accords greatly increasing influence to the rich. Indeed, since we measure transfer rates as a share of the net income of the rich, it is unambiguously the case that net transfers as a share of middle incomes have *risen* over time. This finding is unacknowledged in the current literature, but it is very much in accordance with long-standing traditions in the field, which emphasize the pivotal role of the middle class.

Our results are thus reassuring about the continued importance of democracy for distributive politics. But there are several qualifications to this broad conclusion. Although transfer rates are stable, if we consider the position of the middle in the overall disposable income distribution, we see some erosion in majoritarian, liberal market economies from the mid-1980s. The drop in relative position is small compared to increases in real incomes in the same period, but it is noteworthy nonetheless. Also noteworthy is that real extended income growth has grown increasingly unequal in the United States, which stands out as a major outlier among advanced democracies.

Perhaps more fundamentally, it is important to keep in mind that democratic politics does not guarantee that inequality is adequately addressed. One of the misleading assumptions in some of the contemporary literature is that a working democracy will compensate for inequality, implying that when we see a rise in inequality, we should also expect to see more redistribution. That is not implied by majority rule. Distributive politics is multidimensional, and political alliances determine who benefit and who do not. Since the middle class and its representatives usually stand at the center of the political coalition game, middle-class interests are generally well-attended to. But the poor depend on being invited into government coalitions or else on the generosity of the middle class. The trend since the 1990s toward center-right governments has hurt the poor, and bifurcation of risks and any drop in mobility between the middle and the bottom will undermine insurance motives in the middle class to support bottom-end redistribution. Precisely because democratic governments are so important for redistribution, explaining partisanship and middle-class preferences remains an important task for political economy.

4

Measuring Political Inequality[*]

Larry M. Bartels

Democracy has something to do with equality – but what, exactly? How should we gauge the extent of inequality in democratic political systems? What sorts of inequality are objectionable from the standpoint of democratic theory and why?

In an influential essay on "Measuring Representation," Achen (1977: 806) argued that "The central difficulty is not statistical, but conceptual. Rarely is a measure of representativeness related to the ideas of liberal democratic theory – for example, citizen equality and popular sovereignty. Instead, measures have been plucked from the statistical shelf and employed without much theoretical interpretation." More than forty years later, much the same could be said of the scholarly literature on political inequality. Scholars purporting to measure inequality deploy a variety of very different analyses, perhaps justified with a sentence or two gesturing to democratic theory. They often employ similar terms – "representation," "responsiveness," "congruence," "alignment," "association," "influence" – to describe different analyses and different terms to describe similar analyses. As a result, what appear to be substantive disagreements are often instances of scholars simply talking past each other, not noticing or not caring that they are talking about different things.

This chapter provides a conceptual and methodological roadmap of research on political inequality, with particular emphasis on the grounding of empirical analyses in "the ideas of liberal democratic theory." Like all roadmaps, mine is subjective, with some routes emphasized and others portrayed as backroads or even dead ends. However, my aim is not to resolve normative or empirical disagreements in the field – merely to make the disagreements more productive by clarifying what they are about.

[*] Thanks to Christopher Achen, Mads Elkjær, Martin Gilens, Christopher Wlezien, and the volume editors and contributors for very helpful comments on a preliminary draft of this chapter.

Political inequality has been a subject of scientific study since the time of Aristotle, who classified regimes based on the relationship between political power and economic wealth. In the United States, studies of unequal political power – perhaps most famously, Dahl's (1961) *Who Governs? Democracy and Power in an American City* – were a hallmark of the mid-twentieth-century "behavioral revolution" in political science. However, the pluralist research program embodied in this and other studies of "who actually governs" bogged down in methodological and political controversies, and analyses of inequality increasingly came to focus on narrower but more tractable issues, as with the monumental studies of political participation published by Verba and colleagues over a span of forty years (Schlozman, Verba, and Brady 2012; Verba and Nie 1972; Verba, Schlozman, and Brady 1995).

In the twenty-first century, political scientists have once again aspired to gauge political inequality directly – this time, with the precision of systematic quantitative analysis. The roots of this work lie in two distinct threads of research on political representation: one relating the policy choices of individual elected officials to the preferences of their constituents as measured by survey data, and the other relating policy outcomes to aggregate public opinion across issues or over time.[1] In each case, the key analytical innovation was quite simple: to relate policy choices or outcomes to the distinct preferences of separate subgroups of citizens rather than to the preferences of the public as a whole.

Given this intellectual lineage, contemporary studies of political inequality have inherited much of the conceptual framework – and attendant complexities and confusions – of scholarship on political representation, while adding further complexities and confusions stemming from the application of this framework to a new set of questions. My aim here is to survey the most significant complexities and confusions of both sorts.

CONGRUENCE: SATISFYING PREFERENCES

Perhaps the most straightforward way to gauge the relationship between citizens and elected officials is by assessing the extent of *congruence* between citizens' preferences and policymakers' actions. In her seminal theoretical account of political representation, Pitkin (1967: 163–164) suggested that political leaders "must not be found persistently at odds with the wishes of the represented without good reason":

What the representative must do is act in his constituents' interests, but this implies that he must not normally come into conflict with their will when they have an express

---

[1] My own research on unequal responsiveness in Congress (Bartels 2016: Ch. 8) was grounded in a voluminous scholarly literature elaborating upon the pioneering work of Miller and Stokes (1963) on congressional representation. Gilens (2012: xiii) cited the influence of Monroe (1979), "the first to assess democratic representation by relating public preferences to government policy outcomes across large numbers of issues."

will…. Thus, when a representative finds himself in conflict with his constituents' wishes, this fact must give him pause. It calls for a consideration of the reasons for the discrepancy; it may call for a reconsideration of his own views.

Political theorists sometimes castigate empirical researchers – especially those who do "'large-N,' statistical work" – for adopting a "simplistic normative model of democracy whereby democratic majorities are to get whatever they want, on every issue, and in short order" (Sabl 2015: 345–346). I think a fairer characterization would be that most empirical researchers view the relationship between citizens' preferences and policy outcomes in much the same spirit as Pitkin. Consider, for example, the nuanced statement framing the most influential recent empirical analysis of disparities in representation (Gilens 2012: 47–48):

> The quality of democratic governance in any society must be judged on a range of considerations. Are elections free and fair? Do citizens have access to the information necessary to evaluate their political leaders and competing candidates? Do government agencies perform their duties in a competent and unbiased manner? In this book I concern myself with only one aspect of democratic governance—the extent to which government policy reflects the preferences of the governed…. In documenting the ways in which policy fails to reflect (or reflect equally) the preferences of the public, I do not mean to imply that a perfect (or perfectly equal) responsiveness to the public is best.
>
> There are good reasons to want government policy to deviate at times from the preferences of the majority: minority rights are important too, and majorities are sometimes shortsighted or misguided in ways that policymakers must try to recognize and resist…. Particular segments of the public may hold preferences on particular issues that are harmful to the community, violate important democratic values, or are misinformed and detrimental to the interests of those citizens themselves.

From this perspective, as in Pitkin's account, a pattern of significant discrepancies between citizens' preferences and policy outcomes "calls for a consideration of the reasons." The bases and coherence of citizens' preferences are amenable to empirical research and indeed have generated voluminous analysis and debate. Principles of justice and their application have mostly been treated by empirical researchers as topics beyond their remit, suitable for normative rather than empirical analysis.

Assessments of congruence evaluate representatives as "delegates" rather than "trustees," to employ a venerable theoretical distinction. Rehfeld (2009: 219) suggested that "Empirical scholars may favor delegate views of representation because they are easier to measure: one need only compare roll-call votes of representatives with public opinion surveys, or election outcomes with votes cast, to evaluate whether 'good' representation in this sense is achieved." While "empirical scholars" of representation may chafe at the phrase "one need only," there *is* an appealing conceptual simplicity to the notion that policy outcomes should, at least presumptively, correspond with public preferences. Alas, that conceptual simplicity breaks down rather quickly in practice.

One vexing set of problems turns on the measurement of citizens' preferences. Even when those preferences are not "incoherent" in a common-language
sense, they may be subject to vagaries that complicate the task of assessing the
correspondence between preferences and policies. Opinion surveys may frame
policy issues in ways the call to respondents' minds some relevant considerations rather than others. For example, Americans have much more negative
views regarding government spending on "welfare" than on "assistance to the
poor." Many more would "not allow" a communist to make a speech than
would "forbid" him from doing so. In instances like these, it seems hard to
say exactly what the preferences are that representatives should be weighing
(Bartels 2003).

Even if citizens' preferences are clearly captured by surveys or other data,
assessing congruence requires us to decide whether the behavior of policymakers is consistent with those preferences. When policy choices are framed
in dichotomous terms, congruence with any given citizen's preference may be
thought of as an all-or-nothing matter. The citizen either favors or opposes
adding a prescription drug benefit to a government health program, and policymakers do or don't comply. In many cases, this is straightforward enough;
but sometimes assessing congruence may be a difficult matter of judgment. Is
any prescription drug benefit enough to count?[2]

In other cases, policy outcomes may be arrayed along a continuum, making it natural to think of congruence as a measure of the "distance" between
any citizen's preferred policy and the one her government adopts. Spending
preferences are often portrayed in this way, since the corresponding policy
outcomes are conveniently quantifiable. However, this formalization, too, may
sometimes do considerable violence to reality when, for example, a citizen
who wants her government to spend more on "healthcare" sees the money go
to insurers and pharmaceutical companies rather than to clinics and nursing
homes.

Even greater complexities arise in comparing the positions of citizens on general ideological scales with the positions adopted by or attributed to political
elites. Citizens' understanding of ideological term is often shallow or confused
(Converse 1964; Kinder and Kalmoe 2017). Even when they are splendidly
well informed, it requires a good deal of optimism to assume that one person's
"7" on a zero-to-ten "left-right" scale means the same thing as another's, or
as a member of parliament's, or as a country expert's assessment of a party's

---

[2] Gilens (2012: 63) reported that coders agreed whether a proposed policy change had occurred
91 percent of the time (after excluding some partial change codes), but he did not discuss the
nature of disagreements or how they were resolved. Bartels (2012) examined some of Gilens'
specific cases of responsive policymaking, concluding that "it is seldom straightforward to classify policies as responsive or unresponsive to public preferences" and that, as a result, "responsiveness is a partial and often problematic standard for assessing the role of citizens' preferences
in democratic policymaking."

position on the same scale. This is especially true in times and places when the meaning of ideology is contested or changing due to the emergence of new political issues and cleavages.[3]

Regardless of how policy positions are measured, the notion of congruence seems to require that they be measured identically for citizens and policymakers, or somehow reconciled, in order to allow for comparison between them. In practice, analysts must often make do with imperfect comparisons, relying on assumptions to overcome the limitations of available data. In his work revisiting Miller and Stokes's classic study of congressional representation, Achen (1978: 481, 484–485) acknowledged "some question about comparability" between opinion scales constructed from separate surveys of constituents and representatives. "Although the topics covered were essentially identical," he noted, "the congressional questionnaire was more specific, making reference to specific programs and proposals in some cases." Nonetheless, "For present purposes, one has little choice but to inspect the distribution of opinion on the scales among both Congressmen and constituents, and if no anomalies appear (none do), to follow Miller in standardizing the two scales to the same range and treating them as comparable."

In an ambitious cross-national study of congruence, Lupu and Warner (2022a: 279) applied a similar strategy on a much broader scale. They compiled data on the preferences of citizens and political elites in 565 country years from a wide variety of surveys employing a variety of scales. "To make these responses comparable," they reported, "we rescale them to range from –1 to 1." With this sort of wholesale normalizing, it seems very hard to know whether any resulting pair of citizens' and elites' responses is indeed "comparable," and thus very hard to gauge the extent of congruence or incongruence between them. Alas, concessions of this sort are common, given the scarcity of directly comparable measures of citizens' and policymakers' preferences.[4]

Even in cases where directly comparable measures of mass and elite preferences are available, difficult conceptual issues sometimes arise in comparing them. In legislative systems with single-member districts, we may be

---

[3] Powell (2019) provided detailed analyses and discussion of ideological congruence in parliamentary democracies. Brady (1985) explored the "perils" involved in statistical analysis of "interpersonally incomparable" survey data. Zechmeister (2006) documented substantial variation in the meaning of "left" and "right" among citizens in Mexico and Argentina, which she attributed to different national contexts, "elite packaging," and levels of political sophistication.

[4] Lupu and Warner added, "our analyses control for the scale used in each mass and elite survey and for the differences between the scales provided to elite and mass respondents in each country-year"; but there is no reason to expect measurement error in congruence introduced by incompatible scales to be eliminated, or even mitigated, by including fixed effects for scale formats. Nor is it necessarily the case that biases in measured congruence for distinct income groups will be subject to similar errors (for example, on issues where low-income citizens are generally to the "left" and high-income citizens are generally to the "right" of legislators).

interested in the correspondence between each individual representative's policy choices and the preferences of her own constituents, but the extent of *dyadic* representation sheds little light on the correspondence between citizens' preferences and overall policy outcomes (Weissberg 1978). In electoral systems without single-member districts, scholars have typically compared the preferences of rank-and-file supporters of each party with the preferences of the party's parliamentarians, as in Esaiasson and Holmberg's (1996) remarkably detailed study comparing the views of citizens and members of parliament in Sweden. But here, too, the relationship between party representation and policy outcomes may be complex and variable, depending on legislative institutions (the distribution of agenda-setting rights and resources), party cohesion, and the role of the president or prime minister, among other factors.

Golder and Stramski (2010: 95) distinguished between "absolute citizen congruence," measured by the average absolute distance between the preferences of citizens and those of a single representative, government, or policy outcome, and "many-to-many congruence" based on comparing overall *distributions* of opinion among citizens and legislators. They motivated attention to the latter, in part, by referring to "the importance of having a representative body whose preferences accurately correspond to those of the nation as a whole." However, they noted that "many-to-many congruence" between citizens and legislators is neither necessary nor sufficient to produce congruence between citizens' preferences and policy outcomes. A legislature that is, collectively, splendidly representative of the distribution of public opinion may nonetheless adopt policies that fail to comport with most citizens' preferences – for example, because a governing party or coalition representing one set of views dominates the policymaking process. Thus, it is crucial to distinguish, as Lupu and Warner (2022a: 277) put it, between "congruence or opinion representation – the process of generating a body of representatives that reflects the preferences of the electorate" and "the process by which these representatives generate policies that reflect citizens' preferences."

Even if congruence with majority preferences was a foolproof benchmark for assessing representation, additional conceptual difficulties would arise in adapting it to serve as a benchmark for assessing political inequality. A representative (or, more broadly, a political system) reflecting the preferences of majorities will fail to reflect the preferences of minorities. Thus, individuals who persistently find themselves in the minority will have their preferences satisfied less often than those who are generally in the majority. Some observers may consider this a justifiable form of political inequality because it is produced by the mechanism of majority rule, a familiar feature of democratic political systems, and one with a variety of desirable properties. As is often the case in discussions of inequality, a result that is splendidly egalitarian from one perspective (everyone's preferences count equally in gauging the will of the majority) is plainly unequal and arguably invidious from a different perspective (some people routinely get their way and others do not).[5]

There is also a more prosaic arithmetic problem with attempts to measure differential congruence using aggregated tabulations of group preferences. The fact that policy outcomes are closer to the *average* preference of Group A than of Group B does not necessarily imply that congruence is greater for the *individuals* in Group A than for those in Group B, even on average. In the terminology proposed by Achen (1978: 481–488), congruence depends not only on the "centrism" of policy outcomes relative to a group's average preference, but also on the variance of those preferences. There is little reason to think that "centrism" (relative to the average preferences of a group) is an intrinsic good when the notional "group" is merely a convenient analytical fiction. Thus, in the context of assessing congruence, it seems very hard to attach any real significance to tabulations involving average group preferences.[6]

EQUAL INFLUENCE OVER POLICY

So far, I have surveyed a variety of complications involved in measuring inequalities in congruence between the preferences of citizens and the attitudes or choices of policymakers. But I have not addressed what should be a logically prior question – why care about congruence?

The most obvious answer is that we want our political system to give us what we want. But do we? As we have already seen, Pitkin (1967: 163–164, emphasis added) argued that "What the representative must do is act in his constituents' *interests*." Finding himself "in conflict with his constituents' *wishes*" is not in itself a dereliction of his duty as a representative, though it might "call for a reconsideration of his own views" if constituents' wishes are "normally" a good guide to discerning their interests.[7]

If our wishes are only relevant as indicators of our interests, then preference satisfaction itself is not an intrinsic good from the standpoint of democratic theory. Thus, a political philosopher (Kolodny 2023: 300) considered but rejected the view that "Each of us has a correspondence interest in the satisfaction of his or her policy preferences as such." But in that case, tabulations of

---

[5] Alternative procedures create analogous difficulties. For example, if policy choices are made by citizens chosen at random, everyone's preferences will be equally influential *ex ante*, but those whose views are popular among their fellow citizens will still get their way more often than those whose views are unpopular.

[6] The mean squared distance between a policy outcome and the preferences of group members can be decomposed into two terms – (1) the squared distance between the policy outcome and the average preference of group members and (2) the variance of preferences. Even if the first term is smaller for Group A than for Group B, their sum may be larger for Group A if the variance of preferences in Group A is sufficiently larger than in Group B.

[7] On the relationship between preferences and interests – and the daunting normative and analytical complexities involved in measuring political interests systematically – see Bartels (1990).

inequality in congruence, without careful additional consideration of the correspondence between preferences and interests, are of little normative relevance. What justice demands, Kolodny (2023: 323, 320, 87–145) argued, is not equality of preference *satisfaction* but equality of *influence* over policy outcomes. "Equal Influence," he wrote, "is satisfied insofar as any individual who is subject to superior untampered power and authority [that is, to the power of the state] has as much opportunity as any other individual for informed, autonomous influence over decisions about how that power and authority are to be exercised." Equal influence is intrinsically good, Kolodny reasoned, because "If someone is to have influence, then everyone should have equal influence, lest the inequality convey, or be taken to convey, something disparaging about those with less." In the context of his broader "philosophy of social hierarchy," a demand for equal influence is an instance of "claims against inferiority." Disparities in influence that are correlated with economic and social inequalities seem especially problematic if our concern is about real or perceived "social hierarchy."

Kolodny's emphasis on equal influence as the foundation of just collective decision-making resonates with Dahl's analysis of political equality. Dahl (2006: 4, 9) grounded his normative argument for democracy in the "assumption" that "the moral judgment that all human beings are of equal intrinsic worth, that no person is intrinsically superior to another, and that the good or interests of each person must be given equal consideration" in the determination of public policy. The phrase "equal consideration" seems to imply something like equal weight in the determination of policy, rather than equal probability of winning or equal satisfaction with policy outcome – in the language proposed here, equal *influence* rather than equal *congruence*. That interpretation is bolstered by the fact that Dahl went on to list a series of necessary procedural conditions for "an ideal democracy." The most relevant of these, "Equality in voting," stipulated that "When the moment arrives at which the decision will finally be made, every member must have an equal and effective opportunity to vote, and all votes must be counted as equal." Here, too, the emphasis is on *procedures* rather than *outcomes*; once all votes are counted as equal, presumably some will win and some will lose.

Of course, most policy decisions in real democracies are made not directly by popular vote, but by elected or appointed officials. The closest Dahl (2006: 9) came to addressing this fact was to stipulate that "policies of the association would always be open to change by the demos, if its members chose to do so." But, even leaving aside the vagueness of how that would work, what about all those policies the demos does not choose to decide directly? For those cases, we need a conception of "equal consideration" that does not hinge on the mechanics of casting and counting votes.

The conception of "equal consideration" or "equal influence" animating contemporary empirical research on political inequality has its roots in the same "behavioral revolution" that inspired Dahl's study of *Who Governs?* a half-century earlier. Dahl (1957), Harsanyi (1962), Simon (1953), and other prominent mid-century social scientists contributed to a substantial theoretical literature focusing on the concepts of power and influence. The most important upshot of that work, codified in Nagel's (1975) book, *The Descriptive Analysis of Power*, is that power entails a positive causal relationship between an actor's preferences and outcomes. Nagel proposed using statistical models to represent relationships of this sort. In the context of collective decision-making, we might model a policy outcome as a function of the preferences of various relevant political actors, including citizens, parties, interest groups, and elected or unelected government officials.[8] Contemporary studies of political inequality employing regression analyses relating policy outcomes to citizens' preferences instantiate exactly this approach – or attempt to.

As with attempts to measure *congruence* between opinions and policy, attempts to measure *influence* may be more or less cogent. But the challenges to persuasive measurement are different in kind. One significant advantage of focusing on influence rather than congruence is that the opinions of citizens and the choices of policymakers need not be measured on commensurate scales, as long as the opinions being measured appropriately reflect citizens' relevant policy preferences. Analyses of responsiveness in the United States have employed survey data on ideological self-placements, views on specific issues, and even election returns as measures of citizens' preferences. In the comparative literature, levels of social spending have been related to broad support for the government's role in providing jobs and reducing income differences as well as to preferences for increases or decreases in spending on specific government programs.

While analyses of political influence may be less demanding from the standpoint of measurement than analyses of congruence, taking seriously the notion that influence entails a causal relationship between preferences and policy outcomes raises a host of daunting complications – essentially the same complications that arise in any attempt to make causal inferences based on statistical associations. One problem is that measured public opinion may be an *effect* as well as a *cause* of policy outcomes. This is especially likely to be the case in cross-sectional analyses of relatively stable policies and opinions. For example, Brooks and Manza's (2007: 56) study of *Why Welfare States Persist* tracked public attitudes toward the welfare state in a variety of affluent democracies using broad questions about the government's responsibility to provide jobs and reduce income differences between the rich and the poor. They showed that responses to these questions were strongly correlated with countries' welfare state spending. But did "the policy preferences of national populations

---

[8] Bartels (1985) sketched a statistical framework for analyzing situations involving both power (defined as the impact of actors' preferences on outcomes) and influence (the impact of actors' preferences on other actors' preferences); but that complication has generally been ignored in empirical analyses of political inequality.

strongly influence aggregated welfare state spending," as Brooks and Manza surmised, or did long-standing differences in the scope of countries' welfare states shape their citizens' views about the appropriate role of government?[9]

Another concern is that analyses of political influence may be sensitive to the specification of how citizens' preferences matter. Many studies of inequality focus on disparities in responsiveness to the preferences of affluent, middle class, and poor people, assigning separate regression coefficients to people in each tercile of the income distribution or to preferences imputed to people at a few specific points in the income distribution. As Achen (1978: 480) argued in the context of studies of congressional representation, "estimating a distinct influence coefficient for every individual would be computationally infeasible and theoretically uninteresting." Thus, analyses of this sort implicitly assume that everyone in the same income subgroup is equally influential. But subgroups may be more or less heterogeneous, and the implications of the tradeoff between bias (from treating heterogeneous individuals as identical) and imprecision (from treating them as distinct) deserve careful attention.[10]

Heterogeneity in political influence is almost surely greatest for high-income subgroups. Given the distribution of income in capitalist societies, the long upper tail has its own long upper tail, which has its own long upper tail, *ad infinitum*. Thus, if political influence is proportional to income, a simple average of the policy preferences of people in the top one-third or one-fifth of the income distribution may be a poor approximation of their *effective* preferences weighted by political influence. No one has managed to measure the political preferences of rich people with sufficient precision across space, time, or political issues to produce a systematic analysis of their impact on policy outcomes. However, scholars have gathered more limited descriptive data on the preferences of rich people and have used those data to speculate about the political power of the wealthy (Page, Bartels, and Seawright 2013; Page, Seawright, and Lacombe 2019).

It is also worth bearing in mind that even the most careful delineation of citizens' preferences along one dimension may be misleading if it overlooks other bases of inequality. Most contemporary research has focused on the translation of economic inequality into political inequality; but in some settings, differences in income may be less consequential than racial, ethnic, or other social distinctions. Moreover, the effects of distinct but correlated bases of inequality may easily be confounded. Are poor people underrepresented because they are poor, or because they are disproportionately women and members of racial and ethnic minority groups?

---

[9] Kenworthy (2009) noted that cross-national differences in welfare state effort are quite stable over long periods of time, making it very difficult to discern whether supportive public attitudes are a cause or an effect of government policy.

[10] On the statistical considerations arising in pooling disparate observations, see Bartels (1996a).

More broadly, policy outcomes are shaped by a wide variety of factors besides citizens' preferences. Kingdon's (1989) study of roll call voting in the U.S. Congress portrayed constituents' opinions as one among several important considerations shaping members' voting decisions.[11] But while it may be possible to construct a general list of potentially important actors in policymaking, the specific factors that may confound any particular analysis are likely to vary from case to case. Public employee unions loom large in some local policy domains, developers and business interests in others; ignoring these groups will make it hard to get sensible estimates of political influence (Anzia 2022). In setting defense budgets, policymakers are likely to be sensitive to the magnitude of external security threats. Those threats may also affect citizens' defense spending preferences, producing a spurious correlation between citizens' preferences and policy outcomes even if policymakers act solely on the basis of their own strategic judgments (Hartley and Russett 1992). Once we approach the problem of measuring political inequality as a problem of causal inference, the variety of potentially relevant factors to be considered is no less complex than the policymaking process itself.

One ubiquitous potential confounding factor in analyses of this sort is the preferences of the policymakers themselves. Perhaps affluent citizens only *appear* to be influential because their preferences happen to coincide with what policymakers were going to do anyway. Elkjær (2020: 2232, 2238) related Danish government spending in a variety of policy domains to the preferences of affluent, middle-class, and poor citizens. He found that "political representation appears to increase monotonically with income"; but his interpretation of that finding was that high-income groups have preferences that better reflect current economic and political circumstances. Accordingly, when governments pursue standard macroeconomic policies, such as stabilizing fiscal policies, these short-term policy changes more closely reflect the preferences of high-income groups. But the bias is coincidental, driven by better information, rather than a substantive overrepresentation of the "interests of the rich."

A direct test of this interpretation would require adding measures of policymakers' own preferences to Elkjær's "influence" analyses and seeing whether the apparent impact of high-income preferences was reduced or eliminated. Unfortunately, analysts of responsiveness rarely have access to reliable measures of policymakers' own preferences.[12] A more feasible approach would be

---

[11] Kingdon (1989: 18) tabulated members' spontaneous mentions of various actors in explaining their decisions on a series of specific roll call votes. Constituencies were mentioned in 37 percent of the cases, fellow members in 40 percent, interest groups in 31 percent, and the administration in 25 percent, with party leaders, staff, and "reading" mentioned less frequently.

[12] Some analysts have employed rough proxies for policymakers' own preferences, such as partisanship or statements in party manifestos. Examining the roll call votes cast by US senators, Bartels (2016: 235–249, 347) interpreted substantial differences in the voting behavior of Democrats and Republicans representing similar constituencies as reflections of "partisan ideologies," concluding that "the specific policy views of citizens, whether rich or poor, have less impact in the policy-making process than the ideological convictions of elected officials."

to augment the analysis with measures of government partisanship, macroeconomic conditions, and other factors potentially relevant to spending decisions. If those factors are consequential and positively correlated with the preferences of high-income citizens, then accounting for them would indeed reduce the apparent influence of high-income citizens' preferences on government spending.

In another article, Elkjær and Iversen (2020: 269–270) related long-run social spending in twenty-one affluent democracies to average support for redistribution in different income classes. They interpreted their results as "point[ing] to the critical role of the middle class" and indeed as "suggest[ing] that the level of redistribution is largely decided by the middle class." However, adding a measure of average government partisanship in each country produced a much better fit to the data, while the apparent impact of middle-income preferences evaporated, suggesting that the preferences of political elites were more consequential than those of the middle class – and mostly *not* themselves accounted for by the preferences of the middle class.[13]

Of course, the impact of government partisanship on policy is likely to vary significantly by country and policy domain. One advantage of analyses focusing on specific policy domains, like Elkjær and Iversen's, is that they facilitate assessing the direct impact on policy outcomes of partisanship and other factors correlated with but distinct from citizens' preferences. Capturing these effects in catch-all analyses including dozens of different policies will generally be much more difficult. For example, Mathisen and colleagues in this volume explore the impact of government partisanship on linkages between citizens' preferences and policy outcomes, but the main effects of "left government" in their analyses capture general orientations for or against policy change, not the leeway of governments to promote or block specific policies based on their own ideological proclivities. An additional complexity, addressed by Becher and Stegmueller in this volume, is that governments' own ideological proclivities may be shaped, in part, by citizens' preferences through both electoral selection and lobbying.

The ubiquity of concerns regarding potential confounding factors in analyses of political influence is daunting; as Wlezien (2017: 562) observed in surveying research on political responsiveness, "It is simply hard to demonstrate causality in observational studies." It is no more likely that analysts will agree about the theoretical and statistical assumptions required to make persuasive causal inferences in this realm than in any other. Thus, there is good reason to be modest about our conclusions. Yet that is no good reason to refrain from drawing conclusions, with due allowance for uncertainty – or to use the difficulty of the task as an excuse for pretending that simpler analyses will suffice.

---

[13] Cross-national analyses of changes in social spending using similar data (Bartels 2017: 57–59) likewise found most of the variation accounted for by factors other than citizens' preferences, though the estimated effects of high-income preferences were also, in several cases, substantial.

MULTICOLLINEARITY, PREFERENCE
DIVERGENCE, AND INEQUALITY

Having sketched in general terms the significance of congruence and influence as dimensions of potential political inequality, it may be helpful to consider some examples of how these concepts have been employed in the scholarly literature. One common bugaboo in analyses of this sort is that the policy preferences of distinct subgroups of citizens are often highly correlated across time or space. From the standpoint of assessing congruence, that is not really a problem, though it can be a source of confusion when analysts mistake correlation for similarity. As Gilens (2015b: 1068) noted, "even a strong correlation between two groups' preferences need not imply similar levels of congruence between preferences and outcomes." In studies of social spending, for example, the preferences of distinct income subgroups are often highly correlated across countries or over time, but with substantial, ubiquitous preference gaps between subgroups producing greater congruence for some subgroups than others.

From the standpoint of assessing political influence, multicollinearity is both a real problem and a pseudo-problem. Statistically, the effect of multicollinearity is to produce less precise estimates of the impact of each subgroup's preferences. For some purposes, that is a substantial disadvantage, for others not so much. If our scientific interest is really in *inequality* rather than in the extent of responsiveness to each group considered separately, it may be feasible to recast our analyses (by redefining our explanatory variables) to focus directly on the impact of *differences* in subgroup preferences, which are less likely to be highly correlated. Schakel, Burgoon, and Hakhverdian (2020) and Mathieson et al. (in this volume) provide examples of that approach.[14]

But aside from its statistical implications, multicollinearity has also produced a good deal of conceptual confusion and misdirection. While *perfect* collinearity between two (or more) explanatory variables in a multiple regression analysis makes it impossible to distinguish their separate effects, high levels of collinearity short of this extreme violate none of the standard assumptions of regression analysis; neither the regression parameter estimates

---

[14] These analyses, like Gilens' employ estimated preferences of citizens at the 90th, 50th, and 10th percentiles of the income distribution, denoted P90, P50, and P10. While P90, P50, and P10 are likely to be highly correlated, P90 can be rewritten as (P90–P50)+P50 and P10 can be rewritten as P50–(P50–P10). Relating policy outcomes to P50, (P90–P50), and (P50–P10) rather than to P50, P90, and P10 captures the same information about preferences, but isolates the *differential* impact of affluent and poor citizens' preferences *relative* to those of middle-income citizens. The parameter estimate for P50 in this analysis reflects a combination of the influence of all three groups, so is no longer directly interpretable as the impact of middle-income preferences. Analyses with only two explanatory variables, P50 and one of (P90–P50), (P50–P10), or (P90–P10), will also be difficult to interpret, since they impose implausible constraints on the estimated influence of one or more of the three groups.

nor their standard errors are biased.[15] The standard errors will be larger than they would be with less-correlated regressors – just as the standard errors will be larger than they would be with more observations. In either case, if the results are too imprecise to answer the questions being asked, the solution is straightforward: find more data.

Unfortunately, finding more data can be hard. Thus, scholars have sometimes attempted to sidestep the problem of having too little data by resorting to statistical shortcuts. Soroka and Wlezien (2010: 161–165), for example, proposed a model in which annual changes in government spending in each of several policy domains are related to the spending preferences of subgroups of citizens (differentiated by party, education, or income), with distinct weights translating each subgroup's preferences into policy change. "Applying this approach here," they wrote, "is complicated by very high multicollinearity" among preferences for change in the distinct subgroups. "To assess differential responsiveness, therefore, we separately model the effect of each group's preferences."

It is hardly surprising that regression analyses with fifteen to thirty-three slow-moving annual observations of preferences and spending are insufficient to estimate disparities in responsiveness to a variety of distinct subgroups. Unfortunately, there is no reason to think that the alternative of comparing parameter estimates from separate models focusing on each subgroup's preferences in isolation can shed any reliable light on the question of "whether policy responds more to the preferences of some groups than others." Each of these mutually contradictory analyses is biased by the omission of other subgroups' preferences (aside from any other factors) from the set of relevant explanatory variables. Moreover, the higher the correlations among the subgroup preferences are, the more severely biased the bivariate regression parameter estimates will be. There is simply nothing useful to be learned from analyses of this sort about disparities in political influence.

The implications of correlated subgroup preferences are further muddled by a tendency to mistake statistical imprecision for evidence in favor of null hypotheses. Using spending and survey data from the United States, Wlezien and Soroka (2011: 299, 302, 298) assessed income-group differences in dynamic representation across thirty-five years and six different policy domains. Only three of the resulting eighteen estimates of responsiveness (for each of the three income groups in each of the six domains) were "statistically significant," and the authors concluded that "it is difficult to distinguish responsiveness to particular groups." So far, so good. However, by the end of their chapter,

---

[15] The notion that "Gilens and Page's analyses are questionable based on concerns about collinearity among the independent variables" (Branham, Soroka, and Wlezien 2017: 58) is sometimes attributed to Bashir (2015), overlooking fatal flaws in Bashir's simulation analysis noted by Gilens (2016). Winship and Western (2016) provided a Bayesian analysis of how multicollinearity can exacerbate biases stemming from misspecification, but no reason to think that omitting relevant variables would mitigate those biases.

this statistical uncertainty was somehow transmuted into substantive equality: policymakers, they concluded; "appear to be guided as much by the median voter as anyone else. This is about all that we would expect if people had equal weight in the policymaking process." In fact, their estimates of responsiveness to the rich, averaged across policy domains, were almost 50 percent larger than those for the "median voter," while the average estimated responsiveness to low-income people was slightly negative.[16] Given the limitations of the data and analysis, this is certainly not conclusive evidence of unequal influence, but it is even less indicative of "equal weight in the policymaking process."

Another way to generate inconclusive statistical results is to limit the analysis to small subsets of cases. Branham, Soroka, and Wlezien (2017: 60, 56) analyzed 185 of Gilens' 1,779 proposed policy changes,[17] those where majorities of affluent and middle-income people disagreed. The result of truncating the sample was to inflate the standard errors of the key parameter estimates by a factor of four or five, leading the authors to conclude that "it is nearly a coin flip as to which group wins," a result they interpreted as "more encouraging (normatively speaking) than recent scholarship." Statistical analyses that are too underpowered to shed light on quantities of interest are not "encouraging," they are simply uninformative.

Why focus on cases in which majorities of income subgroups disagree? According to Branham, Soroka, and Wlezien (2017: 56, 60), "We know that disagreement in policy preferences is a necessary condition for differential representation. If majorities in different income cohorts prefer the same policy, we cannot distinguish whose preferences are being represented." "Differential representation" here seems to mean differential congruence between preferences and policy outcomes. But clearly, disagreement between subgroup majorities is not a necessary condition for differential congruence. If a policy is adopted with 80 percent support from one subgroup and 51 percent support from another subgroup, clearly more people in the first subgroup than the second got their way. Nor does agreement between subgroup majorities imply equality of influence. Indeed, when the authors examined cases where majorities of affluent and middle-income people agreed, they found strong evidence of unequal influence.[18]

---

[16] The average responsiveness estimates were 0.187 for the high-income group, 0.128 for the middle-income group, and –0.034 for the low-income group. Elsewhere in the same edited volume, Bhatti and Erikson (2011: 241) provided a rather more nuanced interpretation of ambiguous empirical results, writing that "Conclusive statistical evidence could not be found in favor of the differential representation hypothesis."

[17] Gilens (2012), for the most part, and Gilens and Page (2014) focused on 1,779 policy questions asked in U.S. opinion surveys between 1981 and 2002, relating the opinions of survey respondents at various points in the income distribution (imputed from the quadratic relationship between preferences and reported incomes for each survey question) to subsequent changes in policy.

[18] In 1,594 cases with coincident majorities, the estimated impact of "Rich Preferences" (from a structural equation model taking account of measurement error in subgroup preferences) was

Some analysts have focused on cases of preference divergence in the apparent hope that doing so would mitigate statistical biases resulting from employing mutually contradictory bivariate analyses of influence. An analytical shortcut in Gilens' book seems to have served as an encouraging example in this respect. His most persuasive evidence of unequal influence was derived from regression analyses simultaneously incorporating the preferences of affluent, middle-class, and poor people and allowing for correlated measurement error in the estimated preferences of the three income subgroups (Gilens 2012: 85–87, 256).[19] However, in much of his book, he presented the results of simpler bivariate statistical analyses relating policy outcomes to the preferences of each income subgroup separately, first for his entire sample of 1,779 policy questions and then for subsets of issues where the subgroups' preferences differed. He was clear about the inferential limitations of the latter approach. "To assess the ability of citizens at different economic levels to influence government policy," he wrote (2012: 78), "we need to know not the strength of the overall preference/policy link for each income group, but rather the strength of this association net of the impact of other income groups." Nonetheless, he offered parallel analyses of subsets of issues where subgroups' preferences diverged as "an alternative to multivariate analysis," noting that "this technique produces results comparable to a multivariate model when the multivariate approach is feasible."

The similarity to his more sophisticated statistical findings notwithstanding, I know of no reason to think that limiting analyses to cases of preference divergence will overcome the bias resulting from misspecified bivariate models. While sample selection may reduce the correlation between subgroup preferences, and thus the bias resulting from misspecification, the bias would only be eliminated if that correlation were reduced to zero – and in that case, the cost in precision of including multiple subgroups in the analysis would also be eliminated, so there would still be no reason to prefer a bivariate model.

Gilens' shortcut was relatively benign, in that the key results of his bivariate analyses were corroborated by more sophisticated analyses, either in the appendix of his book or in subsequent work by Gilens and Page (2014). However, there is no comparable corroborating evidence for many other bivariate analyses of subsets of issues on which the average preferences of income subgroups diverge, either in absolute terms or in the sense that a majority of

---

0.757 (with a standard error of 0.079); the estimated impact of "Middle Preferences" was 0.032 (with a standard error of 0.082).

[19] Gilens' correction for measurement error employed estimates of error variances and covariances derived from the subset of cases in which substantively similar policy questions were asked of independent survey samples in the same calendar year. The persuasiveness of his results was bolstered by careful examination of a variety of potential alternative explanations for his findings of unequal influence, including differences across income subgroups in the reliability, intensity, and homogeneity of policy preferences and in levels of education.

one subgroup favored a proposed policy change that a majority of another subgroup opposed.[20]

Sometimes, bivariate analyses have been presented not just as shortcuts for assessing disparities in political influence, but as significant in their own right. For example, Enns (2015: 1055) proposed "relative policy support" as a benchmark for assessing representation, arguing that a positive correlation between the strength of a subgroup's support for various policies and the probability that they are adopted constitutes "straightforward – perhaps even axiomatic … evidence of representation." But it is very hard to see why subgroup members should be gratified by a correlation that implies neither congruence nor influence. This is a conception of representation with little apparent grounding in any theory of democracy.[21]

In other cases, it is unclear whether bivariate statistical associations are supposed to be measuring congruence, influence, or something else. In their study of the relationship between support for redistribution and levels of social spending in twenty-one democracies, Elkjær and Iversen (2020: 267–268) estimated "simple bivariate responsiveness models to examine how well social spending aligns with the preferences of each income class." They found that the bivariate relationship was "strongest for the middle class, suggesting that the middle class is instrumental in setting the level of redistribution." This sounds like a simple conflation of "alignment" with influence. However, Elkjær (2020: 2228) separately offered a different-sounding interpretation of "policy alignment": "Unequal policy responsiveness should be disaggregated into two concepts: policy alignment and policy influence. Policy alignment conceptualizes the extent to which policies correspond to subgroup preferences, whereas policy influence conceptualizes the degree of independent influence of subgroup preferences on policies." Here, "policy alignment" seems intended to capture something like congruence, distinct from influence. But what? The estimated slopes from bivariate regression analyses – indeed, from *any* regression analyses – shed no light on how well policy outcomes satisfy any individual's or subgroup's preferences.

On the other hand, if the bivariate "alignment" between policy outcomes and subgroup preferences is supposed to be significant in its own right, as with Enns's notion of "relative policy support," the logic is equally murky. Why should a person living in any one of Elkjær and Iversen's twenty-one democracies be expected to care how closely spending policies in other countries "align" with the average preferences of people in the corresponding income groups in those countries? If "alignment" is not a measure of congruence or influence, it seems to be a statistical measure looking for a theoretical rationale.

---

[20] Bowman (2020) provided a comprehensive assessment of analyses of various subsets of Gilens' data employing alternative "preference gaps" and "preference thresholds."

[21] On the logic of "relative policy support," see Gilens (2015b: 1066–1068).

CONGRUENCE, INFLUENCE, AND
COINCIDENTAL REPRESENTATION

Even if analysts of political inequality could agree about how to conduct their empirical analyses, they would still be left to wrestle with the implications for democracy of findings regarding congruence and influence. Gilens' data from the United States revealed substantial disparities in apparent influence across income groups, but only modest differences in the extent to which citizens got the policy outcomes they preferred. Parallel analyses of European data by Mathisen and colleagues (this volume) reveal a similar pattern, as do a variety of other studies employing different research designs. As Soroka and Wlezien (2008: 325) wrote of the first wave of such studies, "we take that research to imply that policy would represent the median voter *only* because the preferences of people with middling income are much like the preferences of those with high incomes. From this perspective, representation of the middle would be indirect."

These findings raise two distinct issues, one empirical and the other normative. The empirical issue turns on the prevalence of what Soroka and Wlezien referred to as "indirect" representation and Gilens and Page (2014: 573) termed "democracy by coincidence, in which ordinary citizens get what they want from government only because they happen to agree with elites or interest groups that are really calling the shots." Soroka and Wlezien (2008: 325) acknowledged that "there are differences in preferences across income levels in some important policy domains," but argued that "regardless of whose preferences policymakers follow, differences across income groups are often rather small, and policy will end up in essentially the same place." Gilens (2015b: 1070, 1065) was more pessimistic, acknowledging that "'democracy by coincidence' is an important feature of contemporary American politics," but emphasizing specific "important and highly salient issues on which the power of the affluent and interest groups has pushed policy away from the preferences of the majority."[22]

Statistical analyses aggregating hundreds of distinct policy issues tend to occlude detailed consideration of differences among them, including differences

---

[22] In some cases, scholars have employed selective citation to bolster broad claims that policy disagreement between income subgroups is "relatively rare." For example, Elkjær and Iversen (2020: 257, 258) argued that "unequal representation is naturally quite limited on most policies with no redistributive aim, since class preferences barely diverge." In support of this claim, they cited Soroka and Wlezien's (2008: 319) tabulations of responses to eight spending questions in the United States over twenty-four years, ignoring Gilens' (2009: 339) response documenting substantial gaps between the average preferences of income subgroups across hundreds of survey questions drawn from a wide range of policy domains, including not only social welfare, taxes, and economic policies, but also moral issues and foreign policy and national security. Similar preference gaps appear elsewhere; for example, European survey data reveal significant differences between income subgroups in attitudes toward gay rights, the role of science in addressing environmental problems, trust in the legal system, and other issues.

in the similarity of preferences across subgroups and potential differences in the influence of specific actors in different policy domains. Gilens' examinations of variation across policy domains (2012: ch. 4) and political contexts (2012: ch. 6–7) are a notable exception in this regard, but much more work of this sort will be necessary to clarify the empirical significance of "democracy by coincidence."

The normative significance of coincidental representation is an equally important issue, but much harder for empirical analysts to adjudicate. Gilens (2015b: 1070) argued that "democracy by coincidence is a debased and conditional form of democracy (if it is a form of democracy at all)." Kolodny (2023: 304) reached a similar conclusion on philosophical grounds, arguing for "a democratic ideal not of correspondence, but instead of influence: not of satisfying the People's policy preferences, but instead of ensuring the People's control over policy." For the most part, however, and despite its seeming prevalence, "democracy by coincidence" has received rather little attention from theorists of democracy.

CONCLUSION

As Gilens (2012: 47) observed, "There is no single right way to assess something as complex as government responsiveness to public preferences; alternative approaches offer different sets of trade-offs and limitations." From the standpoint of research design, studies in which the units of analysis are distinct policy proposals – like those described by Gilens, and by Mathisen and colleagues in this volume – rest on rather different assumptions and offer rather different analytical opportunities than those focusing on temporal or cross-national variation (or both) in a single policy domain. Cross-sectional studies relating citizens' preferences to the preferences or choices of specific policymakers or parties may help to overcome ubiquitous data limitations, but they require careful attention to the question of how policymakers' choices are aggregated into policy outcomes.

No one analytical template will or should monopolize the study of political inequality. However, in designing research, it behooves us to be as clear as possible about what we hope to learn, how, and why. My focus here has been on two key aspects of political inequality – *congruence* and *influence*. Each of these concepts has a (relatively) coherent theoretical pedigree with (relatively) unequivocal methodological implications. While I do not mean to suggest that these two concepts exhaust the ways in which we might study political inequality, alternative approaches have yet to find comparable grounding in democratic theory. Attaching significant-sounding labels to measures "plucked from the statistical shelf and employed without much theoretical interpretation," as Achen (1977: 806) put it more than forty years ago, is unlikely to produce much real insight.

For analysts aspiring to measure inequality in the extent of congruence between citizens' preferences and policy outcomes, the key challenge will be to calibrate preferences and policies, either by coding policy outcomes to harmonize with existing survey data (the approach taken by Gilens and by Mathisen and colleagues) or by employing survey data that take the policy status quo as an explicit point of reference (as in studies of governmental spending). Both of these approaches suggest that the preferences of affluent citizens are better satisfied than those of poor citizens, though the differences are often modest in magnitude.

If our interest is in measuring differences in political power or influence, we will succeed to the extent that we can produce credible inferences regarding the impact of citizens' preferences on policy outcomes. The potential pitfalls here are of two broad sorts. On the one hand, there is the temptation to evade substantive difficulties by oversimplifying. As in most realms of social research, bivariate analyses are not a promising basis for inferring causality. Analyses representing the policymaking process as a simple contest among the preferences of distinct subgroups of citizens will generally be somewhat more informative, though still less credible than more sophisticated analyses taking account of political parties, interest groups, and other salient actors in the policymaking process. Analyses that also take account of the potential indirect influence of citizens via parties, interest groups, and other salient actors will be most persuasive of all.[23]

On the other hand, there is the temptation to evade substantive difficulties by imposing unrealistic standards of perfection on our data analyses. While experimental research has occasionally shed valuable light on responsiveness, its utility in this realm is likely to be limited, given the scale and complexity of the political processes involved.[24] For the most part, we will have to do the best we can with empirical analyses that reflect the policymaking process sensibly rather than precisely, producing inferences that are never wholly persuasive. Given the rudimentary state of knowledge in the field, even experienced scholars will often disagree about the persuasiveness of any specific analysis. Disagreement is to be expected, a natural feature of the scientific process of criticism and successive approximation. Nonetheless, we can hope that results from multiple studies with distinct strengths and weaknesses in different political contexts will gradually produce a clearer picture of the unequal distribution of political influence in contemporary democracies.

When Gilens and Page's (2014) analysis was published, I argued that "their findings should reshape how we think about American democracy."[25] That

[23] Of course, citizens' preferences are also shaped by parties, interest groups and other salient actors, raising additional normative and empirical complexities that are generally ignored in this literature.

[24] Butler (2014) and Kalla and Broockman (2016b) used field experiments to assess biases in the responsiveness of congressional offices to constituents' requests for assistance and access, respectively.

[25] Larry Bartels, "Rich People Rule!" *Washington Post*, Monkey Cage, April 8, 2014 (www .washingtonpost.com/news/monkey-cage/wp/2014/04/08/rich-people-rule/).

assessment may have been too modest. Subsequent research on other countries suggests that substantial disparities in political influence are ubiquitous in affluent democracies (Bartels 2017; Elsässer, Hense, and Schäfer 2021; Mathisen and colleagues in this volume; Schakel, Burgoon, and Hakhverdian 2020). Those findings imply that political inequality is *not* primarily attributable to specific features of the US system, such as permissive campaign finance regulations, weak unions, and a policymaking process with myriad veto points. Its roots apparently lie much deeper in the social and political soil of democracy than even pessimistic analysts have supposed.

Political science, like politics, involves a lot of slow boring of hard boards. In the past two decades, the scientific study of political inequality has advanced considerably. Nonetheless, we have only begun to scratch the surface of the problem, and much more work will be necessary to confirm and extend our understanding of the magnitude and bases of inequality in putative democracies. The challenges are formidable, but it is difficult to think of a more vital set of questions.

5

Why So Little Sectionalism in the Contemporary United States?

The Underrepresentation of Place-Based Economic Interests[*]

Jacob S. Hacker, Paul Pierson, and Sam Zacher

The United States has a long history of political conflicts emerging out of the shifting spatial distribution of economic activity. From the first stirrings of industry in the nineteenth century through the era of mass production in the twentieth, the country's diverse economy fostered sectional divisions over national policy. Today, another revolution in economic and political geography is taking place – the shift from an industrial to a knowledge economy. This transformation is feeding both economic polarization (between advantaged and disadvantaged places) and political polarization (between "red" Republican-leaning jurisdictions and "blue" Democratic-leaning ones). As a result, each party is increasingly drawing support from areas with distinct economic needs based on their place within the knowledge economy.

We call these differing needs "place-based economic interests" (PBEIs) – the interests of voters that emerge out of their local economic contexts. In this chapter, we investigate the extent to which they are reshaping the priorities and performance of the nation's two major parties. The basic geographic divide on which our analysis centers is between metropolitan areas that have thrived in the knowledge economy and rural and exurban areas (hereafter, "nonmetro" areas) that have not. Metro America is, of course, increasingly blue, while nonmetro America is increasingly red. However, both have distinct economic needs that require active national policy, albeit of a different form.

[*] For thoughtful comments on earlier versions of this chapter, we gratefully thank Larry Bartels, Dan Carpenter, Sid Milkis, and Kathy Thelen. We also received many useful suggestions from participants in Harvard's "State and Capitalism Since 1800" seminar series and the University of Virginia Miller Center's "Democracy and Capitalism" seminar series. Finally, we are grateful to fellow contributors to this volume for their feedback and to the editors of this volume and an anonymous reviewer for their guidance.

The question is whether those needs are being articulated and met within each party's coalition and the US policy process as a whole.

Like other chapters in this volume, then, we are interested in the quality of representation. Our distinctive focus, however, is on the representation of voter interests rooted in geospatially differing economic circumstances – an approach we explain further in the next section. We consider this a revealing area of focus for at least three reasons. First, the parties are rapidly becoming more sectionally distinct, and these sectional divides are associated with powerful economic forces that have reshaped the geography of US prosperity, as well as the social, racial, ethnic, and economic character of both metro and non-metro America. Second, these forces have raised the stakes for voters, whose health, income, well-being, and opportunities are increasingly connected to where they live. Finally, key features of the American political system – particularly federalism, single-member districts, and a territorially based Senate and Electoral College – are widely seen to encourage responsiveness to such place-based interests. Indeed, sectional economic coalitions have been among the most powerful forces animating US federal policymaking in the past (Bensel 1984; Katznelson 2013; Sanders 1999; Schickler 2016). To use a national security metaphor, American political institutions are well designed to "stovepipe" local demands up to higher levels of government. In short, there are compelling reasons to expect that the knowledge economy is reshaping voters' PBEIs and equally compelling reasons to expect that these shifting PBEIs are reshaping national representation.

Despite these strong expectations, however, we find that PBEIs are strikingly *underrepresented* in contemporary American politics. The knowledge economy has wrought enormous changes. Yet we find little evidence that the PBEIs it has generated are strongly reflected in either overall policy outcomes or the stances of the parties. In a variety of ways, national policymakers are failing to provide robust support for the expansion of the knowledge economy. Nor have the parties reoriented around the differing PBEIs of their geographic bases as expected. The sectionalism that has animated politics and policy in the American political past seems more often muted or puzzlingly distorted in the American political present.

Far from mirroring local economic interests, we find that each party has failed to respond to a fundamental set of PBEIs associated with core voters within its coalition. Against expectations, national Republicans have failed to reorient their economic agenda around the needs of red jurisdictions that would benefit from increased transfers from blue jurisdictions. Instead, they have placed priority on lavish tax cuts favorable to corporations and the affluent that offer little to these areas. Also against expectations, national Democrats have proved strikingly willing to promote policies that redistribute resources *away* from blue places that vote for them and toward red places that do not. Meanwhile, they have largely left blue jurisdictions to cope on their own with the huge collective action problems that plague urban knowledge hubs, particularly the problem of affordable housing, which hurts both metro economies and core Democratic voters.

Thus, each party's economic priorities exhibit strong sectional disconnects, which we term the "red PBEI paradox" and "blue PBEI paradox," respectively. These two paradoxes may seem very different from each other, and in important respects they are. Yet they also reflect the same underlying reality: while both blue metro areas and red nonmetro areas need federal help to overcome problems that cannot be tackled through localized action alone, the party allied with each of these respective locations has shown limited inclination to pursue that course, despite high costs of inaction to its core voters.

In neither case, we argue, is the main reason for the disconnect that these voters have failed to recognize their economic interests. Confusion, misdirection, and motivated reasoning are rife, but there is ample evidence of voter dissatisfaction with the status quo and desire for a more PBEI-consistent course. Instead, we point to the ways in which the PBEIs associated with each party's geographic base are refracted through a set of "filters" that are historically and/or comparatively distinct. Three filters loom large: (1) the increasing antimetro and status quo biases of American political *institutions*; (2) the nationalization of US *party coalitions*, including the intense organized interests allied with each party; and (3) the path-dependent character of America's unusually decentralized and fiscally fragmented social and economic *policies*.

Together, these institutional, party, and policy filters mute voters' expression of PBEIs, limit the extent to which these PBEIs have reshaped party agendas, and reduce the degree to which any shifts in party agendas have been reflected in public policy. Crucially, these filters operate on both the "supply" and "demand" sides of representation. Thus, for example, the nationalization of party coalitions has facilitated the agenda control of party elites and these elites in turn have shaped the way in which voters assess parties, candidates, and policies. On both sides of the partisan divide, we shall see, elites have offered bundles of appeals that are relatively unresponsive to PBEIs, with the disconnect particularly striking on the GOP side, where "second dimension" issues of cultural and racial identity have loomed large.

In the next section, we expand on our approach to representation and then draw out the implications of the US transition to the knowledge economy for PBEIs, building on recent influential accounts. Having established a set of grounded expectations, we turn to our core task: explaining why these expectations have not been met. To do so, we first lay out the red and blue PBEI paradoxes and then our concept of filters. Finally, we show how these filters help explain the puzzling (non)response to geographic economic polarization. We conclude by drawing out some of the broader lessons of our account for the study of representation.

THE REPRESENTATION OF SHIFTING PBEIS

The approach we take to representation in this chapter departs from that employed by most studies of representation, especially within the subfield of American politics.[1] Thus, we start with a brief discussion of its logic.

Filtered vs. Unfiltered Approaches to Representation

We offer what might be called a "filtered" approach to representation. We start with a set of previously theorized and empirically studied citizen interests – in this case, PBEIs – and see how well they are represented. Because we find they are underrepresented, we propose a set of explanations focused on key filtering features of the representative process. We see the enumeration of these filters as our central contribution: a means of understanding why some citizen interests (and not just PBEIs) are stovepiped into national politics while others are not.

By contrast, most students of representation offer an "unfiltered" view of representation. They start with some measure of voters' preferences based on opinion surveys and then map those views onto some measures of politicians' or parties' stances. A common finding is that, at least in critical contested races, voters punish politicians with extreme stances, suggesting that the "electoral connection" (Mayhew 1974) is strong (see, e.g., Hall 2015).

As the contributions to this volume show, this approach has become more sophisticated and multifaceted (and, in the process, more skeptical about the electoral connection). Among other things, scholars are now attentive to differences in voters' opinions across class lines and to the differential responsiveness of politicians to richer voters relative to poorer ones (Gilens 2012). They are also more attuned to the biases and limits of voter awareness, including the strong filtering effects of the media (as in Mathews, Hicks, and Jacobs's chapter for this volume). And they are now more likely to judge representation by looking at policy outcomes, rather than broad measures of ideological alignment between voters and elected officials.

Still, there remains a serious gap between what these analyses can show and what students of representation aim to know. At its core, representation concerns whether citizens have control over governance: the things that government does and doesn't do to shape people's lives. But most studies of representation pay only limited attention to governance. Even when the outcome of interest is public policy, investigations are limited to asking whether policies reflect the expressed views of voters on those policy issues and positions that prior surveys have covered. Of course, this means that many issues and

---

[1] Our basic approach is more common within comparative political economy, as suggested by the interests-oriented analysis by Elkjær and Iversen in this volume (which also raises questions about the quality of US representation).

positions are never examined because they failed either to make it high on the political agenda or to elicit the interest of pollsters. Moreover, this approach implicitly assumes that all issues are of equal weight to voters and equal impact on society, when in fact some are far more valued, consequential, or both.

As a result, the dominant approach to representation has little to say about a fundamental feature of representation: agenda setting – which issues and alternatives get on the agenda and which do not. As E.E. Schattschneider (1960: 71) famously put it, a central aspect of politics is the process by which "some issues are organized into politics while others are organized out." Even if we see congruence between opinion and policy, we still need to know whether the issues on the agenda are those citizens care about and the alternatives considered are those citizens prefer (on congruence, see Bartels's chapter). Indeed, we might see congruence even though very few of the policy shifts that citizens want actually occur, either because the preferred shifts weren't the focus of surveys or because the few changes that *did* happen were popular.[2]

A last thorny question concerns what public opinion polls tell us about what citizens want. We will not belabor these issues, which are discussed extensively in other chapters in this volume. Suffice it to say that opinion polls provide only a partial and distorted picture of citizen preferences. Preferences, in turn, may be considerably removed from what scholars call "interests" (in Dahl's influential formulation [1989], "whatever that person would choose with fullest attainable understanding of the experience resulting from that choice and its most relevant alternatives"). Whether we call these underlying demands "interests" or "enlightened preferences" (Bartels 1996b), they may be quite distinct from what surveys end up measuring.

Without minimizing the challenges involved, we think there is value in starting from a different place. Our concept of PBEIs is meant to capture one set of citizen interests that have the potential to reshape governance. Indeed, as we discuss in the next section, prominent scholars have argued that voters on both the left and right are developing a new set of priorities rooted in their spatial relationship to the metro-oriented knowledge economy. In part because existing scholarship has highlighted PBEIs, we are able to form research-backed expectations about how they are likely to evolve in the knowledge economy. This in turn makes it easier for us to investigate whether these key interests make the transition into governance without assuming that all issues of concern to citizens make it high onto the agenda (or find expression in reliable surveys). However, we see PBEIs as just one area – albeit an important one given recent economic changes – where a filtered approach can deepen our understanding of patterns of representation in rich democracies.

---

[2] Gilens (2012), for example, finds greater congruence between the opinions of the nonrich and national policy change when there is greater gridlock, because the things that do happen are more likely to be universally popular.

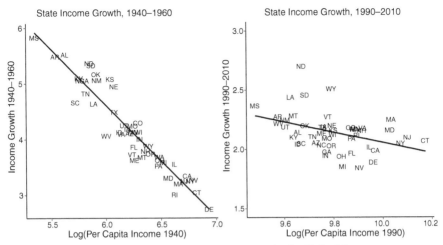

FIGURE 5.1 The end of state economic convergence in the United States
Source: Grumbach, Hacker, and Pierson (2022)

The Knowledge Economy and PBEIs

The United States is on the leading edge of the affluent world's transition from a "Fordist" economy built around manufacturing to a "post-Fordist" knowledge economy (often shorthanded as KE). At the heart of this reorganization is the increased prominence of metropolitan areas – cities and their suburbs. Value creation and economic opportunity are increasingly concentrated in favorably placed urban agglomerations (Moretti 2013).

The flip side of this transformation is the relative economic decline of locations far from these agglomerations. This decline is associated with import competition and deindustrialization, as well as the consolidation of a wide range of enterprises that once supported nonurban communities, from corner stores to factories. For workers and communities lacking the human and physical capital to compete effectively in the KE, the toll has been massive.

A vivid change illustrates the broader trend. Traditionally, economists expected to see convergence in living standards within an economic union. For most of the twentieth century, the American political economy met this expectation, as incomes in the nation's poorest states steadily made up ground. Around 1980, however, a century-old trend of convergence in state incomes stalled (see Figure 5.1). Between 1997 and 2018, real GDP per capita actually *diverged* across the states (Ram 2021) – a stark departure from as recently as 1977–1997. As noted, other indicators of well-being have also diverged between metro and nonmetro areas. Between 2010 and 2019, for example, Americans living in rural areas of the country experienced an unprecedented *decline* in life expectancy, while urban areas experienced continued gains (Abrams et al. 2021).

Equally striking are the changes in *political* geography that have accompanied this shift. To a degree unparalleled in American political history, the population density of a locale now reveals its partisan affiliation: the denser the community, the higher the vote share for the Democratic Party (Rodden 2019). More and more, the metro/nonmetro divide that cleaves the economy also cleaves the parties (Cramer 2016; Gimpel et al. 2020). One result is that the American political map looks remarkably fixed from election to election (Hopkins 2017). There are not just fewer swing voters; there are fewer swing places.

In short, the rise of the KE constitutes a profound political-economic rupture. It brings with it not just a radical reorganization of economic space, but also a radical transformation of the association between place and partisanship. We should expect, then, that it has also raised the salience and stakes of conflicts over PBEIs. As scholars of American political development have long argued, the nation's territorially based electoral and governing institutions foster the representation of spatially generated economic interests. "Sectionally-based political conflict," in the words of Bensel (1984), "constitutes the most massive and complex fact in American politics and history." This "fact" powerfully shaped partisan dynamics and domestic policy outcomes in the nineteenth and early twentieth centuries (Bensel 1984; Sanders 1999). Later in the twentieth century, Southern economic interests fused with the defense of white supremacy to forge a heightened sectional divide that shaped nearly all features of national politics (Katznelson 2013). In each case, the American institutions of federalism, single-member districts, and a state-based Senate and Electoral College magnified the salience of PBEIs and facilitated their stovepiping into party positions and public policy.

It is not just these current and historical realities that provide grounds for expecting new voter and party cleavages rooted in PBEIs. In addition, prominent political analysts have also voiced such expectations. In the next section, we consider these new theoretical and empirical accounts, which offer two basic sorts of arguments: (1) a median-voter-style argument in which the PBEIs of pivotal voters are reflected in overall policy outcomes; and (2) a distributional-conflict-style argument in which clashing parties come to represent the differing PBEIs of their core voters. These accounts identify PBEIs resulting from the knowledge economy, link them to shifting voter behavior, and argue that they are driving key policy outcomes (argument 1) or partisan dynamics (argument 2). The expectations they provide are logical, rooted in present circumstances, and consistent with the long history of American sectionalism. They are also, for the most part, not borne out by contemporary American politics.

Pivotal Voters and the Knowledge Economy

Surely the most ambitious effort to chart the politics of the KE is Iversen and Soskice's (2019). Comparing rich democracies, they argue that the knowledge economy creates a distinct set of PBEIs based on the role of urban agglomerations, and that these interests are expressed by "decisive voters" who are part of (or aspire to be part of) this new arrangement. In response, governing parties gravitate toward policies that support the KE.

The crucial policies are those supporting knowledge hubs that anchor the high value-added sectors of the economy, according to Iversen and Soskice. Workers and firms in dynamic metro areas need a continuing supply of skilled workers, public investments, and risk-tolerant capital. They also need to embrace the cultural, racial, and ethnic diversity that characterizes high-growth metros and is essential to innovation and growth. Perhaps most important, they need help coping with the collective action challenges associated with population density (Iversen and Soskice 2019; Soskice 2022), including congestion, lack of affordable and available housing, and inadequate access to high-quality education. For reasons to be discussed later, a good share of this help must come from higher levels of government.

Iversen and Soskice (2019: 12) make fairly strong claims about representation. However, both together and separately, they have noted that this optimistic story may falter in the United States. There, the deep inequality of opportunity created by geographic divergence and economic segregation may provide fertile ground for a populist backlash. Meanwhile, the US system of territorial representation, with its strong antimetro bias, may give this backlash coalition disproportionate influence, as well as make it difficult to deliver concentrated spatial benefits to support agglomerations, however large their positive spillover effects.

These worries appear warranted. Figures 5.2 and 5.3 summarize several pieces of relevant evidence. Figure 5.2 shows that public investment – spending on infrastructure, R&D, education, and training at all levels of government – is at its lowest point in over sixty years. Figure 5.3 shows that federal spending on cities is also starkly down. The data can be parsed in many ways, but none suggest a major response to metro PBEIs in the knowledge economy.

Perhaps, however, we are looking for the representation of PBEIs in the wrong place. The parties are responsive, but not to the PBEIs of pivotal voters but to the PBEIs of their geographic bases. This is the second type of argument introduced earlier: parties are in *conflict* over PBEIs, based on the differing sectional interests of their core voters. We now turn to this second model.

Partisan Conflict and the Knowledge Economy

In Iversen and Soskice's argument, governing parties face pressure to support the knowledge economy regardless of partisan hue. In arguments reviewed in this section, by contrast, competing parties represent *differing* spatially generated interests. This work dovetails with a large body of work on American

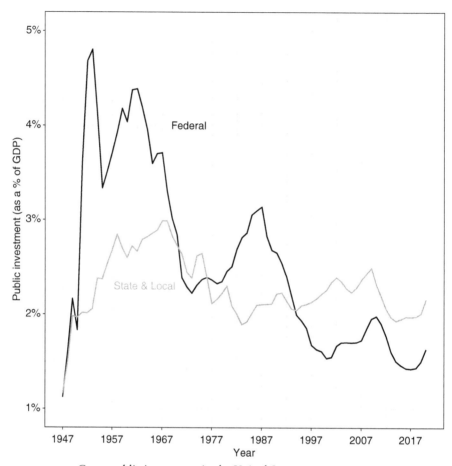

FIGURE 5.2 Gross public investment in the United States
Source: U.S. Bureau of Economic Analysis, National Income and Product Accounts,
Table 3.9.5.

politics that emphasizes the local economic roots of legislative representation
(e.g., Becher et al. 2018). Yet it goes beyond that focus by linking overall patterns of party competition to the shifting PBEIs emerging in the knowledge
economy.

Rodden (2019), for example, argues that the territorial basis of US representation has accentuated partisan conflict over PBEIs. Much attention has focused
on Rodden's analysis of the antimetro bias that accompanies single-member
districts (a bias we discuss later in this chapter). Equally important, however,
is his argument that the parties have realigned around the "odd bundles of
policies [that] came together because of economic and political geography.
The Democrats ... have evolved into a diverse collection of urban interest

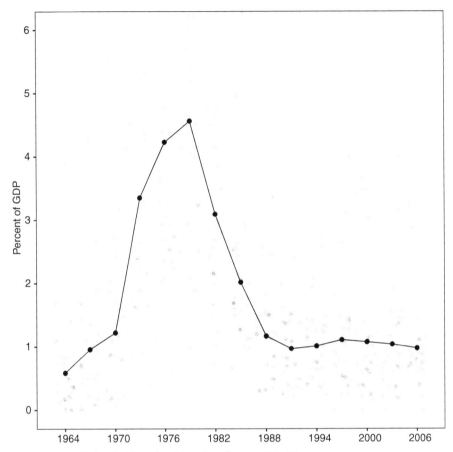

FIGURE 5.3 Federal aid to the thirty-four biggest US cities
Notes: Chart line connecting black dots represents annual average (not sum) transfer to group of thirty-four biggest cities.
Source: Historical data from US Census Bureau's Annual Survey of State and Local Government Finances.

groups, and the Republicans into an assemblage of exurban and rural interests" (Rodden 2019: 9).

Ansell and Gingrich (2022) offer a complementary analysis focused on the nature of those "urban" and "exurban and rural" interests. Like Rodden, they argue that there is a strong tendency for the American political system to stovepipe PBEIs into national politics. In contrast to many European systems, the American system encourages spatially contiguous coalitions. Voters in PR systems do not need to form coalitions that can win local majorities, so they can support (smaller) parties that draw diffuse support from like-minded voters across the country. United States voter coalitions are instead territorially based and, according to Ansell and Gingrich, reflect the growing divide between the PBEIs of rising and declining locations.

Ansell and Gingrich are helpfully specific about what these PBEIs should be. They argue that Democrats, as part of a cross-class metro coalition, should become more favorable to policy bundles that include *local* redistribution (what they call "decommodification") to hold their diverse coalition together. The same voters, however, should become less favorable to policies that allocate resources *beyond* metro areas (what they call "deconcentration"). Thus, even relatively affluent Democrats should embrace decommodification within metro blue America, but resist shifting resources toward nonmetro red America. In contrast, nonmetro voters – that is, Republicans – should favor such deconcentration, since it will reward their economically struggling territories. As we will discuss later, this last expectation is especially plausible given that incomes are higher in blue areas, so Democratic rather than Republican voters will finance the bulk of these benefits.[3]

These are expectations about voter preferences, but like Iversen and Soskice and Rodden, Ansell and Gingrich suggest the parties will reshape their national party priorities in response. Indeed, a critical implication of all of these accounts is that both metro and nonmetro regions require policy supports from higher levels of governing authority. This is obviously true for non-metro areas that lack resources: left on their own, they are acutely vulnerable to ongoing decline. But it is also true for metropolitan areas. The urban knowledge economy's local agglomerations require extensive public good provision (for transport, education, public safety, and social services) that is vulnerable to free riding. Addressing these challenges requires federal authority (Ogorzalek 2018). For voters and parties on both sides, then, the challenges and opportunities reflected in PBEIs require an active response from leaders at higher levels of government.

Thus, we have clear expectations: the red coalition will shift toward supporting deconcentration (interregional redistribution); the blue coalition toward decommodification (*intra*regional redistribution). Here, too, these strong expectations confront striking paradoxes. In the remainder of this section, we briefly lay out these paradoxes. We then turn to the institutional, partisan, and policy filters that help explain them.

The Red PBEI Paradox

Red is increasingly the color of places the knowledge economy is passing by. Yet even as Republicans have become increasingly reliant on voters in non-metro areas, national party elites have shown little inclination to transfer federal resources toward these constituencies. There are exceptions we will discuss, such as Republican support for fossil fuel extraction. The bottom line,

---

[3] In explaining the original setup of federal systems, Beramendi (2012) makes a parallel argument.

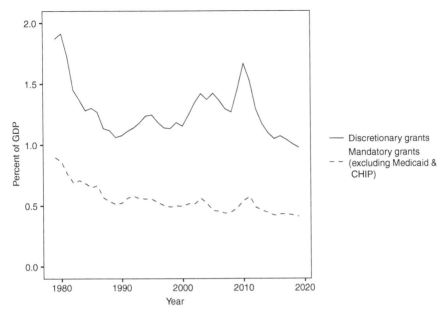

FIGURE 5.4 Federal grants for states and localities, 1980–2020
Source: Grumbach, Hacker, and Pierson (2022).

however, is that deconcentration is almost nowhere to be seen within the GOP policy repertoire.

Instead, the signature party priority for at least three decades has been tax cuts for corporations and the rich – a goal that is unpopular even among Republican voters. These cuts have consistently offered their greatest benefits to big businesses and the super-wealthy, not rank-and-file GOP voters. Moreover, a large majority of these beneficiaries are located in blue metro areas rather than red nonmetro regions.

At the same time, Republicans have supported stark cuts in federal transfers to the states, which have fallen by roughly half since 1980 (see Figure 5.4). Given the progressive structure of federal taxes and spending, these transfers are highly favorable to nonmetro regions.[4] Republicans have also sought to cut social spending disproportionately received by voters in these regions. The most striking example is Medicaid, which GOP leaders have repeatedly sought to scale back – most recently, in early 2023, when they sought to tie Medicaid restrictions to a necessary extension of the so-called debt ceiling, a demand that threatened the first credit default in US history. In 2017, they came remarkably

---

[4] We exclude Medicaid. The unique skyrocketing of US health costs makes spending a poor proxy for benefits. Indeed, such spending would not even be included in regional transfers if Medicaid, like Medicare, were federal.

close to achieving even bigger cutbacks that would have been particularly devastating for nonmetro areas and red states (Levey 2017).

The Blue PBEI Paradox

Blue is the color of the knowledge economy in the United States. Given the increasingly tight link between population density, KE activity, and Democratic partisanship, we should expect Democratic elites to push for policies that support metro agglomerations. Meanwhile, they should embrace decommodifying policies (i.e., local redistribution) and reject deconcentrating ones. For the most part, however, these expectations have failed to pan out too.

Like the red PBEI paradox, the blue paradox has a positive and a negative side: unexpected policies that elites support and expected ones they do not. The key example of the former is interregional redistribution in favor of red America. As the fight over the ACA suggests, it is Democrats, not Republicans, who push for bigger transfers to nonmetro regions. Democratic elites have not simply backed existing fiscal policies that favor red nonmetro areas; they have pushed to *increase* this pro-red tilt, both by raising rates for top taxpayers (again, located mostly in blue America) and by expanding social policies that are particularly anemic in red America. If there is a party of deconcentration, it is the metro-oriented Democratic Party – precisely the opposite of what Ansell and Gingrich anticipate.

What about the other side of the ledger: PBEI-consistent policies that have failed to materialize? Here, what stands out is the relatively low priority placed by national Democrats on the challenges facing metro hubs that cannot be solved through local action alone. The key example is housing. Dynamic metro areas face a triple crisis of unaffordability, inadequacy, and inequality. Opinion polls suggest that the skyrocketing cost of housing is a huge concern of voters living in these regions, with strong support for various kinds of federal action (Demsas 2021; Hart Research Associates 2019). Housing supply shortages make productive urban centers much less productive (Hsieh and Moretti 2019), shut out millions of Americans who would benefit from proximity to knowledge hubs, and impose huge costs and risks on nonaffluent residents, including the growing specter of homelessness. These are exactly the sort of local inequalities that Ansell and Gingrich style decommodification could address.

To be sure, housing affordability is a problem of "superstar cities" worldwide. Yet the breadth of the US crisis and weakness of the US federal response stand out in cross-national perspective (Le Galès and Pierson 2019). It can be seen not only in the continuing failure of national Democrats to remedy local policy failures in this area – despite stepped-up efforts to do so in 2021, which we shall discuss later – but also in trends in federal housing outlays, which

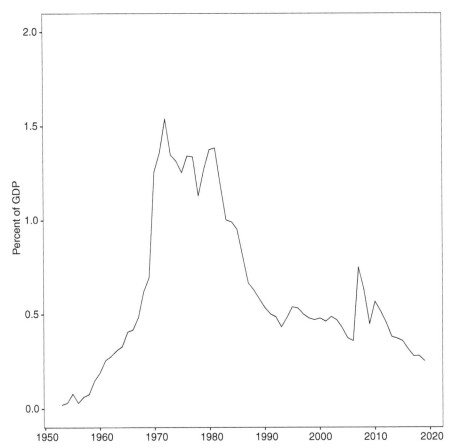

FIGURE 5.5 Federal housing and urban development spending
Source: Office of Management and Budget; Federal Reserve Economic Data. Includes the agency's total annual budget (as a percentage of GDP).

have declined dramatically from historic highs even as home prices and rental costs have moved sharply the other way (see Figure 5.5).

Table 5.1 summarizes the discussion thus far. The two types of arguments we have reviewed focus on different outcomes (overall policy outcomes vs. party stances). Yet they both foresee voters reorienting around the PBEIs that accompany the emergence of the KE. As the last column indicates, these expectations appear largely unmet.

The next section considers why. We first describe our concept of filters. We then show how these filters help account for the underrepresentation of PBEIs in the contemporary era.

TABLE 5.1 *Representation of Pbeis in the US knowledge economy*

Focus of Account	Clearest PBEI(s)	Actual Outcomes
Iversen & Soskice – pivotal voter power in the KE		
Overall policy	Pivotal voters support KE investments	Declining public investment in KE
Ansell & Gingrich/Rodden – partisan divergence in the KE		
"Red" (Republican) Coalition's Stance	"Deconcentration" (interregional redistribution)	Red PBEI Paradox: Resistance to deconcentration; tax cuts that are the opposite of deconcentration
"Blue" (Democratic) Coalition's Stance	"Decommodification" (local redistribution), not deconcentration	Blue PBEI Paradox: Support for deconcentration; weak support for decommodification, esp. re. housing

THE FILTERING OF PBEIS

By filters, we mean institutional, partisan, and policy structures that refract, redirect, or block the expression of citizen interests as they move through the representative process. We divide our filters into three categories: political institutions, party coalitions, and policy regimes. Although students of representation appreciate the role of political institutions, the enormous power of this filter – especially in the United States – is not always appreciated. Less widely appreciated are the filters of party coalitions and policy regimes. Yet like formal institutions, these arrangements serve to organize some issues into national policymaking and organize others out.

Political Institutions as Filters

When thinking about representation solely in the US context, it is easy to take for granted the distinctive features of American political institutions or to treat them as historical constants. We shouldn't, especially because the biases that these institutions produce have intensified and become more consequential. We focus on two biases in particular: the bias in favor of nonmetro interests (and the party that represents them) and the bias in favor of the status quo (and the party that seeks to preserve it). Each form of bias has grown in recent decades. Each also has enormous implications for the representation of Pbeis.

The underrepresentation of metro areas emerges out of several interlocking features of American institutions. Taken together, these impose what might

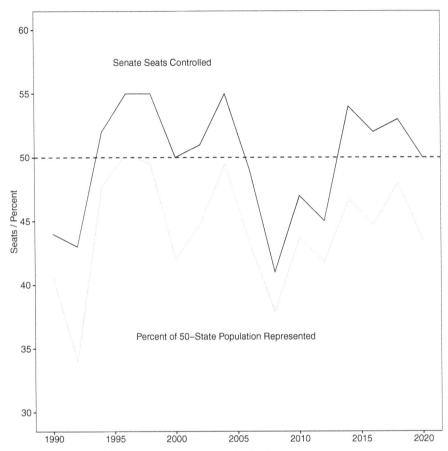

FIGURE 5.6 Republican overrepresentation in the US Senate
Source: DailyKos: www.dailykos.com/stories/2021/2/23/2013769/-How-minority-rule-plagues-Senate-Republicans-last-won-more-support-than-Democrats-two-decades-ago

be called a "density tax": the denser a population, the less well represented it is. As the metro/nonmetro divide has widened, the density tax has not only increased; it has also become more aligned with partisanship.

The heaviest density tax, of course, applies in the Senate, the most malapportioned upper house in the rich world. The effects include, but are not limited to, giving the GOP a substantial seat edge (see Figure 5.6). In recent decades, Republicans have frequently enjoyed a Senate majority despite representing fewer people and receiving fewer votes in Senate elections.

Antimetro bias is not limited to the Senate. As Rodden (2019) argues, a system of single-member districts also imposes a density tax. Parties drawing their support from urban areas will be less efficient in translating votes into

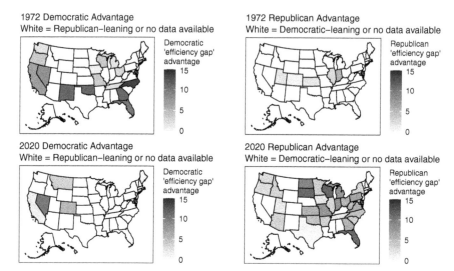

FIGURE 5.7 Partisan skew in statehouse district maps, 1972 vs. 2020
Source: Planscore.org; the "efficiency gap" is calculated by taking one party's total "wasted" votes in an election (votes in excess of a majority for winning candidates; all votes for losing candidates), subtracting the other party's total wasted votes, and dividing by the total number of votes cast.

seats. As the parties have cleaved between metro and nonmetro areas, this tax has fallen on Democrats, awarding Republicans something like an extra dozen seats in the closely divided House (Powell, Clark, and Dube 2020). Though there are signs the density tax has lessened as the suburbs of rich metros have become more blue, the penalty remains, and it is particularly pronounced in state legislatures. As Figure 5.7 shows, the average bias of statehouse maps toward Republicans has increased dramatically, driven by the density tax as well as the increasing frequency of GOP control over redistricting it helps produce.

The second crucial institutional filter is status quo bias. As students of comparative politics have long noted (Stepan and Linz 2011), no other affluent democracy places so many constitutional obstacles in the path of legislated policy change. In addition – and it is not a small addition – the Senate filibuster means that a supermajority of an already highly skewed institution is required to advance legislation.[5] Needing only forty-one votes, a minority that might

---

[5] It is worth noting that the United States also has the largest barriers to constitutional amendment, locking in all these arrangements except the filibuster. In addition, the overrepresentation of small states is the only constitutional arrangement that explicitly cannot be altered by amendment.

represent less than 20 percent of the US population can block legislative action. In practice, narrow minorities block legislation, including very popular legislation, all the time.[6]

Status quo bias is far from neutral. First, it empowers those who had power in the past. Existing policy can be seen as a kind of congealed influence, reflecting earlier power configurations (Moe 2005; Pierson 2016). Anything that makes these policies hard to change is likely to disadvantage those who were weakly represented in these earlier periods. This is particularly evident when it comes to racial and ethnic minorities, who are both concentrated in metro areas and now approach a majority of Democratic voters. For these voters – and the party seeking to represent them – the hurdle of American political institutions is often more like a wall.

Second, status quo bias empowers those who do not rely on national legislation to advance their interests. In general, this favors those who advocate minimalist government, or at least minimal regulation and redistribution – stances that often line up with the positions of the contemporary GOP. Like antimetro bias, the status quo bias of American institutions is favorable to one party over the other.

The interaction of these two biases draws our attention to the potential for "compounding bias," when one institutional skew generates additional ones. As already noted, Republican state majorities, benefiting from the density tax, can gerrymander their own electoral maps, as well as those used to apportion seats in the US House. In another form of compounding bias, Republican Senators can exploit their chamber's extreme skew to block Democratic judicial nominees, while racing their own to confirmation. The contemporary 6–3 conservative Supreme Court (which also reflects the antimetro bias of the Electoral College, which has elected two Republican presidents lacking popular vote majorities since 2000) is a vivid illustration of cumulative bias. The Court is also a far more powerful economic policymaker than often recognized, reinforcing the already-high barriers to an active response to both metro and nonmetro PBEIs. In each case, biases in one site create the capacity to enhance biases in others, even in a set of institutions expected to resist consolidations of partisan power (Pierson and Schickler 2020).

We can sum up the discussion of institutional filters quickly. In the contemporary political environment, American political institutions operate in ways that greatly diminish the voice of metro interests in national policymaking, while also giving the Republican Party a representational edge that it can use to pursue its own aims or resist those of Democrats.

---

[6] Over the past three decades, more than three-quarters of the bills blocked by a Senate filibuster were bipartisan (with an average of five senators from the other party); and nearly a quarter were supported by Senators who represented over 60 percent of the US population (Scholars for Reform 2021).

Party Coalitions as Filters

Party systems represent a second significant filter. Traditionally in American politics, it was assumed that national politicians would have an incentive to respond to strong place-based interests – that "all politics is local," as Tip O'Neill famously put it. Yet as American politics has become more national-ized and polarized, local interests have faced a rockier path.

Two filtering effects are most important here. The first is the way polariza-tion discourages elite efforts to serve local interests that are not aligned with party programs. American politics has always been based on two parties. But it has not always been based on two highly polarized and nationalized parties. In a context where two parties are not only dominant but polarized, they become powerful gatekeepers of national policymaking. Both voters and politicians are presented with increasingly binary choices, and the space to diverge from national priorities shrinks (Rodden 2019). Indeed, to the extent voters' hard-ening allegiances are "affective" (driven by animus toward the other side), national party elites have much greater room to sidestep even deeply felt PBEIs, since voters are likely to stick with them even if they do.

At the same time that polarization decreases the scope for localized policy ventures, it increases the potential for priority setting by policy-demanding groups (Bawn et al. 2012). Groups that once might have floated between the parties now have incentives to side with one or the other, since their best oppor-tunity for shaping policy is to enter into long-term coalitions with the party closest to them (Pierson and Schickler 2020). In turn, party elites can use their increased running room with voters to serve these intense organized interests. In short, the power of resourceful party-allied groups relative to strong party identifiers is likely to increase.

It is important to emphasize that this filtering process may be quite func-tional for a party. Getting local issues expressed nationally may well create intraparty cleavages. Party leaders seek to institutionalize beneficial "trades" among intense allies, such as the Republican Party's foundational trade of corporate-friendly tax cuts for conservative cultural stances. Because these deals are always vulnerable to destabilizing new issues, party leaders have strong incentives to keep such issues off the agenda. Traditionally, however, this has been difficult, which has repeatedly led to the breakdown of national issue-based coalitions (Schickler 2016). Parties struggled to keep divisive issues off the agenda because *local* politicians faced different incentives and constitu-encies than *national* ones. As this has become less true, the capacity of parties to keep disruptive local concerns off the table has grown.

We mention this last possibility because a central feature of the party filter today is that elite management of intraparty cleavages have tended to suppress, rather than foster, the representation of PBEIs. We have already mentioned the Republican Party's prioritization of conservative pro-business policies. This has encouraged party elites to play on cultural grievances and white racial identity to mobilize voters, given that their economic priorities are largely inconsistent with nonmetro voters' PBEIs. A very different but also very consequential intraparty cleavage has increasingly characterized the Democratic Party as it has come to rely on highly unequal metro regions. Affluent whites in these areas now largely back the Democratic Party, and as Ansell and Gingrich argue, they are relatively supportive of redistribution so long as it does not impose large costs on them. But they are much warier, we shall see, of policies that would threaten the privileges they enjoy because of local segregation and the resulting differential access to economic opportunities and public goods – a policy divide that cleaves the Democratic coalition along lines of both race and class. For Democratic party elites, this potential land mine encourages an emphasis on broader, if also less metro-beneficial, priorities.

Policy Regimes as Filters

Policy regimes represent our last and least-recognized filter. By policy regimes, we mean the inherited complex of rules and programs that determine the allocation of resources and authority in particular policy areas. While policies can, in theory, always be revised, they are highly path-dependent. Not only are those defending the status quo advantaged, but policies themselves make some changes easier to effect than others. Indeed, as the literature on "policy feedback" suggests, they shape whether certain changes are seen as possible or desirable at all, in part because they determine which allocations of valued resources are visible to voters and which are not.

Two features of the policy landscape are of particular relevance. The first is the degree to which policies automatically update to reflect changing circumstances. Revising entrenched policies is hard. Thus, default rules – whether, for example, policies expand to reflect the number of people eligible – matter enormously for how likely it is that they will continue to perform as expected, or "drift" away from their original purpose (Hacker, Pierson, and Thelen 2015). This, we shall see, helps explain the anemic US response to the shifting contours of the KE.

The second crucial feature is the extreme decentralization of US policymaking, especially in core areas of policy that affect the knowledge economy, such as housing, land use, education, infrastructure, and policing. This extreme decentralization coexists with weak measures to even out the administrative and budget capacities of differing localities, such as fiscal equalization and revenue sharing. In cross-national perspective, American policymaking is not merely decentralized; it is decentralized in ways that accentuate inequalities across jurisdictions.

Little in these arrangements is constitutionally required. Unmentioned in the nation's founding charter, localities are creatures of the states. Instead, these arrangements are constituted by longstanding policies that reflect the mutually reinforcing effects of path dependence and the distribution of power

(Trounstine 2018; Weir et al. 2005). The resulting regime divides authority between localities and higher levels of government in ways that are both relatively invisible and pose high hurdles to positive-sum collective action.

Most notably, property-tax financing of local public goods and highly decentralized authority over land use – along with the ability of suburban communities to evade the tax and regulatory reach of cities – reinforce the influence of affluent white homeowners and give them strong incentives and ability to oppose policies that would allow less-affluent outsiders access to hoarded public goods or housing. Simultaneously, this regime makes it very hard to push these issues up to higher policy levels, where these forces of resistance would be less advantaged.

We can see how these three sets of filters play out by revisiting our two paradoxes. In the next two sections, we look again at the paradoxical positions of the Democratic and Republican Parties, showing how key filters help explain the weak (and sometimes upside-down) relationship between the stances of the parties and the PBEIs of red and blue America.

THE RED PBEI PARADOX REVISITED

Republicans have pursued policies that offer little or nothing to their geographic bastions or even hurt these areas. Meanwhile, they have failed to pursue policies that might transfer resources toward declining red regions. The filters – particularly the institutional antimetro and status quo biases and the nature of the GOP coalition – help us understand these puzzling patterns.

The Institutional Filter

The role of the institutional filter is hard to overstate. First, as noted, it helps explain why Republicans have dominated legislatures in many states that would be closely divided, or controlled by Democrats, absent the density tax and aggressive gerrymandering. Second, at the national level, it has given Republicans a stronger hand than their popular vote totals or support for their agenda would suggest. The Senate filibuster has proved especially useful for Republicans, allowing the party to tie up governance in ways that are very hard for voters to understand or punish. In particular, it has short-circuited the kind of cross-party coalitional efforts that often undergirded sectional policy in the past.

Although our focus is on national representation, we should stress that these institutional biases also play out at the state level. In another chapter written by two of us with Grumbach (Grumbach, Hacker, and Pierson 2022), we argue that GOP leaders have generally pursued policies ill-suited to a globalized knowledge economy. Indeed, we find that, controlling for prior education levels and manufacturing strength, red states that have pursued the most conservative economic policies have the lowest workforce participation, wages, and median incomes. One reason why red-state Republicans have managed to pursue such policies and still retain strong majorities is that the antimetro bias is at least as strong at the state level as at the national level.

The Party Coalition Filter

While the institutional filter is helpful in understanding Republicans' outsized governing influence – and, in particular, their ability to block even popular policies – it is less helpful for explaining what they *do* with their influence. Here the party filter – the peculiar shape of the GOP's party coalition – becomes much more important.

In brief, the Republican Party has become a national coalition uniting two sets of groups: "plutocratic" organizations, such as business lobbies and billionaire donors, that shape the party's economic policies; and "right-wing populist" organizations, such as conservative religious groups and the National Rifle Association, that shape the party's electoral strategies and social issue priorities. Stretching the definition of groups, the latter organizations also encompass right-wing media (which has no real counterpart on the left). The stability of this "plutocratic populist" coalition has rested in part on the willingness of leaders on the populist side – notably, those allied with the Christian right – to jettison demands for economic policies that would have benefited their mass base but were opposed by the party's plutocratic allies (Hacker and Pierson 2020).

Whenever and wherever such conflicts have arisen, the PBEIs of red America have given way to the priorities of rich America. We have already mentioned high-end tax cuts, the cornerstone of GOP economic policy. Given the spatial distribution of affluence in the United States, the direct beneficiaries of these tax cuts disproportionately reside in blue states (or abroad). Moreover, these cuts not only bypass most Republican voters. They also pose a clear fiscal threat to the GOP electorate over the long term, generating acute pressures on major social programs on which aging red-state voters disproportionately rely, including Social Security, Medicare, and Disability Insurance. In short, tax cuts not only disproportionately go to blue America; they restrict the fiscal space for "deconcentrating" initiatives that could help red America.

As noted, a version of this dynamic has already played out on healthcare. GOP "repeal and replace" plans for the Affordable Care Act (ACA) would have had a devastating impact on nonmetro America. Yet almost all national Republicans supported them. They did so in part because repealing the ACA would have allowed a rollback of the high-end taxes that provided the program's progressive financing. Moreover, the associated Medicaid cuts could be leveraged into even deeper tax cuts in the future. Only the defection of a handful of Senate Republicans saved the ACA.

The rise of Donald Trump did not much change this dynamic. While doubling down on right-wing populism, Trump embraced both massively skewed tax cuts and the ill-fated ACA repeal. He talked about but did little to press for adequate federal spending to deal with the opioid epidemic – a core dimension of the "deaths of despair" disproportionately ravaging areas of GOP strength (Case and Deaton 2020). Nor did he follow up on repeated promises of infrastructure or prescription drug proposals that might have helped nonmetro voters.[7]

Indeed, even the one clear area of PBEI-party affinity suggests the importance of coalitional considerations. National Republicans have taken increasingly aggressive stances with respect to energy deregulation, the use of federal lands, and resistance to action on climate change. These stances have certainly helped a handful of red states (in particular Alaska, North Dakota, and Wyoming), but they have proved even more lucrative for the fossil fuel industry. Indeed, given the extreme geographic concentration of energy production in a few red states, these stances are better seen as successful rent-seeking by corporate backers of the GOP than as a viable growth strategy for red America.

Are Voters, Not Filters, the Source of the Paradox?

Before we move to the Democratic side of the story, we want to address an objection that analyses of the Republican Party like ours invariably provoke: the disconnect is not between GOP voters and their representatives; it is between GOP voters' economic interests and how they vote. As noted, however, we do not think the explanation for the patterns we find is that GOP voters are committed to policy positions at odds with the shifting PBEIs of red America.

To be sure, voters operate in a complex environment in which party elites and allied groups provide powerful cues and no small measure of misinformation. Most people have limited understanding of policy, and partisanship and social identities heavily color what they think they know. For example, Republicans are much more likely to associate government spending with Black Americans, immigrants, and means-tested benefits (Krimmel and Radar 2021). Growing negative affect toward the other party further limits the scope for policy issues to matter in electoral politics. To this list of complications, we should add the ability of party elites to use second-dimension issues – particularly those concerning religious and racial identities – to reduce the salience

---

[7] We have not discussed the GOP stance on trade. For one, it is an issue that still divides the party, though the more populist forces clearly have the upper hand. For another, the immediate effects of the Trump trade wars on GOP regions were sharply negative. Trump did extend agricultural subsidies (seemingly the clearest example in recent years of a red-state-focused economic policy), but at best these served only to offset the impact of his own trade and immigration policies, and the long-term trend in such subsidies has been downward.

of voters' economic stances (Hacker and Pierson 2020). Given the relatively homogenous racial and religious identities of GOP voters, a significant share can be motivated primarily by the cultural, racial, ethnic, and regional resentments that party elites have stoked. Indeed, a core reason we focus on PBEIs is that we want to avoid treating answers to survey questions – which necessarily incorporate these factors – as synonymous with preferences, much less interests.

Nonetheless, there is substantial evidence that Republican voters are not driving GOP economic policy and, indeed, that many of the party's PBEI-inconsistent stances are unpopular among its own voters. For at least two decades, elite Republicans have made the combination of high-end tax cuts and sharp spending cuts the centerpiece of their fiscal plans. This was the formula embodied, for example, in Paul Ryan's high-profile budget blueprints of the early 2010s. According to national polling, the Ryan plan lacked majority support not only among Democrats but also Republicans – and, indeed, even among GOP donors. Only among donors with annual incomes greater than $250,000 did support outweigh opposition (Hacker and Pierson 2020).

More recently, the failed effort to repeal the ACA and successful effort to pass highly skewed tax cuts in 2017 were both overwhelmingly unpopular, failing to command strong support even from Republican voters. Indeed, they were the two least popular major federal initiatives considered and/or passed between 1990 and 2017 (Hacker and Pierson 2020).

Perhaps most revealing, however, are state-level ballot questions. Six of the eleven red states where ballot initiatives are allowed have held votes on Medicaid expansion – a policy universally opposed by national Republican elites, as well as most state GOP leaders. *Every one of these states* voted in favor of Medicaid expansion. Similarly, Republican elites have strongly resisted increases in the minimum wage. Since 2006, however, eleven red states have held ballot questions to raise the state minimum. All eleven passed by very large margins.

These results suggest that red state legislatures are blocking popular initiatives, and the behavior of these legislatures only reinforces this conclusion. In Michigan, Republicans enacted their own legislation to preempt an initiative – and then promptly repealed it once the election was safely past. In Idaho, the Republican legislature responded to a successful initiative expanding Medicaid by radically restricting the initiative procedure. Missouri may well follow suit. In other red states, legislatures have ignored proposals to expand the minimum wage, among other popular initiatives.

In sum, the disconnect between the PBEIs of red America and the policy agenda of the Republican Party does not seem to be voter-driven. Instead, it bears the imprint of both America's distinctive institutions and the particular character of the GOP coalition. Together, these simultaneously motivate nonresponsive party stances (party filter), undercut accountability (institutional filter), and increase the governing strength of the Republican Party relative to its popularity (institutional filter). The result is a nationalized interest group coalition that places top priority on business- and affluent-friendly policies regardless of their sectional impact.[8]

THE BLUE PBEI PARADOX REVISITED

What we have called the blue PBEI paradox constitutes at least three puzzles. First, Democrats have not strengthened – or even sustained – KE investments. In part, this is simply a reflection of the Republican Party's institutional edge. Nonetheless, we do not think GOP blocking can fully explain the notable fall in public investment discussed earlier.

The second and third puzzles squarely concern party stances, rather than policy outcomes: Why have national Democrats proved so eager to embrace deconcentrating policies that distribute outsized benefits to red America? And why have they proved so reluctant to address the collective action challenges of metro areas, particularly with regard to housing?

Not surprisingly, the institutional filter again looms large. However, both the character of the Democratic coalition and of the US policy regime play an important role as well.

The Institutional Filter

Both the antimetro and status quo biases of American political institutions weaken the capacity of national Democrats to update economic policies to reflect the changing needs of the knowledge economy. They do so, moreover, in ways that reflect specific features of the US policy regime we will discuss shortly. For now, the key point is that all the advantages enjoyed by the party that represents nonmetro regions and seeks to block government action are disadvantages for the party that represents metro regions and seeks to expand government action.

Moreover, these disadvantages have been growing. Urban America once enjoyed relatively strong representation in American national politics (Ogorzalek 2018). But the density tax has been rising. Even as blue metros have gained

---

[8] A telling example we have not discussed is defense. While it is often assumed that elite GOP support for higher military spending reflects a desire to funnel resources to Republican regions and voters (who are, of course, much more likely to serve in the military), the vast majority of military outlays are for defense contracts rather than personnel. Of the five states with the highest share of GSP comprised of military spending (Harper 2021) – contracts plus personnel – three are strongly Democratic: Virginia (10.6 percent), Hawaii (7.7), and Connecticut (6.8). Within the top ten, only four are solidly Republican: Alabama (6.9), Alaska (6.4), Kentucky (5.7), and Mississippi (5.3). To the extent that there are strong economic interests driving the GOP stance on defense spending, they seem as likely to reflect the priorities of intense policy demanders – the defense industry has given more to Republicans in every election cycle since 2010 (Open Secrets 2021) – as the PBEIs of Republican voters.

more and more economic ground – Joe Biden won counties that produced 70 percent of US GDP in 2020 (Muro et al. 2020) – they have lost more and more political ground. The biases of Senate apportionment, House, and state districts naturally favoring nonmetro areas, and aggressive gerrymandering and other measures (often sanctioned by stacked courts) compound to tilt the playing field farther and farther.

The eroding political clout of metro interests is not simply a reflection of the institutional filter. Urban representatives have never been a majority in the national legislature. They relied for their power on a capacity to form *party coalitions* with representatives from nonmetro districts. Today's weakness of metro America also reflects profound changes in the party system.

The Party Coalition Filter

Cities have not always been solidly blue. Since the New Deal, however, their political fortunes have been tied to the national Democratic Party. During the New Deal Era, the power of the nation's major urban centers rested on their ability to form logrolling agreements with Southern representatives, facilitated by shared partisanship (Ogorzalek 2018). This arrangement unraveled after 1975 as the South (and eventually nonmetro districts outside it) realigned to join the Republican Party. Indeed, the earliest policy impact of this realignment was the collapse of the coalition that had supported major national urban initiatives in the 1960s and 1970s (Caraley 1992). Conservative Democrats (mostly from Southern and/or nonmetro places) joined the "Reagan revolution" and gutted these programs – in retrospect, an intermediate step as those electoral jurisdictions transitioned into Republican hands.

Trends since the early 1980s have further diminished the voice of cities in national policymaking. As Ogorzalek (2018) has argued, the Southern Democratic retreat from its New Deal alliance with cities, the growth of the suburbs, and the decline of urban political machines all weakened the strong place of cities within the party's organized coalition. The problem is not merely that cities now have a weaker hold on the Democratic Party than they once did. Republican politicians who represent urban areas have all but vanished, and with them, the incentives to fashion cross-party compromises in support of metro PBEIs.

The character of the Democratic coalition can also help explain why Democrats in power have pursued an agenda heavy on deconcentration. To some extent, the antimetro bias of American institutions can help to explain this: due to the density tax, Democrats must reach beyond their core metro supporters to win elections. Yet it is hard to see how the institutional filter can explain why Democratic priorities envision redistributing so many resources to deeply red regions of the country where the party has no real chance of success. Nor do Democratic voters appear to be the main catalysts here. Most are probably unaware that the policies their elected officials advance entail such substantial spatial redistribution (though, unlike the case of the red state paradox, there is little sign that they would actively oppose such initiatives).

The subject requires far more research, but we would stress the role of party coalitions here, too – specifically, the role of intense policy demanders within the Democratic coalition. These include labor unions, civil rights organizations, progressive economic groups, and a variety of allied social movements. As is true on the Republican side, these organized elements of the coalition are increasingly national in their focus, increasingly working with "their" party alone, and increasingly at odds with the other party's social and economic policies. And as is also true on the Republican side, these organized actors mostly "float above" local and regional differences: their funding comes from nationally oriented donors and foundations, their leadership and headquarters are generally based in DC, and their activities – even if sometimes focused below the national level – are rooted in their increasingly tight alliances with an increasingly nationalized party. Indeed, the Democratic Party arguably lacks some of the localized connections that have animated GOP politics in recent years (mostly on the cultural side of the Republican agenda). With the partial exception of organized labor, Democrats lack the widespread community infrastructure embodied in the Christian Right, nor have Democratic-aligned groups and movements proved as adept at using American federalism to advance their goals on a state-by-state basis (Hertel-Fernandez 2019).

The vision of party-aligned groups on the left is not just national in focus but also universal in aspiration. By this we mean they tend to advance goals – from greater ability to form a union to improved access to affordable health-care to sustained reductions in poverty – that aim to provide greater support for low- and middle-income Americans, whatever their backgrounds and wherever they live. This vision of a universal policy floor is what you might expect from nationally focused groups with stated commitments to equality, especially the party's mass-membership backbone: organized labor. Yet there is also a strategic rationale that seems important to many of their leaders: that the party's multiracial coalition is best held together through appeals and proposals that center shared economic interests, rather than those specific to place, race, or other salient divides.[9] In another recent analysis (Hacker et al. 2023), for instance, we find that both Democratic Party platforms and the tweets of recent Democratic presidents and members of Congress have overwhelmingly emphasized economic issues and universal economic policies (in contrast with Republican leaders, who emphasize cultural appeals on Twitter).

For these policy demanders, then, Ansell and Gingrich's decommodification – downward redistribution within richer areas – is not enough. They want a generous policy floor nationwide. Given America's highly uneven and

---

[9] We base this conclusion in part on a series of (mostly off-the-record) interviews with group leaders and policymakers we have conducted as part of a larger project on the changing character of the Democratic coalition.

decentralized fiscal federalism, that floor can be created only by strengthening federal redistribution in ways that offer disproportionate benefits to declining areas where supports are weak. In other words, national redistribution of the sort advocated by groups aligned with the Democratic Party tends to produce substantial deconcentration, and this deconcentration in turn tends to benefit states aligned with the Republican Party. By way of illustration, only one of the ten states with the highest ratio of federal benefits to federal taxes – that is, whose residents get back more from the federal government than they pay to it – has consistently voted for the Democratic presidential candidate since 2000 (Hawaii), while nine of the ten with the lowest ratio of federal taxes to benefits have consistently voted for the Republican candidate.[10]

The Policy Filter

Many of the problems facing metro America boil down to one: cities lack the tools or authority to deal with collective action challenges they face. The erosion of federal funding for key investments in metro economies has deprived these areas of vital resources on which they once relied to manage the exigencies of urban interdependence. Of course, the institutional biases already discussed are major causes of this trend. But the structure of public policy is also implicated. As noted, different programs are more or less vulnerable to erosion over time depending on whether they require periodic legislative updating. While some federal spending programs are "mandatory" – meaning their benefits cover everyone eligible and expenditures rise automatically in response to demand – many are "discretionary" and must be reauthorized regularly. Most of the major spending programs of importance for the knowledge economy fall into the discretionary category, including support for science, education, housing, and mass transit. To grasp the full effect of the institutional filter, then, requires looking at the way existing policies privilege some kinds of policy updates while discouraging others.

The policy filter is even more clearly implicated in the final PBEI puzzle – the failure of the Democratic Party to respond adequately to the collective action challenges facing metro America, particularly with regard to housing. There is a broad consensus among economists that land use and zoning rules are the principal causes of the housing crisis. These are not national or even state policies; they are local policies, with each of the nation's tens of thousands of local governments controlling development within its borders. This fragmented system allows suburbs to free ride on cities, magnifies the influence of affluent white homeowners (Einstein et al. 2020), and empowers "home-voters" who are most likely to show up in low-visibility local elections and have extreme and intense preferences on this dimension (Marble and Nall

---

[10] Gordon, Deb, "The States That Are Most Reliant on Federal Aid," moneygeek, April 2, 2023.

2020). The result is widespread use of exclusionary zoning, inadequate afford-able housing, and stark racial and economic segregation within and across jurisdictions (Trounstine 2018). Much of the burden falls on those denied access to high-productivity places. But it also imposes huge costs on the most disadvantaged residents of metro America, disproportionately non-white, as well as the economy overall.

Here again, voter preferences do not seem to be the decisive factor. There is strong support for measures to provide more affordable housing (Demsas 2021; Hart Research Associates 2019). The problem is unfavorable political dynamics at the local level, rooted in a highly decentralized and entrenched policy regime, in which intense minority interests are privileged at the expense of broader majority interests. The result is a set of increasingly dire problems that affect millions of Democratic voters and cry out for national leadership.

Yet Democratic elites at the national level have largely failed to respond to these critical needs. To do so would require challenging localized policy-making, and that has proved something that party leaders have shown limited ability or inclination to do. The entrenchment of localized control makes the task hard to begin with. On top of that, it also creates a huge potential wedge within the Democratic coalition between affluent, white, home-owning voters and less-affluent portions of the party's metro-based electorate. For Democrats, there are good reasons to organize this issue out of their agenda, or at least to focus on symbolic or half-hearted measures that do not threaten to activate intense potential cleavages within the party's electorate.

In short, the *institutional*, *party*, and *policy* filters all help explain the under-representation of the PBEIs of blue metro areas, even as the knowledge econ-omy has made their policy interests and party allegiances increasingly distinct.

CONCLUSION

The rise of the knowledge economy has produced a growing economic fissure between metro and nonmetro America, and this fissure has mapped closely onto the polarized divide between the Republican and Democratic parties. In a territorially organized polity, these changes might be expected to create pres-sures for elected officials to shift their priorities to reflect the evolving place-based interests of their constituents – a recurrent historical pattern in American politics that prominent scholars have argued is happening again today.

Despite these pressures, however, we find more refraction than reflection. There is limited sign of Iversen and Soskice's predicted realignment of partisan competition around promotion of the knowledge economy. Indeed, the last two decades have witnessed a marked *decline* in policy support for the knowl-edge economy – a potentially fateful development.

Nor have the parties reoriented themselves toward the PBEIs of their geo-graphic bastions as might be expected. Despite increasing reliance on nonmetro voters, the Republican Party has done little to support Ansell and Gingrich's "deconcentration," focusing its priorities on the demands of wealthy voters and corporate interests rather than those of its broad voting base. Instead, if there is a party backing deconcentration, it is the Democrats – driven in part by their own organized allies, who emphasize the need to raise the social policy floor in nonmetro regions. At the same time, even as the Democratic Party has come to dominate the nation's metro agglomerations, national Democrats have failed to robustly address the hugely costly dilemmas associated with local control that threaten these blue locales' continuing success.

To explain these paradoxes, we have argued for a greater focus on what we call "filters" – durable features of a polity that mediate the influence of citizens on governance. In asking whether PBEIs make this transit, we seek to avoid the assumption common in the prevailing filter-free view of representation that all issues of fundamental concern will become manifest in policymaking. Because of the institutional, party, and policy filters, there is no guarantee that voters will see a clear link between their electoral choices and their PBEIs, or that politicians will respond to those PBEIs even if voters articulate them. In particular, there is no guarantee that local economic interests will be stovepiped up to higher levels of government where effective action can be taken.

Our filtered approach to representation emphasizes three refracting features of contemporary American politics. First, geographic partisan polarization has accentuated longstanding biases in US political institutions that impose a density tax on voters in metro areas and privilege the policy status quo. This, in turn, has made ongoing policy adaptation to the knowledge economy difficult and shifted the partisan balance of power toward the Republican Party. Second, in an increasingly nationalized and polarized party system, the character of party coalitions is another powerful filter of local economic interests. Organized groups operating on a national scale have strong incentives to pick sides, orient their activities around national party agendas, and take advantage of parties' increased agenda-setting power. Especially with affective partisan identities increasingly driving voter behavior – identities that map onto and have roots in racial and ethnic conflict as well as growing geographic inequality itself – party elites may well feel empowered to pursue policies with support from organized allies even when those policies are at odds with voters' local concerns.

Finally, the distinctive structure of the US public policies weighs heavily on the representation of metro interests today. Localized control over zoning and other vital policy levers places a formidable barrier in the way of national action to support the knowledge economy and help urban agglomerations overcome collective action problems. The party filter also matters here, too, for unsettling these costly arrangements could also unsettle the Democratic Party's alliance between the privileged and the disadvantaged and between urban and suburban residents of metro America. Thus, Democrats too face distributional tensions between the most affluent portions of their coalition and their broader voting base.

Whether those tensions can be resolved depends in part on the heated battles taking place in Washington as we write. In 2021–2022, the razor-thin Democratic majority in Congress failed to enact an ambitious package of domestic social policies. However, it did pass three bills (two with modest Republican support, one enacted on a party-line vote) that began to address the huge backlog of urban infrastructure needs and the long-term stagnation of investment in advanced R&D. It is important to recognize, though, that these new initiatives were paired with a great deal of investment in nonmetro areas, in part because the pivotal Democrat in the Senate was Joe Manchin of (rural) West Virginia. Notably, the investments envisioned so far include substantial funding for infrastructure and clean energy in red areas of the country. For example, nearly four-fifths of the clean energy investments announced by May 2023 under the 2022 Inflation Reduction Act are set to take place in Republican House districts. Meanwhile, the new House Republican majority has voted to repeal these incentives (a symbolic step, given Democratic control of the Senate, but one that could get caught up in the aforementioned debt ceiling fight). As the veteran journalist Ronald Brownstein aptly notes, "This opposition contravenes the traditional assumption that politicians almost always support the economic interests creating opportunity for their constituents."[11]

We do not think the filters we have examined completely explain this striking disconnect, much less all the patterns of representation we see. A focus on the institutional, party, and policy filters does not fully capture the role of race, for example – though distinctive elements of that role do come into view, as we hope we have shown. Nonetheless, the filters play a fundamental role in explaining why PBEIs occupy such a limited and often paradoxical place in American politics today. National party priorities cannot be simply "read off" of voters' preferences – we need to see how they are refracted through the filters. Because of the nationalization and polarization of the parties within a distinctive electoral system, neither Democrats nor Republicans are likely to be penalized if they neglect PBEIs as they would have in the past.

To be sure, there is scope for PBEIs to come to play a larger role, and party coalitions can and do change over time. A crucial question is whether the investments being made today might bolster Democrats' standing outside their metropolitan base, in turn pressuring Republicans to be more responsive to the PBEIs of their constituents. Another is whether organized elements of the business community that benefit from such investments might become more willing to actively back the Democratic Party and even perhaps push it to focus more on metro investments. Ultimately, the question is whether the filters will continue to dampen the incentive for US representative institutions to produce active federal policies responding to the dramatic shift in the geography of prosperity that the transition to the knowledge economy has fostered.

---

[11] Brownstein, Ronald, "More green investment hasn't softened red resistance on climate," CNN, May 2, 2023.

This is not a question for American policymakers alone. All advanced democratic societies are grappling with it in one way or another. Many of the features of the American political landscape that we highlight are unusual. Those features may well help to account for the growing cross-national evidence that the United States is a significant outlier with regard to the representation of citizen preferences in an increasingly unequal economy. Yet we believe a filtered approach to representation has relevance beyond the American case. Our hope is that this paper can contribute to the ongoing effort to consider how countries' institutions, party systems, and policy inheritances influence the degree to which the concerns of ordinary citizens are translated into public policy.

PART II

POLITICAL INEQUALITY AND REPRESENTATION

6

Organized Interests and the Mechanisms behind Unequal Representation in Legislatures[*]

Michael Becher and Daniel Stegmueller

What explains unequal representation in contemporary democracies? In the wake of rising economic inequality, a recent literature has cumulated evidence that legislators in representative institutions, ranging from the US Congress to legislative assemblies in Europe and Latin America, are more responsive to (or more congruent with) the preferences of high-income constituents and business interests than to the preferences of those with average incomes and particularly the poor (e.g., Bartels 2008; Elsässer, Hense, and Schäfer 2017; Gilens 2012; Gilens and Page 2014; Lupu and Warner 2022a; Mathisen et al., volume; but see Elkjær and Iversen 2020). However, there is no consensus on the main mechanisms driving unequal representation. Surprisingly divergent views are combined with only limited evidence on the impact of organized interests on political inequality in legislatures.

In this chapter, we start by reviewing the scholarly debate and identify a central area of disagreement about the relative importance of interest groups and the mechanism through which they shape substantive political inequality. Then, we present a synthetic model that captures a representative democracy with organized interests that can seek to influence policy through electoral selection and postelectoral lobbying. We use the model to derive positive implications on the context-varying nature of interest group influence and to clarify the challenges faced by scholars trying to uncover interest group influence and to unbundle competing mechanisms using empirical observations.

Broadly speaking, a fundamental difference among theories of unequal democracy is their relative emphasis on electoral selection or postelectoral

[*] We are grateful to Charlotte Cavaillé, Thomas Christiano, Ben Page, Noam Lupu, Imil Nurutdinov, Jonas Pontusson, Jan Stuckatz, Georg Vanberg, and participants at APSA 2020, IAST workshop "Knowledge, Power, and the Quest for Political Equality," and the Unequal Democracies speaker series (Vanderbilt University and University of Geneva) for comments and suggestions.

influence as drivers of unequal representation. Prominent explanations that take an electoral *selection* perspective include partisan differences and descriptive representation (Bartels 2008; Carnes 2013; Carnes and Lupu 2015; Curto-Grau and Gallego, this volume; Mathisen et al., this volume; Rhodes and Schaffner 2017). This analytical perspective focuses scholars' attention on explaining unequal influence over election outcomes (e.g., based on campaign finance, electoral laws, organized labor, or voter psychology). Alternative explanations highlight the importance of *postelectoral* channels of influence and focus on lobbying, broadly construed (Flavin 2015b; Hacker and Pierson 2010; Hertel-Fernandez, Mildenberger, and Stokes 2019; Kelly et al. 2019).

Interest groups may influence political representation through both channels, electoral selection and postelectoral influence. But we know little about the relative importance of these two channels. Moreover, there is no agreement on the overall contribution of interest groups to political inequality. A better understanding of possible mechanisms provides foundations for studying the total impact.

One the one side, organized groups that represent business interests and high-income professionals are an important explanation for why policy outcomes deviate substantively from the preferences of average citizens. This perspective is called *Biased Pluralism* (Gilens and Page 2014). While direct tests are still rare, the study of Gilens and Page (2014) covers nearly two thousand policy issues in the United States. It concludes that organized interests have a substantial impact on public policy, beyond the preferences of average citizens and economic elites, and that this is especially pronounced for business-oriented groups. Related research on legislative voting rather than policy adoption uses an instrumental-variable approach and finds evidence that labor unions can dampen the pro-rich bias in the US Congress (Becher and Stegmueller 2021). The view that organized interests matter for political equality is of course not restricted to American politics. Mancur Olson's theory of collective action implies that narrow, concentrated interests are more likely to be represented in the interest group universe than broad-based groups of citizens (Olson 1965). It is not hard to find scholars of contemporary democracy in Europe who, after looking at the available data, are worried about biased pluralism. For example, recent comparative research shows that European campaign finance systems are unequal, benefiting the rich and corporations more than the poor through tax exemptions and other rules, and that higher campaign spending is linked to electoral results (Cagé 2020).

On the other side, the quantitative empirical literature on the role of money in politics has grappled with the difficulty of showing that interest groups' financial contributions affect legislative votes. Reviewing dozens of roll-call studies on the link between interest group contributions and legislative voting in the United States, Ansolabehere, Figueiredo, and Snyder (2003: 116) conclude that the evidence that financial contributions to candidates affect their votes "is rather thin." Rather, based on their own analysis they conclude that

"Legislators' votes depend almost entirely on their own beliefs and the preferences of their voters and their party." They add the methodological recommendation that scholars trying to assess the impact of money on votes using observational data should include legislator fixed effects to control for legislators' own preferences, party, and constituency influence. By doing so, scholars are implicitly or explicitly trying to isolate a postelectoral channel of influence. However, this strategy can be problematic and lead to misleading inferences when electoral selection and postelectoral influence are complements.

We argue that electoral selection and postelectoral influence are likely to go hand in hand in polarized environments. Ignoring this complementarity, researchers may wrongly conclude that only electoral politics matters as a channel through which interest groups affect political equality in legislatures. This issue matters both for tests of positive theories of unequal democracy as well as normative evaluations. Without a better understanding of mechanisms, it remains difficult to devise strategies to mitigate substantive political inequality against the backdrop of economic inequality and populist challenges to democratic institutions.

We set forth our argument using a simple formal model that is then used to generate simulated legislatures. It captures a two-stage political process with an electoral and a postelectoral stage. The model assumes a political process where electoral influence and postelectoral influence are not perfect substitutes. An organized interest – whether pro-poor or pro-rich – aiming to shape policy has to first ensure that their preferred politician is elected. But the story does not end on election night. Legislators have a constrained agenda and will carefully choose which issues to prioritize even among those they principally agree with. So the organized group will also have to lobby (friendly) legislators (Austen-Smith and Wright 1994; Hall and Deardorff 2006).

Our model illuminates how the strategies of organized interests vary across context. When party polarization is relatively low, they can focus on swaying legislators through postelectoral lobbying. Increasing polarization incentivizes organized interests to focus some of their energy on helping to select like-minded politicians. However, lobbying will not be fully substituted by electioneering. Rather, when polarization is high, and with politicians facing competing demands, organized interests will have to engage in both activities. This leads to an important but largely neglected challenge for empirical research on unequal representation (and the related, but largely separate, literature on lobbying): what can be learned about mechanisms from the data alone might be limited by the strategic actions of political actors.

The problem of analyzing mechanisms is not simply due to confounding or omitted variable bias. Assume that a researcher can identify the causal effect of the group on legislative behavior (e.g., via an exogenous or instrumented measure of group strength, or a natural experiment). The key question then is *how much* of the treatment effect is due to electoral selection of a friendly legislator versus postelectoral lobbying. To empirically illustrate this point, we simulate thousands of possible legislatures arising from a known data generating process (our theoretical model) where *without* postelectoral lobbying legislators would *not support* an interest group's preferred policy. We then apply statistical models commonly used in the literature and show that researchers risk drawing incorrect conclusions from such analyses, overstating the relevance of elections as a channel through which groups affect legislative responsiveness. Furthermore, we illustrate the issue using roll-call votes in the US House of Representatives.[1]

Empirical research on lobbying usually faces the problem that postelectoral effort cannot be inferred from observable data. However, as we show in this chapter, our conclusion still stands even when researchers can fully observe postelectoral effort (or correct for the known lack of reliability of a measure). The reason is that the group lobbies friendly legislators. In equilibrium, the selection of a friendly legislature and lobbying can be highly (but not perfectly) correlated. Empirically, this leads to a form of simultaneity bias. As a result, based on standard empirical analyses, scholars may erroneously conclude that all that matters for unequal representation is electoral politics. Again, this empirical problem exists even though scholars can causally estimate the total effect of group power on legislative responsiveness.

INCOME AND LEGISLATIVE RESPONSIVENESS

The idea that all citizens should count approximately equally in the political process underpins various normative theories of democracy since antiquity (Müller 2021). Political equality is conceived as the "equal advancement of interests" (Christiano 2008: 95) and is about substantive or de facto representation, not just equal political rights. This is what Dahl (1971) calls equal responsiveness and the social choice literature calls the anonymity axiom. Political equality is a yardstick, not a prediction. Several positive theories of democratic politics suggest that pervasive socioeconomic inequalities can limit equality in policymaking. For example, interest groups' monetary contributions can influence postelectoral policymaking (Grossman and Helpman 2001) as well as electoral outcomes (Cagé 2020). In the wake of rising economic inequality (Lupu and Pontusson, this volume; Piketty 2014), political scientists and other social scientists have paid increasing attention to the implications of economic inequality for substantive political equality.

Building on pioneering research on the US Senate (Bartels 2008) and policy adoption in the United States (Gilens 2012), numerous studies have found evidence that elected policymakers in legislative assemblies are more responsive to the preferences of relatively rich constituents at the expense of middle-income

---

[1] Evidence from the United States shows that electoral effort (to influence selection) and postelectoral lobbying are linked (Ansolabehere, Snyder, and Tripathi 2002; Kim, Stuckatz, and Wolters 2020).

and poor constituents (e.g., Elsässer, Hense, and Schäfer 2017; Gilens 2016; Hertel-Fernandez, Mildenberger, and Stokes 2019; Kalla and Broockman 2016a; Lupu and Warner 2022a; Mathisen et al. in this volume; Peters and Ensink 2015; Rigby and Wright 2013). Responsiveness here refers to the relationship between the opinions of constituents differentiated by income and legislative actions of officeholders, usually legislative votes[2], or the relationship between national public opinion differentiated by income and policy outcomes. When policy questions are polarized by income, many of these studies suggest that the views of the rich matter more, whereas the views of the poor matter little or not at all (but see Brunner, Ross, and Ebonya 2013; Elkjær and Iversen 2020). Perhaps not surprisingly, populist parties and politicians have capitalized on the perception that democracy favors the affluent (Müller 2021).

The degree and relevance of unequal responsiveness is a matter of ongoing debate (Erikson 2015). One view is that elected representatives should not pander to the views of the largely uninformed public. Rather, good representatives ought to lead by making choices that are in the enlightened interest (however defined) of citizens. We agree with *Federalist Paper 71* and game-theoretic models of pandering (Canes-Wrone, Herron, and Shotts 2001) that there can be too much responsiveness. However, these models cannot justify complacency about *unequal* responsiveness in the democratic process that lies at the center of this volume and chapter. Many disagreements about policy between rich and poor citizens concern economic bread-and-butter issues and are based on differences in material conditions or ideals. Indeed, an established political economy literature predicts and documents rational sources of disagreement. For example, consider income redistributive policies, minimum wage increases, or stimulus spending in the wake of an economic depression. On these and similar economic issues, individuals in the United States and Europe with lower incomes are, on average, significantly more in favor of government action (Gilens 2009; Rueda and Stegmueller 2019; Soroka and Wlezien 2008). Based on current textbook economics, one would be hard pressed to argue that citizens supporting these policies should somehow get less weight than citizens opposing them.

Assessing the degree of unequal responsiveness requires addressing challenging measurement and estimation issues that are discussed in more detail elsewhere (e.g., see Bartels in this volume). Our interpretation of the literature is that there is sufficient (if contested) evidence for the existence of unequal responsiveness to warrant investigation of its mechanisms.

Initial research on congressional or state-level representation in the United States was limited by small survey sample sizes, which poses the risk that estimates of unequal responsiveness are mostly due to sampling noise in the measures

---

[2] Less widely studied, but other aspects like bill sponsorship, speeches, or committee work are clearly relevant as well.

of (correlated) group preferences (Bhatti and Erikson 2011).[3] However, larger surveys, such as the Cooperative Election Study (CES, formerly the Cooperative Congressional Election Study), have reduced this problem. For instance, Bartels (2016: Ch. 8) uses the 2010 and 2012 CES with more than 100,000 respondents and finds differential responsiveness in the Senate. Senators' roll-call voting behavior is positively responsive to average constituent opinion, but this is mainly driven by responsiveness to the upper third of the income distribution. Bartels' estimates imply that senators are five times more responsive to high-income than middle-income constituents and not at all responsive to low-income constituents. Subsequent work on the US House draws on additional CES waves and corrects for possible imbalances between the survey sample and district populations using micro-level census data (Becher and Stegmueller 2021). On average, the pattern in the House is very similar to the one found for the Senate by Bartels (2016).

Field experimental research has added important insights by helping to identify in a more controlled fashion biases that tend to work against the poor and in favor of the affluent. Kalla and Broockman (2016a) find that legislators are more likely to meet donors than nondonors, which bolsters the argument that money buys access. Another study sends messages from (fictional) constituents to politicians, randomly varying name and ethnicity but keeping the same content (Butler 2014). It reveals that politicians exhibit a significant socio-economic bias when evaluating constituent opinion. Focusing on legislative staffers in Congress, Hertel-Fernandez, Mildenberger, and Stokes (2019) find that staffers systematically misestimate public preferences in their district. This mismatch is partially explained by personal views and contacts with business groups. Through an experiment, the study also documents that staffers are less likely to view correspondence from ordinary citizens as being representative of constituent preferences than correspondence from businesses.

Importantly, scholars extended the study of unequal representation to assemblies in Europe, Latin America, and elsewhere (e.g., Bartels 2017; Elkjær and Iversen 2020; Elsässer, Hense, and Schäfer 2017; Lupu and Warner 2022a; Mathisen et al. 2021; Peters and Ensink 2015). One approach in the comparative literature is to match data on government spending with data on public spending preferences by income groups from multiple survey waves and multiple countries. Estimating time-series cross-section models on such data, some studies find that changes in policy are positively related to changes in spending preferences of the rich but not the poor (Bartels 2017; Peters and Ensink 2015). On the other hand, Elkjær and Iversen (2020) show that these findings can be model-dependent. In their preferred regression specification, policy appears to respond only to middle-income preferences. Lupu and Warner (2022a) combine elite and mass surveys in fifty-two countries over three decades to calculate the distance between the views of citizens and legislators. They find that legislators' views are more congruent with those of the rich.

---

[3] On question wording and framing effects, see Gilens (2012, ch. 1); Hill and Huber (2019).

While future research will surely refine estimates of the degree of unequal representation in a larger set of democracies, one can conclude that much of this preliminary evidence runs counter to normative theories of democracy stressing substantive political equality at the policymaking stage.

INTEREST GROUPS AND THE HUNT FOR MECHANISMS

It remains an open question why there is so much political inequality in the legislative arena and what can be done about it. Surveying the literature, Bartels notes that there "is clearly a great deal more to be learned about the mechanisms by which economic inequality gets reproduced in the political realm" (2016: 267). The analysis of mechanisms in this body of scholarship has often focused on the importance of unequal political participation, knowledge, or individual campaign contributions (Bartels 2016; Erikson 2015; Gilens 2012).

We take a complementary perspective and ask how organized interests shape substantive political inequality. Interest groups may focus their efforts on shaping election outcomes or on swaying incumbent policymakers, whatever their partisan stripes. To what extent is unequal legislative responsiveness driven by an electoral *selection* channel rather than a postelectoral *lobbying* channel? So far, the existing evidence does not provide a clear answer about the relative importance of these two mechanisms. We will demonstrate that common empirical strategies may fail to provide a clear answer, and potentially also underestimate the overall impact of interest groups on unequal responsiveness.

One of the few studies that directly examines the relevance of organized interest for unequal responsiveness concludes that national policy in the United States is significantly biased toward economic elites and organized groups representing business interests (Gilens and Page 2014). Related research at the subnational level finds that US states with stricter lobbying regulations exhibit less political inequality at the policymaking stage (Flavin 2015). However, these results stand in contrast with findings from a separate literature on lobbying and money in politics. It concludes that interest groups' monetary contributions have little discernible impact on legislative voting (Ansolabehere, Figueiredo, and Snyder 2003) and that groups with more resources do not necessarily have much higher success rates than other groups (Baumgartner et al. 2009).

Political Selection as a Pathway to (In)equality

Partisanship

From an electoral selection perspective, unequal responsiveness in lawmaking is driven by what types of politicians are elected to office. Partisanship is often the strongest predictor of legislative voting (Bartels 2008; Lee, Moretti, and Butler 2004; McCarty, Poole, and Rosenthal 2006), and the partisan composition of governments shapes key public policies over which people with different incomes tend to disagree (Pettersson-Lidbom 2008). In partisan theories of political competition and public policy, different parties represent different socioeconomic groups and political competition does not lead parties to convergence to the median voter (Hibbs 1987). Once in office, politicians try to implement their policy agenda and are not very sensitive to lobbying efforts to do otherwise. The account implies that reducing political inequality in a legislature requires first and foremost to balance the electoral arena.

Are legislators from different parties unequally responsive to rich and poor constituents? Examining the US Congress, Bartels (2016: 248–249) finds that Republican House members and senators are more responsive to high-income than to middle-income constituents and largely irresponsive to the poor. While Democratic members of Congress are generally also responsive to high-income constituents, they do respond to the views of low-income and middle-class constituents (sometimes to the extent that there is no statistical difference in rates of responsiveness). An analysis drawing on rich individual-level voter registration data confirms this basic pattern (Rhodes and Schaffner 2017).[4] A comparative analysis of policy adoption in four European countries finds that unequal responsiveness is less pronounced when Left parties are in power in three out of the four countries (Mathisen et al., this volume).

Descriptive Representation

Political selection does not only concern partisanship. Individuals vary on many attributes and some of them are bound to shape how they behave in the political arena. In particular, descriptive representation matters because the composition of many legislatures is imbalanced in terms of gender and tilted toward the highly educated and well-off. Thus, one might ask, as did John Stuart Mill in his Considerations on Representative Government, if "[p]arliament, or almost any of the members composing it, ever for an instant look at any question with the eyes of a working man" (Mill 1977 [1861])? There is ample evidence that the occupational class background of politicians matters for legislative voting in the United States (Carnes 2013) and, comparatively, for the positions endorsed by legislators (Carnes and Lupu 2015) and the fiscal policy choices of mayors (Curto-Grau and Gallego, this volume). Politicians with a working-class background are more responsive to the views of the relatively poor, even after controlling for political party. Similarly, characteristics like gender and race shape the responsiveness of politicians (Butler 2014; Swers 2005).

This line of research on the link between descriptive representation and inequality in legislatures implies that barriers to entry in politics for less advantaged individuals are part of the process driving unequal political responsiveness.

---

[4] Gilens' study of system-level responsiveness in the United States does not find the same partisan gap (Gilens 2012). While inferences are limited by the relatively small number of years, the most responsive period was during the presidency of George W. Bush, driven in part by support for the Iraq war and the 2001 tax cuts.

What Shapes Selection?

Economic inequality may favor the selection of policymakers more inclined to consider the opinions of the affluent. For example, increased economic inequality may incentivize higher contributions by those who have most to lose from redistribution and thus change the partisan composition of the legislature (Campante 2011).

It may be tempting to think that the electoral influence of resource-rich interest groups is predominantly an American phenomenon due to its outsize levels of campaign spending. But what matters in electoral contests is the relative financial advantage of one group over another. For example, Cagé (2020) documents that in Europe, funding is not equally distributed across political parties; it tends to favor conservative over Left parties. The richest sections of society and corporations contribute the bulk of private political contributions, and their spending is not electorally neutral. For instance, while Germany has a public campaign finance system, it imposes no limits on corporate donations (with carmakers being leading contributors). In the UK, election spending is strictly regulated, but parties can receive large amounts of cash in the form of donations.[5]

Electoral institutions may also matter for selection. In the absence of credible commitments by parties, one theory goes, majoritarian electoral systems experience a bias in favor of low-tax and low-redistribution parties on the Right (Iversen and Soskice 2006). The bias may vary with economic inequality because Left parties will have more incentives to solve their commitment problem as inequality increases (Becher 2016).

Organized labor can also be a force for more political equality. In our own previous work, we find that stronger local labor unions enhance political equality in the US House of Representatives (Becher and Stegmueller 2021), consistent with state-level evidence (Flavin 2018). While unions are endogenous to politics, we use an instrumental variable approach to reduce concerns about omitted confounders. In line with the evidence on partisan gaps in responsiveness just discussed above, we also find evidence that the impact of unions works at least in part through the electoral selection channel. Relatedly, Carnes and Lupu (this volume) show across countries that unionization is positively correlated with the proportion of legislators with a working-class background.

Postelectoral Influence as a Pathway to (In)equality

Other accounts of unequal democracy emphasize the importance of postelectoral politics. While campaign contributions shape elections, they and other material inducements (e.g., dinners, vacations, well-paid board appointments,

---

[5] For France and the UK, Cagé (2020) finds evidence that private money is associated with more votes.

revolving doors) are often thought to make the incumbent, who looks forward to the next election, more pliable to the views of well-organized groups
(Grossman and Helpman 2001). Economic inequality entails resource advantages for corporations and the wealthy over average citizens and mass organizations. As a result, even supposedly pro-poor politicians may join the
legislative coalition in favor of the economically advantaged (Hacker and
Pierson 2010).

Postelectoral influence can take various forms, such as exchange or persuasion. Due to well-known measurement and causal identification issues,
empirically testing the political efficacy of lobbying is difficult (Baumgartner
et al. 2009; Figueiredo and Richter 2014). The literature has paid particular
attention on how to isolate the impact of organized groups' monetary contributions on legislators' behavior from that of legislators' party, ideology,
and constituency. To improve the veracity of regression analyses of legislative votes in this respect, the review article of Ansolabehere, Figueiredo,
and Snyder (2003) recommends controlling for legislators' party affiliation
or, if possible, to include legislator fixed effects that capture policymakers'
time-invariant attributes. While intuitively appealing, it is noteworthy that
this approach equates interest group influence with postelectoral lobbying.
This strategy can fail to estimate the relevance of the postelectoral channel if preelectoral influence and postelectoral influence are strategic complements. Below, we argue that this is likely to be the case in times of party
polarization.

Field experiments support the idea that money (or even the promise thereof)
provides access to legislators (Hertel-Fernandez, Mildenberger, and Stokes
2019; Kalla and Broockman 2016a). Also consistent with a postelectoral influence view, observational research has found that the revenue of lobbyists connected to legislators drops substantively once their former employer leaves the
legislature (Blanes i Vidal et al. 2012). A study of the congressional agenda
based on legislative speeches finds that corporate contributions are associated with lower attention by legislators to issue like inequality and wages and
higher attention to upper-class issues (Kelly et al. 2019). Labor contributions
are associated with higher attention to inequality and wages and lower attention to upper-class issues. These results hold conditional on partisanship and
committee assignment.

Theories differ on whether organized groups should mainly lobby opposed
legislators, legislators that are on the fence on the issue, or legislators who
are friendly toward their position (Austen-Smith and Wright 1994; Grossman
and Helpman 2001; Hall and Deardorff 2006). Following the formal model
of Hall and Deardorff (2006) and an older interest group literature, we argue
that organized groups will often concentrate their lobbying efforts on friendly
legislators.

Why should organized groups lobby friendly legislators? One useful way
to think about lobbying is as providing a matching grant or legislative subsidy

that assists like-minded legislators to achieve their own objectives (Hall and Deardorff 2006). For example, a conservative legislator may generally believe that the corporate tax rate should be cut, but there are numerous issues on the legislative agenda that require her attention. Given limited time and resources in a legislature that considers thousands of issues each term, providing assistance (e.g., resources and information) enables the legislator to actively support the issue: drafting bills or amendments, convincing constituents, convening with cross-pressured colleagues, and finally casting a corresponding vote. In addition, lobbying friendly legislators counteracts lobbying of opposing groups (Austen-Smith and Wright 1994).

Selection and Postelectoral Influence as Complements

Rather than being alternative drivers of political (in)equality, electoral selection and postelectoral lobbying may go hand in hand. Organized interests maximizing their influence over the policy outcome pursue two objectives. First, ensuring that legislators already friendly to its interests are elected and, second, providing the elected friendly legislators with support to achieve their goals in the postelectoral arena. Then it will be especially difficult to unbundle the mechanisms empirically and applying standard statistical approaches to study mechanisms is likely to lead to wrong conclusions.

To clarify this argument, the section below introduces a simple formal model of a two-stage political process with an electoral and a postelectoral stage. Assuming that both channels may be complementary, the model highlights the resulting behavior of organized interests and legislators. The political equilibrium is then used as input for generating simulated legislatures. The main point of the model is to provide clear analytical foundations for the data generating process used in the simulation, and for this purpose, it prioritizes accessibility and transparency over technicality. Each of the model's key components is based on a rich literature and more elaborate game-theoretic analysis. The strategic interaction of electoral selection and postelectoral lobbying we present here is relatively novel and has implications for empirical research on unequal responsiveness in legislatures that are not as apparent without the guiding light of the model.

A TWO-STAGE MODEL

An organized group, G, cares about the policy action of an elected policymaker, P. The policymaker may be an individual legislator or a collective legislative body. Group G may represent the interest of the relatively poor (e.g., organized labor), or that of the relatively rich (e.g., corporate interest groups). P faces a binary policy choice $X \in \{A, B\}$. G's utility from policy A versus policy B is given by $u(A)$ and $u(B)$, respectively. To fix ideas, we assume throughout that $u(A) > u(B)$, so that G strictly prefers policy A to policy B. The model can be interpreted in two ways without affecting the analysis. First, think of G as a labor union support-ing a policy, A, of more social protection for individuals in the lower half of the income distribution over policy B that would remove such protections. Here, the group will balance the proclivity of the policymaker to side with economic elites and business interests documented in the literature. One possible implication is that the decline in organized labor as a countervailing power is an important driver of political inequality. Second, one can think of G as corporate interests pushing for lower taxes on corporations or top incomes. Here, G wants legisla-tors to support a policy that is not preferred by middle-income and low-income constituents. For concreteness, we will focus on the first interpretation in the text. But it is important to keep in mind that the model also applies to the second case.[6]

Policy is made in a representative democracy, where G can influence policy in two distinct stages of the political process: via lobbying elected represen-tatives and by affecting what type of legislator is elected in the first place. To impact the latter in an election, G can take some costly action, such as cam-paign contributions, get-out-the-vote campaigns, or advertisement, to stochas-tically improve the chances that its preferred type of policymaker is elected. To impact the former, G can lobby elected representatives to increase the prob-ability of them supporting a given policy. Policymakers differ in their policy priorities, be it due to party membership or categories such as gender, race, or class background. We assume that there are two types of legislators, $P \in \{L, R\}$, where L indicates left and R right, to capture the most important aspect of cur-rent partisan polarization. Then group G may choose to lobby a policymaker after the election and P then chooses either policy A or B. The model developed below considers a strategic group and agent-based policymakers acting under political uncertainty.

The Electoral Stage

During the election, G chooses a level of mobilization effort, denoted by m, that may be low ($m = m_0$) or high ($m = m_1$). All that we need to assume is that a higher mobilization effort translates into a higher probability that the group's preferred type of politician wins the election. In a two-candidate race in a first-past-the-post system, this requires winning just more than 50 percent of the vote. Say G's policy interests are more in line with Left policymakers so that G prefers $P = L$ over $P = R$. We model an electorate with a large number of voters (i.e., there are no ties). Denote by v_L the share of votes obtained by a candidate of type L. The mobilization assumption made above then translates to $Pr(P = L \mid m_1) = Pr(v_L > 0.5 \mid m_1) > Pr(P = L \mid m_0) = Pr(v_L > 0.5 \mid m_0)$.

A group's mobilization capacity depends on two key factors. First, the cost of mobilization, which is represented by a nonnegative scalar, c_m. Second, the

---

[6] In this case, party labels should be switched.

group's exogenously determined strength, for example, its membership size or capital stock. We represent the total of the latter by nonnegative scalar β. Groups with larger mobilization capacity have a larger impact on electoral politics:

$$Pr(P = L \mid m_1) = (1 + \beta) Pr(P = L \mid m_0).$$

The Postelectoral Stage

As already argued above, we consider the situation where electoral mobilization (and the resulting selection of P) and postelectoral lobbying are not perfect substitutes. Managing to get a number of type L politicians elected is not necessarily enough for G to achieve its policy objectives. While L policymakers are a priori more favorable toward A than type R policymakers, their support for the policy cannot be taken for granted by G. Policymakers vary in their ideological or partisan constraints and commitments. Think of type L politicians as having a large policy agenda and facing offers from other groups on other dimensions, so that they have to make a decision of whether to exert costly effort (e.g., drafting a proposal) to support A. Thus, after the election, G considers whether and how much to lobby any given elected policymaker. Lobbying may take varying forms such as exerting pressure or providing information and resources. We represent lobbying effort by a nonnegative real number, l. Note, that due to the aforementioned heterogeneity in priorities and constraints, not all politicians are equally responsive to being lobbied by G.

Rather than modeling the full complexity of postelectoral politics, we capture this logic in a reduced form by using a contest success function (Cornes and Hartley 2005; Tullock 1980). The probability that a policymaker chooses A over B is characterized by the effectiveness of group G's lobbying in favor of A relative to countervailing influences (such as lobbying efforts of competing interest groups or the opportunity cost of not pursuing other issues), which are captured by a hurdle factor z_P:

$$Pr(X = A \mid P, l) = \frac{\beta l}{\beta l + z_P}.$$

Here β is G's exogenous strength and l is the endogenous lobbying effort as defined above. The hurdle factor z_P is a nonnegative real number that depends on the type of politician. For a given lobbying effort, Left politicians are more willing to support A than Right politicians: $z_R > z_L$. An instructive case is that only L types are positively responsive to G's lobbying (i.e., z_R is sufficiently large to render lobbying R types prohibitive). Should G decide not to lobby L then policy B is the certain outcome. Lobbying is costly and, following much of the literature using contest functions, we assume a linear cost structure.

Analysis

Given the sequential nature of the interaction, the analysis starts in the post-electoral stage. For a given type of the policymaker, G chooses lobbying effort l to maximize the payoff:

$$\left(\frac{\beta l}{\beta l + z_P}\right)u(A) + \left(1 - \frac{\beta l}{\beta l + z_P}\right)u(B) - l.$$

The first order condition implies that G chooses l until marginal expected benefits of lobbying equal marginal cost:

$$\frac{\beta z_P}{(\beta l + z_P)^2}(u(A) - u(B)) = 1.$$

For nonnegative values of l, group G's optimal behavior is well defined and has a unique best response (Cornes and Hartley 2005). Solving the equation above yields the optimal lobbying effort:

$$l^* = \max\left\{\frac{1}{\beta}\left(\sqrt{\beta z_P(u(A) - u(B))} - z_P\right), 0\right\}.$$

Two intuitive results emerge. First, higher policy stakes for the interest group, captured by a larger utility differential for policies A and B, $(u(A) - u(B))$, induce more lobbying effort. Second, the effect of the hurdle factor z_P on postelectoral lobbying is nonmonotonic. As opposing forces make a legislator less inclined to support the policy preferred by G for a given amount of lobbying, increasing G's lobbying effort pays off when the initial hurdle is relatively low ($z_P < (u(A) - u(B))/4\beta$) but not when the hurdle is already high ($z_P > (u(A) - u(B))/4\beta$).

Given the optimal postelectoral lobbying behavior, we now show G's choice of costly mobilization effort. To simplify notation, consider the probabilities of the key outcomes. Denote by π_{L1} the probability of seeing a Left legislator elected given high mobilization effort, $\pi_{L1} = Pr(P = L \mid m_1)$, and by π_{L0} given low mobilization effort, $\pi_{L0} = Pr(P = L \mid m_0)$. Denote by τ_L the probability of obtaining the preferred policy given optimal lobbying of a type L legislator, $\tau_L = Pr(X = A \mid P = L, l^*)$, and by $\tau_R = Pr(X = A \mid P = R, l^*)$ the respective probability for a legislator of type R.

Group G exerts costly mobilization effort at the electoral stage if and only if the expected value of mobilizing is larger than the cost:

$$\left[\pi_{L1}\tau_L + (1 - \pi_{L1})\tau_R\right]u(A) + \left[\pi_{L1}(1 - \tau_L) + (1 - \pi_{L1})(1 - \tau_R)\right]u(B) - c_m >$$
$$\left[\pi_{L0}\tau_L + (1 - \pi_{L0})\tau_R\right]u(A) + \left[\pi_{L0}(1 - \tau_L) + (1 - \pi_{L0})(1 - \tau_R)\right]u(B)$$

This simplifies to:

$$\beta > \frac{c_m}{\pi_{L0}\left(\tau_L - \tau_R\right)\left(u(A) - u(B)\right)}.$$

Mobilization thus requires that the group is sufficiently strong (i.e., β is sufficiently large), that the policy stakes $(u(A) - u(B))$ are sufficiently high relative to the cost of mobilization (c_m), and that there is party polarization captured by the partisan gap in responsiveness to postelectoral lobbying effect $(\tau_L - \tau_R)$.

Party polarization is low when legislators of either party have a similar probability of supporting policy A for a given amount of postelectoral lobbying. If party polarization is sufficiently low, then even a strong group will focus all its efforts on postelectoral lobbying. In the context of sufficiently high party polarization, the interest group will first engage in electoral mobilization on behalf of its preferred candidate, and then engage in postelectoral lobbying if its preferred candidate wins the election. This logic implies that interest group strategies systematically vary across context.

Consider the interaction of both stages in the case of high polarization such that only type L politicians are responsive to G's lobbying (i.e., z_P is sufficiently large such that $Pr\left(X = A \mid P = R, l\right) = 0$ for feasible values of l). Then, a strong G will exert mobilization effort and, if L wins the election, postelectoral lobbying effort to achieve its preferred policy, A. On the one hand, mobilization alone is not sufficient to affect the policy outcome. On the other hand, a rational group will not solely rely on lobbying. Everything else equal, the strength of G, as parameterized by β, improves both the electoral and the postelectoral chain of influence: L is more likely to prevail in the election and more likely to choose policy A. In equilibrium, the selection of the preferred type of politician and the use postelectoral lobbying are strongly correlated.

EVIDENCE FROM SIMULATED LEGISLATURES

We trace the implications of our model for empirical analysis using a simulation approach. We create 5,000 simulated legislatures, each with 435 legislators, whose composition is the result of an electoral process including strategic mobilization and whose policy choice is the result of strategic postelectoral lobbying. Each legislator faces the choice of supporting one of two policies, A or B, in a roll-call vote (or prior action such as cosponsorship).

The simulation captures a situation where policy A is preferred over policy B by citizens in the middle and lower part of the income distribution, but economic elites and business interest groups generally have opposing preferences. In this environment, mass-based organizations like labor unions may be a force for more political inequality in legislatures (Becher and Stegmueller 2021; Flavin 2018). Continuing with this running example, we would like to

TABLE 6.1 *Parameter values*

Parameter	Label	Value
β	Group strength	U (0.05, 0.21)
$u(A) - u(B)$	Policy polarization	5
z_L	Lobbying hurdle	0.06
c_m	Mobilization costs	0.15
v_{L0}	Left vote share under m_0	U (0.30, 0.61)
N	Number of legislators	435

know to what extent the effect of organized labor on legislative responsiveness works through political selection rather than postelectoral bargaining. Nothing changes with respect to the identification challenges for unbundling the mechanisms if one prefers to interpret unions as enhancing inequality or if one thinks of the organized group G as a business group that has preferences add odds with the majority of voters (Gilens 2012; Gilens and Page 2014; Grossman and Helpman 2001).

Table 6.1 shows the parameter values used in our simulation. To generate variation in the ability of the group to affect legislative behavior and thus substantive political equality, the group strength parameter across the 435 districts is drawn from a uniform distribution ranging from 0.05 to 0.21. This represents district-level variation in union strength (e.g., number of union members). We base this range on district-level membership estimates found in the data of Becher, Stegmueller, and Kaeppner (2018).

In the absence of any mobilization effort by the group, the vote share of Left legislators can vary from 0.3 to 0.61; the expected value of Left vote share is 0.46.[7] Thus, Left candidates are electorally disadvantaged compared to their Right competitors but with a narrow enough margin to make electoral mobilization worthwhile in expectation for a well-organized group.[8] Realistically, there is significant political polarization, as represented by the utility difference between policy A and policy B. Organized interests face a complementarity between partisan selection and lobbying. The positive lobbying hurdle for Left politicians (z_L) implies that without being lobbied by G, even like-minded

---

[7] In the simulation, we assume that vote shares are drawn from a uniform distribution that is shifted by the group's mobilization effort. Without mobilization ($m = m_0$), the vote obtained by L, v_{L0} is drawn from a uniform distribution with support on the interval $\left[v_{L0}^{low}, v_{L0}^{high} \right]$. With mobilization ($m = m_1$), the distribution for v_{L1} is shifted to the Right with support on $[(1 + \beta)v_{L0}^{low}, (1 + \beta)v_{L0}^{high}]$. In the simulation, the average Left vote share with mobilization is 0.54; counterfactually, without mobilization, it is 0.45.

[8] In our simulations of the model, the group decides to mobilize for about 64 percent of all candidates, on average.

legislators would not support policy *A*; right politicians are never willing to support *A* for feasible lobbying efforts by *G*.[9] This setup produces partisan voting patterns that are in line with many key votes.[10]

Common Statistical Specifications

We now turn to analyses of the simulated legislatures using standard regression approaches used in the literature on legislative voting and representation. A key parameter of interest is the regression coefficient for β, which captures the average effect of *G*'s strength in a legislator's district on representational inequality. A common specification would regress a legislator's support for policy *A* (i.e., a recorded roll-call vote) on the group strength variable and a set of district characteristics. We have constructed the data-generating process such that there is no endogeneity problem with respect to group strength and legislative behavior.[11] This is to focus on the mechanism problem. It illustrates the difficulties that can arise even when researchers have an exogenous measure of the group's power in each district.[12] A key decision when deciding on a model specification is the choice of how to treat the partisan identity (or descriptive characteristics) of the legislator, captured by an indicator variable equal to 1 if $P = L$. We begin with a specification that does not include this indicator, followed by a specification where it is included. The reasons for its inclusion are usually given in terms of either "controlling for partisanship" or in an informal attempt to capture the selection channel and distinguish it from a residual "direct" channel.[13] Partisanship has a key practical advantage for researchers. It is directly observable and measured with little error. This contrasts with a group's lobbying effort, which can use multiple instruments and only some of them are observable to researchers (Figueiredo and Richter 2014).

Table 6.2 shows the resulting estimates obtained from linear probability models (accompanied by the required heteroscedasticity-consistent standard errors). Column (1) shows that group strength significantly increases the support for policy *A*. A marginal increase in group strength increases the probability of a legislator supporting the policy by 1.6 ± 0.5 percentage points. Expressed in substantive terms, a one standard deviation increase in group strength increases the probability by about 7 percentage points. This represents the "total impact" of an increase in group strength on policy adoption both

---

[9] The latter assumption simplifies the analysis but is not needed.

[10] In our simulations, policy *A* receives no support from Right legislators, but is supported by about 76 percent of Left legislators on average.

[11] Thus, we ignore district-level controls in what follows. One may think of this as a situation where a natural experiment (e.g., redistricting) makes this assumption plausible. Similarly, with some modification of the statistical analysis, researchers may leverage an instrumental variable.

[12] For the same reason, we also abstract from measurement problems with respect to preferences (Becher and Stegmueller 2021; Hill and Huber 2019).

[13] We will investigate a more sophisticated empirical decomposition of causal channels below.

TABLE 6.2 *Group strength, electoral selection, lobbying, and legislative responsiveness*

	(1)		(2)		(3)	
	Est.	s.e.	Est.	s.e.	Est.	s.e.
Group strength $[\beta]$	1.559	(0.484)	0.327	(0.307)	0.005	(0.143)
Left legislator $[P = L]$			0.753	(0.031)	0.919	(0.159)
Postelection effort[a]					−0.108	(0.106)

Notes: Based on $M = 5000$ simulated legislatures with 435 members. Intercepts not shown. Estimates from linear probability model with heteroscedasticity-consistent standard errors.
[a] Postelection effort observed without measurement error (or measured via proxy with known and adjusted reliability). Correlation of postelection effort with electoral mobilization, $\mathrm{Cor}(m_1, l^*) = 0.023$; correlation with left election winner, $\mathrm{Cor}(L, l^*) = 0.962$.

via changing the likelihood of the election of Left legislators and via changing their support for the policy via lobbying once elected. A researcher including the partisan identity of legislators in the specification would obtain the results displayed in column (2). The estimate for the partisanship variable is large and clearly statistically different from zero (0.75 ± 0.03). The coefficient for group strength is drastically reduced and almost five times smaller compared to specification (1). Given the size of its standard error, one would have to conclude that it is statistically indistinguishable from zero. Faced with these empirical results, a researcher might reach the conclusion that only partisan selection matters for the support of policy A – which is clearly incorrect given the model that generated the data, in which the selection channel alone is *not sufficient* to change substantive representation in the legislature. Recall that without any lobbying of friendly legislators (something that does not occur in equilibrium), all legislators would support policy B.

Just Omitted Variable Bias?

Are these stark results simply the result of omitted variable bias, namely omitted postelection lobbying effort? Specification (3) of Table 6.2 includes a measure of the intensity of lobbying after the election. More precisely, we include the level of optimal postelection effort (parameter l^* in our model). Usually, researchers will not have access to this variable, but work with an imperfect proxy or one or several of its components, which raises issues of errors-in-variables bias. Here, we show a *best-case* scenario, where a researcher either fully observes l^* or corrects for known reliability of the variable measured with error. As the estimate for β signifies, the inclusion of lobbying effort does not recover the impact of group strength when the true data-generating process exhibits strategic complementarities.

Can Mediation Analysis Recover the True Effect?

Given advances in the statistical analysis of causal mechanisms, researchers explicitly interested in mechanisms may go beyond the regression analysis above and opt for an explicit effect decomposition. The goal of this approach is to decompose the effect of group strength on policy choice into an indirect component channeled via partisanship and a direct or remaining component (e.g., Pearl 2001). Imai et al. (2011) define the former as an average causally mediated effect (ACME) and the latter as an average direct effect (ADE). We follow their definition and their guidance about best empirical practice (Imai, Keele, and Yamamoto 2010).

Panel (A) of Table 6.3 shows the resulting causal effect decomposition estimates.[14] The ACME is 1.2 ± 0.4 indicating a substantively and statistically significant impact of group strength via the selection of a Left legislator. In contrast, the ADE of group strength is only 0.3 ± 0.31 and not statistically distinguishable from zero. Almost 80 percent of the total effect of group strength is mediated by the selection of a Left legislator. Again, these findings would tempt a researcher into drawing a conclusion contrary to the true model generating the data. Namely, they might conclude that it is the partisanship of the legislator, and thus the selection mechanism, that matters most for the support of a policy in the legislature and that, as indicated by the remaining effect of group strength, postelectoral influence plays a comparatively small (even "insignificant") role.

A careful decomposition analysis will always include a sensitivity analysis for omitted confounding variables. A researcher realizing that unobserved variables (including postelectoral effort) are likely confounding the

TABLE 6.3 *Mediation analysis*

	Estimate	s.e.
A: Causal decomposition estimates		
ACME of group strength [β] via Left legislator [$P = L$]	1.232	(0.387)
ADE (remaining effect of β)	0.327	(0.307)
Proportion of total effect of β mediated by L	0.783	
B: Omitted M-Y confounder		
Sensitivity analysis: $\tilde{\rho}$ where $ACME = 0$	0.813	
True value of $\rho \left[Cor\left(L, l^*\right) \right]$	0.962	
Test $\rho > \tilde{\rho}$ [p-value]	0.000	

Notes: Based on $M = 5000$ simulated legislatures with 435 members. Causal decomposition estimated following Tingley et al. (2014) with standard errors based on 500 bootstrap draws.

[14] The included variables are the same as in specification (2) before.

mediator-outcome relationship would conduct a sensitivity analysis by simulating various degrees of residual correlation, $\tilde{\rho}$, between the mediator and outcome equation (Imai, Keele, and Yamamoto 2010). In Panel (B) of Table 6.3,
we report a common quantity that emerges from this exercise: the value of $\tilde{\rho}$
where the estimated ACME becomes zero. In our simulated data, this occurs
when $\tilde{\rho}$ is about 0.8. Because of the large size of this correlation, a researcher
might well conclude that only an unrealistically large correlation induced by
omitted confounders would negate the strong estimated role of the partisan
selection channel. But again, under a true data-generating process with strategic complementarity, this empirical result provides a false sense of security: the
true ρ value is larger than 0.8 – on average the correlation between an elected
Left legislator and postelectoral lobbying effort is 0.96.

ROLL CALL VOTING IN THE US CONGRESS

A reader might wonder if the issues discussed in this paper do indeed show
up in common empirical applications. While we attempted to choose realistic
parameter values in our simulations, it is possible that empirical research might
not encounter similarly stark patterns. In Table 6.4, we summarize typical
analyses of four key votes in the 110th and 111th Congress. We chose votes on
issues that enjoyed broad support among low-income constituents, such as the
Fair Minimum Wage Act of 2007 or the Foreclosure Prevention Act of 2008.
The first specification regresses roll-call votes on union strength (measured as
district-level union membership calculated from administrative data in Becher,
Stegmueller, and Kaeppner 2018) to capture the impact of group strength on
the behavior of elected representatives. Union strength does indeed have a positive impact on representation: the coefficient of (logged) union membership is
of sizable magnitude and statistically significant for all four key votes.

  The final column of Table 6.4 presents a specification likely to be explored
by many researchers at some point (or to be demanded by reviewers): an analysis of roll-call votes and union strength while "controlling" for a legislator's
party. We have shown above that this strategy yields misleading inferences for
the impact of group strength when postelectoral influence and selection are
strategic complements. This is likely the case in our empirical example given
high levels of party polarization in the US Congress, where the addition of
legislator partisanship drastically changes the group strength coefficient. For
many key votes, the impact of logged union membership is essentially nil with
coefficients statistically indistinguishable from zero. Interpreting these results
as evidence for the overwhelming importance of partisan selection or of the
irrelevance of unions would be misleading.

  Using arguably exogenous variation in union strength based on historical
mining locations, Becher and Stegmueller (2021) find, in line with theoretical
intuition, that stronger unions make it more likely that Democratic candidates
win congressional elections. However, it is possible that postelectoral lobbying

TABLE 6.4 *Estimates of group strength on roll-call votes for some key bills with high support among low-income constituents*

			Group strength estimates	
Roll-call vote	Low inc. support[a]	Democratic legisl. votes[b]	Union size[c]	Union size + Democrat[d]
Lilly Ledbetter Fair Pay Act	0.62	223 (96%)	0.140 (0.030)	−0.000 (0.006)
Fair Minimum Wage Act	0.82	233 (100%)	0.097 (0.025)	0.011 (0.012)
Foreclosure Prevention Act	0.70	227 (96%)	0.109 (0.028)	−0.001 (0.020)
Affordable Care Act	0.64	219 (87%)	0.156 (0.033)	0.046 (0.018)

Note: Linear probability models with state fixed effects. Robust standard errors clustered at the state level.
[a] Average share of low-income citizens in 435 districts supporting the policy. Constituency preferences derived from Cooperative Election Study questions corresponding to roll-call vote. District-level small area estimation via matching to the Census population using random forests. See Becher and Stegmueller (2021).
[b] Number of yea votes among Democrats. Percentage of Democratic caucus voting yea in parentheses.
[c] Coefficient of logged district union membership numbers. District-level union membership calculated from administrative data in Becher, Stegmueller, and Kaeppner (2018).
[d] Coefficient of logged district union membership numbers after adding an indicator variable for partisanship of legislator.

remains a relevant mechanism at play. Theory and evidence suggest that electoral selection and lobbying may go hand in hand when parties exhibit divergent ideologies.

Using individual-level data linking contributions and lobbying by firms, Kim, Stuckatz, and Wolters (2020) find that a campaign donation to a member of Congress by a firm increases the probability that the same legislator is also lobbied by 8–10 percentage points, on average. Our theoretical model highlights that even a fairly small correlation between electoral and postelectoral *effort* can lead to a very high correlation between electoral selection – having a friendly legislator win the election – and lobbying.

CONCLUSION

Interest group influence is sometimes perceived as the main source behind unequal representation in legislatures around the world. For example, the power of corporations to shape policies that diverge from the interests of much of the population is a frequent topic of news stories. Relatedly, the weakening of organized labor may have critically reduced the political voice of non-elite workers. However, academic scholarship on the issue is far from settled.

Trying to understand why there appears to be so much substantive political inequality in the policymaking process, the rapidly growing unequal democracies literature has paid only limited attention to the role of organized interests. This is in part due to data constraints but may also reflect lack of theoretical attention. For European observers, it is tempting to think that interest groups and the money they bring to politics are mainly a problem for democracy in America and less institutional presidential systems in other parts of the world. While comforting, this is a deceiving thought. Recent research has revealed remarkable inequalities in campaign finance systems in European countries and positive theory highlights the potential power of special interest groups in proportional electoral systems commonly found in continental Europe.

We have highlighted through a simple model and model-based simulation the value of analyzing interest groups' incentives on how to use their resources in the electoral and postelectoral lobbying stage. Our analysis shows that when party polarization is low, interest groups have incentives to focus on lobbying incumbent politicians, regardless of their partisan affiliation. When parties are polarized, efforts to shape the selection of partisan policymakers in elections and postelectoral lobbying go hand in hand in political equilibrium. Thus, electoral selection becomes more important as party polarization increases. This testable implication from our model may help to explain variation in interest group strategies across countries. Furthermore, ignoring this relationship may lead scholars to underestimate the importance of interest groups for political inequality.

The model also clarifies that interest group efforts to shape selection complement lobbying efforts rather than substitute them. Thus, even in times of high polarization, lobbying remains substantively important even though it can be empirically difficult to untangle its effects from that of the selection mechanism. With respect to policies aiming to enhance the ideal of substantive political equality, the logic outlined in the chapter implies that reforms aiming to limit the scope of the selection channel do not render the lobbying channel ineffective and must not be ignored. It also stands to reason that well-endowed interest groups face less of a trade-off between the two mechanisms, electoral selection and postelectoral influence, possibly explaining their clout.

Our argument and empirical illustration also highlight a neglected methodological issue with implications for our understanding of unequal representation. When analyzing data on legislative behavior or policy adoption, researchers may wrongly conclude that interest group influence mainly works through electoral selection. Furthermore, if interest group influence is equated with postelectoral lobbying, as is sometimes done implicitly or explicitly in efforts to mitigate concerns about confounding, then researchers can wrongly conclude that there is no interest group influence on policy and political inequality at all. When the regression coefficient appears to assign large weight and statistical significance to a variable like party that was determined in an election, the obvious interpretation may be that interest groups do not really matter much. But this conclusion is wrong for data that are generated from a political process similar to the one we studied here. This point is relevant for research on political inequality, but it also applies to the lobbying literature at large. Admittedly, we offer no easy fix for this problem. But theoretical awareness helps researchers to triangulate different types of data and come up with innovative research designs. For instance, findings on the importance of political selection must be interpreted against evidence on the link between contributions and access.

Extending our theoretical framework, one avenue for future research would be to derive comparative statics about the effect of electoral institutions on interest group strategies and how they impact unequal representation. Doing so requires additional modeling choices about institutional variation, the internal organization of political parties, and multiparty systems. Suppose for a moment that the effectiveness of lobbying is reduced by higher party discipline, which itself varies with electoral rules. Then an increase in party discipline can shift in the balance of total effort toward postelectoral lobbying. Because a focus on electoral selection alone is not sufficient to achieve the desired policy outcome, the group (think, if you would like, of a labor union) has to increase its lobbying effort. This occurs if the group has sufficient exogenous resources. Up to a point, the result still holds even if returns to electoral mobilization are also comparatively lower under PR. This implication appears broadly consistent with the empirical finding that firms' lobbying efforts in closed-list PR systems appear to increase with district magnitude (Campos and Giovannoni 2017). However, an opposing view suggests a different prediction: under higher party discipline, lobbying can be rationally targeted at party leaders and party organizations as a whole and thus be more efficient. For organized interests, the result may be more bang for the buck in PR systems. Thus, the impact of the institutional environment may hinge assumptions made about within-party organizational features and details of the electoral rules.[15]

---

[15] Differences in electoral rules may also be modeled using variation in the elasticity between votes and seats (Rogowski and Kayser 2002).

7

How Do the Educated Govern?

Evidence from Spanish Mayors

Marta Curto-Grau and Aina Gallego

Politicians have on average much higher levels of education than citizens (Bovens and Wille 2017; Gaxie and Godmer 2007; Gerring et al. 2019). This empirical regularity is consistent across countries and over time, but is the overrepresentation of highly educated citizens in office justified? A long tradition sees highly educated politicians as more desirable on the basis that education is a sign of competence or "quality" (Dal Bó and Finan 2018): highly educated individuals are considered as better able to understand politics, as better managers, as having more authority on others, and as being more committed to the well-being of their communities than the less educated. In empirical research, numerous studies use the education of politicians as a proxy of their unobserved "quality" (e.g., Artiles, Kleine-Rueschkamp, and Leon-Ciliotta 2021; Baltrunaite et al. 2014; Becher and Menendez 2019; Gagliarducci and Nannicini 2013; Galasso and Nannicini 2011). This argument would provide a normative defense for the overrepresentation of some types of citizens in politics. In turn, this overrepresentation of some points of view is at the core of some elite-centered explanations of unequal representation, as discussed in the introduction of this volume (see also Bartels in this volume).

However, existing evidence about the actual consequences of having highly educated politicians on policy outcomes is scarce and conflicting. Some studies have argued that educated political leaders produce positive outcomes such as better economic performance (Besley, Montalvo and Reynal-Querol 2011; Congleton and Zhang 2013) or an increase in the provision of public goods (Martinez-Bravo 2017). But other studies find that the education of politicians is irrelevant for policy outcomes (Carnes and Lupu 2016b; Freier and Thomasius 2015) or find mixed evidence (Lahoti and Sahoo 2020).

This chapter studies if the education level of politicians in government affects fiscal policies and performance using detailed local government data.

While previous empirical research either views education as a sign of the quality of politicians or finds that highly and less-educated politicians implement similar policies, our research introduces a third possibility, which is that governments led by more-educated politicians implement more conservative fiscal policies. This idea is complementary to other elite-centered explanations in this volume, including the chapter by Mathisen et al. on the importance of parties; the chapter by Hacker, Pierson, and Zacher on the importance of communication; and Becher and Stegmueller on the role of interest groups to help understand why politicians fail to represent the views of citizens.

To study how the education of politicians affects government performance, we present detailed analyses based on data from Spanish municipalities between 2003 and 2011. We construct an original dataset with information about the gender, age, and education of all mayoral candidates in local elections and match it to local policy outcomes, including fine-grained information about budget items, tax rates, and spending in several policy areas. To address endogeneity concerns, we follow previous research that applies regression discontinuity designs to study the effects of partisanship and the characteristics of politicians on various outcomes (e.g., Ferreira and Gyourko 2009; Gerber and Hopkins 2011). Our identification strategy, which is tailored to the PR system employed in Spanish municipal elections, exploits close races between mayoral candidates with and without a university degree to examine if performance and fiscal policy differed in municipalities where a candidate with a university degree just won or just lost an election.

The RD estimates suggest that when highly educated politicians closely win an election, municipalities do not have better outcomes in respect to unemployment, population growth, primary deficit, or a close match between projected and realized spending, nor are these governments more likely to be reelected. Our analysis of budget items and spending categories provides evidence that, on average, less-educated mayors choose higher levels of capital spending and increase spending in basic infrastructure projects. In ancillary analyses, we also find that the positive effect of electing left-wing governments on capital spending is reduced when the mayors of left-wing parties have a university degree. Overall, our results suggest that educated and noneducated politicians differ on preferences rather than on ability.

This chapter complements recent work on how the social class background of politicians affects government outcomes (Carnes 2013; Carnes and Lupu 2015; Pontusson 2015; O'Grady 2019). Our study joins others that claim that a lack of descriptive representation by socioeconomic status is normatively problematic, as argued by Bartels in this volume. The large overrepresentation of highly educated citizens in office does not produce obvious benefits in terms of better government performance, and our findings suggest that it can introduce a conservative bias in public policy.

THEORY

Our work is motivated by studies which demonstrate that public policies are not determined by the median voter and political institutions alone, but also by the identity of political leaders (Bhalotra and Clots-Figueras 2014; Chattopadhay and Duflo 2004; Jones and Olken 2005; Pande 2003). This claim has wide-ranging implications. Above all, when the composition of governments and legislatures differs from the composition of the population, policies will deviate from the counter-factual situation in which politicians resemble the population. Policy bias will, in all likelihood, favor the overrepresented groups. The most important respect in which politicians stand out in advanced industrial democracies is their privileged socioeconomic background, as discussed in the chapter by Carnes and Lupu in this volume. Whereas the underrepresentation of women and minorities has improved markedly over time, it has only worsened for workers, the less educated, and low-income citizens (Bovens and Wille 2017; Carnes 2013; Gaxie and Godmer 2007; O'Grady 2019).

Different dimensions of socioeconomic advantage such as income, occupation, and education are highly correlated, but education has differential features that justify a separate assessment.[1] Highly educated governments have been defended based on the purported higher ability of their members. However, education is not only the result of higher ability and a vehicle of social mobility, but also a mechanism for the reproduction of inequality (Lee and Seshadri 2019). Having parents of a higher socioeconomic and educational background predicts educational attainment and ultimately income, beyond differences in ability.[2] Education can affect the preferences of citizens through a variety of channels, some of which are separate from income or occupation (as we discuss in detail later). The distinctive features of education justify the need for a careful analysis of both valence and positional outcomes that could reveal trade-offs.

PREVIOUS STUDIES: BETTER PERFORMANCE OR NO EFFECTS?

A first strand of studies finds that highly educated politicians are more competent. Besley, Montalvo, and Reynal-Querol (2011) exploit the death of leaders due to natural causes to identify the effects of their education

---

[1] As Pontusson (2015) points out, little is known about the distinct effect of income, occupational background, and education on the preferences and behavior of politicians and this paper cannot establish if these effects differ. We deem education as relevant on its own right. Given that educational credentials are required for most white-collar occupations, we also see it as implausible that the effects of education and social class differ dramatically. As we discuss in the conclusions, the content of education and the occupations it gives access to may also be influential and further analyses are needed to address this question.

[2] In a related study about the intergenerational transmission of inequality in Spain, Bernardi and Ares (2017) find that the offspring of highly educated parents such as university professors have higher incomes, even controlling for the offspring's education level between competence and representation (for a discussion about this trade-off, see Gulzar 2021).

on economic growth and find that the departure of highly educated leaders from office reduces economic growth. Martinez-Bravo (2017) exploits a large education program in Indonesia and finds that highly educated village heads govern more efficiently and deliver more public goods than less-educated village heads. Lahoti and Sahoo (2020) find that educated politicians produce better educational outcomes in developed states in India, but not in less-developed states.

There are several reasons why highly educated politicians may perform better. Educated people score higher on cognitive and noncognitive traits which predict job performance, including crystallized and fluid intelligence and personality traits such as openness to experience, conscientiousness, and emotional stability (Heckman and Kautz 2012). Skills acquired through formal training or job experience, such as accounting skills, team management, or legal knowledge, can be transferred to government tasks. The correlation of education and desirable abilities and traits may be due to a mixture of self-selection of people with these traits to pursue postsecondary education and to formal education enhancing abilities such as mathematical, verbal skills, or grit. Whatever the direction of causality, if this positive correlation holds among politicians, we should expect highly educated politicians to deliver better outcomes than less-educated politicians on indicators of economic performance.

The dominant view that highly educated politicians perform better than less-educated politicians has been challenged empirically by Carnes and Lupu (2016b) who reanalize Besley, Montalvo and Reynal-Querol's (2011) data using a broader set of outcome measures and fail to find a positive effect on performance. They confirm these null results using further evidence from close elections in US congressional elections and mayoral elections in Brazil. Similarly, Freier and Thomasius (2015) do not find an effect of education on local spending and debt in German municipalities.

Two reasons stand out that may explain these null effects. Politicians may simply not be able to influence policy outcomes much, perhaps because other factors are more important or because governments have little power. The lack of effect of education on performance may also be due to self-selection. As in the case of female politicians (Anzia and Berry 2011), less-educated citizens may be less likely to run and to obtain support, holding quality equal. As a consequence, only the most exceptional less-educated citizens will run in elections and win office. Adverse selection may operate among highly educated citizens. If the salaries of politicians are lower than the salaries of highly educated workers in the private sector, perhaps only those with a low ability among the highly educated choose to run. As a result of both processes, even if there is a positive correlation between education and ability in the population, this correlation could be weakened among politicians. The prediction of this argument is that the education of politicians should not affect governmental performance.

EDUCATION AND ECONOMIC PREFERENCES

A third possibility is that educated politicians have different preferences and implement more fiscally conservative policies than less-educated politicians. This view links the strands of literature that link the preferences of citizens about redistribution (see Cavaille, Ares and Häusermann in this volume) to unequal representation in elite-centered explanations, also discussed in this volume. Perhaps individuals with different characteristics have different preferences. If some are more likely to be representatives than others, this introduces a bias in the political process that helps explain unequal representation.

The more general theoretical argument, in line with citizen-candidate models of representation (Besley 2006), is that the individual characteristics of politicians are informative about their preferences and shape their actions in office. The main testable hypothesis is that the identity of politicians predicts public policies, a general claim that has been applied to multiple individual characteristics (Burden 2007).

Education can shape preferences through multiple channels, some common to other socioeconomic characteristics and others specific to education. The first is the income channel: Educated people have higher incomes and income potential and hence different material interests. As an illustration of this well-known correlation for the Spanish case, according to the yearly Survey on Life Conditions conducted by the National Statistics Institute, citizens with university degrees had incomes more than twice as high, on average, as citizens with lower secondary education. Given the progressive structure of the tax system, this means that more-educated citizens pay relatively more taxes than less-educated citizens. Higher incomes also give educated citizens better access to privately provided healthcare, education, and other services. Because they pay more in and get less out, they should have a preference for a smaller size of the state.

A slightly different material interest channel relates to the risk of unemployment. Less educated citizens face much higher economic risks (Hacker, Rehm and Schlesinger 2013) and hence are more reliant on social protection. In Spain in 2007, people aged between 25 and 64 who had primary education were twice as likely to be unemployed than people with university education. The unemployment rate was 9.9 and 4.8 respectively. In 2010, the gap was even larger at 28 and 10.5. As a consequence of both their different incomes and risk levels, citizens – and politicians – with low levels of education should prefer a larger and more generous state.

There are several nonmaterial channels through which education can produce more fiscally conservative preferences, some of which are particularly relevant in the case of politicians. First, education strongly affects the composition of people's networks. Educated politicians will have fewer acquaintances in their networks in situations of unemployment and economic hardship, which should limit the salience of these issues. Vicarious exposure to economic hardship also affects perceptions about the deservingness of those affected and hence views on economic issues (Newman, 2013). A second reason why the educational composition of the networks of policymakers is important is that less-educated politicians should be more likely than highly educated politicians to be approached and lobbied by less-educated citizens (because networks facilitate access). Note that this "access channel" does not operate through the preferences of politicians.

Independently of income, risk, and networks, educated politicians may have more conservative economic views because of their different socialization experiences in educational environments during their formative years. Independently of their background, educated politicians have been socialized in secondary and university environments, in which peers of privileged backgrounds abound. Experiences lived in privileged educational environments lead to the development of more conservative worldviews (Mendelberg, McCabe, and Thal 2016). In addition, educated citizens (either because of self-serving biases or because of exposure to the rigors and delayed gratification of schooling) may be more likely to endorse "just-world" beliefs and view inequalities as a result of meritocracy.

Empirically, education has been repeatedly found to predict preferences for economic and welfare policies among citizens. For instance, education is associated with less support for redistribution (Rehm 2009) and social policies (Häusermann, Kurer, and Schwander 2016), more support for economic globalization (Naoi 2020), and opposition to protectionism (Hainmueller and Hiscox 2006).[3] Also in Spain, education is associated with right-wing economic policies (Calzada and Del Pino 2008).

We expect governments led by educated politicians to reduce the size of the state and use less interventionist and expansionary policies. The most relevant evidence supporting this expectation is provided by Carnes and Lupu (2015) who find that politicians with a working class background (which correlates very strongly with education) sponsor more "leftist" bills and have more leftist ideal points. These authors look at legislative activity and do not examine if the class of legislators ultimately affects policy outcomes. There is some indirect evidence that the educational background of decision-makers may affect the fiscal conservatism of the policies they adopt and the economic results they obtain. For instance, the education and professional background

---

[3] We do not provide a full overview of the vast empirical literature on education and political preferences here, but note two important points. First, the correlation between education and self-placement in the left-right spectrum varies across countries and is often small. This in part reflects the multidimensionality of ideology, which includes social issues such as abortion on which educated citizens are more left-wing. Second, there is some disagreement in the literature about the relative importance of education vis a vis other socioeconomic characteristics. Horse races between competing variables are misguided in this case because alternative measures of socioeconomic position such as income and occupation are themselves partly affected by education, which is temporally prior to these variables.

of central bankers affect monetary policies (Adolph 2013; Gohlmann and Vaubel 2007), as well as the resulting inflation and unemployment rates. These studies focus mostly on the type of university education achieved and do not examine elected politicians but high-level economic decision-makers. Dreher et al. (2009) examine the effect of the educational level and background of the heads of government on the adoption of market-liberalizing reforms and find that, in some specifications, educated heads of government are more likely to initiate such reforms. Our main hypothesis is thus that governments led by educated politicians implement more conservative fiscal policies.

Testing this hypothesis poses an important identification challenge because of the correlation between the education of the population, of politicians, and of municipal- and party-level characteristics. Our research attempts to disentangle the effect of educated governments using a quasi-experimental regression discontinuity design focusing on municipal elections in Spain.

INSTITUTIONAL BACKGROUND AND DATA

To examine the impact of education on government performance and fiscal policies, it is crucial to understand the constraints faced by politicians in a particular context. As our empirical analyses are focused on Spanish local governments, in this section we describe their main features with emphasis on how the members of the city council are elected, the structure of local public finances, and the capacity of local politicians to influence fiscal policy. We also discuss the data used to test the hypotheses and the construction of our main variables.

Spanish Local Elections

Spain has a decentralized political system with elected governments at the national, regional, and municipal level. Since 1979, citizens elect local councils every four years in about 8,000 municipalities, but our analysis only includes municipalities with more than 1,000 inhabitants.[4] Depending on their size, municipalities elect nine councilors or more using a closed party list proportional representation system (PR). In the first meeting, the local council elects a mayor, which is usually the first candidate of the party list with the most votes. The city council is the main decision-making body during the legislature and is responsible for approving the budget, tax codes, laws, regulations, and zoning.

Spanish local governments have considerable influence on the well-being of citizens. By law, municipalities are required to provide a number of services such as waste collection, street cleaning, public lightning, sewerage, and roads pavement. In addition, larger municipalities must provide other services depending on their size. They can also provide additional goods and services

---

[4] Data on several key variables are missing in municipalities with less than 1,000 inhabitants.

on a voluntary basis. Municipalities manage about 14 percent of total public expenditure. This figure is similar to countries like Belgium, Austria, Portugal, or Germany. They are, however, an important employer at 647,000 employees in 2015 according to the Ministry of Territorial Policy and Administration. Section S1.1 in the supporting information complements this description with further details about Spanish electoral law.

Local Public Finances

The revenues of local governments come from own resources and transfers from other levels of government. Municipalities can levy a number of taxes and fees, and receive fixed shares of the revenues of indirect taxes and the income tax. In 2009, taxes and fees amounted to 43 percent of total revenues. Current transfers amounted to 27 percent of revenues, with the main grant being the revenue-sharing grant transferred by the central government using a fixed formula based on population size and other parameters. Most other grants, including European grants, are earmarked for specific purposes. Regarding expenditures, the bulk of local expenditure (84 percent) was approximately equally distributed between three categories: personnel (29.4 percent), current goods and services (28.3 percent), and real investment (26.9 percent). The empirical analyses focus mostly on the largest categories.

As in other countries, the discretion that local governments have over expenditures is greater than their capacity to raise revenues. Municipalities have a limited capacity to issue debt and can mostly influence revenues by raising or reducing local taxes and by attracting grants.[5]

DATA: POLITICIANS, PERFORMANCE, AND FISCAL POLICY

Our analyses draw on an original dataset with individual-level information about the characteristics of local councilors elected in Spain in 2003 and 2007. Municipalities collect the data and send it to the Spanish Ministry of Finance (Ministerio de Hacienda y Administraciones Publicas), which granted the authors access. The dataset details the education, gender, age, and occupation of local council members.[6] Our dataset contains information on around

---

[5] Specifically, they can set tax rates for some direct local taxes, with the most important being the property tax. In contrast to formula-based current transfers, municipalities can attract capital transfers, which are largely distributed at the discretion of the granter government. Hence, local politicians can mostly influence total revenues by setting taxes and fees, and attracting revenues from capital transfers.

[6] Unfortunately, the occupational data contain many missing values and we do not use it in the main analyses. We provide some descriptive analyses in the supporting information. More-educated politicians typically have backgrounds in professional occupations such as law, health, or education. Less-educated politicians often have industrial or agricultural occupations, hence supporting our claim that education is associated with different material interests and socialization experiences.

1,200 municipalities with more than 1,000 inhabitants for two terms of office (2003–2007 and 2007–2010). This coincides with a broadly expansionary economic cycle during the Spanish housing boom which lasted approximately until 2008, which was then followed by a deep economic crisis.

In our dataset, as expected, highly educated citizens are overrepresented among politicians. On average, the education of local councilors in our sample is thirteen years with a standard deviation of 2.42. The level of education of mayors is slightly higher at fourteen years. This is significantly higher than the education of the Spanish adult population, which according to the census is less than ten years on average.[7]

We complement the dataset about the individual characteristics of local politicians with extensive municipal-level information on electoral results, performance outcomes, and fiscal data. The share of votes for the different parties is obtained from the Spanish Ministry of Home Affairs (Ministerio del Interior), which also provides data about population size, the number of registered voters, and the party of the mayor. We collect a variety of performance indicators to test whether educated mayors perform better,[8] suggesting that they have higher "quality."

We view unemployment as an important indicator of economic performance. Although unemployment is not directly affected by municipalities, they can create jobs through public hiring or stimulating the local economy. Another performance indicator is population growth, which may be a proxy for the attractiveness of the municipality. We use deficit per capita as an additional measure of performance, although we acknowledge that this is debatable given that municipalities could use deficit to counteract economic cycles. Our next indicator of quality is the share of the vote for the incumbent party at the next election. Finally, we calculate the deviation between the budget approved for a given year (forecasted) and the actual amount spent in that year. This measures the ability of governments to administer their budgets as they intend to.

For our analyses about the effect of education on fiscal policies, we gather data from the annual budgets (*liquidaciones*) provided by Spanish municipalities and collected by the Ministry of Finance (Ministerio de Hacienda y Administraciones Publicas). We focus on the most important categories, these are total nonfinancial revenues and expenditures per capita and their main categories: capital transfers, current transfers, taxes and fees, capital spending, and spending on current goods and personnel.

Each observation in our dataset represents one municipality during a mayoral term. Compared to the original sample, our final sample is reduced

---

[7] The supporting information describes the evolution of the average years of education of politicians and the population aged 25 or older since 1979. Over the whole period, politicians are consistently more educated than the population, and the gap is stable over time.

[8] In 2012, a new law was passed which forced municipalities to balance budgets and curtailed the ability of governments to influence outcomes through fiscal policy. Moreover, the categories of reported fiscal data changed, making longer series not comparable. Hence, we limit our analyses to the prereform period.

significantly for several reasons. First, we exclude all municipalities with less than 1,000 inhabitants because, as mentioned, many variables are not available for these municipalities. We also exclude places where the mayor is not among winner and runner-up (2 percent) and where both the winner and runner-up have a university degree.

EMPIRICAL STRATEGY

As educated politicians are not randomly assigned to municipalities, many time-invariant and time-varying unobservable factors can be correlated with both the education of mayors and economic outcomes. For example, changes in voter preferences or in the composition of the population may influence both demand for different fiscal policies and for more-educated politicians. Thus, empirical approaches such as fixed-effects models are unable to establish causal links. To overcome concerns about endogeneity, we employ a Regression Discontinuity (RD) design to estimate the effect of the education of mayors on government performance and fiscal policies in Spanish municipalities. The intuition of the RD design is that municipalities where the party with the most educated candidate wins are very similar to municipalities where the most educated candidate lost (i.e., the latter are a good control group for the former). At the limit, the outcomes of these elections can be treated as random, which allows obtaining quasi-experimental estimates of the effects of interest.

We focus on municipalities in which the two parties with the highest and second highest number of seats (usually the main government and opposition parties) vary in the university attainment of their leading candidates. That is, we include only municipalities where one of the two main candidates had a university degree, while the other did not have it. To construct our forcing variable, we calculate the vote margin (vit) of the party with a university-educated candidate as the percentage of votes this party needs to win (lose) to become the winner (the runner-up) in terms of seats.

The RD approach has been mostly applied to majoritarian electoral systems such as the United States. By contrast, Spain has a PR system in which the party that wins an election may not be in government if it has less than 50 percent of seats and other parties can form a coalition with a majority of seats. In about 94 percent of municipalities in our sample, the mayor belongs to the winning party. We follow Curto-Grau, Sole-Olle, and Sorribas-Navarro (2018) and Folke (2014) and implement a fuzzy set regression discontinuity design adapted to PR systems.

More formally, we estimate the following equations:

$$u_{it} = \beta_1 d_{it} + f\left(v_{it}\right) + \eta_t + \epsilon_{it} \tag{1}$$

$$y_{it} = \alpha_1 u_{it} + g\left(v_{it}\right) + \eta_t + \upsilon_{it} \tag{2}$$

where u_{it} equals 1 if the mayor in municipality i at time t has a university degree. The variable y_{it} refers to the outcomes of interest in fiscal year t. Our forcing variable – the margin of victory of the candidate with a university degree – is represented by v_{it} and we construct a dummy variable d_{it} that equals 1 if this margin is positive and 0 if it is negative. The margin of victory is based on the outcomes of the most recent election.[9] The function $f(v_{it})$ is a function of the forcing variable fitted on each side of the threshold.

We report estimates using local linear regressions and a data-driven optimal bandwidth as per Calonico, Cattaneo, and Titiunik (2014a, 2014b). All specifications report cluster standard errors at the municipality level and include time and region fixed effects as Spain presents significant regional heterogeneity in political and economic characteristics. The coefficient of interest, $\alpha 1$, is the Local Average Treatment Effect (LATE), which is a robust estimate of the causal effect for observations near the threshold.

VALIDATION OF THE RD STRATEGY

The validity of the RD estimates relies on the assumption that the forcing variable, in this case the margin of victory of the party with a university-educated candidate, is not manipulated by political parties. When the margin of victory is very narrow, winning or losing the election should be a random event not influenced by electoral fraud. To check this assumption, we use the manipulation test proposed by Calonico, Cattaneo and Titiunik (2015). Figure 7.1 shows that, at the threshold, the density of the forcing variable is not discontinuous. This means that when candidates of different education levels compete in a close election, neither the more-educated nor the less-educated candidate has a significantly higher likelihood of winning.

In Table 7.1, we test for the presence of discontinuities for key political and socioeconomic variables. We find discontinuities in the mayors' gender. This reflects the fact that female candidates tend to be better educated than male candidates. To address concerns that differences in the gender of mayors might affect our results, we control for this variable on both sides of the threshold in the main analyses. We also find a discontinuity in the percentage of retired citizens living in the municipality and control for this in the analyses.

In addition, the descriptive analyses provide information about the education of the politicians involved in the mayoral races. Almost 46 percent of mayors have a university education and the figure is very similar for politicians who ended up in the second position.

Additional analyses show that in 49 percent of municipalities, the percentage of local government politicians educated in university is higher than

---

[9] Recall that the budget of a specific fiscal year, *t*, is approved in *t-1*. This means that officials elected in 2003 are responsible for the budgets of fiscal years 2004, 2005, 2006, and 2007 and those elected in 2007 set the budgets of fiscal years 2008, 2009, 2010, and 2011.

TABLE 7.1 *Discontinuities in political and socioeconomic covariates*

	Coef.	SE
Female mayor	0.273[*]	(0.111)
Mayor's age	4.624	(2.695)
Party alignment with regional government	0.176	(0.152)
Party alignment with central government	0.208	(0.157)
Party alignment with provincial government	0.085	(0.153)
Left-wing mayor	0.182	(0.152)
Majority government	0.082	(0.159)
Mayor is manager	−0.152	(0.122)
Turnout	−0.020	(0.031)
Initial debt per capita	−24.99	(15.66)
Population	7.338	(4.963)
Density	731.0	(474.7)
% Population <14	1.068	(0.995)
% Population >65	−4.716[*]	(2.107)
Income	−0.063	(0.0474)
Weight of tertiary sector	4.074	(4.355)
% Foreigners (EU)	0.0773	(0.658)
% Foreigners (non-EU)	−0.955	(0.118)
% College education	−1.150	(2.631)

Note: [*]$p < 0.1$.

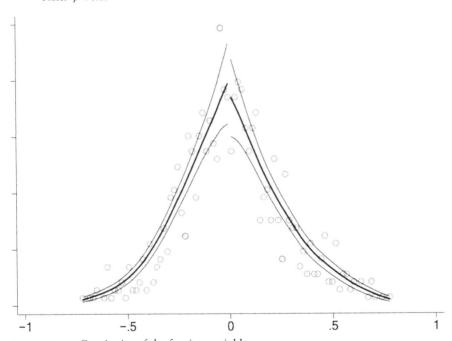

FIGURE 7.1 Continuity of the forcing variable
Note: Density plot of the forcing variable computed with rddensity Stata program.

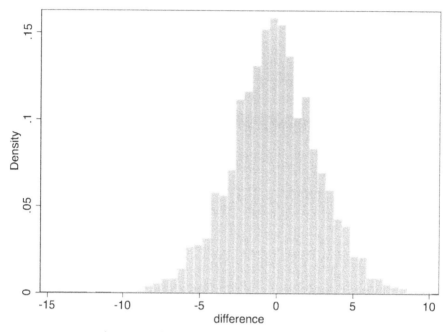

FIGURE 7.2 Distribution of difference in average years of education of government and opposition members

the percentage of local opposition politicians educated in university. This finding suggests that mayoral races are on average balanced in terms of the education of politicians who win or lose the election (i.e., it is not the case that more-educated politicians managed to win close races at a higher than expected rate). This finding is confirmed when we look at an alternative indicator, the average years of education of government (thirteen years) and opposition members (13.2 years). Although the average is close to zero, Figure 7.2 shows that there is sizeable variability in the education levels of government and opposition members in individual races. On average, government members have 0.17 fewer years of education on average than opposition members (the mean difference is negative), but the standard deviation is 2.9 years, suggesting significant variation across municipalities.

RESULTS

In the empirical analyses, we first examine if educated politicians perform better in office using a variety of indicators. After showing that this is not the case, we present the main empirical analyses which test the hypothesis that the educated governments choose more conservative policies with extensive data on local finances.

TABLE 7.2 *Effect of mayors with university degrees on performance outcomes*

	Unemployment rate	Population growth	Incumbent vote at t+1	Deviation from exp. budget	Primary deficit pc
Education	0.357	−0.215	−0.646	−1.148	2.163
	(0.194)[*]	(0.634)	(1.003)	(1.296)	(5.526)
Bandwidth	0.185	0.190	0.158	0.168	0.173
Mean outcome	8.29	4.99	−1.40	1.38	−5.47

Notes: Standard errors clustered at the municipality level in parentheses, $^*p < 0.1$, $^{**}p < 0.05$, $^{***}p < 0.01$. All RD estimates are obtained by local linear regression and optimal bandwidth as per Calonico, Cattaneo, and Titiunik (2014a). All specifications include time and region fixed effects. Unemployment growth = percentage change in unemployed people (as a share of working-age population) between the first and last year of the legislature. Primary deficit and total expenditures (columns 3 and 4) are expressed in euros per capita. Deviation from exp. budget = percentage difference between the actual expenditure budget and its initial forecast approved by the local government.

Education and Government Performance

This section provides evidence about the causal effect of education on several performance indicators. To start, in column 1 of Table 7.2, we regress unemployment rates on the level of education of the government and find that electing mayors with a university degree leads to an increase of 0.36 percentage points in local unemployment rates, a 4 percent increase in unemployment. As discussed earlier, given the characteristics of the Spanish economy, we regard unemployment as a particularly important indicator of performance. Educated politicians perform worse in this respect.

We also test whether the government's education affects population growth, which can signal quality if people are attracted to municipalities with a better provision of public goods and services. In column 2 of Table 7.2, we present the estimates of regressing municipal population growth from the start to the end of four-year electoral terms (hence the smaller number of observations) on the average education level of the government and find no statistically significant effect. Balanced budgets can also be regarded as indicators of good government performance, although deficit and surplus can also be a counter-cyclical fiscal policy used by governments. In column 3, we show the results of regressing the level of primary deficit per capita on the level of education. There is no evidence that more educated governments run smaller deficits.

Another indicator of government performance is the vote share of the incumbent in the next election. Voters should reward good governments such that the vote share of a well-performing incumbent party should be higher than the average incumbent. We test this hypothesis in column 4 and find that more-educated politicians do not perform better. Lastly, we examine whether more-educated governments are better at forecasting the spending needs of the municipality and able to stick to their own proposed budget. We construct a variable that measures the percentage difference between the actual expenditures and their initial forecast approved by the local government at the start of the fiscal year. The estimates in column 5 show that the education of the government has no statistically significant effect on this indicator.

The Effect of Education on Fiscal Policies

This section analyzes if the education of politicians affects the choice of fiscal policies. Table 7.3 presents LATE estimates using key spending and revenue categories of the local budget as dependent variables. We focus on the largest budget chapters, as discussed earlier. Except for current revenues, local governments have considerable discretion to influence these chapters.

The results indicate that more-educated mayors reduce expenditures and revenues per capita. Mayors with university degrees decrease total spending per capita by 36 euros (3.8 percent lower expenditures) and total revenues per capita by 32 euros (3.3 percent less funds). The negative effect of mayors' education on local public spending is driven by lower capital spending, while the effect on current spending (expenditures on both personnel and current goods) is statistically insignificant. We find that electing a university-educated mayor decreases capital expenditures by 35 euros per capita (11 percent lower investment, on average). With regards to revenues, only capital transfers are affected by the education of mayors. University-educated mayors decrease capital transfers by13 euros per capita (7 percent). Given that capital transfers are used to finance public investment, the negative effect we observe can be attributed to lower capital spending. Although we

TABLE 7.3 *Effect of mayors with university degrees on fiscal outcomes*

Variable	Coef.	SE	Mean outcome
Nonfinancial expenditures	−36.114	$(12.493)^{***}$	949.98
Personnel spending	−5.57	(4.94)	290.48
Goods and services spending	−8.52	(5.24)	281.77
Capital spending	−15.71	$(7.18)^{**}$	288.59
Nonfinancial revenues	−32.41	$(11.67)^{***}$	965.24
Current transfers	−6.23	(5.18)	289.69
Capital transfers	−12.60	$(5.41)^{**}$	180.86
Taxes and fees	−8.85	(8.94)	410.23

Notes: Standard errors clustered at the municipality level in parentheses, $^{*}p < 0.1$, $^{**}p < 0.05$, $^{***}p < 0.01$. All RD estimates are obtained by local linear regression and optimal bandwidth as per Calonico, Cattaneo, and Titiunik (2014a). All specifications include time and region fixed effects. The dependent variables are expressed in euros per capita and the figures represent averages over the four-year term of office.

cannot demonstrate that increased investment reduces unemployment, this is a plausible possibility. By contrast, our results suggest that it is unlikely that less-educated mayors reduce unemployment by increased public hiring, a classical clientelistic strategy.

These analyses suggest that better educated governments are more fiscally conservative, in the sense that they prefer smaller governments than less-educated politicians. Lower total revenues and expenditure are driven by the fact that educated governments invest less and receive lower capital transfers. To shed some light on the areas to which this increased investment may be going, the next section examines spending by "functional" area. This is also informative about the revealed policy priorities of politicians.

The Effect of Education on Key Revenue Categories

Besides capital transfers, city councils can influence some other revenue categories, the most important being revenues from fees and direct taxes. In Table 7.4, we present the RD estimates of the effect of the education of governments on those categories. In contrast to capital transfers, we do not find any effect on the other revenue categories at conventional significance levels.

To investigate the influence of education on taxation, we narrow the analysis to the taxes on which city councils have most discretion: the urban and rural property tax. The coefficients are positive, but they are insignificant and the magnitudes are very small. Thus, it is unlikely that the education of governments influences tax revenues to a large extent.

The findings about taxes and fees are relevant because they once more disconfirm the claim that less-educated governments have a lower quality. We found earlier that less-educated governments spend more, but these analyses suggest that they are not incurring more deficit nor are they increasing fiscal pressure. Hence, their higher spending is not financed through strategies that could be detrimental

TABLE 7.4 *Effect of mayors with university degrees on key revenue categories and tax rates*

	Coef.	SE	Bandw.	N	Mean outcome
Revenues from: Fees	8.587	(9.373)	0.13	1,016	177.57
Direct taxes	−19.258	(21.388)	0.17	1,262	250.63
Tax rates: Urban property tax	0.006	(0.008)	0.13	1,169	1.38
Rural property tax	0.009	(0.011)	0.16	1,208	0.65

Notes: Standard errors clustered at the municipality level in parentheses. $*p < 0.1$, $**p < 0.05$, $***p < 0.01$. All RD estimates are obtained by local linear regression and optimal bandwidth as per Calonico, Cattaneo, and Titiunik (2014a). All specifications include time and region fixed effects.

in the long term. Rather, it seems that less-educated governments finance higher spending by attracting capital transfers from other administrations.

Effects on Spending Areas

Our dataset provides information about how total spending is distributed across policy areas. These functional data are rare and valuable, but much noisier than the data about types of spending presented earlier. First, many municipalities do not report this data, leading to a higher number of missing values. Second, the classification of budget items to policy areas is often subjective and the internal organization of areas in policy departments varies substantially across municipalities, leading to more measurement error.

In 2009, two out of eight investment items, production of public and social goods and production of economic goods absorbed 87.4 percent of local capital expenditures and 62 percent of total spending. The most important areas in budgetary terms are housing, community welfare (including waste and water management), culture, and basic infrastructure. By contrast, spending on areas such as health and education is low because municipalities only have residual powers on these policy areas.

Table 7.5 presents the findings regarding the effect of the education of mayors on total expenditures (including capital spending and other types of

TABLE 7.5 *Effect of governments' education on key areas*

Expenditure by function	Coef.	SE	Mean outcome
Production of public and social goods	1.216	(0.746)	47.02
Health	0.189	(0.245)	1.68
Education	0.209	(0.178)	3.87
Housing and urban planning	0.558	(0.532)	14.14
Community welfare	0.034	(0.313)	10.87
Culture	0.218	(0.314)	13.00
Other social and community services	−0.081	(0.270)	3.63
Production of economic goods	−1.008	(0.497)**	10.96
Basic infrastructure and transportation	−0.890	(0.481)*	9.91
Communications	0.019	(0.018)	0.13
Agrarian infrastructure	−0.115	(0.060)*	0.63
Research	0.019	(0.014)	0.034
Basic information and statistics	−0.031	(0.031)	0.15

Notes: Standard errors clustered at the municipality level in parentheses, $*p < 0.1$, $**p < 0.05$, $***p < 0.01$. All RD estimates are obtained by local linear regression and optimal bandwidth as per Calonico, Cattaneo, and Titiunik (2014a). All specifications include time and region fixed effects. The control variables included in all regressions are: % female government members, mayor's education, average years of education of the opposition members, and a binary variable for left-wing mayors. Revenues from fees and direct taxes are measured in euros per capita.

spending) in the two main functional categories and their corresponding sub-categories. For each expenditure area and each year, we compute the share of total expenditures allocated to that function. Following previous work (e.g., Gerber and Hopkins 2011), we use this measure because it reflects policy preferences better than per capita spending. The results indicate that electing a mayor with a university degree decreases spending on basic infrastructure, transportation, and agrarian infrastructure. These results are also important. Basic infrastructure and transportation projects may be one of the targets of the increased investment we detected in previous analyses. This again is consistent with our interpretation that less-educated politicians adopt more Keynesian policies.

ROBUSTNESS CHECKS

Placebo Tests

We conduct a series of placebo tests in order to increase confidence in the validity of our findings. The most relevant test is to examine the effect of the education of mayors on dependent variables lagged one period.[10] The estimates presented in Table 7.6 show that the education of mayors elected in certain year does not have any statistically significant effect on fiscal outcomes of the previous term as politicians do not have the capacity to influence such outcomes. This increases our confidence that the results presented in this chapter are not due to chance.

The results confirm that the education of governments has no statistically significant effect either on the revenues obtained through direct taxation or on financial expenditures.

Who Is Driving These Results?

We examine whether the effects of the education of mayors on economic outcomes and fiscal policy differ for left- and right-wing governments. To estimate heterogeneous local average treatment effects (HLATE), we interact the explanatory variable of interest (university-educated mayor) with a dummy variable that equals one if the mayor is left-wing (Left). Table 7.7 shows these results. The estimates suggest that the role of education in affecting nonfinancial and current expenditures does not differ significantly for left- and right-wing governments, although we note that all interaction coefficients are negative. Columns 3 shows that the preference of left-wing governments for more capital spending is lower when the mayor is more educated. Specifically, electing a mayor with a university degree reduces the

---

[10] Electing a mayor with a university degree in 2003 is regressed on fiscal outcomes between 2000 and 2003, and in 2007 it is regressed on fiscal outcomes between 2004 and 2007.

TABLE 7.6 *Effect of mayors with university degrees on lagged fiscal outcomes*

Variable	Coef.	SE
Total expenditures	–15.50	(17.22)
Personnel spending	1.63	(5.70)
Goods and services spending	–4.61	(6.43)
Capital spending	–14.09	(11.25)
Total revenues	–19.16	(17.44)
Capital transfers	–1.47	(8.36)
Current transfers	2.02	(6.24)
Financial revenues	–3.33	(3.94)
Taxes and fees	–13.74	(12.09)

Notes: Standard errors clustered at the municipality level in parentheses, $^*p < 0.1$, $^{**}p < 0.05$ $^{***}p < 0.01$. All RD estimates are obtained by local linear regression and optimal bandwidth as per Calonico, Cattaneo, and Titiunik (2014a). All specifications include time and region fixed effects. The dependent variables are expressed in euros per capita with one period lag (i.e., the education of governments during term t is regressed on fiscal outcomes of the previous term that this government cannot influence).

TABLE 7.7 *Heterogeneous effects of governments' education: left- and right-wing parties*

	Nonfinancial expend.	Current expend.	Capital expend.	Nonfinancial rev.	Capital rev.
Education	–49.448	–6.133	–14.082	–23.048	14.859
	(60.023)	(20.223)	(30.701)	(51.658)	(23.560)
Left	610.845	9.510	478.887	441.623**	251.832
	(367.438)*	(136.194)	(197.334)**	(316.019)*	(138.052)*
Education × Left	–44.466	–1.204	–35.293	–41.615	–17.577
	(27.785)	(10.359)	(15.070)**	(23.860)*	(10.486)*

Notes: Standard errors clustered at the municipality level in parentheses, $^*p < 0.1$, $^{**}p < 0.05$, $^{***}p < 0.01$. All RD estimates are obtained by local linear regression and optimal bandwidth as per Calonico, Cattaneo, and Titiunik (2014a). All specifications include time and region fixed effects.

large effect of having a left-wing government on spending by 35 euros per capita. The interaction term Education × Left is also significant for nonfinancial and capital expenditures and indicates that the effect of having a left-wing mayor on revenues is decreased by 42 euros per capita when the mayor has a university degree. All in all, the results suggest that highly educated left-wing mayors choose more fiscally conservative fiscal policies.

While these results are suggestive, the reasons why they are driven by left-wing parties are unclear. One possibility is that the pathways to political office are different for individuals in left-wing parties with high or low levels of education. Traditional working-class organizations, such as trade unions or other organization, such as agrarian cooperatives, may affect the political preferences and policy priorities of less-educated politicians (making them more likely to embrace what we label "Keynesian" policies) and also be ways in which individuals are recruited and helped to achieve a runner-up position in mayoral races. While this is an interesting possibility, other data would be needed to explore it.

CONCLUSION

Some scholars believe that educated citizens are more capable political leaders (Dal Bó and Finan 2018). Recent empirical research echoes this elitist view and uses education as a proxy measure of leader quality. Using a detailed dataset about performance outcomes and fiscal policies at the local level, we find that highly educated leaders do not perform better on a variety of indicators. Instead, we find evidence supporting the claim that more educated politicians implement more fiscally conservative policies, both raising less revenue and spending less money. Our database allows us to pin down some aspects of how the actions of more- and less-educated politicians differ. We find that less-educated governments are more expansionary, in the sense that they increase both revenues and spending, but we do not find that they use strategies that may be harmful in the long run. These results suggest that education should not be used as a proxy of leader quality.

Our substantive findings have broad-ranging implications. In sharp contrast to gender or ethnicity, the descriptive representation of less-educated citizens has worsened over time in lockstep with the declining influence of trade unions. Our analyses suggest that the secular decline in the share of less educated politicians within left-wing parties can shift the policies of these parties in a more conservative economic direction (see also O'Grady 2019). The result could be a mismatch between the preferences of the party leadership and their constituencies, leaving the door open for political entrepreneurs to appeal to the traditional supporters of the left. While we cannot provide direct evidence about the political consequences of the changing composition of politicians, it is noteworthy that the ongoing realignment in advanced industrial democracies (Beramendi et al. 2015) is driven in part by changes in how more- and less-educated citizens vote. It is plausible that the increasingly elitist educational makeup of politicians is one reason, among others, why the traditional constituencies of center-Left parties feel disconnected from mainstream parties and search for alternatives such as populist parties.

Our results are also relevant for research about the unequal responsiveness of politicians to the preferences of affluent citizens (Bartels 2016; Giger,

Rosset, and Bernauer 2012; Gilens and Page 2014). A well-known finding is that when the preferences of citizens with a high or low socioeconomic background differ, politicians are more responsive to the preferences of the rich. The mechanisms that generate unequal responsiveness are largely unexplored, though (see Becher and Stegmueller, this volume). One possible mechanism suggested by our findings is the similarity in educational backgrounds between privileged citizens and elites. If educated citizens and elites share preferences and worldviews, it is unsurprising that when the preferences of the public diverge, elites side with people who are descriptively like them.

To be sure, our empirical analysis has limitations. We cannot tease out the relative effect of education, income, and occupation. An important follow-up question is if different types of education and degrees affect preferences in different ways. For instance, the share of lawyers, engineers, or economists in governments may have different effects on policies. Our work focuses on local elections in Spain in a specific time period and further research should establish if the results hold in other political arenas, geographic contexts, and time periods. Although we scrutinize a wide range of outcome measures, we lack some relevant measures of performance such as economic growth, which is not measured at the local level, or corruption. As is well known, RD estimates are internally valid, but they may not apply to contexts in which the margin of victory was not close.

Despite these limitations, the results of our analyses support the view that the education of who is in government affects fiscal policies. According to Hanna Pitkin, having representatives with a similar distribution of politically relevant characteristics as the represented population is important not on its own sake but mainly because we "tend to assume that people's characteristics are a guide to the actions they will take" Pitkin (1967: 89). Our results show that education does guide the actions of politicians and suggest that increasing the substantive representation of these disadvantaged citizens would change fiscal policies and make them less conservative.

8

Working-Class Officeholding in the OECD[*]

Nicholas Carnes and Noam Lupu

Working-class citizens – people employed in manual labor, service industry, clerical, informal sector, and labor union jobs – rarely go on to hold elected office in the world's democracies. Whereas workers typically make up majorities of most countries' labor markets,[1] people who had working-class jobs when they got into politics rarely go on to hold more than 5 percent of the seats in most national legislatures (e.g., Best 2007; Best and Cotta 2000; Carnes and Lupu 2015; 2023b; Joshi 2015; Warburton et al. 2021).

These kinds of inequalities in the social class makeup of governments can have important consequences for public policy.[2] Politicians from the working class – like working-class citizens in most democracies – are more likely than other legislators to have proworker or leftist views about economic issues, preferring state intervention into the economy and a robust social safety net, and they tend to behave accordingly in office, at least to the extent that they have some personal discretion in their official decisions. These differences in politicians' attitudes and choices – coupled with the sharp numerical underrepresentation of leaders from the working class – seem to tilt policy outcomes in favor of the more rightist preferences of white-collar professionals on economic issues (Alexiadou 2020; Borwein 2021; Carnes 2013; 2018; Carnes and Lupu 2015; Curto-Grau and Gallego, this volume; Hemingway 2020, 2022; O'Grady 2019).[3] This may help

[*] For their comments and advice, we are grateful to Larry Bartels, Aina Gallego, Davy-Kim Lascombes, Jonas Pontusson, Kris-Stella Trump, the other contributors to this volume, and seminar participants at the University of Geneva.
[1] For the sake of variety, we sometimes refer to working-class people simply as workers.
[2] Where worker representation is lower, moreover, democratic institutions are perceived as less legitimate (Barnes and Saxton 2019), and political systems that exclude less-affluent citizens may be less racially and ethnically diverse as well (Bueno and Dunning 2017).
[3] This phenomenon is not confined to working-class politicians; numerous studies have found evidence that other occupational and economic background characteristics of politicians predict

to explain why rising inequality in recent decades has not been met with the kind of compensatory redistribution that canonical theories might expect (see Lupu and Pontusson, this volume).[4]

Why, then, are working-class citizens so sharply underrepresented in the world's legislatures? If holding public office can have significant consequences for public policy, it is natural to wonder: *What keeps workers out office?*

As it stands, no one really knows. Some studies have tested hypotheses that might shed light on why so few working-class citizens go on to hold office in the world's democracies. Most have been inconclusive; they have yielded null results, or the associations they have uncovered have stopped far short of accounting for the vast underrepresentation of workers. Moreover, all of the existing studies that might help explain why workers are so badly underrepresented have focused either on small numbers of countries (e.g., Carnes and Lupu 2016a; Hemingway 2020; Joshi 2015; Vivyan et al. 2020) or on just one country at a time (e.g., Carnes 2018; Dal Bó et al. 2017; Griffin, Newman, and Buhr 2019; Matthews and Kerevel 2022; Wüest and Pontusson 2018).

The time seems right for broader cross-national research that explores why so few working-class people go on to hold public office. In that spirit, this chapter takes stock of what scholars know about the causes of working-class officeholding and uses new data on the social class backgrounds of national legislators in the OECD to present initial analyses of several common *country-level* explanations that have never been tested before using data from a large sample of countries.

Our findings suggest that some hypotheses have promise and warrant future research: working-class people more often hold office in countries where labor unions are stronger and income is distributed more equally. However, some common explanations do not pan out in our data – neither Left-party strength nor proportional representation are associated with working-class officeholding. Moreover, the various country-level explanations that scholars have put forward in the past do not take us very far toward a complete explanation of the phenomenon of working-class underrepresentation; they account for at most 30 percent of the gap between the share of workers in the public and in national legislatures.

---

important differences in their choices in office (e.g., Adolph 2013; Fuhrmann 2020; Han and Han 2021; Hansen, Carnes, and Grey 2019; Kallis and Diaz-Serrano 2021; Kirkland 2021; Stacy 2021; Szakonyi 2021). There is a growing consensus – beyond just the literature on *working-class* politicians – that the economic or class backgrounds of politicians can have important consequences for public policy (see Carnes and Lupu 2023b).

[4] Research on the class backgrounds of politicians has largely focused on differences in substantive representation but not congruence per se or responsiveness more generally (see Bartels, this volume; Mathisen et al., this volume). The reason is that in the datasets suitable for studying congruence or policy responsiveness, there have not been enough politicians from working-class occupations to test for differences (e.g., Lupu and Warner 2022a). We know of no study that has been able to test the hypothesis that the shortage of politicians from working-class jobs is responsible for the well-documented inequalities in congruence or policy responsiveness.

Future research would do well, we think, to explore some country-level explanations in more detail, but there may also be limits to what we can learn from country-level analyses. If scholars wish to understand why working-class people so rarely go on to hold office in the world's democracies, it may be helpful to focus comparative analyses on individual- and party-level explanations as well, and to consider the possibility that there are factors common to all democracies that limit working-class officeholding.

UNEQUAL OFFICEHOLDING AND THE WORKING CLASS

Research on the numerical underrepresentation of any social group generally tries to answer two questions: *when* are members of the group screened out of the candidate selection process at disproportionately high rates, and *why* are they screened out at those stages?

The question of when is the more straightforward of the two, since it is essentially a descriptive question. Broadly speaking, the candidate selection process can be thought of as a series of semidiscrete stages (see e.g., Carnes 2018; Fox and Lawless 2005; Lovenduski 2016; Norris and Lovenduski 1995): (1) a person must have the qualifications and abilities that allow someone to run (i.e., they must be what scholars sometimes refer to as *potential candidates*); (2) they must have some intrinsic desire to run or hold office (what scholars call *nascent political ambition*); (3) they must formally declare their candidacy (*expressive ambition*); (4) in many countries, their party must select them and decide how strongly to support them; and, finally, (5) they must win enough votes to take office. Scholars differ in how granular their accounts of this process are, but at bottom, to determine *when* a social group is screened out, researchers simply divide the candidate entry process into stages and then measure the group's representation at each stage in order to determine when, exactly, that group is disproportionately removed from the process of political selection.

The question of *why* social groups are screened out is more complicated. We can generally divide scholars' hypotheses into three categories based on the kinds of political phenomena they study: micro- or individual-level explanations, macro- or polity-level explanations, and meso-level explanations.[5]

Individual- or micro-level explanations posit that groups are screened out because of the attitudes and choices of individual citizens, usually potential

---

[5] The other common framework scholars use for thinking about why a social group might be underrepresented is supply and demand (e.g., Lovenduski 2016; Norris and Lovenduski 1995), which collapses these categories. In this view, a social group will be underrepresented if there is a supply problem, a shortage of qualified candidates from that group (these are primarily individual-level explanations focused on potential candidates), or if there is a demand problem, if others in the candidate entry process discourage that group (these are individual-level explanations focused on voters and party- and country-level explanations).

candidates or voters. This research aims to understand the most immediate reasons why members of a given social group are less interested in running, less capable campaigners, less likely to win votes, and so on. Most scholarship in this category focuses either on the characteristics of potential or actual candidates (Why are qualified women in the United States less interested in running for office? Are attorneys more likely to run because they are better at fundraising?)[6] or on the characteristics and motivations of voters (Do voters see working-class candidates as more relatable?). In either case, the focus is on the attitudes or choices of ordinary citizens and the immediate antecedents to those choices.

Of course, scholars recognize that individual choices and attitudes are driven by larger *macro-level* forces like political institutions or economic and social conditions. Researchers who carry out macro-level studies attempt to determine whether there are features of entire cities, states, or nations that might help explain the shortage of candidates or officeholders from a given social group. The most common explanations focus on things like election rules, unionization rates, and economic conditions; studies in this category often begin by simply examining whether the numerical representation of a social group is associated with the aggregate-level characteristics of entire polities. Whereas an individual-level study will usually focus on one discrete stage of the candidate entry process, macro-level research often focuses broadly on whether the characteristics of a country or state is associated with the rate at which a social group holds office, or perhaps the rate at which members of that social group run.

Some explanations are positioned in between the polity and the individual; the most common of these *meso-level* explanations focus on *political parties*, hypothesizing that party rules or platforms or the attitudes and behaviors of the leaders of formal party organizations help explain the shortage of a social group in the candidate pipeline (e.g., Norris and Lovenduski 1995; Thomsen 2017). Of course, the importance of parties in the candidate entry process varies from country to country, but parties are at least influential – if not the exclusive drivers of – the candidate entry process in virtually every democracy. As such, when many scholars seek to understand why a given social group is underrepresented, they focus on the biases and behaviors of political parties and other large, stable organizations within countries.

These different levels of explanation are not mutually exclusive, of course, or inherently in tension with one another. To the contrary, they are often complementary, differing more in terms of where in the theorized causal process they focus (e.g., individual choices, or the groups and institutions that structure those choices). In any given country, theories at all three levels might be useful: people from a given social group might be reluctant to run because they

---

[6] See, for instance, Fox and Lawless (2005) or Bonica (2020).

worry that they will not receive needed support (an individual-level explanation) because party leaders so rarely recruit or support them, fearing that they will make worse candidates (a meso-level explanation), which in turn happens because fundraising is so important in elections in that country (a macro-level explanation). In most democracies, we would expect the underrepresentation of a social group to be linked to processes that occur at all three levels. When studying the reasons why a social group is numerically underrepresented in public office, all three levels of analysis can help illuminate the obstacles the group faces.

These frameworks for thinking about *when* and *why* a social group is screened out of the political selection process can be used to study any social group in any country. To date, however, there are few studies that use these approaches to shed light on why so few working-class citizens go on to hold office in the world's democracies. Some of the gaps in the literature are simply geographic: there are roughly 120 electoral democracies in the world, but to date, research on working-class officeholding has only been conducted in around twenty of them. More broadly – and more pressing – there simply are not many studies in this literature in the first place.

On the question of when workers are screened out, most existing studies focus on a single country or a single stage of the political selection process. They usually find no evidence that working-class citizens are screened out because of differences in qualifications or nascent ambition: workers seem just as likely as nonworkers to have characteristics that make them attractive potential candidates (Carnes 2016; 2018), and they appear to be just as interested as nonworkers in running for office (Carnes and Lupu 2023a). Numerous studies have also looked at whether working-class candidates perform worse than nonworkers in elections. While some find evidence that workers perform worse (Matthews and Kerevel 2022; Wüest and Pontusson 2018), others find that they perform about as well as – and sometimes better than – nonworkers (Albaugh 2020; Campbell and Cowley 2014; Carnes 2018; Carnes and Lupu 2016b; Griffin, Newman, and Buhr 2019; Kevins 2021; Hemingway 2020; Sadin 2012; Vivyan et al. 2020).[7] Related studies also find that working-class candidates are often evaluated more positively (Carnes and Lupu 2016a; Hoyt and DeShields 2021), especially by working-class voters (Heath 2015).

Even if some of the explanation has to do with the election stage, workers seem to be mostly screened out of the candidate entry pipeline at the *decision to formally run or apply to run*. In England, Norris and Lovenduski (1995, 121)

---

[7] We think part of the explanation for these contradictory findings has to do with the research design. In general, observational studies of election outcomes seem more likely to find evidence that workers are screened out at the election stage, while experimental studies with voters find no such effect. This suggests that it is not that voters are biased against working-class candidates, but that other aspects of the electoral process – campaigning, fundraising, media attention, etc. – may account for the observational result.

find that nonprofessionals (a close approximation to working-class people) were less likely to apply to be candidates for the House of Commons (but no less likely to be selected by the party), and in the United States, Carnes (2018) finds that in state and local elections, working-class people made up over half of the labor force, but less than 5 percent of the people who actually ran for state, county, and local offices (and 3 to 5 percent of the people who won).

Although this body of "when" research points generally to one stage in the candidate pipeline (expressive ambition), there are still many gaps in this literature. So far, the work has been piecemeal, focusing on just one country and just one stage at a time. To our knowledge, no study has ever comprehensively analyzed the candidate pipeline from start to finish in a single country; that is, no study has analyzed a single sample of citizens to check for social class gaps in qualifications, nascent ambition, expressive ambition, party selection, and winning, all in a single, directly comparable group of people. Moreover, almost every published study has focused on just one country; we know of just three that have studied more (Carnes and Lupu 2016a; Hemingway 2020; Kelly 2019). There is still a great deal of room for research that asks the basic descriptive question of when working-class people are screened out of the political selection process.

The research on *when* workers are screened out is still emerging, so naturally, research on *why* they are screened out is scarce and piecemeal as well. We know of just two studies that present positive evidence to support an individual-level explanation about resource constraints (Carnes 2018; Hemingway 2020) and just a few that test party-level explanations (Carnes 2016; 2018; Hemingway 2020; Norris and Lovenduski 1995). Some studies note that certain types of parties appear more likely to recruit working-class candidates (Best and Cotta 2000; Joshi 2015; Matthews and Kerevel 2022; Tarditi and Vittori 2021). In particular, leftist parties typically have less affluent core constituencies (Garrett 1998; Huber and Stephens 2001; Korpi and Palme 2003), so their voters may prefer working-class candidates, or these parties may be more likely to recruit workers as candidates.

The most common explanations focus on the macro level, highlighting four key factors. One such factor is the *strength of labor unions* (Carnes 2016; Feigenbaum, Hertel-Fernandez, and Williamson 2018; Hemingway 2020; Sojourner 2013). Where unions are strong, they may have formal arrangements with certain political parties that make it more likely that workers will get on the ballot (Aylott 2003; Høyer 2015; Norris and Lovenduski 1995). Alternatively, since unions often mobilize votes for leftist parties (e.g., Korpi 1983), they may simply help workers already on leftist party lists get elected just by increasing the vote share of leftist parties.

Another macro explanation has to do with features of the *electoral system* (Carnes 2018; Hemingway 2020; Joshi 2015). For instance, proportional representation (PR) systems are often thought to ensure that a larger proportion of the electorate is represented (e.g., McDonald and Budge 2005), promoting a closer connection between voters and representatives (Bernauer et al. 2015). And PR is also associated with better descriptive representation for other social groups (e.g., Kittilson and Schwindt-Bayer 2010; Schwindt-Bayer and Mishler 2005).

Campaign costs, which vary tremendously across countries, are routinely cited by scholars of US politics as obstacles to working-class candidacy and officeholding (Carnes 2018). Finally, places where *economic resources* are distributed unequally may give more affluent citizens disproportionate political influence (Erikson 2015; Rosset et al. 2013).

To date, however, most studies of macro explanations focus on just one country or, at best, a handful (see Best and Cotta 2000; Hemingway 2020), making it hard to draw general inferences about the global phenomenon of working-class underrepresentation. The time seems right, then, for scholars interested in the shortage of working-class politicians to expand their focus to a broader range of democracies and to delve more deeply into the questions of both when and why working-class people are screened out of the political selection process. There is still a lot of ground to cover here.

As a step in that direction, in this chapter, we ask how working-class officeholding varies with four types of *macro-level forces* that have been cited by scholars in the past as possible drivers of working-class underrepresentation: the strength of Left parties, electoral rules (proportional vs. majoritarian), the costs associated with campaigning (the availability of public financing), and labor market conditions (economic inequality and unionization rates). Using a new dataset, we study the thirty-seven OECD member nations, the largest sample of countries in which these macro-level explanations have been analyzed.

What can we learn from a large cross-national analysis of working-class representation? Can macro-level characteristics like these help explain why so few working-class people hold office in the world's democracies?

WORKING-CLASS OFFICEHOLDING IN THE OECD

To find out, we collected an original dataset with a team of collaborators (Carnes et al. 2021). This dataset includes individual-level information about the last occupation held by each member of the unitary or lower chamber of the national legislature in each of the world's 103 large electoral democracies[8] during one legislative session between 2016 and 2018 – a total of over 20,000 individual legislators.

Like past research on politicians (e.g., Carnes and Lupu 2015; O'Grady 2018) and social class analysis more generally (see Oesch 2013), we focus here on occupations as our measure of social class. Occupational information about politicians is universally observable (unlike income and wealth data),

---

[8] The dataset only includes countries with a population over 300,000 that were electoral democracies, according to Freedom House, as of 2016.

even if the data are not always easy to collect. Moreover, alternative measures like income can vary over a person's life cycle (a construction worker and a PhD student might earn similar annual incomes but belong to very different social classes) and education often does not determine labor market outcomes (e.g., Bill Gates does not have a college degree). And although politicians often discuss their parents' occupations, research on parental occupations is mixed at best; studies of lawmakers find that parental occupations are not associated with legislative conduct (e.g., Carnes 2013; Carnes and Lupu 2015) or only associated under certain conditions (e.g., Grumbach 2015; Pilotti 2015), and studies of ordinary citizens find that for people with similar adult social classes, there is little evidence of a link between the social class of their parents and their adult political views (Barber 1970; Langton 1969). As Manza and Brooks (2008, 204) explain:

> Occupation provides the most plausible basis for thinking about how specifically class-related political micro processes and influences occur.... Workplace settings provide the possibility of talking about politics and forging political identity, and work also provides a springboard for membership in organizations where class politics are engaged: unions, professionals associations, business associations, and so forth.

As such, we focus here on lawmakers who had working-class occupations as adults.[9]

We focus in this chapter on data on the occupational backgrounds of legislators in the thirty-seven OECD member countries. With these data, we can carry out simple tests of several hypotheses about the factors that discourage working-class officeholding using new, accurate, aggregate-level data on national legislatures (which to our knowledge did not previously exist; we know of no prior database that includes complete information about the share of working-class lawmakers in the national legislatures of a large number of democracies).[10]

Figure 8.1 plots the rates at which working-class people held office in these thirty-seven countries. For each country, we plot the percentage of lawmakers who were primarily employed in working-class occupations when they were first elected to public office (darker bars) and the percentage of the country's labor force

---

[9] For a longer discussion of these points, see Carnes (2013) and Carnes and Lupu (2023b). Even if many nonworkers with working-class parents go on to hold public office, it would still leave open the question of why workers themselves do not.

[10] We are not the first to collect occupational data on political leaders, of course. There are publicly available databases that include unstandardized information about national legislators in a handful of countries, but they require tremendous effort to standardize. Other datasets focus on national executives, a population that is interesting, but less closely related to the idea of descriptive representation. Finally, there are datasets on national legislators that include occupational information that is not detailed enough for an analysis of politicians from the working class. None of these are suitable for our purposes; if our goal is to study the rate at which working-class people hold office in the world's national legislatures, we know of no prior dataset that fits the bill.

FIGURE 8.1 Working-class representation in the OECD
Sources: Carnes et al. (2021), International Labor Organization (2020a).

made up of working-class jobs (lighter bars). We define the working class as people who work in manual labor, service industry, clerical, and informal sector jobs, and people who work for unions that represent these kinds of occupations.[11]

---

[11] Appendix 8.B describes in detail the occupations we defined as working class in each dataset we use in this chapter. In general, our approach was to count as working-class jobs those that were coded as ISCO 08 categories 4 (clerical support workers), 5 (service and sales workers), 6 (skilled agricultural, forestry, and fishery workers), 7 (craft and related trades workers), 8 (plant and machine operators and assemblers), and 9 (elementary occupations). Our definition of "working-class" is ultimately quite similar to other popular ways that academics classify occupations. This approach aligns with Kitschelt and Rehm's (2014) description of jobs that entail low dispositional capacities and autonomy. It is also essentially a combination of Oesch's (2006) skilled and unskilled worker categories, or Erikson and Goldthorpe's (1992) categories (3b) routine nonmanual employees,

As the figure illustrates, working-class citizens are vastly numerically under-represented in OECD legislatures. In the average country, working-class jobs make up 56 to 58 percent of the labor force, but former workers make up just 3 to 5 percent of the national legislature, a 53-percentage-point gap in the absolute numerical representation of working-class people in elected institutions.[12] The size of the disparity varies from country to country, of course; it is smallest in Luxembourg, a country that reports below-average rates of working-class jobs in its labor force (due to its exceptionally high rates of employment in white-collar or professional occupations, in particular banking). But even in this best-case scenario of sorts, working-class citizens still make up around four out of every ten employed citizens but just one out of every ten elected legislators, and nonworkers – who we refer to as professionals or white-collar citizens – still make up 90 percent of the legislature, only a little less than what they make up in the average OECD country.

As other studies have argued, the shortage of working-class politicians seems to be essentially orthogonal to the well-documented underrepresentation of women in public office (see also Carnes 2015; 2020). In the individual-level OECD data summarized in Figure 8.1, 4.4 percent of male legislators and 4.9 percent of female legislators came from working-class jobs. If we focus only on the legislators who had working-class occupations, 29.7 percent were women; among nonworkers, 27.2 percent were women. Unfortunately, at this time, we cannot check for racial or ethnic balances with these data.

Does the variation across OECD countries seem to track major macro-level characteristics of countries like Left-party strength, electoral systems, campaign costs, economic inequality, or unionization rates? Do traits like these have the potential to help us understand why so few working-class people hold office in most electoral democracies?

MACRO-LEVEL EXPLANATIONS

Left-Party Strength

Figure 8.2 begins to answer these questions by plotting the representation of working-class people in OECD legislatures (vertical axis) against the rate at which Left parties[13] hold office in the same national legislatures (horizontal

---

lower grade (sales and services); (5) lower-grade technicians; supervisors of manual workers; (6) Skilled manual workers; (7a) semiskilled and unskilled manual workers (not in agriculture, etc.); and (7b) agricultural and other workers in primary production.

[12] Figure 8.A1 in the appendix breaks out people who work for labor union organizations (i.e., not unionized workers, but employees in the labor union organization). There are no obvious patterns that would lead us to question our basic interpretation of Figure 1.

[13] We count as Left parties those that the Comparative Manifestos Project (Volkens et al. 2020) code as left, ecological (green), or social democratic. When a party was not included in the

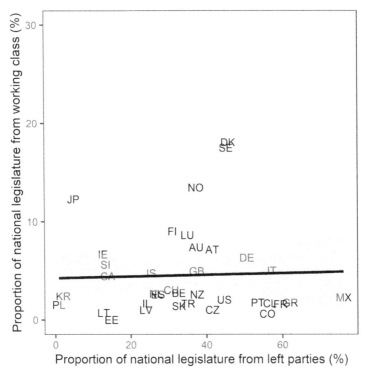

FIGURE 8.2 Left-party representation and worker representation
Sources: Carnes et al. (2021), Comparative Manifestos Project (Volkens et al. 2020).

axis). There is no relationship: workers are no more or less likely to hold office in countries with more Left-leaning national legislatures.

Some patterns seem evident, however, in more fine-grained data on the *types* of Left and Right parties in OECD countries. Among the three leftist party families identified by the Comparative Manifestos Project (ecological, left, and social democratic), the proportion of working-class legislators was 4.3 percent, 6.5 percent, and 6.6 percent, respectively; for the rightist parties, it was 1.7 percent (liberal), 4.3 percent (Christian democratic), 3.1 percent (conservative), 8.1 percent (nationalist), and 4.7 percent (agrarian). In the OECD countries, there is no broad or narrow category of political party in which a large percentage of legislators are drawn from working-class occupations, but the variations here also seem to square with basic intuitions about party families. Left and social democratic party legislators – those from the traditional party families associated with the working

Comparative Manifestos Project, we researched other sources to determine whether it was regarded as a Left or center-left party. Excluding these cases does not change our findings.

classes – are two percentage points more likely to be from working-class occupations than green party legislators, which tend to represent more affluent constituencies. Among the rightist parties, legislators from nationalist parties (many relative political newcomers) are four percentage points more likely to come from working-class occupations, and legislators from liberal parties (the traditional parties of business and capitalism) are three percentage points less likely than others to come from working-class occupations. The differences are modest, but there seems to be a basic logic to the distribution of working-class politicians across party families. These differences do not align with a simple expectation that Left parties will tend to have more working-class politicians, but they suggest that certain party families may be associated with more working-class representation.

Of course, the differences are only marginal; in the OECD countries, the gap between the party families with the most and least working-class legislators in just six percentage points, far smaller than the overall shortage of workers (roughly 53 percentage points). Something beyond simple differences in the party makeup of national legislatures is driving the shortage of working-class legislators.

Electoral Systems

What about electoral systems? Proportional representation systems tend to be associated with greater representation for groups like women and racial or ethnic minorities, and scholars often speculate that PR systems may be more accessible to candidates from the working classes. Pilotti's (2015, 247, emphasis added) research on Sweden found hopeful evidence that "the ratio of elected representatives from working-class *families* increased after the introduction of PR: less than 10% before the constitutional change to about 15–17% after the reform and until the 1970s–1980s" (see also Joshi 2015). Are legislators who had working-class occupations *themselves* better represented in proportional representation systems in the OECD?

Figure 8.3 plots the average representation of working-class people, disaggregating OECD countries by the broad category of electoral system they use (proportional, majoritarian, or mixed) and the narrower electoral rules listed in the V-Dem dataset (Coppedge et al. 2021).[14] In contrast to research on the

---

[14] These are single-transferrable vote multimember districts (STV MMD), list proportional representation systems with large multimember districts (List PR large MMD), list PR systems with small multimember districts (List PR small MMD), compensatory PR systems with single-member districts (Compensatory PR + SMD), parallel proportional representation systems used alongside single-member districts (Parallel PR + SMD), single transferrable vote elections with single-member districts (STV SMD), two-round elections with single-member districts (Two-round SMD), and first-past-the-post elections with single-member districts (FPTP SMD).

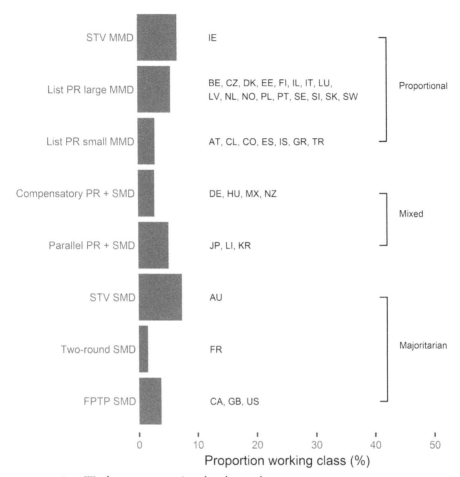

FIGURE 8.3 Worker representation, by electoral system
Sources: Carnes et al. (2021), V-Dem (Coppedge et al. 2021).

representation of other social groups in proportional representation systems, there is no evidence that PR systems tend to have more working-class politicians in their national legislatures (and none of the differences documented in Figure 8.3 are statistically significant). We do not find evidence that the ratio of elected representatives from working-class occupations is higher or lower in proportional or mixed systems relative to countries with majoritarian elections. (Figure 8.A2 in the online appendix reports similar analyses comparing countries by district magnitude and the number of seats in the national legislature.) As far as we can tell, there is nothing about the broad form of national electoral systems that helps account for why so few working-class people hold office in the OECD.

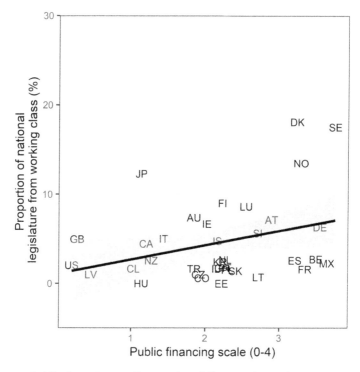

FIGURE 8.4 Public financing predicts modest differences in worker representation
Sources: Carnes et al. (2021), V-Dem (Coppedge et al. 2021).

Public Financing

Public financing, in contrast, is at least weakly associated with working-class officeholding. Figure 8.4 plots our original data on the occupational backgrounds of elected leaders in the OECD against V-Dem's measure of public financing liberalism.[15] In countries where public financing funds a large share of most parties' expenditures (closer to a 4 on the underlying scale), workers hold office slightly more often, although the difference is not statistically significant ($p < 0.06$).

---

[15] Country experts were asked, "Is significant public financing available for parties' and/or candidates' campaigns for national office?" and given these response options: 0: No. Public financing is not available; 1: Little. There is public financing but it is so small or so restricted that it plays a minor role in most parties' campaigns; 2: Ambiguous. There is some public financing available but it is unclear whether it plays a significant role for parties; 3: Partly. Public financing plays a significant role in the campaigns of many parties; and 4: Yes. Public financing funds a significant share of expenditures by all, or nearly all parties. The survey researchers then used a measurement model to create weighted average scores across several expert coders.

Like the differences between the party families with the most and fewest working-class members, the differences between countries with the most and least generous campaign finance systems are modest. Extrapolating from the data in Figure 8.4, workers make up close to 0 percent of the average national legislature in a country with no public financing but only about 6 percent of the national legislature in the average country with the most generous public financing system, still almost 50 percentage points short of a complete explanation for the shortage of working-class politicians in the world's democracies. That is, the campaign finance landscape seems to explain (at most) only a marginal difference in working-class officeholding – far less than a complete explanation for why so few working-class citizens go on to hold office.

Economic Environment

Of the four kinds of macro-level characteristics we examined, the economic characteristics of countries were by far the most strongly associated with working-class officeholding. In Figure 8.5, we focus on three important economic characteristics of the OECD member nations: GDP, economic inequality (measured here as the share of total posttax/transfer income earned by the lowest-income half of the country; results are similar with pretax income), and the country's unionization rate. All three are statistically associated with working-class officeholding, and the differences are substantial: countries with higher GDPs, more egalitarian income distributions, and more heavily unionized labor forces[16] do, in fact, have more working-class people in their national legislatures.

Of course, this kind of analysis – like all the preceding findings – cannot discern the nature of the causal relationships, and in this preliminary study we will not attempt to push the data further than simply documenting these bivariate relationships. It could be that the better economic fortunes of the working classes in these countries cause workers to go on to hold office at higher rates, or it could be that working-class officeholders encourage countries to adopt policies that promote shared prosperity, or both (or neither, if the associations are spurious).

Even if we assume that any of these economic characteristics truly *cause* working-class representation, these kinds of explanations seem to have the potential to take us only part way to an explanation for why so few workers go on to hold office. Increasing GDP from $20,000 to the maximum in this sample, $80,000, is associated with an increase of 10 percentage points, under one fifth of the total gap between working-class representation in the labor forces and national legislatures of these countries. As unionization rates approach 100 percent or bottom 50 percent income shares approach 50 percent, working-class representation

---

[16] This association holds even if we control for Left-party seat share.

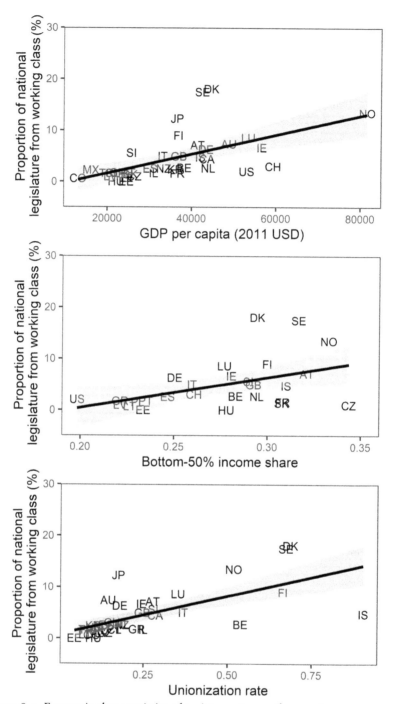

FIGURE 8.5 Economic characteristics of society matter on the margin
Sources: Carnes et al. (2021), International Labor Organization (2020b), V-Dem
(Coppedge et al. 2021), World Inequality Database (Alvarado et al. 2020)

is still projected to be below 20 percent. Even considered in tandem, these three economic variables do not take us far; they are all positively correlated, so if we regress the working class's percentage in the national legislature on all three variables, then predict worker representation setting all variables at their theoretical or observed maximums (100 percent unionization, 50 percent income going to the bottom 50 percent, and $80,000 per capita GDP), the expected share of workers in the national legislature is just 20 percent. That is, together, these variables only seem to explain about 30 percent of the observed gap between workers and politicians, even when we make the heroic assumption that all three are true causes of working-class representation.

Of course, 30 percent is not trivial. These country-level explanations each warrant future research. But there is still far more to the story of why so few working-class people go on to hold office. Perhaps the country-level variables scholars have often discussed interact in important ways: perhaps proportional representation makes more of a difference in countries where elections are also inexpensive, or perhaps Left-party government matters more in states with strong labor unions. And maybe there are country-level variables we have yet to consider. Or, perhaps there are traits that are common across all modern democracies that discourage working-class officeholding.

WHERE SHOULD WE GO NEXT?

Our aim with this simple analysis was not to close the case on why so few working-class people hold office in the world's democracies, but rather to open it in the first place. There has never been broad cross-national research on the question of why so few working-class people go on to hold elected office in the world's democracies. Our analyses suggest that scholars could learn a great deal from comparative studies that analyze large samples of countries. There is meaningful variation across countries (see Figure 8.1) that differs in some promising ways (like the analysis of economic conditions in Figure 8.5) and also that does *not* differ much in ways that defy some ideas scholars have put forward about the factors that might be discouraging working-class people to hold office (like the analyses of Left-party strength, proportional representation, and public financing in Figures 8.2, 8.3, and 8.4). The simple first-cut analysis seems to suggest that some popular scholarly explanations may provide a partial explanation for why workers so rarely hold office (but only a partial one), while others may not ultimately be borne out in the data.

Where does this leave us? There is still a great deal that scholars need to learn about the basic question of *when* in the candidate pipeline working-class people are screened out in most democracies. In almost every democracy in the world, no one actually knows whether working-class citizens are less qualified, less interested in running for office, less likely to run, less likely to be chosen by parties, and/or less likely to win.

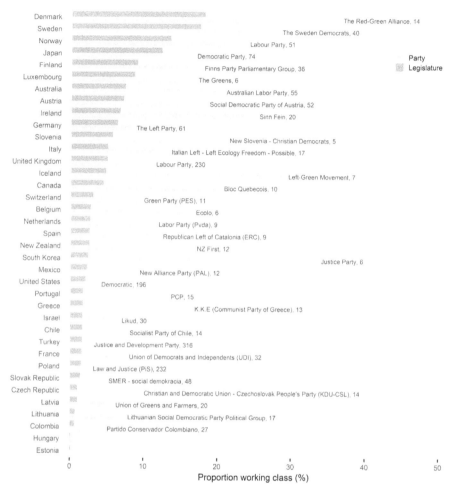

FIGURE 8.6 Worker representation varies more in parties than countries
Note: Bars report the share of working-class lawmakers in the national legislature (darker bars) and in the party with the highest rate of working-class officeholders (excluding parties with fewer than five members; lighter bars), along with the names of parties and the total numbers of legislators they elected.
Source: Carnes et al. (2021).

The results of this first cross-national analysis suggest, moreover, that scholarship on *why* so few working-class people hold office should continue exploring in more detail the country-level factors that discourage working-class officeholding. Here we have looked at just four kinds of variables – there are, of course, many more characteristics of countries that deserve our attention. The variables we studied here also beg for more detailed analyses to determine the extent to which the associations (and nonassociations) we document are causal and generalizable.

The fact that *all* OECD countries have large shortages of working-class officeholders also raises a possibility that transcends even country-level analyses, namely, that perhaps there are universal features of democracies that discourage working-class officeholding. In addition to individual-, meso-, and macro-level analyses, scholars should consider universal-level analyses. Understanding the traits *common to* democracies will almost certainly require more advanced methodologies than the simple cross-sectional comparisons that have been a staple of research on this topic in the past.

Another way forward might be to engage in cross-national analyses of meso-level forces, in particular the role of political parties and interest groups in facilitating or discouraging working-class representation. Figure 8.6 replots the country-level data on working-class officeholding from Figure 8.1. But now we compare the share of working-class lawmakers in each country's national legislature (darker bars) and the share of working-class lawmakers in the political party with the highest rate of worker representation in each country's national legislature (excluding parties with fewer than five delegates; lighter bars).

Viewed this way, it is easy to see that political parties are far more varied in how well-represented working-class citizens are than countries as a whole. These differences do not seem to track neatly onto existing left-right distinctions or party typologies, nor are they confined only to smaller parties. Something else is driving some parties to run large numbers of working-class politicians and others to sidestep workers in favor of white-collar candidates. Understanding these party-level gatekeeping processes – as scholars have sometimes done in individual countries (e.g., Norris and Lovenduski 1995) – should be a high priority.

Above all, the work must simply move forward. As Thomsen (2019, 576) recently put it, "It is rare for scholars to have such an open empirical terrain." Every approach to studying working-class officeholding – descriptive work on when workers are screened out, and micro-, meso-, macro-, and universal-level research on why workers are screened out – is currently in short supply. The empirical terrain is indeed open, and it is high time for cross-national research to move forward.

9

Political Participation and Unequal Representation
Addressing the Endogeneity Problem

Ruben Mathisen and Yvette Peters

Research has demonstrated that public policy in many advanced democracies is biased toward the preferences of affluent and highly educated citizens. They respond little to the interests of the uneducated and poor – or even to those of the average citizen. These findings present a severe challenge for democracy, in which, theoretically, political equality is required. It is thus no surprise that scholars have sought to understand the workings of unequal representation. While there are various mechanisms that could potentially account for these outcomes, including the role of money in politics, descriptive representation, and a supply gap in the party system, we here focus on one complementary mechanism that traditionally has gotten the most attention in the literature: unequal political participation. Political research going back to the early 1970s has argued that systematic inequalities in, for example, who votes, contacts elected officials, demonstrates, and signs petitions, are bound to produce a political system that caters more to citizens who actively voice their opinions. Although the logic of this argument appears sound and much empirical work points to its credibility, scholars have noted a problem of endogeneity. Namely, is responsiveness unequal because of unequal participation, or is participation unequal because of unequal responsiveness? It might very well be that citizens who rarely see their preferences translated to policy are discouraged from participating in politics, and likewise, that citizens who feel that the government is listening to them view participation as effective and meaningful.

Determining the direction of the causal arrow is hard. In this chapter, we make an attempt at estimating the extent to which the reversed causality scenario (unequal representation affecting participation) occurs. Specifically, under the key assumption that unequal representation produces differences in participation mainly through citizens' subjective perceptions of the system, we can calculate to what extent these beliefs account for gaps in participation across income and educational groups. That is, we can estimate to what extent participation gaps are caused by gaps in perceptions on whether the system can offer adequate representation. To this end, we use Oaxaca-Blinder Decomposition to decompose education and income gaps in participation and estimate counterfactually how large these gaps *would have been* if low-educated and poor citizens had the same beliefs about the system as the more-educated and affluent citizens. Using nine different measures of system satisfaction and looking at nine different forms of political participation, we find that the gap in voting between the bottom and top education/income quintile would be around 15 to 20 percent smaller if those groups were equally optimistic about the workings of the system and their possibilities for influence. Gaps in other forms of participation would change even less, or not at all. These results provide some evidence that unequal participation is mainly attributable to other factors than the system being perceived as unequally responsive.

Our chapter proceeds as follows. We first discuss previous findings regarding unequal representation, outlining the various approaches in this research as well as the scope of the problem. We then highlight the main findings regarding participation gaps in many developed democracies, including various forms of political participation. Further, we outline why participation would be expected to affect the representation of preferences before dealing with the potential reversed causality puzzle.

DIFFERENTIAL REPRESENTATION BASED ON INCOME AND EDUCATION

The last fifteen years have seen an increasing number of studies exploring if, and to what degree, rich citizens are better represented politically than the less well-off in modern democratic states. Some of these studies compare public opinion with subsequent changes in public policy. Gilens (2005, 2012) and Gilens and Page (2014), the most extensive studies of the kind (but see Jacobs and Page 2005), estimate the relationship between policy outcomes and the opinions of affluent, middle-class, and poor Americans with a dataset of nearly 2,000 policy issues. They conclude that economic elites have "substantial independent impacts on U.S. government policy," while average citizens "have little or no independent influence" (Gilens and Page 2014, p. 564). Importantly, however, ordinary citizens "often get the policies they favor," but only because they often agree with economic elites, "who wield the actual influence" (576). Some scholars have criticized their methods and conclusions (Bashir 2015; Branham et al. 2017; Elkjær and Iversen, this volume; Enns 2015; Soroka and Wlezien 2008), and the authors have in turn responded to the critiques (Gilens, 2009, respectively; Gilens 2015a, b, 2016; Gilens and Page 2016). Other studies of the United States have demonstrated responsiveness bias in favor of the rich with respect to roll-call voting in Congress (Bartels 2016), specific policies at the state level (Flavin 2012), and the broader policy orientations of the Democratic and Republican parties across the states (Rigby and Wright 2013).

Outside of the United States, single-country studies using more or less the same research design as Gilens (2012) have been undertaken in Germany (Elsässer and Schäfer 2018), the Netherlands (Schakel 2021), Sweden (Persson 2023), Norway (Mathisen 2023), as well as comparatively (Mathisen et al., this volume). All find similar results as Gilens, the only partial exception being Norway, where Mathisen (2023) finds the poor to have some independent influence on economic issues.

Other studies have taken a cross-national approach to unequal responsiveness using more aggregate policy measures, such as spending or the ideological orientation of governments and parties. Peters and Ensink (2015, p. 596) match income-disaggregated support for redistribution with subsequent changes in government social spending for twenty-five European countries. They find that "[l]ower-income groups tend to be under-represented while higher-income groups appear over-represented" and that "low levels of turnout seem to emphasize" this pattern. Bartels (2017) similarly finds what he calls a "social welfare deficit" of 10 to 15 percent in affluent democracies due to government spending being biased in favor of the preferences of the affluent. Examining congruence around the world by matching citizen and elite surveys, Lupu and Warner (2022a) also find that the rich are generally over-represented compared to the poor, specifically on economic issues. Moreover, Giger et al. (2012, p. 57) find that "generally, the poor are represented worse than the rich" in terms of their distance to the nearest party and the government on a left-right scale. However, they observe "considerable variation in the effect" across twenty-one Western democracies. In subsequent work, the authors find that the unequal ideological proximity is smaller in PR systems (Bernauer et al. 2015) and in countries with lower levels of economic inequality (Rosset et al. 2013).

So far, this relatively young empirical literature has produced robust evidence suggesting that rich citizens are substantially better represented politically than the average citizen and the poor in Western states. This finding is strengthened by the wide variety of empirical strategies that scholars have utilized, all leading to similar conclusions. Indeed, Bartels (2017, p. 10) notes that except for his unpublished manuscript on immigration in Europe (Bartels 2017), he has found no study "providing positive evidence of egalitarian responsiveness to the preferences of affluent and poor people." Recent work by Lupu and Warner (2022a), however, does find that the poor are overrepresented on certain cultural issues.

Compared to the work on differential responsiveness based on income, there is little work on the issue with respect to educational differences. Gilens (2012) showed that in the United States, responsiveness does not increase with education the same as he found with income. On the other hand, Schakel (2021) and Mathisen (2022) find that responsiveness is actually more contingent on education than income in the Netherlands and Norway, respectively. Further, an additional study of the Netherlands found that the unequal representation of educational groups extended to both cultural and economic policy issues (Schakel and Van Der Pas 2021). These studies indicate that differential responsiveness is not limited to affluence but extends to educational differences.

UNDERSTANDING DIFFERENTIAL REPRESENTATION

Scholars have identified a range of possible causes for existing political inequality based on income, ranging from an unequal influence of interest groups (Gilens and Page 2014), a supply gap in the policy space covered by political parties (Rosset and Kurella 2021), money in politics (Flavin 2015a), the structural power of business (Young et al. 2018), skewed descriptive representation (Butler 2014; Carnes 2013; Carnes and Lupu 2015), to the way that the media reports economic news (Jacobs et al. 2021). Recently, Lupu and Warner combined different explanations of why some countries experience more affluence-based unequal representation than others and found that economic conditions and good governance are the most important determinants (2022b).

At the same time, scholars of political participation have long argued that the systematic inequality in participation is a main source of unequal representation (e.g., Dalton 2017; Lijphart 1997; Schlozman et al. 2012). We argue that, indeed, unequal political participation is a complementary explanation and likely contributes to unequal representation. Even if the important structural factors would not incentivize politicians to be more responsive to the rich and more educated, politicians would still struggle to represent preferences more equally because poorer and less-educated citizens tend to be less involved in politics. In this section, we provide an overview of the inequalities in participation that previous research has found and present some data to suggest that gaps in participation on the basis of education and income still exist today. Second, we outline the potential mechanisms that would lead unequal participation to cause unequal representation. We consider participation beyond voting alone because, while often less immediately consequential to political careers, other forms of participation emphasize the communication of preferences. Indeed, politicians may learn more about citizen preferences through alternative participation than through voting.

Unequal Political Participation

Democracies need the participation of its citizens in order to function, and because political participation informs governments about the policies that citizens want, citizens should participate in more or less equal ways. Often, however, this is not the case. Research has shown that people with some backgrounds are more likely to be involved than others. In many cases, citizens are not equally likely to engage in active forms of participation. Citizens with more resources, that is, time, money, and skills, are more likely to participate politically than those with fewer resources (see, in particular, Verba and Nie 1972; Verba et al. 1995). For one, citizens need to be able to understand something about politics, both in terms of the contents as well as the participation procedures. Politics can be complex, and not all citizens feel equally capable of participating effectively. Indeed, Gallego (2010) demonstrates that in contexts where voting procedures are easier, and where there are fewer political parties, turnout inequality based on education is reduced. Moreover, with the decline of the welfare state and increasing labor market inequalities (Häusermann, Kemmerling, and Rueda 2020), labor is now also more divided in being either more secure or more fragile. This development affects political preferences but is also likely to affect the available time and energy that some people have. It may, for example, imply that some people work double or even triple jobs in order to earn a sufficient income, leaving these people with little time resources. Labor market inequalities, thus, further emphasize a difference in resources, encouraging unequal participation.

The inequality in resources thus tend to lead to inequalities in participation. In their meta-analysis on the individual determinants of voting, Smets and van Ham (2013) show that most studies find education, income, and social class to be important predictors of voting. It appears that a social-status gap exists in terms of who votes, where higher status individuals are more politically active (Dalton 2017, p. 57) and are thus more likely to communicate their preferences through a vote. These inequalities are not limited to voting, however, but apply to many forms of political participation. Income, education, and citizens' occupation often affect the likelihood of being engaged in contacting, donating money, protesting, and online activism (see, e.g. Dalton 2017; Schlozman et al. 2012). People from a higher social class and with a higher income are also more actively involved in party politics (e.g., Whitely and Seyd 1996).

These types of involvement are important, in part to voice preferences to the political elite, in part to place issues on the political agenda. One important way through which legislators get their information about citizen preferences and the issues that they find important is through contacting (Butler and Dynes 2016; Fenno 1977); and again, not everyone is equally likely to contact politicians. In a clear illustration of such inequality in involvement, a survey among very wealthy Americans showed that these people are politically active through attending meetings, voting, and discussing politics, but are also very active in terms of contacting various politicians (Page et al. 2013). The wealthy Americans tend to have access and be close to public officials, with respondents indicating some form of personal familiarity with members of the political elite.

What is more, while these patterns are often driven by socioeconomic status, they are also reinforced through parental socialization. For instance, research has shown that political interest in part depends on parental socialization (Neundorf et al. 2013) and that conversations about politics in the family directly affect the frequency of participation of the children (Cornejo et al. 2021).

Moreover, Schlozman et al. (2012) show that besides their own level of education and family income, the education of parents and their exposure to politics at home when younger affect the political activity by Americans. This research suggests that persistent socioeconomic inequalities through generations are, to some extent, also accompanied by persistent intergenerational inequalities in political participation.

The overall unequal patterns of participation have raised concerns for the health of democracy (Dalton 2017; Lijphart 1997; Schlozman et al. 2012; Verba et al. 1978). It is important to note, however, that gaps in political participation are not equally large in all countries, and there are even places where the pattern is reversed. Kasara and Suryanarayan (2015) show, for example, that the rich tend to turn out more than the poor in countries where redistribution preferences of the rich and poor diverge more, and where the state has the capacity to tax the rich. In a way, this implies that when the rich do not see a credible threat to their wealth, they also tend to participate less. Moreover, Amat and Beramendi (2020) show that the poor tend to turn out to vote at higher rates when inequality is high and capacity is low. In these cases, parties see a benefit and an easy opportunity to mobilize poorer voters, conditioning "the political voice of the poor as opposed to excluding them altogether" (p. 860). Gallego (2015) further highlights that the gap in voting based on education varies considerably between countries, to the extent that some countries do not experience an educational bias or that the bias is reversed. She demonstrates that institutional structures affect inequality in voting, including electoral procedures, party systems, and unionization. This literature emphasizes that unequal participation among citizens can be remedied (or worsened) by how politics and participation are structured institutionally.

Figure 9.1 displays average levels of voting across the twenty-nine European countries in the ESS (2018) and Figure 9.2 provides this information for alternative forms of participation. They show that overall, there are substantial participation gaps between the rich and poor, and between the more and less educated. This is true for all forms of participation, sometimes with differences of around 20 percent on average. This is especially the case for forms that are overall less used, such as signing a petition. Figures 9.1 and 9.2 further highlight that gaps in participation tend to be larger between the more and less educated, than between the rich and poor, emphasizing the importance of the role of education in politics (Bovens and Wille 2017).

How Unequal Participation Can Translate to Unequal Representation

Political participation can affect political representation through (1) the selection of parties and candidates into office, (2) the communication of preferences, and (3) the representatives' strategic behavior in response to known participation patterns (see also Griffin and Newman 2005). First, citizens effectively select political parties and candidates who will make up the legislature and government

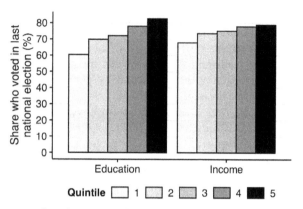

FIGURE 9.1 Voting, by education and income

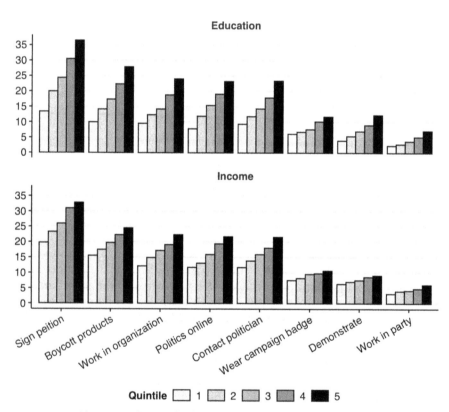

FIGURE 9.2 Alternative forms of political participation, by education and income

through elections. To the extent that preferences in part depend on citizens' wealth and educational background, this implies that nonvoters' preferences are underrepresented in the legislative and executive bodies. With the larger absence of poorer and less-educated citizens, the pivotal median voter is richer and more educated than the median citizen contributing to representational biases (Larcinese 2007). This may hold in terms of both policy and ideological considerations, as well as the specific candidates that are elected. Since people tend to appreciate candidates that are similar to them in certain relevant personal characteristics (Arnesen and Peters 2018), one may expect that a bias in who votes also translates to who is elected to office. Furthermore, *how* people vote when they do vote may contribute to representational inequality. Some scholars have, for example, shown that some citizens tend to vote "incorrectly", that is, not in the way that their preferences or interests would suggest they would vote (e.g., Ha and Lau 2015). Predictions in the vote choice are less accurate for people with less education and less political interest. Moreover, Bartels (2008) finds that the vote choice of the less wealthy is in part dependent on how much the wealthy improved their economic situation in an election year – not on their own economic situation. While there may be valid explanations for the deviations in expected vote choice, this research suggests some people may be more fortunate in the results of the elections than others in terms of preference reflection.

Second, various forms of political participation serve to communicate preferences to the political elite. In order for legislators to represent accurately, they require more or less accurate perceptions of public opinion (Miller and Stokes 1963). Research has found that representatives tend to align more with constituent opinion when they have more accurate information about it (Butler and Nickerson 2011). Yet, some research has shown that legislators are indeed not always very accurate in knowing what citizens want (e.g., Belchior 2014; Hedlund and Friesema 1972). United States legislators, for example, appear to have a systematic conservative bias in their perception constituents' preferences, which can be attributed to a bias in who contacts (Broockman and Skovron 2018). A systematic bias in who participates politically would then also translate into a bias in the information that politicians have about their constituents and may consequently lead to a bias in representation. Communication of preferences, here, can include various forms of participation, and especially contacting and involvement in parties may be important in this respect.

Third, participation may matter through the strategic considerations of political candidates. If candidates are motivated by (re-)election, they would primarily be motivated to please people who may help them to get elected. On the one hand, this may be citizens with larger voting power, that is, groups that are (a) more likely to vote, (b) are less decided on who to vote, and (c) larger groups (Griffin and Newman 2013). This suggests that the persistent inequalities in voting form, in part, the basis for decisions on who politicians *aim* to represent. On the other hand, politicians may be motivated to cater to the preferences of those who make political donations and/or campaign contributions, something that candidates need in some election contexts. Indeed, joining campaign work and/or donating money is often undertaken with the motivation to increase one's impact beyond one's own vote (Schlozman et al. 2012: 239).

Some research has attempted to connect unequal participation to unequal representation, often suggesting that participation may have some effect, but that it is not the main driver of differential representation. Some scholars find that voters are better represented (Griffin and Newman 2005) and that turnout levels affect the representation gap between the rich and the poor (Larcinese 2007; Martin and Claibourn 2013; Peters and Ensink 2015), although it does not seem to be the main explanatory factor (Bartels 2008; Lupu and Warner 2022b). At the same time, Leighley and Oser (2018) show that roll-call votes correspond better to the preferences of the politically active, and Adams and Ezrow (2009) show that parties in Europe respond better to the preferences of those who are politically engaged. Bartels (2008) finds some evidence that contacting reduces the inequality gap. Aligning with some of the arguments regarding the role of money in politics, Barber (2016) finds that US senators are in general not very congruent to their constituents, though they do tend to respond to the preferences of the average financial contributor.

In addition to the potential mechanisms through which participation affects representation, the context of political supply may further affect this relation. On the one hand, there is the pool of candidates that run for office, effectively defining who can be elected by voters. Carnes and Lupu (this volume) show that workers are strikingly underrepresented both in the pool of candidates and among the elected legislators in many European countries. Indeed, looking at the composition of several European parliaments, Best (2007) also shows that few representatives have a background in the primary sector and most have a university degree. Carnes (2013) shows that in the United States, such gaps also exist: citizens are much more likely to have a working-class background, be without a college degree, or own less than a million dollars, than the political elite. The notion that not all citizens are likely to become part of the political elite is perhaps further supported by the change that political parties have experienced. European-focused research has indicated that parties are increasingly outside of civil society, the political elite has specialized and professionalized, and are more focused on output legitimacy (Mair 2013). This suggests that the political elite has become a sphere on its own, without too strong ties to the citizenry in general terms. This type of bias, however, does not seem to be driven by specific citizen preferences for these higher socioeconomic candidates (Carnes and Lupu 2016a; Griffin et al. 2019), nor do working class citizens have less of a nascent political ambition (Carnes and Lupu 2023). It appears that citizens are presented with a choice at the outset that limits the possibility to approach descriptive representation of poorer and less-educated citizens; something that may facilitate equal representation (e.g., Bratton and Ray 2002; Carnes 2012; Hakhverdian 2015).

On the other hand, research has shown that the political offer in terms of policies and ideology is biased toward higher socioeconomic citizens. Rosset and Kurella (2021) show that preferences of the poor are less well reflected in the political offer that parties present. They show that parties cover different combinations of preferences for the middle incomes best, while both the rich and poor need to make a trade-off. In addition, they find that poorer voters take policy less in consideration, so that they do not make up their disadvantage in offer in the way that the rich tend to do. Furthermore, Weber (2020) discovers that party platforms cater mostly to male, educated, and affluent citizens while attempting to appear agreeable to others. This shows again that already *before* electoral choices are made, the political landscape favors citizens with a higher socioeconomic background.

At the same time, this political supply issue does not exist exogenously from citizens' participation. Through their participation, citizens can affect who runs for office and what issues parties put on the agenda. But they also affect who gets elected, that is, even though the pool of candidates is in part given to voters, they select who represents them. Seeing how this may be affecting the composition of the parliament in that there is an overrepresentation of affluent and more-educated legislators (Carnes and Lupu; Curto-Grau and Gallego, both in this volume), it implies that descriptive representation and political participation would have both complementary and interactive effects on unequal representation.

THE ENDOGENEITY PROBLEM: IS PARTICIPATION UNEQUAL BECAUSE REPRESENTATION IS UNEQUAL?

Can we conclude from the earlier discussion that policy outcomes are biased toward the preferences of the affluent and educated partially because they participate more in politics? Not necessarily. While we have discussed several reasons why one would expect unequal participation to translate into unequal representation, the causal arrow might very well go in the other direction. Figure 9.3 demonstrates this point. As we can see, the top three mechanisms in the figure imply that it is participation that influences representation (as we discussed earlier), while the bottom two imply that the causal relationship is the other way around. That is, participation could be unequal precisely because representation is unequal. If elected officials systematically favor the preferences of some citizens over others, one would expect this to have consequences for how citizens perceive the political system. Specifically, citizens who rarely see their preferences enacted in policy might feel that the system is rigged against them, that elected officials ignore their needs, and mainly attend to the interests of the privileged. Therefore, they might see little hope for changing the system through traditional forms of political participation. Conversely, citizens whose views are well represented might feel that the system is working as it should and view participation as effective and

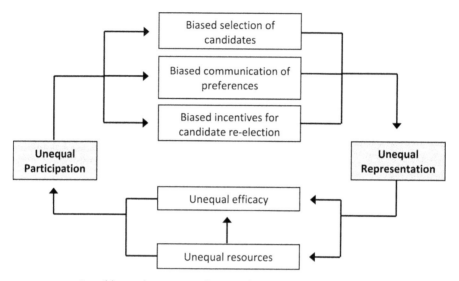

FIGURE 9.3 Possible mechanisms explaining the association between unequal participation and unequal representation

Notes: The top three mechanisms imply that it is participation that influences representation, while the bottom two imply that the causal relationship is the other way around: representation affects participation. In our empirical analysis, we estimate how much of the relationship that can maximally be attributed to unequal efficacy. That is, how much unequal participation would change under perfectly equal efficacy.

meaningful. Hence, the presence of unequal representation could produce unequal efficacy among the public.

Unequal representation might produce unequal efficacy both directly – as described earlier – but also indirectly. Indirectly, when the voices of the well-to-do dominate the policymaking process, this is likely to produce policies that exacerbate existing inequalities in access to resources. The policy outcomes resulting from unequal representation might thus have important feedback effects on politics (Pierson 1993). Specifically, it might discourage certain strata from participating politically (Brady et al. 1995). As argued by Solt (2008: 58), when economic inequality increases, the nonrich are more likely to conclude that "politics is simply not a game worth playing" because the resources needed to play the game are so unevenly distributed.

In sum, we are left with an endogeneity problem (see Anderson and Beramendi 2008), that is, does the lower participation rate of poor and less-educated citizens lead to unequal representation; or does unequal representation lead to lower participation rates among those these groups? Realistically, the causal arrow probably goes in both directions – so one could imagine a vicious cycle by which unequal participation creates unequal responsiveness, which in turn exacerbates future inequality in participation. Yet it matters whether the relationship is mainly driven by participation or representation. If participation is the driving factor, then equalizing political participation might produce more egalitarian representation. On the other hand, if unequal political participation is merely a consequence of unequal representation, then equalizing participation should not be expected to have any effect on representational inequality.

Tackling this question empirically is challenging. For example, trying to isolate the causal effect of unequal representation on participation is hampered by factors including a lack of comparable cross-country measures of unequal representation and the rarity of exogenously induced changes. However, under the key assumption that unequal representation, to the degree that it leads to unequal participation, would mainly do so through citizens' subjective perceptions of the system (i.e., through unequal efficacy in Figure 9.3), we can estimate the effect. Specifically, we then estimate to what extent differential *perceptions* of the system account for gaps in participation across income and educational groups. We believe the assumption to be highly plausible. Of course, it cannot be ruled out that unequal representation could discourage the low educated and poor from participating without them knowing about it: Unequal representation might produce unequal access to resources, which might influence participation independently of citizens' beliefs.[1] That is, worse access to resources could hamper the participation of certain strata, even if they believe the government is actually listening to them. It seems more likely, however, that if unequal representation produces unequal access to resources, then this would adversely affect citizens' feelings of political efficacy and consequently reduce participation. That such an effect must mainly run through citizens' subjective perceptions is tacitly assumed by Rennwald and Pontusson (2021) when they argue that "growing class bias in responsiveness can hardly be invoked to explain growing working-class support for populist parties" if "citizens have failed to register this development in their perceptions of political representation" (p. 21).

In order to examine to what extent gaps in participation across income and education can be accounted for by different beliefs about how the system works, we employ Oaxaca-Blinder Decomposition. Oaxaca-Blinder Decomposition (Blinder 1973; Oaxaca 1973) has become a standard method in economics for estimating how much of a wage gap (typically between males and females) is attributable to a set of predictors (typically occupation, working hours, and experience). However, the method can be used to explain any average difference in a numeric variable between two groups. The method has so far seen limited use in political science (for exceptions, see e.g., Dow 2009; Kostelka et al. 2019). We here use what is known as a "twofold" decomposition, which will decompose a difference in participation between two groups into the share that is attributable to group differences in a set of predictors, and the

---

[1] Notice in Figure 9.3 that unequal resources have a direct effect on participation in addition to that which goes via unequal efficacy.

remaining, which is unexplained. The explained share is determined by counterfactually imputing the predictor levels of one group onto the other and
then predicting with a regression model the level of participation under this
scenario. The difference between this prediction and the actual observed level
of participation is what is attributable to group differences on the predictors.
Standard errors for the estimates are calculated (Jann 2008).

Our data source is the European Social Survey Round 9 for twenty-nine
European countries. This survey is well suited for our purposes since it contains multiple measures of both concepts in which we are interested: political participation and perceptions of the political system. Our decomposition
model includes three types of predictors from the ESS: nine predictors tap into
satisfaction with the political system, four predictors measure internal efficacy
(i.e., personal abilities, confidence, etc.), and four predictors are sociodemographic variables about the respondent. Most of our predictors are measured
on Likert scales from strongly agree to strongly disagree, which we treat as
numeric variables in the analysis.

RESULTS

We begin by examining the relationship between beliefs about how the political system works and propensity to participate. If it is indeed the poor and
less-educated citizens' lower satisfaction with the political system that drives
their lower rates of participation, then satisfaction with the system needs to be
positively associated with participation in the first place.[2] We use nine variables
from the ESS to measure satisfaction with the political system: Agreement that
the system allows people "like you" to have (1) influence and (2) say, (3) that
everyone can participate, (4) that government considers the interests of all citizens, (5) satisfaction with the country's democracy, (6) that the respondent
feels closer to any of the parties, and lastly, trust in (7) politicians, (8) parties,
and (9) parliament (see Table 9.A1 in the Appendix). To test in a simple manner whether these perceptions are related to participation, we made an index
by linearly transforming the variables to the same scale and then averaging
them for each respondent. We then assigned the respondents into quintiles
based on the index distribution in their respective countries.[3] When it comes
to voting, there are clear differences between the people who think the system
is working properly and the ones who do not. People in the bottom quintile of
the index are 65 percent likely to vote, while this number is 82 percent for the

---

[2] Not only that, this association needs to be at least partially causal (something we are not able to
test here, but which seems a reasonable assumption). To the degree to which it is not causal, we
are overestimating the effect of equalizing beliefs about the system on the income/educational
gaps in participation. See the Discussion for details.

[3] Hence, a respondent in quintile five would be among the 20 percent most satisfied with the
political system in his/her country.

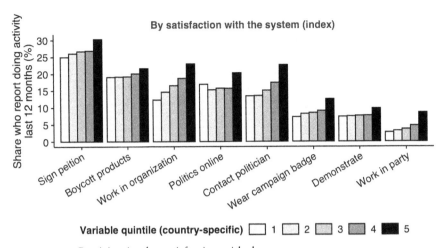

FIGURE 9.4 Participation by satisfaction with the system
Notes: Index averaging the nine measures of satisfaction with the system. Quintiles are based on each country's respective distribution. See Table 9.1.

people at the top quintile, and 76 percent for the middle quintile. Furthermore, Figure 9.4 shows the estimated share of respondents who engage in different alternative forms of participation for different quintiles on the satisfaction with the system index. The results show that respondents who are more optimistic about the system are more likely to participate. This is especially the case for respondents who are in the top quintile on the index for their country. Differences are particularly large when it comes to working in organizations and parties or contacting politicians.

Next, Table 9.1 presents results from the Oaxaca-Blinder Decomposition for voting. Starting from the top of the table, it shows the average gap in voting between the top and bottom education quintile (18.3 percentage points) and between the top and bottom income quintile (10.7 percentage points). Furthermore, the results show that all the predictors we have included in the model (listed in *italics*) together explain 18 percent of the educational gap and 40 percent of the income gap. Simply put, this means that if the low educated and high educated had had the same values on all the predictors, the difference in voting would be reduced by 18 percent (from 18.3 pp to 14.9 pp; the income gap would go from 10.7 pp to 6.5 pp).

If we look at the first block of predictors – those measuring satisfaction with the system – we see that they together account for 14 percent of the educational gap and 21 percent of the income gap. Among the survey items in this group, it is, *The system allows people like you to have influence* and *Feel closer to any of the parties* that explain the most on their own. Still, in the counterfactual world where citizens with very different levels of income and education have

TABLE 9.1 *Oaxaca–Blinder decomposition of the voting gap between high income/highly educated and low income/low educated*

	Education		Income	
	Contribution (Std. Err.)	% of gap	Contribution (Std. Err.)	% of gap
Overall				
Gap in voting between bottom and top quintile	18.29	100.0	10.67	100.0
Total explained	3.35 (1.21)	18.3	4.22 (0.08)	39.5
By variable				
Satisfaction with the system	0.86 (0.19)	4.7	1.03 (0.35)	9.7
System allows people like you to have influence	−0.03 (0.08)	−0.2	0.00 (0.09)	0.0
System ensures everyone can participate	0.45 (0.05)	2.5	0.43 (0.26)	4.1
Government considers interests of all citizens	−0.05 (0.05)	−0.3	−0.28 (0.07)	−2.6
Satisfied with working of democracy in country	−0.02 (0.01)	−0.1	0.10 (0.02)	0.9
Feel closer to any of the parties	1.28 (0.07)	7.0	0.74 (0.14)	6.9
Trust in politicians	−0.37 (0.25)	−2.0	−0.15 (0.20)	−1.4
Trust in parties	0.01 (0.16)	0.0	0.09 (0.15)	0.9
Trust in parliament	0.50 (0.30)	2.7	0.23 (0.02)	2.1
Sum		14.3		20.6
Internal efficacy				
Able to take active role in political group	0.16 (0.17)	0.9	0.52 (0.13)	4.9
Confident in own ability to participate in politics	0.37 (0.31)	2.0	−0.01 (0.02)	−0.1
Interest in politics	3.06 (0.21)	16.7	1.76 (0.12)	16.5
News consumption	−0.01 (0.01)	−0.0	0.06 (0.08)	0.6
Sum		19.6		21.9
Sociodemographic				
Income (education) quintile	2.18 (0.43)	11.9	4.85 (0.10)	45.5
Age	−4.75 (0.04)	−26.0	−5.97 (0.02)	−56.0
Gender	0.03 (0.01)	0.1	−0.50 (0.15)	−4.7
Born abroad	−0.31 (0.12)	−1.7	1.31 (0.05)	12.3
Sum		−15.7		−2.9

Note: Percentages are interpreted as the expected share of the voting gap that would disappear if the bottom education/income quintile had the same levels on a given explanatory variable as the top quintile (or visa-versa, both scenarios weighted equally). Negative values suggest that the gap would be even larger if the two groups had the same levels.
Source: European Social Survey Round 9.

the exact same beliefs on all these nine opinion variables, at least 80 percent of the gap in voting would remain.

For comparison, we also included a set of predictors measuring a respondent's internal efficacy, that is, one's ideas on own political abilities and interests. These variables explain a little more of the voting gap than the previous block (20 percent for education; 22 percent for income). If we look closer, however, it is clear that within this block, one survey item – *Interest in politics* – does almost all the work (17 percent for both income and education).[4]

Further, to separate the explanatory power of sociodemographic variables that are correlated with the first two blocks of opinion variables, we include a set of socio-demographic variables in the model. These are presented in the third block. They show, unsurprisingly, that equalizing income would reduce some of the educational gap in voting, and vice versa.[5]

In the next step, we used the Oaxaca-Blinder method to decompose income and educational gaps in the alternative forms of participation. The results of this are summarized in Figure 9.5, which plots for each form of participation the percentage of the gaps explained by differential satisfaction with the system (i.e., the sum of the first block of predictors in Table 9.1). Two of the activities – working in organizations and wearing a campaign badge – would see the income/education gaps reduced about as much as voting (15–20 percent) if satisfaction with the system were equalized. The other six activities, however, would see less of a reduction or almost none. Inequalities in terms of who contacts politicians, works in parties, and signs petitions would be almost unchanged.

In the last part of the analysis, we look at variation across countries in terms of how participation gaps would change if people at high/low income and education had the same satisfaction with the system. We do this for voting since it showed some of the largest reductions among the different forms of participation. Furthermore, since the Oaxaca-Blinder models are computationally demanding, we employ a simpler way of estimating the effect of equalizing beliefs about the system. Specifically, we estimate an OLS model for each country where the dependent variable is a vote dummy, and the main independent variable is a dummy for whether the respondent is in the first or

---

[4] It seems unlikely that unequal representation would cause differences in political interest independently (i.e., unrelated to the fact that people who feel the system is not working might lose interest in politics). However, if this somehow were the case, then we could add the 17 percent reduction to the sum of the satisfaction with the system-block, and we would get a 31 percent reduction for the educational gap and 38 percent for the income gap. This does not seem justifiable from a theoretical perspective, however.

[5] The large negative effects of age suggest that voting gaps would be even larger if the poor and low educated had had the same age as the affluent and highly educated. This is because older people have relatively low income and education (the latter is probably a generational aspect), but are more likely to vote than younger people, offsetting some of the voting gap across income and educational levels.

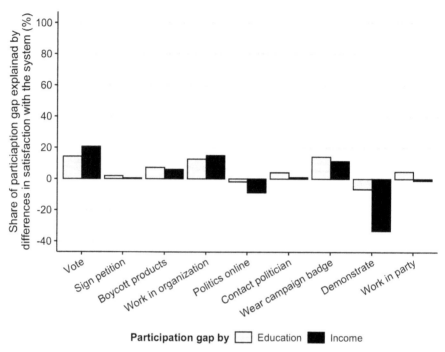

FIGURE 9.5 The power of differential satisfaction with the system in explaining differences in participation across income and education
Note: Estimated with Oaxaca-Blinder Decomposition using the same model as presented in Table 9.1 for different forms of participation.

fifth education quintile (only respondents in one of the two groups are included in the analysis). We also include the set of sociodemographic variables from the third block in Table 9.1. From there, we compare the coefficient for the education dummy with the same coefficient after we add the nine variables measuring satisfaction with the political system to the model. The difference represents the amount that the voting gap between the first and fifth education quintiles is reduced when holding constant these nine variables. We then do the same for income.

Figure 9.6 shows the results of this analysis. As one would expect, most of the countries follow the general pattern of little difference before and after taking satisfaction with the system into account. This goes for countries such as France, Germany, Sweden, and the Netherlands. On the other hand, in some of the Eastern European countries, such as Bulgaria, Lithuania, and Latvia, differential beliefs about the system explain more of the voting gaps than in most other countries. However, in none of the countries that have substantial

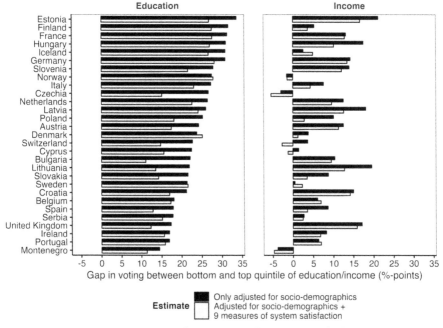

FIGURE 9.6 Country variation in the voting gap by income and education

voting gaps in the first place (e.g., above 5 pp), would the gap reduce by more than half if satisfaction with the system had been equal for income and educational groups?

DISCUSSION

Over the past two decades, research has shown that representation of political preferences in established democracies tends to favor the richer and more-educated citizens. Since these findings present a severe challenge to the democratic idea of political equality, scholars have sought to find the various causes for the gaps in representation. One of the main explanations that has been discussed, even before the actual representational inequalities were demonstrated, is unequal participation. There tend to be structural inequalities that make it more or less likely for citizens to participate, mainly centering around the idea that individuals are facilitated in their political engagement through their resources (i.e., time, money, and skills). Consequently, those who participate more determine election outcomes, communicate their preferences, and are strategically better catered to by politicians who seek reelection. Indeed, while this area needs more research, there are some studies that have found a link between unequal participation and representation – even if it may not be the main explanatory factor.

However, because there are good arguments for the idea that people decide not to participate because they do not experience representation (while they may observe it for others), we are presented with an endogeneity problem. In this chapter, we sought to address this problem, at least in part, by examining whether participation gaps would narrow if the rich and poor, and more and less educated, would view the political system as equally well functioning. We find, in overall terms, that these participation gaps would likely be reduced in such a scenario – but only in limited ways.

Although there seems to be some support in the data for the argument that the poor and low educated participate less because they feel the system is not working properly, such perceptions account for a rather small part of the gaps in political participation across income and educational groups (15–20 percent for voting; less for other forms of participation). And in fact, if anything, we are probably overestimating rather than underestimating the effects. The reason for this is that the results from the Oaxaca-Blinder models assume that *all* of the relationship between satisfaction with the system and participation is causal. To the degree this is not the case (and the relationship is, for instance, explained by people viewing the system more favorably *as a result of* participating), the gap would see an even smaller change as a result of equalizing beliefs about the system. Moreover, it is not certain that having perfectly equal political representation at the system level *would* in fact equalize beliefs about the system. The poor and low educated could distrust the system for other reasons than unequal representation. Therefore, we should be careful when inferring from our analysis a specific amount by which unequal participation would be reduced if the political system was perfectly equally representative. Given the ways in which we are likely to overestimate that quantity here, a gap reduction on the order of 15 to 20 percent should be viewed as an upper bound.

While the reduction in the gap does not appear that large, it needs to be noted, however, that even such smaller effects may be consequential. We mentioned that the relationship between representation and participation is likely to go in both directions, at least to some extent. This means that if unequal participation exists, it may lead to (more) unequal representation. This in turn would affect gaps in participation somewhat, which then again translates into increased representational inequality. So, even if the effect of unequal representation on participation is minimal, we may be observing a part of the vicious cycle we highlighted earlier. Importantly, this cycle may reach a (an unspecified) threshold level, with potentially severe consequences for democracy. On the one hand, we could conclude that certain systems are in fact no democracies at all, but rather oligarchies (or plutocracies). On the other hand, however, we may in the future observe a strong, potentially revolutionary reaction among citizens who do not accept to be underrepresented while being told they are. Such processes have uncertain outcomes and may lead to even worse situations.

Finally, while most studies have found unequal representation of richer citizens, we see that, especially, education is a dividing factor regarding participation. And indeed, some research has already suggested that, at least in some contexts, the educational representational gaps are more important than the ones based on income (Mathisen 2022; Schakel 2021). Other research has also highlighted the importance of educational divides in politics (e.g., Bovens and Wille 2017; Gallego 2010), and it suggests that cleavages may have shifted within society. It also suggests that research should perhaps focus more deeply on the relation between education and politics, paying also special attention to potential country difference.

PART III

VOTERS AND DEMAND FOR REDISTRIBUTION

10

Fairness Reasoning and Demand for Redistribution[*]

Charlotte Cavaillé

A shared expectation among both pundits and scholars is that more inequality will be met with more demand for redistribution. Pundits couch this expectation in moral terms: while Left-leaning pundits expect voters to be outraged by "unfair" income differences,[1] Right-leaning commentators dispute the unfairness charge and expect envy and resentment to drive rising demand for redistribution.[2] For scholars in political economy, expectations of rising support for redistribution often have little to do with the type of fairness concerns voiced by pundits. These expectations are rooted instead in a set of assumptions regarding human behavior (people prefer more disposable income than less), the redistributive design of the welfare state, and people's extensive knowledge of the latter's implications for their own pocketbook (Meltzer and Richard 1981). Under these assumptions, as inequality increases, so does the share of voters who stand to benefit from redistribution and who update their policy preferences in line with their material self-interest (e.g., see Lupu and Pontusson, this volume).[3] This chapter demonstrates how incorporating the type of fairness concerns voiced by pundits into existing political economy models can help explain the absence of a redistributive policy response to rising inequality, despite expectations of growing support for such policy.

An important step in this demonstration is conceptualizing and operationalizing "fairness." I define fairness reasoning as the thought process through

---

[*] This chapter draws on Cavaillé (2023).
[1] "Sorry Washington Post, Bernie Sanders Is Right About Economic Inequality" by John Nichols, in *The Nation*, July 2, 2019
[2] "Income Inequality and <u>Bullsh*t</u>" by William Irwin, in *Psychology Today*, November 15, 2015.
[3] When fairness concerns are included in the analysis, it is often to better highlight the role material self-interest plays in shaping them (e.g., Hvidberg et al. 2020).

which individuals act as if a third-party judge ruling on the fairness of a given situation and acting to maximize fairness accordingly. In this case, maximizing fairness means expressing support for a policy that moves the status quo closer to what is prescribed by shared norms of fairness. Based on this definition, to study fairness reasoning, researchers first need to identify the finite set of fairness norms widely agreed upon by all members of a given polity. Having done so, they can then measure people's beliefs about the extent to which the status quo deviates from what these norms prescribe, *fairness beliefs* for short. Fairness beliefs I show introduce a wedge between changes in the distribution of market income and support for redistribution, explaining why rising income inequality has a less-than-straightforward impact on attitudes toward redistributive policies.

This chapter unfolds in four sections. First, I argue that fairness reasoning, as defined earlier, is the individual-level manifestation of a moral system. I describe the moral system underpinning redistributive institutions and policies in Western democracies and identify the two key norms of fairness that characterize it. I show that these two norms receive broad support. In sections 2 and 3, I turn to fairness beliefs. Fairness beliefs function as an anchoring proto-ideology, a mental map helping people interpret a complicated and uncertain world and pick redistributive policies that increase the fairness of the status quo. As I show in section 2, the conceptualization of fairness reasoning proposed in this chapter suggests a mental map that is very different from the one hypothesized in existing work on the topic. In section 3, I propose a friendly horse race between existing work and the conceptualization presented in this chapter: the evidence overwhelmingly supports the latter. The last section discusses implications for our understanding of the demand side of redistributive politics in times of rising inequality.

FAIRNESS REASONING, MORAL SYSTEMS, AND SOCIAL ORDER

Studies across the social sciences show that the impulse to do what is collectively recognized as the "right thing" is central to human cognition. This impulse is the individual-level observable manifestation of a moral system, that is, a social technology that helps regulate the constant toggle between cooperation and opportunistic behavior characteristic of social life. This moral system contributes to social order[4] and the provision of stable institutional solutions to social dilemmas (Baumard 2016; Binmore 1994; Gintis et al. 2005; Graham, Haidt, and Nosek 2009; Tomasello 2016). In this section, I unpack the moral system underpinning redistributive institutions in Western democracies. In doing so, I will provide a more precise definition of a moral system and sketch its role in the provision of social order and large-scale cooperation.

---

[4] This claim is purely descriptive: the fact that a moral system helps foster social order and cooperation does not mean that the resulting equilibrium is inherently good and/or coercion-less.

Famous examples of moral systems are discussed in the work of Margaret Levi on taxation and mass mobilization as well as that of Eleonor Ostrom on the monitoring of common pool resources (Levi 1991; Ostrom 1998). Given their centrality, not including fairness reasoning in workhorse models of redistributive politics represents a significant oversight. This is especially true when it comes to forming an opinion on redistributive policies: for most people, stakes are too low or too uncertain for selfish material concerns to distract them from doing the fair thing. First, because social programs are "locked-in" (Pierson 1996), policy changes tend to be incremental, affecting existing institutions only on the margin, often with delayed effects, which are themselves hidden by deficit spending and complicated budget arbitrations. Fearing a backlash from affected constituents, politicians have only limited incentives to provide clarifying information on a policy's diffuse pocketbook implications. Second, in representative democracies, expressing an opinion on a given policy, most often in the context of a survey, is itself a low-stakes task. In such context, the assumption that voters are fully informed selfish income maximizers is heroic at best.[5] Instead, most people satisfice, that is, settle on a "good enough" policy position using cognitively less demanding decision heuristics that provide satisfactory outcomes. Fairness reasoning is one form of satisficing. It manifests itself as a simple decision rule: "if fair then support," "if unfair then oppose." Understanding how people evaluate a policy change as fair or not requires first unpacking the moral system underpinning redistributive institutions in postindustrial democracies.

In Western democracies, the allocation of economic resources is affected by a complex bundle of institutions and policies. A central distinction is the one made between the "market economy" on the one hand and the "welfare state" on the other. The market economy generates income that is taxed to fund the social transfers distributed by the welfare state. The welfare state organizes social solidarity, that is, the collective endeavor through which individuals are insured against life's main risks (unemployment, old age, illnesses...).[6] Governments can affect the distribution of income in a given society through three channels: (1) predistribution policies, which affect how market income is generated and distributed, (2) taxation policies, which affect how much market income people get to keep, and (3) changes to the design of the welfare state, which affect the extent to which social insurance is redistributive. With regards

---

[5] Contrast this with the situation economic actors face when confronted with high-stakes economic decisions (e.g., a consumer buying a car, and entrepreneur expanding their company, a worker choosing between two jobs). Given high-stakes, economic actors face strong incentives to collect information on existing alternatives and choose the one that will maximize their economic well-being (Roth, Settele, and Wohlfart 2022).

[6] The market economy's existence as an autonomous institutional sphere separate from the welfare state is part institutional reality, part shared cultural myth. To the extent that I am interested in people's beliefs about the status quo, whether or not this description of the status quo is true is somewhat irrelevant, what matters is that people share this representation of the world.

to the latter, governments can increase the generosity of means-tested benefits, tweak the relative mix of earnings-dependent and nonearnings-dependent benefits (more or less "giving") and change the legal definition of who is included in the welfare state (more or less "sharing"). Institutional stability is more likely when a majority finds the existing institutional bundle "fair," or at least "fair enough" according to shared norms of fairness. Institutional change is more likely when a majority perceives the status quo as unfair. What exactly does "fair" mean in this context? Or to put it differently, what are the norms of fairness people rely on to justify their support or opposition to status quo-changing policy proposals, whether related to predistribution (1), income taxation (2), or social policy design (3)?

A dominant line of research emphasizes the following allocation principle: a fair allocation is one in which economic rewards are related to effort (i.e., "effort pays"). In the words of Benabou and Tirole (2006), support for income redistribution is affected by the views people hold about "the causes of wealth and poverty, the extent to which individuals are responsible for their own fate, and the long-run rewards to personal effort." This common approach to fairness reasoning in Western democracies does not explicitly engage with the market economy/welfare state dualism mentioned earlier. Yet, as I argue next, the manufacturing of consent is achieved very differently depending on the institutional realm under consideration.

In the market economy, mass consent implies the shared agreement that the status quo abides by what the proportionality norm prescribes, namely that rewards be proportional to merit, itself a combination of personal decisions as a free agent, individual work ethic, acquired skills, and innate talent. Milton Friedman himself emphasized its centrality to the market economy's system of justification: "payment in accordance to product," he writes, is part of the "basic core of value judgments that are unthinkingly accepted by the great bulk of [a society's] members" and enables "resources to be allocated efficiently without compulsion" (p. 167). This is the norm captured by the "does effort pays?" literature. But it is only half of the story: what people experience as actors in the market economy is separate from what they experience as stakeholders in a resource pooling effort embodied by the welfare state. One key difference is the importance of free-riding concerns: while mostly irrelevant for thinking about how economic resources are allocated by the market economy, they are central to how people think about how economic resources are allocated by the welfare state. This suggests the existence of a second norm, the reciprocity norm, which prescribes that all members of a group contribute to the collective effort and that free riding does not go unpunished.

Numerous studies have documented the importance of the reciprocity norm when people are engaged in joint cooperative endeavors (Axelrod 1980; Ostrom and Walker 2003). This norm is both simple to describe and surprisingly difficult to theorize. Simply stated, the norm turns people into conditional cooperators. People willingly contribute to a collective endeavor if they feel others are not free riding (positive reciprocity). They punish free riders by either ceasing to cooperate or by excluding them from accessing the goods generated by cooperation (negative reciprocity). Behavior attached to the reciprocity norm is thus inherently two-faceted and can be presented in one of two lights. The more positive light casts it as a form of conditional altruism: people's default position is to help others unless others are "antisocial" (Fong, Bowles, and Gintis 2006; Henrich et al. 2001). Viewed in a negative light, it is a form of conditional punishment: people's default position is to deny help to others unless they are prosocial.

If the proportionality and reciprocity norms are indeed manifestations of consent-inducing moral systems, agreement with these two norms should be quasi-universal. Specifically, people applying the same norm to the same situation will unanimously agree on whether or not this situation is fair and in need of corrective intervention. Such unanimity is routinely observed in experimental settings where the features of a given situation are carefully explained and communicated to participants (Cappelen et al. 2013; Konow 2003; Petersen 2012). It is unfortunately beyond the scope of this chapter to review this literature in full: the interested reader can turn to the summary of this evidence provided in Cavaillé 2023 (Chapter 2). Another type of evidence comes from cross-national surveys. The World Value Survey, for example, includes items that plausibly measure agreement with the proportionality norm: "Imagine two secretaries, of the same age, doing practically the same job. One finds out that the other earns considerably more than she does. The better paid secretary, however, is quicker, more efficient, and more reliable at her job. In your opinion, is it fair or not fair that one secretary is paid more than the other?"[7] This question holds constant attributes one is not responsible for (age, tasks being given to accomplish) and only varies factors one has control over (i.e., effort). In all countries, more than four out of five respondents find it fair that one secretary is paid more than the other. Relatedly, the 2008 wave of the ESS asked respondents whether they agreed with the statement that "(a) society is fair when hard-working people earn more than others." On average over 80 percent of respondents agree with this statement, with a high of 92 percent in Austria and a low of 70 percent in the Czech Republic.

Unfortunately, survey items documenting widely shared agreement with the reciprocity norm in postindustrial democracies are not available. One exception is a recent set of studies by Michael Bang Petersen and coauthors focusing on two most-different cases, namely the United States and Denmark. In one study, Petersen et al. (2012) randomly assign representative samples of American and Danish respondents to one of three treatment conditions. Respondents in all three groups are presented with a male welfare recipient and then asked: "To what extent do you disagree or agree that the eligibility

---

[7] To the best of my knowledge, no such item exists for the reciprocity norm.

requirements for social welfare should be tightened for persons like him?" In one treatment, no cues are provided about the recipient's labor market attachment and effort. In another treatment condition, respondents are told that he "never had a regular job" and that, while "he is fit and healthy," he is not "motivated to get a job." In a third treatment condition, respondents are told that the recipient "always had a regular job" but was affected by a "work-related injury" and is "motivated to get back to work again." Assuming individuals in both countries reason in similar ways based on the reciprocity norm, there should be little to no difference in how respondents treat the "deserving" recipient relative to the "undeserving" one. In line with expectations, the authors find that, "despite decades of exposure to different cultures and welfare institutions, two sentences of information (...) make welfare support across the U.S. and Scandinavian samples substantially and statistically indistinguishable."

To sum up, the existence of moral systems compel people to behave fairly, that is, justify one's actions (and policy preferences) according to shared norms of fairness. The proportionality norm is most often mobilized when evaluating the fairness of market outcomes and policies that interfere with such outcomes. It constrains envy and resentment from those who have "less than others" and promotes consent over policies that take from those who have more than others. The reciprocity norm is most often mobilized when evaluating the fairness of redistributive social insurance. It helps a group cooperate over the provision of social solidarity and promotes consent over design features that make social solidarity more or less redistributive.[8] Note that the distinction between deviations from what the proportionality norm prescribes on the one hand, and deviations from what the reciprocity norm prescribes on the other is partly obscured by the generic terms available to discuss the fairness of a given situation, and relatedly the fairness of the status quo. Specifically, two outcomes can be both judged as fair or unfair, with each evaluation referring to different norms of fairness. Relatedly, the same concept of desert or deservingness can apply to very different fairness judgments as illustrated in Figure 10.1.

In the realm of mass attitudes toward redistributive social policies, behaving fairly in line with the proportionality norm will mean, for example, opposing (supporting) high taxes because differences in market income (do not) reflect differences in effort and talent. Behaving fairly in line with the reciprocity norm will lead some to oppose social spending cuts because it unfairly affects "deserving" cooperators. Others, in contrast, will support cuts to programs that unfairly reward free riders over those who, in contrast, "carry their weight." This implies that people rely on prior knowledge regarding the status quo's

---

[8] As a reminder, these include means-tested programs as well as the design features that make some social benefits accessible to all irrespective of past contributions (e.g., universal access to public healthcare in Great Britain).

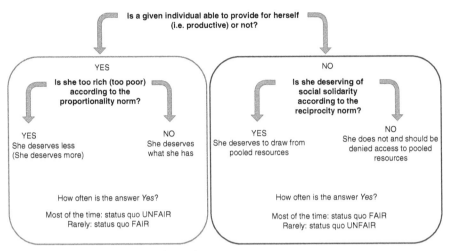

FIGURE 10.1 What is fair? Who is deserving?
Reprinted with permission from Cavaillé (2023). Copyright © 2023 by Cambridge University Press.

defining features. Put differently, they hold empirical beliefs about the nature of the status quo, specifically about the prevalence of deviations from what norms of fairness prescribe (see Figure 10.1). I turn to this point next.

FAIRNESS BELIEFS AND DEMAND FOR REDISTRIBUTION

Moral systems help promote both stability (consent) and change (dissent). Stability is more likely when enough individuals (1) share the same understanding of what is fair and (2) share the perception that the status quo is fair according to this definition. Change is more likely when enough individuals (1) share the same understanding of what is fair and (2) share the perception that the status quo is unfair according to this definition.[9] In other words, the existence of a stabilizing moral system implies not only that people agree on shared norms of fairness (what ought to be) but also that people hold beliefs about the fairness of the status quo (beliefs about what is). Yet, while the existence of a stabilizing moral system implies the *existence* of fairness beliefs, it does not imply that people hold the *same set* of beliefs. Put differently, agreement on what ought to be does not imply agreement on what is. Indeed, whether a redistributive system is best described as stable (a majority agrees that the status quo is fair), ripe for change (a majority agrees that the status quo is unfair),

[9] The potential for disorder (as different from change) increases when enough individuals in the group share very different understandings of fairness, one might even question whether these individuals function as a social group in the first place.

or a mix of both is an empirical question: moral systems are a social technology that fosters social order, they do not deterministically induce it.

From individuals' perspective, fairness beliefs function as an anchoring proto-ideology, a mental map helping people interpret a complicated and uncertain world and pick redistributive policies that increase the fairness of the status quo. This suggests that attitudes toward redistributive policies are structured in ways that reflect this mental map. To investigate these empirical patterns, I proceed through a "three-cornered fight" among (1) existing approaches to fairness reasoning (the "does effort pay?" literature), (2) my own framework, and (3) the available data (Hall 2006: 27). I start by showing that the argument presented in this chapter suggests a mental map that is very different from the one hypothesized in existing work on the topic. I then show that the evidence overwhelmingly supports the former.

Fairness Reasoning and Support for Redistribution: State of the Art

The previously mentioned "does effort pay?" literature argues that support for income redistribution is affected by the views people hold about "the causes of wealth and poverty, the extent to which individuals are responsible for their own fate, and the long-run rewards to personal effort" (Bénabou and Tirole 2006). If people are rich (poor) for reasons out of their own control, then effort does not pay, income differences are unfair and income redistribution is justified and even fairness-maximizing. In the words of Fong (2001), "the extent to which people control their own fate and ultimately get their just deserts are first-order determinants of attitudes toward inequality and redistribution, even "swamping the effects of own income and education."

First, a few words on how the literature has conceptualized and measured support for income redistribution, or demand for redistribution for short. One survey item, identified in this chapter as "the traditional redistribution item," has become researchers' go to for measuring individual-level differences in support for income redistribution. It asks respondents whether they agree with a version of the following statement: "the government should redistribute income from the better-off to those who are least well-off." This survey item is also one of the few items that has been asked repeatedly over time in cross-national surveys. As often happens when researchers are constrained by past data collection decisions, this measurement tool has shaped how researchers conceptualize the dependent variable: support for redistribution is now commonly defined as agreement with the policy principle that governments should redistribute income from the haves to the have nots.

As previously discussed, in practice, redistribution occurs through a bundle of heterogeneous policies that affect individuals' material conditions by taking (e.g., through income or payroll taxes) or not taking (e.g., tax credits) on the one hand, giving more or giving less (e.g., in-cash or in-kind benefits) and sharing (e.g., universal access to healthcare in Great Britain) and not sharing (e.g., benefit targeting as with Medicare in the United States). Under that definition, understanding mass support for redistribution implies understanding how people answer not only the traditional redistribution question but also questions such as:

- Should the government financially support those who cannot provide a decent living for themselves? How generous should this support be, and who should pay for it?
- Should healthcare be the same for all, irrespective of income, or is a residual system providing basic services enough?
- Are taxes too progressive? Not progressive enough?
- Can tax cuts come at the expense of social services? If so, should services that benefit the worse off be protected from such cuts?
- Are social programs and the taxes that fund them too large? not large enough?

A common approach in the literature is to look for (and usually find) a latent variable that shapes the answers to most, if not all, of the questions listed above. This latent dimension is often described as capturing left-right preferences on "economic issues," "redistributive issues," or "government involvement in the economy" (Ansolabehere, Rodden and Snyder 2008).[10]

These two measurement strategies (the traditional redistribution item and the multi-item latent dimension) are often assumed to capture the same thing, that is, the extent to which people are inclined to support policies designed to take from those who have more to help those who have less, which Alesina and Giuliano describe as one of "the most important dividing line[s] (…)" in democratic politics (Alesina and Giuliano 2011: 94). According to the "does effort pay?" line of work, one's position on this dividing line is well predicted by one's beliefs about the role of effort for explaining both wealth and poverty. This perspective is sketched on the left-hand side of Figure 10.2.

According to Alesina and Angeletos (2005; see also Bénabou and Tirole 2006), the relationship between demand for redistribution and the belief that effort pays also helps explain why countries differ in their work-to-leisure ratio, levels of income inequality, as well as the share of GDP redistributed through taxes and social spending. Specifically, beliefs, policy preferences, behavior, and institutions all combine to produce a stable outcome, or social equilibrium. Alesina and Angeletos (2005) identify two ideal-typical equilibria: an American Dream equilibrium and a Euro-pessimistic equilibrium. In the American Dream equilibrium, people believe that effort pays and oppose predistribution policies, progressive taxation, and the redistributive features of social insurance because these policies undermine fairness. Predistribution

---

[10] For example, Ansolabehere, Rodden, and Snyder (2008) argue that this latent dimension can be measured "by averaging a large number of multiple survey items," which "eliminates a large amount of measurement error and reveals issue preferences that are well structured and stable."

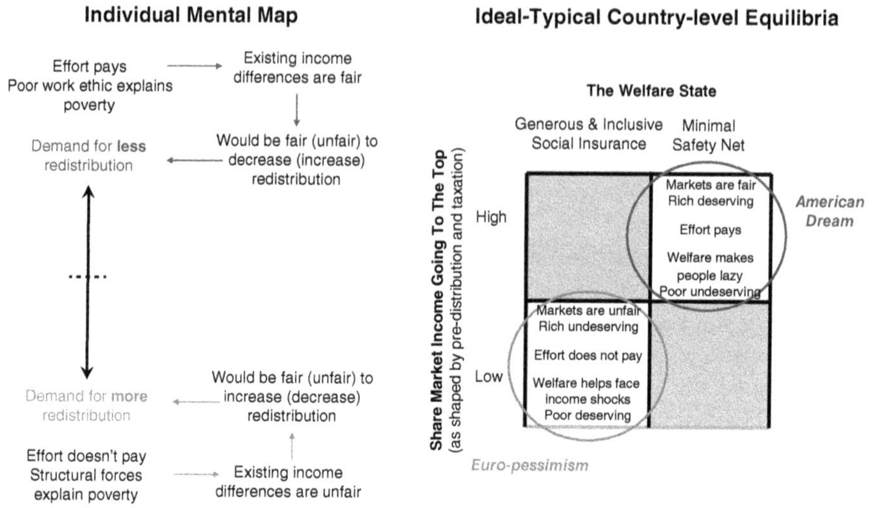

FIGURE 10.2 Fairness reasoning and demand for redistribution: unidimensional approach
Reprinted with permission from Cavaillé (2023). Copyright © 2023 by Cambridge University Press.

policies are unwarranted because economic institutions already reward effort. Similarly, taxing those who earn more market income is unfair given that they have worked harder and, consequently, deserve to keep it. Finally, social insurance programs designed to redistribute to the chronically poor and unemployed are also unfair given that they transfer resources to people who prefer living off benefits than trying their best to improve their plight. In this equilibrium, the poor and unemployed are castigated as lazy, income redistribution is limited to offering a charity-like minimal income floor and total effort (annual hours worked) is high. As a result, income inequality is also high.

In the Euro-pessimistic equilibrium, people believe that "effort does not pay" and, consequently, are more supportive of predistribution policies, progressive taxation, and social insurance that is generous and inclusive because these policies help maximize fairness. Specifically, predistribution policies help correct unbalanced labor relations, progressive taxation is fair because it affects the "undeserving" rich and redistributive social insurance helps recipients who, despite efforts to escape poverty, fail to do so because of an unfair "economic system." In this equilibrium, the poor are less likely to be stigmatized as lazy, income redistribution is extensive, and total effort is comparatively lower than in the American Dream equilibrium. As a result, income inequality is also lower. These two equilibria are summarized in Figure 10.2 (right-hand side). In the next section, I contrast this conceptual framework to the one presented in this chapter.

From One to Two Dimensions

I have argued that what counts as a fair allocation of market income is different from what counts as a fair allocation of social benefits, meaning that beliefs about the fairness of the former can differ from beliefs about the fairness of the latter. The reason for this disconnect extends beyond the existence of two norms instead of one and also follow from the relationship between fairness beliefs and status. People derive status from being "productive members" of society. The distinction between a market economy and the welfare state suggests at least two distinct understandings of "productive." One draws on an individual's market value made visible to all through one's market income: the higher the income, the higher the status. People tend to form proportionality beliefs that make them feel good about their own income level: if high, then they are more likely to believe that effort pays, if low, then they are more likely to think that it does not (Hvidberg et al. 2020). The other understanding of "productive," overlooked by the "effort pays" literature, draws on an individual's membership in the welfare state, a resource pool of historical scope. In this case, being a productive member involves "carrying one's weight" and not free riding on shared resources. Being a productive member is also status-enhancing because of what the members of the pool "owe to one another and to no one else, or to no one else in the same degree," namely welfare. This implies a distinction between high(er) status members who can access welfare and lower status strangers who cannot. Such distinction makes little sense in a market economy, an "indifferent association, determined solely by personal preference and market capacity" and "open to whoever chooses to come in" (Walzer 1983). People tend to form reciprocity beliefs that make them feel good about being themselves as a deserving member of this resource pooling endeavor. This implies a distinction between oneself and the undeserving other, which can lead to overestimating the prevalence of free riding, even among those most likely to rely on social benefits (Lamont 2002). It can also lead to distorted perceptions of immigrants as welfare shoppers and the perception that access that is not conditional on full membership as inherently unfair.[11] In other words, there are no reason to expect a priori that status-boosting proportionality beliefs align with status-boosting reciprocity beliefs as hypothesized by the "does effort pay?" literature.

As a result of this disconnect between proportionality and reciprocity beliefs, for some people, fairness reasoning also implies a disconnect between attitudes toward policies that take market income from those who have more (e.g., predistribution and taxation policies) and attitudes toward policies that give to people who can no longer provide for themselves (e.g., generous and inclusive social insurance). As a shorthand, I will call the first type of policy

---

[11] For ethnographic evidence on the relationship between racial boundaries, racism, and reciprocity beliefs in the United States, see also Cramer, this volume.

redistribution from policies and the second type *redistribution to* policies. Below, I provide examples of both types of policies:

Redistribution from Policies

- New antitrust legislation or regulations that increase drivers' bargaining power vis-a-vis a platform like Uber
- A progressive wealth tax or closing tax loopholes that benefit rich corporations
- A cap on CEO salary
- Equal-pay-for-equal-work reforms

Redistribution to Policies

- Increase (decrease) in spending on social programs that maintain the living standards of the able-bodied unemployed
- Making access to benefits conditional on past contributions and/or on length of residency (if immigrant)
- Extending existing generous policies (healthcare, unemployment insurance, pensions) to previously excluded individuals with weak labor market attachment

Because of fairness reasoning, attitudes toward policies that affect the distribution of market income on the one hand can differ from attitudes toward policies that affect the redistributive features of social insurance on the other. This perspective, sketched on the left-hand side of Figure 10.3, implies that individuals sort across four ideal-typical proto-ideological profiles: (1) consistently pro-redistribution (bottom-left quadrant), (2) consistently antiredistribution (top-right quadrant), (3) in favor of more generous *redistribution to* but skeptical of more *redistribution from* (top-left quadrant), and (4) inclined to support more *redistribution from* while opposed to more *redistribution to* (bottom-right quadrant).

This two-dimensional conceptualization of demand for redistribution stands in contrast to the mainstream unidimensional conceptualization of demand for redistribution and fairness reasoning sketched on the left-hand side of Figure 10.2. The latter implicitly assumes that proportionality and reciprocity beliefs reinforce each other: the belief that the world is fair (unfair) according to the proportionality norm goes alongside the belief that the world is unfair (fair) according to the reciprocity norm. Specifically, if effort pays, then market income is distributed fairly and net beneficiaries of social transfers are free riders who are not trying hard enough. Conversely, if effort does not pay, income differences are unfair and net beneficiaries cannot be blamed for a situation they cannot control. Relatedly, if the rich are deserving (undeserving) of their high earnings and should not (should) be

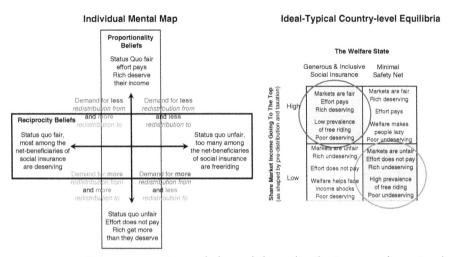

FIGURE 10.3 Fairness reasoning and demand for redistribution: two-dimensional approach
Reprinted with permission from Cavaillé (2023). Copyright © 2023 by Cambridge University Press.

taxed, then the poor are deserving (undeserving) of their plight and should not (should) be helped. In other words, in this framework, fairness reasoning contributes to what scholars call "issue constraint" (Baldassarri and Gelman 2008; Converse 2006), that is, ideological consistency across beliefs and policy preferences within a given issue area. In contrast, I hypothesize that institutional dualism, as well as free riding and membership concerns that are uniquely salient to the welfare state, imply a disconnect between proportionality and reciprocity beliefs.

Relatedly, the existence of two norms of fairness or two separate institutional spheres suggests not two but four ideal-typical social equilibria (right-hand side of Figure 10.3). To the high redistribution and low redistribution equilibria hypothesized by the "does effort pay?" literature (top-right and bottom-left corners), I add two other combinations: one that limits income inequality at the top but fails to offer generous social insurance cover for the poor and the unemployed (bottom-right corner) and another that does not affect top income inequality but nevertheless engages in large risk pooling through universal and generous social insurance (top-left quadrant). This is summarized on the right-hand side of Figure 10.3.

In the remainder of this chapter, I use survey data to examine which of the unidimensional or two-dimensional conceptualizations of fairness reasoning and demand for redistribution provides the best fit, focusing first on individual-level mental maps and next on country-level differences in support for *redistribution to* and *redistribution from*.

EVIDENCE FOR A TWO-DIMENSIONAL MENTAL MAP

Because people carry a diverse set of considerations regarding the fairness of the status quo, using more than one survey item is necessary to better differentiate individuals holding mostly "status quo unfair" considerations from people holding mostly "status quo fair" considerations. To proxy for an individual's proportionality beliefs, researchers can rely on at least three types of survey items. A first type includes items used by the "does effort pay?" literature. Respondents are asked to what extent they believe that economic institutions reward talent and effort. These items need to be complemented with questions asking about the prevalence of norm-violating/conforming outcomes and behaviors. Indeed, the goal is to measure not only whether one believes that effort pays but also whether one believes that effort pays for most people, most of the time. A third type of item directly elicits respondents' perceptions of the size of the disconnect between existing income differences (what is) and fair income differences (what ought to be).[12] Below, I provide example of survey items that can be used to measure proportionality beliefs:[13]

Fairness of Market Institutions

- "In COUNTRY, people get rewarded for their intelligence and skill. Agree/disagree?" ***
- "In COUNTRY, people have equal opportunities to get ahead. Agree/disagree?" ***
- "In COUNTRY, with hard work and a bit of luck most people can succeed financially. Agree/disagree?"
- "The stock market is mostly there to help rich people get richer. Agree/disagree?"
- "The economic system mostly benefits a privileged minority. Agree/disagree?"

Prevalence of Norm-Violating Outcomes

- "In your opinion, what share of rich (poor) people are rich (poor) for reason that have nothing to do with how hard they work? All/most/some/none"

---

[12] One way to do so is to first ask people what is their preferred income difference between individuals in high-earning occupations and individuals in low-earning occupation followed by questions asking about their perceptions of existing income differences between the two. The larger the mismatch between preferred and perceived, the more a respondent is likely to find existing income differences unfair (Osberg and Smeeding 2006).

[13] I have asked versions of items identified with ** in special test pilots. Versions of the items identified with *** are available in national or cross-national surveys including the International Social Survey Programme and the International Social Justice Project.

- "For people born in a poor (rich) family, hard work leads to economic success most of the time/some of the time/rarely/never?" **
- "What share of people born in [COUNTRY] in a [POOR/RICH/MIDDLE CLASS] family get a fair shot at life? All/most/some/none" ***

Fairness of the Income Distribution

- "What is the income difference between a janitor/bricklayer and a doctor/CEO?" "In your opinion, should this difference be larger/smaller/stay the same?" ***
- "Are differences in market income too large/too small/about right?" ***

In the case of the reciprocity norm, norm violation takes the form of people free riding on the common effort. To measure reciprocity beliefs, researchers can ask respondents what they think about benefit recipients' tendency to cheat "the system" and their perceptions of the system's ability to successfully identify cheats. Also important are people's priors regarding how others behave when confronted with the option to free ride on shared resources, something economists like to call "moral hazard." Below, I provide example of three types of survey items that can be used to measure reciprocity beliefs:[14]

Prevalence of Free Riders in the Recipient Population

- "Most unemployed people are trying hard to find a job. Agree/disagree?" ***
- "People on benefits do not really have a choice. Agree/disagree?"

Failure to Identify Free Riders

- "What share of social benefit cheats are successfully identified? Most/some/only a few/none" ***
- "How often does welfare go to people who do not really deserve it? Most of the time/some of the time/rarely" ***
- "What share of people who qualify are wrongly denied benefits? A majority/some/only a few/none" ***

Human Nature and Moral Hazard

- "Social benefits are too generous and make people lazy?" ***
- "To what extent can others be trusted to not abuse and cheat the system? Most of the time/sometime/rarely/never" ***

With enough items similar to those listed earlier, alongside items asking about *redistribution from* and *redistribution to* policies, I can directly test

---

[14] See previous footnote.

which of the two hypothesized mental maps best fits the data using both exploratory and confirmatory factor analysis. To the best of my knowledge, the British Social Attitude Survey (BSAS) is the only representative survey that includes both proportionality and reciprocity items alongside *redistribution from* and *redistribution to* policy items. Using the 2016 wave of the BSAS, I examine whether proportionality beliefs and *redistribution from* policy items load on the same latent factor while reciprocity beliefs and *redistribution to* policy items load on a separate, only weakly correlated factor.[15] If the unidimensional framework better fits the data, then all items will load on the same latent factor, with the latter approximating the latent left-right economic dimension often described in the existing literature. Alternatively, items might load on separate but highly correlated factors. Because cross-national surveys do not ask the same respondents about both reciprocity and proportionality beliefs, I cannot repeat this analysis in countries beyond Great Britain. Instead, I follow alternative empirical strategies (described in more detail later) designed to best leverage the set of items available in the cross-national European Social Survey (ESS). When combined, these tests provide additional evidence that the patterns uncovered in the British context are not unique to this country.

Moving from the individual to the country level, I combine data from the ESS and the International Social Survey Programme (ISSP) and examine whether, in line with the unidimensional approach, countries that find it fair (unfair) to increase *redistribution from* the better off as prescribed by the proportionality norm also find it fair (unfair) to increase *redistribution to* the worse off as prescribed by the reciprocity norm. Against this expectation, I expect two additional clusters of countries to emerge: countries skeptical of more *redistribution from* policies but supportive of extending *redistribution to* on the one hand, and countries enthusiastic about more *redistribution from* but opposed to increasing *redistribution to* on the other.

Individual-Level Results

Since the late 1980s, the BSAS has repeatedly asked a battery of items aimed at measuring core political beliefs regarding income redistribution, labor relations, income inequality, social insurance, unemployment insurance, and welfare recipients (Evans, Heath, and Lalljee 1996). When combined into multiple-item scales, these items have helped researchers place respondents on a "socialist versus laissez-faire – or left-right – dimension" as well as a "prowelfare versus antiwelfarist" dimension (Park et al. 2012). To the best of my knowledge, there has been no attempt to use these items as part of a larger inquiry into the mental maps people use to reason about redistributive

---

[15] I refer the reader to Cavaillé and Trump (2015) and Cavaillé (2023) for evidence from other waves of the BSAS.

social issues. I focus my analysis on the 2016 wave in particular, as it includes additional questions on the topic of progressive taxation alongside questions about social spending for the poor and the unemployed, as well as the traditional redistribution item used in most studies of redistributive preferences. Items are listed in Table 10.1.[16] Specifically, respondents were asked a set of questions about existing tax levels, differentiating between the taxes of the rich and those of the poor. I use these items to classify people based on the extent to which they think that the tax system in 2016 is not progressive enough (tax on the rich too low and on the poor, about right or too high). I assume that this measure provides a decent proxy of support for, or opposition to, a more progressive tax system and examine whether the tax progressivity item loads on the same dimension as items that measure proportionality beliefs.

Best practice, when testing for the existence of a latent structure using survey data, is to divide the sample in two and run an exploratory factor analysis (EFA) on the first half of the dataset and a confirmatory factor analysis (CFA) on the second half. I use the EFA to test the plausibility of a unidimensional versus a multidimensional factor solution. By letting all survey items freely load on any latent factors in the data, an EFA provides information on whether interitem correlations are larger for distinct subset of items. To improve the interpretation of factor loadings, an EFA imposes structure on the relationship between the latent factors.[17] Switching to a CFA provides a more reliable estimate of the correlations between latent factors. Indeed, in contrast to EFA, CFA imposes constraints on the factor loadings, allowing to freely estimate the correlation between latent factors (Costello and Osborne 2005; Matsunaga 2010). In other words, an EFA tells us which items "go together" and to what extent, while a CFA tells us whether the latent factors underpinning each cluster of items are meaningfully correlated or not.[18]

Table 10.1 presents the results from the CFA (for EFA results, see Cavaillé, 2023). They indicate that the two-dimensional conceptualization of fairness reasoning and demand for redistribution sketched in Figure 10.3 better explains the correlation patterns found in the BSAS than the unidimensional conceptualization sketched in Figure 10.2. Indeed, the estimation returns a correlation coefficient of 0.19. Furthermore, when analyzing earlier waves, I cannot reject the null that the two dimensions are orthogonal to each other (see Cavaillé 2023). Policy items load in expected ways. First, questions about transfers to the poor and the unemployed load more strongly on the same latent dimension as reciprocity

---

[16] For more details on model selection, see Cavaillé (2023).
[17] In an EFA, the correlation between the latent factors is highly dependent on the rotation technique applied to extract the factor loadings.
[18] For example, if the EFA returns more than one factor, and the CFA shows that they are highly correlated, then it becomes harder, despite the existence of more than one factor, to reject the unidimensional mental map sketched in Figure 10.2.

TABLE 10.1 *Attitude structure in Great Britain: confirmatory factor analysis*

Item wording	1st Factor	2nd Factor
Reciprocity beliefs		
Benefits for unemployed people: too low and cause hardship vs. too high and discourage job seeking [dole]	0.60	
The welfare state encourages people to stop helping each other [welfhelp]	0.45	
If welfare benefits weren't so generous, people would learn to stand on their own two feet [welffeet]	0.87	
Many people who get welfare don't really deserve any help [sochelp]	0.71	
Most unemployed people could find a job if they really wanted one [unempjob]	0.71	
Most people on the dole are fiddling [dolefidl]	0.69	
Redistribution to policies		
Gov't responsibility: good standard of living for the unemployed [govresp6]	0.51	0.21
More spending on unemployment benefits [morewelf]	0.50	0.20
Proportionality beliefs		
Management will always try to get the better of employees if it gets the chance [indust4]		0.65
There is one law for rich and one for poor [richlaw]		0.71
Working people do not get their fair share of nation's wealth [wealth]		0.87
Big business benefits owners at the expense of workers [bigbusnn]		0.83
Redistribution from policies		
Tax progressivity (combined items) [taxlowsc/taxhisc]	0.53	
It is the responsibility of the government to reduce the differences in income [govresp7]	0.32	0.58
Government should redistribute income from the better-off to those who are least well-off [redistrb]	0.18	0.65
Correlation coefficient between factors (95% CI)	0.19 [0.10, 0.29]	
Standardized root mean squared residual assuming 2 dimensions (shown)	0.075	
Standardized root mean squared residual assuming 1 dimension	0.171	
Sample size	658	

Notes: Results are based on a confirmatory factor analysis; final model relaxes the assumption that policy items load on one dimension only.
Source: British Social Attitudes Survey, 2016.

beliefs items. Second, items asking about taxes load on the same latent dimension as proportionality beliefs items.

TABLE 10.2 *Reciprocity beliefs: factor loadings*

Item wording	ESS 2008	ESS 2016
Beliefs about the ubiquity of shirking		
Most unemployed people do not really try to find a job	0.54	0.65
Many manage to obtain benefits/services not entitled to	0.40	0.49
Employees often pretend they are sick to stay at home	0.47	NA
Beliefs about the disincentive effects of social benefits		
Social benefits/services make people lazy	0.77	0.80
Social benefits/services make people less willing to look after themselves/family	0.80	NA
Social benefits/services make people less willing to care for one another	0.79	0.71
***Redistribution to* policies**		
Role of government to ensure a reasonable standard of living for the unemployed?	0.34	0.28
Eigenvalue	2.65	1.91

Notes: Exploratory factor analysis on the pooled data using a polychoric correlation matrix adapted to ordinal variables. Extracted method: iterated principal factor method, robust to using other extraction methods. Countries included in the analysis are GB, FR, IE, BE, PT, DE, NL, CH, NO, AT, ES, FI, DK, SE, GR, as well as EE, HU, PL, SI, SK, CZ. The latter countries were included because they are market economies with large welfare states. Note however, that given half a century of Soviet occupation, the results for these countries should be analyzed with caution.
Sources: ESS 2008 (round 4) and ESS 2016 (round 8).
Reprinted with permission from Cavaillé (2023). Copyright © 2023 by Cambridge University Press.

Interestingly, attitudes toward income redistribution as traditionally measured most strongly load on this second latent dimension, implying that answers to this item are best explained by differences in proportionality beliefs, not differences in reciprocity beliefs. In other words, and against common expectations in political economy, answers to the traditional redistribution item appear only weakly correlated with beliefs about the work ethic of net beneficiaries of redistribution: support for redistribution measured in this fashion is best interpreted as support for *redistribution from* policies, not *redistribution to* policies.

As previously mentioned, data limitations preclude me from running the same analysis in countries beyond Great Britain. As a result, I focus on testing empirical expectations adapted to the available data. In 2008 and 2016, the ESS included a battery of items similar to the ones used in the British analysis to measure reciprocity beliefs (listed in Table 10.2). Both waves of the ESS also included a version of the traditional redistribution question worded as follows: "The government should take measures to reduce differences in income levels. Agree/disagree?" I examine whether, as found in the BSAS, knowing what someone thinks about the prevalence of free riding among welfare recipients

TABLE 10.3 *Opposition to redistribution is not predicted by reciprocity beliefs*

	Probability of not agreeing that gov't should redistribute		
	Fair – free riding not a concern (10th percentile)	Unfair – Too much free riding (90th percentile)	Delta
2008			
France	0.20	0.21	0.01
Germany	0.31	0.38	0.06
Sweden	0.29	0.45	0.16
Denmark	0.50	0.65	0.16
Netherlands	0.42	0.48	0.06
Great Britain	0.39	0.43	0.04
Spain	0.20	0.20	0.00
Poland	0.21	0.28	0.07
2016			
France	0.24	0.25	0.01
Germany	0.23	0.32	0.09
Sweden	0.26	0.49	0.23
Denmark	NA	NA	NA
Netherlands	0.34	0.46	0.11
Great Britain	0.29	0.41	0.12
Spain	0.10	0.22	0.13
Poland	0.24	0.32	0.08

Notes: People who agree and strongly agree that the government should redistribute income are coded as 0. Other response categories are coded as 1.
Sources: ESS 2008 (round 4) and ESS 2016 (round 8).
Reprinted with permission from Cavaillé (2023). Copyright © 2023 by Cambridge University Press.

says little about their agreement with the claim that the government should redistribute income from the most to the least worse off.

To do so, I use items listed in Table 10.2 to compute individual factor scores that rank respondents according to how prevalent (and concerning) they believe free riding to be.[19] Table 10.3 (top panel) reports the predicted probability of disagreeing with the principle of income redistribution for a hypothetical individual with a reciprocity belief score equal to the 10th and 90th percentile of scores in her country. I repeat this analysis using the 2016 data, results are presented in the bottom panel of Table 10.3. In most countries and in both waves, moving from the 10th to the 90th percentile on the

---

[19] I use factor scores derived from factor loadings obtained after separate country-by-country factor analyses. Results are the same if I use an IRT model to compute individual scores. The same applies if I use country-specific loadings or the same loadings for all countries

reciprocity scores says little about one's level of opposition to income redistribution as traditionally measured. There is one notable exception to this pattern, Sweden, with a differential equal to 23 percentage points for the year 2016. Additional analysis seems to indicate that, in Sweden, the correlation between the two latent dimensions is likely higher than in other countries (Cavaillé and Trump 2015).

Country-Level Analysis

Moving from the individual to the country level, I combine data from the ESS survey of 2008 and the ISSP survey of 2009 to examine country differences in fairness beliefs and policy preferences. First, a few words on the ISSP items, which are listed in Table 10.4. The first measurement item combines answers to a set of questions asking about the perceived and preferred income of a fixed set of occupations. Specifically, I regress items capturing preferred income (what ought to be) over items capturing perceived income (what is). The resulting regression coefficient is equal to 1 if a respondent believes that existing income differences align with their preferred income differences. The closer the coefficient is to zero, the more the respondents believe that existing income differences (as they perceive them) deviate from their preferred benchmark. In other words, this item measures perceived dissatisfaction-satisfaction with existing income differences. The second item captures the extent to which people think blue-collar workers are underpaid. I focus on this occupation

TABLE 10.4 *Proportionality beliefs and "redistribution from": factor loadings*

	2009	1999
1. Labor income: IS versus OUGHT	0.37	0.31
2. Blue-collar worker income: IS versus OUGHT	0.42	0.40
3. Shape of society	0.46	0.50
4. Income differences are too large	0.77	0.78
5. Inequality continues to exist because it benefits the rich and powerful	NA	0.51
6. Wealth important to get ahead	0.24	0.21
7. Effort important to get ahead	0.13	NA
8. Government should reduce income differences	0.74	0.76
9. People with high income pay more taxes than people with low income	0.45	0.55
Eigenvalue	1.97	2.30

Notes: Exploratory factor analysis on the pooled data using a polychoric correlation matrix adapted to ordinal variables. Extracted method: iterated principal factor method, robust to using other extraction methods. Note the small factor loading on items 6 and 7, items which are often used in the "does effort pay?" literature.
Sources: ISSP 1999 and ISSP 2009.
Reprinted with permission from Cavaillé (2023). Copyright © 2023 by Cambridge University Press.

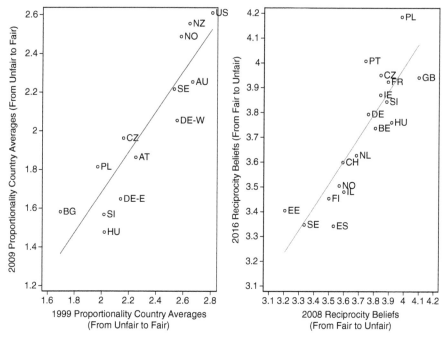

FIGURE 10.4 Changes in fairness beliefs
Note: See text for more detail on the measures.
Sources: ESS 2008 (round 4) and ESS 2016 (round 8), ISSP 1999 and ISSP 2009.
Reprinted with permission from Cavaillé (2023). Copyright © 2023 by Cambridge University Press.

as embodying the quintessential hardworking individual: respondents who believe that this individual is underpaid are less likely to believe that effort alone is enough.[20] The third item is a dummy variable equal to 1 if a respondent perceives the society she lives in as highly unequal, that is, a few rich at the top and most people at the bottom. Items 4 and 5 directly ask about inequality, while items 6 and 7 ask about the role of wealth and effort to get ahead in the country respondents live in. Item 8 is the ISSP's version of the traditional redistribution item, while item 9 asks about support for more progressive taxation.

Table 10.4 includes factor loadings from an EFA on the pooled data: all items load on the same latent factor. I also repeat the analysis on the 1999 wave of the ISSP, which includes many of the same items.[21] I use these items to compute factor scores that measure individual differences in how much

---

[20] Note that the correlation between items 1 and 2 is between 0.3 and 0.5 depending on the country.
[21] Note that in 1999, respondents were asked about income differences for eleven occupations, while in 2009 they were only asked about five occupations.

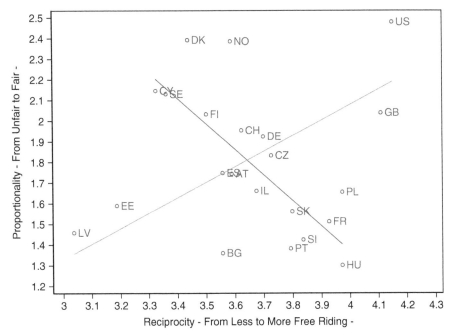

FIGURE 10.5 Correlation between proportionality and reciprocity beliefs
Notes: See text for more detail on the measures. Note that the US score on the X-axis is approximated using Svallfors (2012).
Sources: ESS 2008 (round 4) and ISSP 2009.
Reprinted with permission from Cavaillé (2023). Copyright © 2023 by Cambridge University Press.

people find income differences unfair (fair) and support (oppose) redistribution. I then aggregate these scores at the country level.

Figure 10.4 compares country averages computed using the 2009 wave with country averages computed using the 1999 wave. The correlation between the 1999 country averages and the 2009 averages is 0.90 ($N = 13$). Figure 10.4 also includes the same analysis using the 2008 and 2016 waves of the ESS. Specifically, I use the items in Table 10.4 to compute factor scores measuring individual differences in the extent to which people believe the unemployed and the poor are free riding and oppose transfers that benefit this group. In this case, the correlation between the two waves is 0.86 ($N = 19$). Fairness beliefs appear to be a stable component of a country's attitudinal landscape.

Figure 10.5 combines the 2008 wave of the ESS and the 2009 wave of the ISSP. Note that the ESS does not include the United States. To place this country with regards to the reciprocity norm, I have relied on data collected independently by Clem Brooks and available in Svallfors (2012). Brooks' results show that response patterns in the United States are similar to those found in Great Britain. Overall, very few countries align along the traditional left-right axis (from the bottom-left to the top-right), which runs from consistently pro-redistribution beliefs (fair according to reciprocity, unfair according to proportionality) to consistently antiredistribution beliefs (unfair according to reciprocity, fair according to proportionality). If anything, the key axis appears to be one running from fair to unfair according to both norms.

Given the imperfection of available items, the country-level evidence remains tentative. Nevertheless, it highlights the limits of existing approaches to fairness reasoning as well as the benefits of the two-dimensional framework. First, notice how, despite very different institutional setups, Denmark, Norway, and the United States are in the same ballpark when it comes to proportionality beliefs. Scandinavians find their economic system fair and rightly so: mobility rates are much higher and differences in market income lower. As a result, in these countries, support for income redistribution, as traditionally measured, is often lower than one might expect. In Denmark, for example, agreement with the traditional redistribution item was a low 55 percent, compared to a high 90 percent in Portugal. Where Scandinavian countries differ from the United States is in terms of their reciprocity beliefs: they express high trust and comparatively much lower concerns about free riding and moral hazard. In contrast, the United States (and Great Britain) are much more likely to perceive unemployed workers as undeserving and be concerned about shirking. There is a similar split among countries that find the economic system and income inequality unfair. France and most post-communist countries are closer to the United States and Great Britain than to Scandinavian countries in terms of their level of concern about free riding. The exceptions are Baltic countries who appear satisfied with how welfare spending is disbursed in their country.

Overall, the two-dimensional structure found at the individual level is also found at the country level, echoing the ideal-typical setup sketched in Figure 10.3 (right panel). Jointly, the individual- and country-level evidence demonstrates that the conceptualization of fairness presented in this chapter provides a better fit to the available survey data than existing work on fairness reasoning. In the concluding section, I discuss implications for studying the relationship between income inequality and attitudes toward redistributive policies.

IMPLICATIONS FOR POLICY CHANGE
IN THE AGE OF INEQUALITY

I have argued that in Western societies with mature welfare states, there exist, to paraphrase Michael Walzer, distinct "spheres" of fairness, each with their own social good and distributive principle (Walzer 1983). The "economy" and "markets" produce one type of good – market income – whose allocation is, at least partly, regulated (and contested) through the proportionality principle. "Society," through the "welfare state," pools resources to produce a second type of good – social insurance in the form of social benefits – whose allocation is, at least partly, regulated through the reciprocity principle. The existence of a shared understanding of what constitutes fair inequality and fair social solidarity (i.e., shared norms of fairness) helps regulate envy, minimize resentment, and promote consensual resource sharing. When fairness beliefs, policy preferences, and existing institutional arrangements complement each other, then the system is in equilibrium. On the policy side, this means that fairness beliefs constrain the types of policy reforms that get implemented: those that do not "fit" existing fairness beliefs tend to fail. On the mass opinion side, changes in aggregate preferences should be limited to small fluctuations around a stable mean. What evidence do we have for this?

With regards to policy reforms, one interesting case is that of flexicurity, a type of policy reform first promoted in Scandinavian countries and heralded as the ideal combination of market efficiency and social solidarity. Based on Figure 10.5, Scandinavian countries' combination of fairness beliefs appears particularly hospitable to such reform: the belief that effort pays underpins support for proactive labor market policy, while the belief that abuse of social spending and free riding is the exception, not the norm, underpins support for generous social insurance. Now imagine trying to advocate for such reforms in a country like France, which holds the exact opposite beliefs: these reforms are likely to poll poorly. A combination of vocal opposition from those directly affected by the reform and bad polling will be enough to block proposed reform packages. This has indeed been a recurrent pattern in France since the mid-1990s. France, which taxes high incomes and regulates the market based on the belief that effort does not pay, appears to be less enthusiastic about deepening the redistributive features of social insurance. While there have been no dramatic welfare cuts in France, this might nevertheless preclude welfare reforms that seek to better meet the needs of the growing contingent of labor market "outsiders" (Emmenegger et al. 2011; Rueda 2007; Saint-Paul 1999).

With regards to public opinion, in line with expectations, stability is the norm and change is the exception. Indeed, as shown by Kenworthy and McCall, while aggregate social policy preferences vary across countries, they do not vary nearly as much over time (Kenworthy 2009; Kenworthy and McCall 2008; McCall and Kenworthy 2009; see also Svallfors 2016). These patterns, in line with the hypothesis of fairness reasoning as the manifestation of an order producing social technology, align with the hypothesized existence of self-reinforcing equilibria.

This suggests a key role for fairness reasoning in explaining the disconnect between rising inequality and support for redistribution (specifically, the *redistribution from* a subset of redistributive policies that interfere with the accumulation of market income among the better off). For most people, income inequality is an abstract reality, meaningful only through the lenses of fairness reasoning and prior proportionality beliefs. At the individual level, stable proportionality beliefs introduce a disconnect between changes in inequality and mass perceptions of these changes. At the aggregate level, only a subset of the population (the one that already finds market income unfair) will experience a rise in income inequality as something that needs to be addressed. Ultimately, countries with institutions most favorable (unfavorable) to an increase in income inequality are also those most likely to have a larger share of the population that believes that income inequality is fair (unfair) and are less likely to increase their support for policies that interfere with this distribution (Bénabou and Tirole 2006).

This argument presented in this chapter also has implications for research on demand for redistribution broadly defined.[22] For example, studies that focus on information about inequality as the missing link in the causal chain connecting inequality to demand for redistribution (e.g., Matthews et al., this volume) assume a very specific distribution of fairness beliefs, one in which the median voter finds the status quo unfair, as defined by the proportionality norm. Only then can we expect more information on rising income inequality to translate into a growing demand for more egalitarian policies. However, whether or not a majority perceives income inequality as a violation of the proportionality norm is something to be explained, not assumed.

Researchers should also revisit expectations that disruptive events such as an economic recession or a pandemic have implications for mass policy preferences. Absent ideal conditions, the expectation should be that mass attitudes will not be affected by such events. Instead of puzzling over "too much" stability, researchers might choose to focus their efforts on theorizing what such "ideal conditions" for change might look like. One recent example is given by Scheve and Stasavage (2016). Change, they argue, happens as a result of a unique "shock" (i.e., total warfare) and political entrepreneurs finding the correct fairness appeal to present policy innovations as both necessary and fair. Total warfare constitutes a social dilemma: citizens' individual interest is to defect, at the expense of the collective. In line with the reciprocity principle, their willingness to contribute their blood to the war effort is conditional on the belief that everyone is engaged in a similar sacrifice, that is, nobody is free riding (Levi 1991). In such a context, large economic profits are perceived to violate the reciprocity norm: they reflect an actors' selfish economic gains at the expense of the collective (ultimate) sacrifice. According to Scheve and Stavasage, the ability to (temporarily) frame high-income earners as war profiteers who violate the reciprocity norm helps explain why some countries were able to introduce wealth taxation while others were not. In other words, total warfare opens the door to a new type of critique of high-income individuals as profiteers abusing the joint effort. When mobilized by political actors, this fairness language finds echo in people's personal experiences of hardship and sacrifice.

---

[22] In a formal paper, Iversen and Soskice (2009) examine the implications of transforming redistributive politics into a multidimensional game. This chapter has provided new evidence in support of such critical departure from standard models based on Meltzer and Richard (1981).

11

The News Media and the Politics of Inequality in Advanced Democracies[*]

J. Scott Matthews, Timothy Hicks, and Alan M. Jacobs

This chapter considers the role of economic information in generating political inequality across income groups. Income inequality across many advanced democracies has risen sharply over the last four decades (Lupu and Pontusson, this volume). Not only have market incomes become increasingly concentrated among the very rich in a wide range of national contexts; so, too, have posttax-and-transfer incomes. In other words, many elected governments, notwithstanding the formidable range of market-shaping and redistributive policy instruments at their disposal, have over an extended period of time allowed a narrow and extremely affluent segment of the population to reap a further outsized share of the fruits of economic growth. How has this happened? What has allowed inequalities in material resources to mount in political systems that, nominally, distribute votes equally across adult citizens? Why have basic mechanisms of electoral accountability not induced governments to pursue economic and social policies that better serve the distributional interests of the vast majority of the electorate?

While scholars have identified a wide range of causes of political inequality in advanced democracies (many of them the focus of other chapters of this volume), our focus is on an examination of a key informational prism through which voters learn about the state of the economy: the news media. A vast literature points to the strong influence of citizens' evaluations of the economy on their votes (e.g., Duch and Stevenson 2008; Lewis-Beck 1988).

[*] The authors rotate ordering across their joint publications to reflect equal contributions. We are grateful, for helpful research assistance, to Daniel Rojas Lozano and Camila Scheidegger Farias and, for excellent comments on an earlier version, to the participants in the "Unequal Democracies" seminar series. The authors acknowledge the generous support of the Social Sciences and Humanities Research Council of Canada (Grant #435-2014-0603).

Meanwhile, a substantial body of evidence highlights the powerful role that the news media play in informing citizens' economic evaluations (Blood and Phillips 1995; De Boef and Kellstedt 2004; Boydstun, Highton, and Linn 2018; Garz and Martin 2021; Goidel et al. 2010; Hollanders and Vliegenthart 2011; Mutz 1992; Nadeau, Niemi, and Amato 1999).

Building on our own prior work on the United States (Jacobs et al. 2021) and presenting a set of new cross-national analyses, we investigate how journalistic depictions of the economy relate to real distributional developments. In particular, we ask: when the news media report "good" or "bad" economic news, whose material welfare are they capturing? How does the positivity and negativity of the economic news track income gains and losses at different points along the income spectrum?

Using sentiment analysis of vast troves of economic news content from a broad set of advanced democracies (drawing on data from Kayser and Peress 2021), we demonstrate that the evaluative content of the economic news strongly and disproportionately tracks the fortunes of the very rich. Although we observe somewhat more news responsiveness to the welfare of the middle class in this cross-national sample than we did in our earlier US study, the pro-rich skew in economic news observed in other advanced democracies is highly comparable to that found in the United States. To the extent that economic news shapes citizens' economic evaluations and that evaluations of the economy shape votes, we thus have in hand at least a partial potential explanation of why mechanisms of electoral accountability have failed to deliver more equal economic outcomes.

And yet the finding of class-biased economic news raises one further puzzle: why does economic news content appear to overrespond to gains and losses for the rich? We review a range of potential explanations drawn from the existing media studies literature, most of which posit a set of interests or preferences among news owners, producers, sources, or consumers that lead inexorably to a pro-rich bias in economic reporting.

We then propose an alternative account, arguing that pro-rich biases in news tone could arise from routines of economic reporting in which journalists aim to capture the performance of the economy in the aggregate while paying minimal attention to distributive matters. In this model, the class bias in news content need not arise from a set of pro-rich interests within the news sector, but from the workings of the economy itself: from the fact that, in most capitalist democracies, aggregate expansion and contraction over the last forty years have been positively and disproportionately correlated with the rise and fall, respectively, of the incomes of the very rich. Thus, a news media that seeks merely to cover the ups and downs of the business cycle will generate news that, implicitly, tracks the fortunes of the most affluent. Voters will tend to read "good" economic news in those periods when inequality is rising and "bad" economic news as disparities shrink. We test key predictions of this theory on a large sample of news content from a broad range of OECD contexts, finding that movements in GDP growth, unemployment, and share valuations explain most of the association between news tone and relative gains for the very rich. In addition, we show that pro-rich bias in the economic news is relatively uniform across outlets with varying partisan slants, suggesting that these biases arise at least in part from sources other than journalists' or owners' economic preferences.

In sum, the analyses that we present in this chapter suggest that the democratic politics of inequality may be shaped in important ways by the skewed nature of the informational environment within which citizens form economic evaluations. Moreover, this informational skew appears to be in part a product of the underlying structure of the economy itself. In an economy that distributed aggregate economic gains relatively equally, journalists and voters alike could fairly well assess the changing welfare of the typical household simply by following the ups and downs of the business cycle. In a political economy that generates systematically biased distributions of the fruits of growth, however, the informational demands of our normative model of democratic accountability are steeper, and there is reason to worry that the news media are not currently meeting those demands.

THE ECONOMIC-INEQUALITY PUZZLE

A substantial share of advanced democracies has witnessed rising inequality in posttax-and-transfer income over the last four decades. We illustrate the pattern in Figure 11.1, where we plot change over time (1980–2014) in the posttax-and-transfer income share of the richest 1 percent of individuals for nineteen advanced democracies, grouping countries approximately by welfare-state-regime type (see "Data" for information on data sources). We see that top-income shares, after taxes and transfers, have risen considerably across most of these countries: most steeply in countries with liberal welfare states; somewhat less so, but still markedly in social democracies; and more modestly but nontrivially in continental, corporatist settings. In Southern Europe, we see top-income shares holding about steady over this period (see also Lupu and Pontusson, this volume).

Governments in these nations have had opportunities to shape the allocation of households' consumption possibilities at multiple stages. A range of "predistributive" policies can influence the allocation of income derived from labor and capital, while tax rules and social welfare systems can, and to varying degrees do, compensate for market-driven disparities. Given the powerful tools at the state's disposal for influencing final distributional outcomes, those countries in which disposable income (and wealth) have become increasingly concentrated among the very rich represent a puzzle: how have political systems that are nominally governed under the principle of political equality failed to generate more egalitarian outcomes?

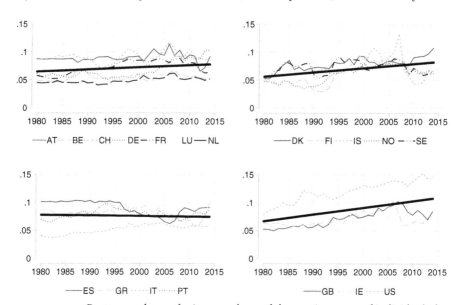

FIGURE 11.1 Posttax-and-transfer income share of the top 1 percent of individuals for nineteen advanced democracies
Note: Thick black lines are overtime trends based on pooled OLS regressions.
Source: World Inequality Database (sdiinc992jp99p100).

Explanations for rising postgovernment inequality (or, similarly, for the incompleteness of compensatory redistribution) abound, and many are considered in this volume. We can distinguish between two broad lines of explanation. One such line emphasizes political inequality, or differentials in influence wielded by the rich and the nonrich: the nonrich might want more equal outcomes, but their demands lose out in the political sphere to those of the most affluent (e.g., Giger, Rosset, and Bernauer 2012; Gilens 2012; Hacker and Pierson 2011, 2020; Peters and Ensink 2015; Bartels, this volume; Mathisen et al., this volume).

A second line of explanation focuses on the "demand side" of the political dynamic and, in particular, on the attitudes and political behavior of the non-rich.[1] We can usefully think of demand-side research on the politics of inequality as coming in two varieties. A majority of demand-side scholarship has focused on citizens' policy preferences, such as their level of support for redistribution (e.g., Cavaillé, this volume; Cavaillé and Trump 2015; Cramer, this volume; Fong 2001; Kenworthy and McCall 2007; Lupu and Pontusson 2011). If we aim to explain elected governments' distributional policy choices, then citizens' attitudes toward those policy choices is a perfectly reasonable place to start.

---

[1] The distinction between these two lines of explanation blurs, of course, once we consider what Lukes (1974) called the "third face" of power: economic elites can exercise power through activities that shape preferences.

At the end of the day, however, incumbents in a democracy who wish to remain in office must win elections, a goal that may depend only weakly on their distributive policies. Voters typically lack strong preferences on all but the most salient policy controversies (Converse 2006, 1964; Tesler 2015) and, in the absence of specific views, may be inclined to adopt the positions of candidates who are favored for reasons unrelated to their policy commitments (Lenz 2012; but see Matthews 2019). When distributional issues do meaningfully influence vote choice, furthermore, that influence may be swamped by other considerations.

On the other hand, among the best-established regularities uncovered in decades of research on electoral behavior is that voters' choices are strongly influenced by economic outcomes, or, at least, by voters' assessments of those outcomes (e.g., Duch and Stevenson 2008; Lewis-Beck 1988). A second line of demand-side inquiry has begun to examine how economic voting interacts with the politics of distribution, asking how electorates respond to different distributions of economic gains and losses. This line of research is motivated by a baseline, normative notion of how economic voting might work: we might in principle expect nonrich members of the electorate to defend their economic interests at the ballot box by voting out governments that oversee patterns of (income) growth that concentrate gains at the very top and rewarding incumbents that spread gains broadly. Even in the absence of conscious demands for redistribution, electoral dynamics should serve as a brake on rising material inequality if citizens cast their economic votes in distributionally sensitive ways, in ways that align in some way with their income stratum's distributional economic interests. Do they?

The answers we have so far suggest that electorates respond to distributional outcomes in a manner directly at odds with this normative model. Not only do nonrich voters appear not to vote their distributional interests, but patterns of economic voting may play a substantial role in incentivizing governments to concentrate economic gains at the top. Studying presidential elections from 1952 to 2012, Bartels (2016) finds that incumbent parties in the United States perform better in election years with higher rates of income growth at the 95th percentile, conditional on mean income growth. In other words, for any given level of per capita income growth, incumbent parties receive an electoral premium when a higher share of that growth flows to the family at the 95th income percentile. At the same time, the US presidential electorate as a whole appears unresponsive to mean income growth after taking into account income growth at the top. Moreover, and most puzzlingly, this broad pattern – which Bartels (2016) terms "class-biased economic voting" – holds specifically for voters in the bottom third and in the middle third of the income distribution. Lower-income voters appear to respond favorably to top-income growth conditional on mean growth, but not at all to mean growth conditional on top-end growth. And while middle-income voters show some responsiveness to mean income growth, they are about twice as responsive to top-income growth.

In an extension of Bartels' work, we find clear evidence of the operation of class-biased economic voting in a broader comparative context (Hicks, Jacobs, and Matthews 2016). Analyzing individual-level election-study data, for instance, we find that lower- and middle-income voters in Sweden and the United Kingdom vote for the incumbent party at higher rates as income growth for the richest 5 percent rises for any given level of mean growth, and appear unmoved by income growth for the bottom 95 percent.[2] Further, analysis of aggregate election data for 200 postwar elections across fifteen OECD countries reveals a substantial average reward to the incumbent party for overseeing rising income shares for the top 5 percent. And, as in the United States, OECD electorates on average fail to reward governing parties for the portion of mean income growth that does not flow to the top.

In short, what we know about the relationship between distributional dynamics and electoral patterns suggests a serious empirical problem with a normative model in which voters defend their (income groups') economic interests at the ballot box. What we seem to be seeing is not the absence of economic voting but a distributionally perverse form of it. The observed patterns suggest the operation of one or more mechanisms that do more than prevent citizens from casting economic votes in distributionally sensitive ways; they seem to turn distributional self-interest on its head.

In the remainder of this chapter, we focus on a mechanism that plausibly intervenes in critical ways between the economy and voter evaluations: the news media. A substantial body of evidence highlights the powerful role that the news media plays in informing citizens' economic evaluations (Blood and Phillips 1995; Boydstun, Highton, and Linn 2018; De Boef and Kellstedt 2004; Garz and Martin 2021; Goidel et al. 2010; Hollanders and Vliegenthart 2011; Mutz 1992; Nadeau, Niemi, and Amato 1999). A key question, then, is how economic news coverage itself relates to objective distributional dynamics in the economy. If the economic news disproportionately reflects the economic experiences of the very rich, then nonrich voters will be operating in an informational environment that is, in an important sense, systematically skewed against their own material interests. In the section that follows, we consider reasons why the economic news in advanced capitalist democracies might tend to be biased in favor of the interests of the most affluent.

POTENTIAL PREFERENCE- OR INTEREST-BASED SOURCES OF CLASS-BIASED ECONOMIC NEWS

It is not difficult to imagine reasons why major news outlets might cover the economy in ways that favor the interests of the rich. One possible source of

---

[2] Notably, we do not find evidence of this same perverse pattern in Canada. Rather, the Canadian electorate displays what we might call an indifference to inequality, neither rewarding nor punishing incumbents on average for rising income shares at the top.

such bias might be the general economic interests of media owners. Since the owners of news outlets tend to be either large corporations or very rich families (Grisold and Preston 2020; Herman and Chomsky 1994), they share an interest in rising concentrations of income and wealth at the top. Moreover, news outlets depend on revenue from advertisers, who themselves may have an interest in policies that promote or permit higher inequality. To the extent that owners and advertisers can influence content, the result may be economic coverage that systematically favors the interests of wealthy households and corporations (for a formalization, see Petrova 2008; though see also Bailard 2016; Gilens and Hertzman 2000: 371).

A further potential source of class bias in economic reporting might arise from the upper-middle-class composition and elite educational background of most members of the journalism profession (e.g., Gans 2004, 124–138; Weaver, Willnat, and Wilhoit 2019). Journalists' interpretation of economic events may be shaped directly by their class interests, and their involvement in upper-middle-class social networks might shape the kind of information about the economy to which they are exposed and, in turn, their beliefs about which economic topics are newsworthy.

On a related note, bias in economic-news content might derive from the skewed perspective of the sources on whom journalists routinely rely when reporting on the economy. As numerous studies have documented, economic reporters looking for commentary and analysis tend to turn disproportionately to elites with close ties to the business community and finance (Call et al. 2018; Davis 2002, 2018; Knowles 2018; Knowles, Phillips, and Lidberg 2017; Wren-Lewis 2018). Dependence on economic-elite and corporate sources might tend to generate coverage that systematically privileges the interests of firms, financial institutions, and investors and that is skeptical of state intervention to redress inequality.

Independently of owners', reporters', or sources' interests and outlooks, readers of economic news may themselves tend to be more affluent than the general population (Davis 2018) and prefer content that reflects their material interests. Gentzkow and Shapiro (2010) find suggestive evidence of the effects of audience partisanship on editorial content in the United States, while Beckers et al. (2021) find that Belgian journalists overestimate the conservatism of the general public, a perception that might dampen any focus on inequality and boost attentiveness to outcomes aligned with the interests of the rich.

A further possibility is that, in many OECD contexts since the 1970s, economic reporting as a whole has been influenced by a general, rightward ideological shift in the political sphere, especially the ascendance of free-market ideas (Davis 2018; DiMaggio 2017; Schifferes and Knowles 2018). Cutting against this view, however, is evidence that journalistic opinion (e.g., Rothman and Lichter 1985) and use of sources (Groseclose and Milyo 2005) reflect a left-wing bias (though see Nyhan 2012) and findings of considerable ideological variation in news outlets' economic content (Arrese 2018; Barnes and Hicks 2018; Larcinese, Puglisi, and Snyder 2011).

A THEORY OF NEWS BIAS INDEPENDENT OF
PREFERENCES: COVERING THE BUSINESS CYCLE

While the material interests and ideological preferences of those who produce, inform, or consume the news might all serve to skew journalistic portrayals of the economy, we will argue that a pro-rich tilt in the economic news can readily emerge from a process in which news outlets seek to do nothing more than faithfully report on the aggregate state of the economy – depending on how the economy itself operates. If journalists seek to assess overall economic performance but economic growth itself is associated with greater relative gains for the rich, then media evaluations of the economy will tend to most closely track the welfare of the rich, even in the absence of pro-rich preferences among media actors themselves.

To be clear, the argument that follows is not a case against the view that ideological or interest-based biases shape economic news coverage. What we seek to elucidate in this section is how features of the economy itself, together with a set of facially neutral journalistic operating routines, could themselves be sufficient to generate bias before the worldviews or class interests of news producers even enter into the equation.[3]

A Focus on Economic Aggregates

We begin by positing the operation among journalists of an understanding – a "mental model" – of the economy that treats the promotion of aggregate expansion as the central, if not exclusive, objective of economic management. In his classic study of American newsrooms, Gans (2004) finds that "responsible capitalism" is among the core values of American journalism and that, in economic reporting, "[e]conomic growth is always a positive phenomenon" (p. 46). Thomas' (2018) analysis of British TV news during the postfinancial-crisis recovery similarly finds that economic growth was depicted as an unalloyed good, while Davis (2018) reports that British economic reporting largely "focuses on a series of headline macroeconomic indicators," including GDP growth and unemployment (p. 165). "Good" and "bad" economic news, then, are defined by developments that signal or reflect an upturn or a downturn, respectively, in the business cycle – especially in output and its close correlate, employment.

In this framework, moreover, distributional questions as such are generally not salient, on the assumption that the benefits of economic growth are typically broadly distributed, with rampant rent-seeking by economically privileged actors rare. As Gans writes of TV news in the United States, journalists display "an optimistic faith that in the good society, businessmen and [business]women will compete with each other in order to create prosperity for all, but that they will refrain from unreasonable profits and gross exploitation of workers or customers." Along just these lines, in their study of coverage of the Bush tax cuts in the

---

[3] Discussion in the next three subsections borrows from Jacobs et al. (2021).

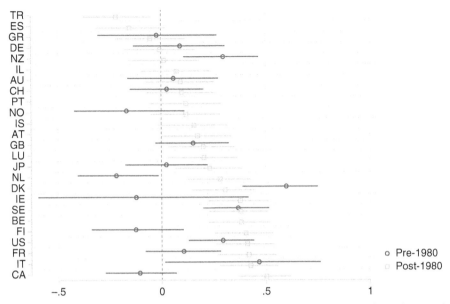

FIGURE 11.2 Correlation between the annual rate of GDP growth and annual change in top-1-percent pretax income shares for a broad set of countries, before and after 1980

Notes: Quarterly observations. Pre-1980 observations unavailable for certain countries.

Sources: World Inequality Database (sptinc992jp99p100); Kayser and Peress (2021).

United States, Bell and Entman (2011) find that news stories emphasized their potential effects on growth, while neglecting their likely impact on inequality.

Aggregate Growth and Distribution

How might a journalistic focus on economic aggregates generate a class bias in economic news? In principle, it need not. Where economic gains and losses were equally distributed, a journalistic focus on the business cycle would generate news that is equally sensitive to the fortunes of all income groups. However, that will cease to be the case in any context in which aggregate income growth is systematically skewed in favor of the most affluent. In particular, if economic growth, its drivers, or its presumed proxies (such as corporate performance) tend to generate higher concentrations of income at the top, then journalists who "cover the business cycle" will, without necessarily intending to, generate portraits of the economy that systematically and disproportionately track the fortunes of the rich.

In Figure 11.2, we plot the post-1980 correlation between the annual rate of GDP growth and annual change in top-1 percent pretax income shares for a broad set of countries, with the pre-1980 correlation plotted where data are

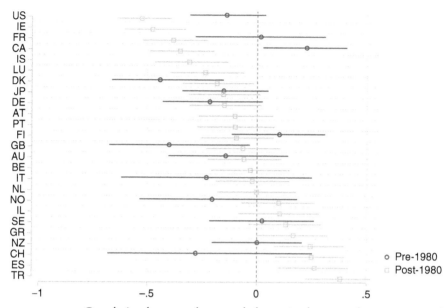

FIGURE 11.3 Correlation between the annual change in the unemployment rate and annual change in top-1-percent pretax income shares for a broad set of countries, before and after 1980

Notes: Quarterly observations. Pre-1980 observations unavailable for certain countries.
Sources: World Inequality Database (sptinc992jp99p100); Kayser and Peress (2021).

available (see "Data" for information on data sources). As we can see, since 1980, there is clear evidence of cyclicality of top-income shares in more than half of the countries in this sample. Put differently, it is incomes at the top that most closely track the business cycle: that grow fastest during periods of aggregate growth and fall most rapidly in recessions. We also note that the group of countries featuring cyclical inequality represents a wide range of political economies, from liberal market economies like Britain, the United States, and Canada to most of the coordinated market economies of Scandinavia. While pre-1980 data are missing for some countries, we also see considerable evidence, on balance, of increasing cyclicality over time.

In Figure 11.3, we turn to another oft-reported economic aggregate, the unemployment rate. The figure plots the correlation of annual change in the unemployment rate with annual change in top pretax income shares for all advanced democracies for which consistent data were available, pre- and post-1980. While unemployment is commonly understood to weaken the bargaining power of labor vis-à-vis capital, we see that change in the unemployment rate has more often been negatively correlated with income concentration at the top, meaning that years with falling unemployment have tended to be years of growing top-income shares – or in which top incomes grow faster than incomes of the nonrich. This is, again, the case for a diverse set of political economies, including the United States, Denmark, and France.[4]

Why do the incomes of the rich tend to grow faster than incomes of the nonrich during economic booms and fall faster during recessions? While we do not seek to unravel this piece of the puzzle in this chapter, we can point to a few possible suspects: reasons why the forces driving economic growth might simultaneously drive greater inequality. Several studies point to changes in the distribution of demand for skills driven by trade and technical change that might generate relatively faster growth (decline) in top incomes as overall output and employment expand (contract). Focusing on the United States, Cutler et al. (1991) argue that, during the recovery of the 1980s, while employment rose – a phenomenon that, on its own, would have benefited lower-paid workers – this aggregate development was overwhelmed by an increase in relative demand for higher-skilled labor, generating a net increase in wage dispersion and income inequality. In broader theoretical work, Aghion, Caroli, and García-Peñalosa (1999) contend that technological change, especially the spread of general-purpose technologies, has become a key driver of both economic growth and earnings inequality by creating a growing skill premium, particularly as the supply of higher-end skills fails to keep pace with demand (see also Goldin and Katz 2009; Parker and Vissing-Jorgensen 2010). Factors such as the increasing financialization of OECD economies (Lin and Tomaskovic-Devey 2013) and the decline of labor unions in many advanced economies (Volscho and Kelly 2012) may play a similar role, simultaneously driving higher rates of economic growth and higher concentrations of income at the top. And, of course, the same forces might not explain the observed correlations across political economies as different as the liberal United States and social democratic Denmark.

Whatever the underlying economic mechanisms, however, we can see that the share of income going to the most affluent has in recent decades been closely tied to key economic aggregates across a broad swathe of advanced democracies. The implication for the economic news is striking: the tone of news focused on economic aggregates, like growth and unemployment, will be characterized by a bias toward the interests of the very rich – even without any conscious intention, on journalists' part, to deliver a skewed portrait of the economy. To the extent that growth and income inequality arise from a common source, "good" economic times – understood in aggregate terms – will tend to be accompanied by rising concentrations of income at the top. We should, on this logic, expect economic news focused on the business cycle to more closely track the incomes of the very rich than the incomes of the nonrich, and we should expect the news to become more positive as income

---

[4] A more detailed discussion of the evidence on the exceptional (relative to other income groups) cyclicality of top incomes in the United States can be found in Jacobs et al. (2021).

inequality – understood as an income skew toward the top – rises. Given the steep concentration of company shareholding among the very rich, economic assessments tied to corporate or stock market performance will likewise be disproportionately correlated with welfare at the top of the income scale.

This argument (if true) would not imply that class-biased economic news emerges apolitically or via the ineluctable operation of market forces. In the United States, for instance, there is strong reason to believe that political choices in areas such as trade, education, labor relations, and taxation have played a substantial role in tying growth and inequality more closely together in recent decades (see, e.g., Hacker and Pierson 2011). Moreover, one could understand a journalistic focus on economic aggregates at the expense of distributional dynamics as itself ideological in nature – as a "blind spot" underwritten by a political worldview or material interests. Our claim, however, is that class-biased economic reporting itself need not involve any deliberate effort by reporters to overattend to the interests of the rich. Given the underlying distributional biases in the broader political economy, the emergence of class-biased news merely requires that journalists cheer the economy on during periods of aggregate growth and lament its decline in aggregate downturns.

Why would class-biased economic news matter for the politics of inequality? Recall that voters' choices are shaped to a substantial degree by sociotropic assessments of the economy and that those assessments are influenced by signals from the news media. If economic reporting is driven overwhelmingly by changes in economic aggregates, and the incomes of the nonrich are less closely correlated with aggregate growth than are the incomes of the rich, then the signals received by nonrich voters in many OECD contexts will most closely track the fortunes of the rich. The implication is not just that nonrich voters' economic assessments are less likely to capture welfare changes among the nonrich. It is also that nonrich voters are, on average, taking in more favorable assessments of economic performance at precisely those times when inequality is increasing – and less favorable signals as inequality is falling. To the extent that the economic vote is shaped by the news media, then, journalism that covers the business cycle – in a context in which the fruits of growth are concentrated at the top – will tend to generate an electoral environment favorable to rising income disparities between the rich and the rest.[5]

---

[5] The counterfactual implicit in this claim is one in which economic reporting *attends in a specific way to income changes among the nonrich*, rather than capturing such changes only insofar as they affect overall averages. We can readily imagine two forms in which the economic news might directly reflect income developments below the top. One possibility is that, rather than just seeking to characterize the aggregate economy, the media might differentially assess economic developments affecting different income groups – such as by characterizing welfare gains and losses separately for the rich and the nonrich or separately for the bottom, the middle, and the top of the income scale. Each income group in the electorate would then receive a distinct signal about how "their" economy is doing and would have the opportunity to vote on the basis of

Empirical Predictions

We can summarize our core argument with this simple causal graph:

$$\text{NewsTone} \leftarrow \text{GrowthAndEmployment} \leftarrow \text{X} \rightarrow \text{Inequality}$$

where X denotes a set of inequality-inducing drivers of growth and employment (e.g., trade, skill-biased technological change, financialization, union decline). In this model, the drivers of growth simultaneously generate aggregate expansion and higher inequality (i.e., higher income shares for the very rich). Economic aggregates, in turn, drive the positivity of economic news, resulting in a positive correlation between inequality and news tone. Importantly, inequality itself has no causal effect on news tone in this model, and class-biased economic news does not emerge from a journalistic response to inequality. Rather, class-biased news arises here from media actors placing a positive value on features of the economy that are systematically correlated with rising inequality, owing to common causes of these features of the economy and rising inequality.

Part of the analysis that follows is focused on the descriptive question of whether class bias is operating: whether the news tracks gains and losses for different income groups in a manner that is disproportionately sensitive to the welfare of the rich. In addition, we examine a number of empirical implications of our theorized causal mechanism. Specifically: (1) News tone should be positively correlated with inequality. (2) News tone should be correlated positively with GDP growth and negatively with unemployment rates. (3) A final prediction – one more specific to the aggregate-centered-journalism explanation for class-biased economic news – is that any correlation between inequality and news tone should be weaker conditional on the macroeconomic aggregates than it is unconditionally. In the language of Pearl (2009), conditioning on the macroeconomic aggregates should, under this causal model, "block" the path running between news tone and inequality, eliminating any correlation between the two that arises from this path (while potentially preserving other sources of correlation not captured in the model).

Further, in their efforts to find indicators of the performance of the overall economy, journalists may be expected to devote special attention to the health of the corporate sector – with corporate performance itself an important driver of inequality:

$$\text{NewsTone} \leftarrow \text{CorporatePerformance} \rightarrow \text{Inequality}$$

Under this argument, (4) corporate performance should be correlated with news tone, and (5) controlling for corporate performance should reduce

this more targeted signal. Another possibility is that economic reporting might attend to the distribution of income itself, such that economic evaluations are "discounted" for distributions of gains and losses that operate against the relative interests of less-affluent income groups. In either scenario, media evaluations of the economy would be more closely tied to changes in both the absolute and relative welfare of the nonrich.

the size of the correlation between top-end inequality and news tone, since conditioning on corporate performance blocks a path connecting these two variables.

EMPIRICAL EVIDENCE OF CLASS-BIASED ECONOMIC NEWS

We now consider empirical evidence on both the presence of class-biased economic news in advanced democracies and the mechanisms driving it. A growing literature, drawing on increasingly sophisticated data collection and measurement techniques, has examined how the economic news – usually captured by the positivity and negativity of the tone of coverage – responds to changes in the real economy. This has included analysis of the sensitivity of the news to levels and changes of various economic parameters, such as growth, unemployment, and inflation, over different time horizons (Kayser and Peress 2021; Soroka 2006, 2012; Soroka, Stecula, and Wlezien 2015). There has been little analysis to date, however, of whose material welfare the economic news reflects or of whether and how the news captures the distribution of aggregate economic gains and losses.

The media studies literature has yielded significant qualitative evidence, derived from close readings of modest corpora of news content, of how journalists represent distributional issues. On the whole, these studies suggest that news coverage of economic issues generates a discursive environment that is not merely unfavorable to proequality policies, but also favorable to policies that might aggravate existing material disparities. For instance, in the US context, Bell and Entman (2011), drawing on a qualitative assessment of television news coverage of the highly regressive Bush tax cuts, argue that reporting created an informational environment favorable to their passage. Kendall (2011), analyzing the frames used in US newspapers to describe people of different classes, finds more sympathetic portrayals of the affluent, even when engaged in wrongdoing, than of the working class and the poor. Schifferes and Knowles (2018), in a qualitative content analysis of British economic commentary on austerity in the wake of the Global Financial Crisis, find that it overwhelmingly legitimized austerity measures and devoted little attention to its impacts on poverty or household income. Grisold and Preston (2020), in a four-country study of newspaper coverage of the debate unleashed by Thomas Piketty's book, *Capital in the Twenty-first Century*, report that while inequality is largely represented as a problem, there remains a strong focus on inequality's quasi-automatic causes (e.g., technology, globalization) at the expense of its political sources. They also find that journalists tend to emphasize the goals of meritocracy and equality of opportunity over that of equality of material outcomes; characterize growth as beneficial for all; and depict redistributionist policies in unfavorable terms. Further, they identify important silences in coverage, including an absence of attention to the failure of earnings to keep pace with productivity growth and to the adverse consequences of inequality.

While these studies shed light on the substantive frames and considerations shaping news coverage, they are unable to speak to broader systematic patterns in news responsiveness. In particular, they cannot tell us how news coverage of the economy on the whole relates to real developments in the distribution of resources. Studies that systematically examine the relationship between a large corpus of news content and objective material-distributional conditions have been sparse and mixed in their findings. Kollmeyer (2004) analyzes a modest sample of Los Angeles Times articles from the late 1990s and finds that negative economic news focused disproportionately on difficulties faced by corporations and investors as compared to those faced by workers, at a time when corporate profits in California were skyrocketing relative to wages. On the other hand, taking a longer time period and examining a European setting, Schröder and Vietze (2015) analyze postwar coverage of inequality, social justice, and poverty in three leading German news outlets, finding that coverage of these topics rises with inequality itself.

In the remainder of this section, we present analyses that relate the tone of large corpora of economic news content over extended periods of time to real distributional dynamics in the economy across a substantial set of OECD economies. These analyses build on those reported in Jacobs et al. (2021), where we examine biases in the economic news in the United States. In that study, drawing on an original dataset of sentiment-coded economic news content from thirty-two large-circulation US newspapers, we uncover a set of descriptive relationships strongly consistent with the operation of a pro-rich bias in the economic news as well as evidence consistent with the empirical predictions of the "covering the aggregates" mechanism. However, the US political economy and media environment are different from those of other OECD nations in many highly consequential ways; relationships uncovered in the United States tell us little on their own about whether class-biased economic reporting is a widespread or general phenomenon in advanced capitalist democracies. Our aim in the remainder of this chapter is thus to ask whether we find similar patterns – in regard to both the descriptive question of whether class bias is operating and the causal question of why – across a broader set of OECD countries. To do so, we bring together a massive new cross-national, time-series dataset of economic news tone from Kayser and Peress (2021) and data on the distribution of income from the World Inequality Database.

Data

The dependent variable in all analyses – the tone of the national economic news – derives from Kayser and Peress's (2021) cross-national, time-series dataset. Based on a sample of roughly 2 million newspaper articles about the economy, this dataset provides monthly readings of economic news tone – the degree of positivity or negativity of sentiment in economic news articles[6] – for sixteen countries for the period 1977–2014 (coverage windows vary by country; see Table 11.A1 in the Appendix). Complete details regarding data collection can be found in Kayser and Peress (2021: 7–12). For our purposes, two critical features of the Kayser and Peress (KP) dataset are worth noting.

First, the data were collected with the aim of studying, among other things, whether media with different ideological leanings portray economic developments differently: whether left-wing outlets report more positively on the economy when a left-wing government is in power, and whether the reverse holds for right-wing outlets under right-wing governments. A key element of the data structure, accordingly, is that tone is observed in two media outlets in each country: one left-wing and one right-wing newspaper. The data consist, thus, of thirty-two time series (16 countries × 2 newspapers per country) of monthly economic-tone observations.[7]

Second, as in Jacobs et al. (2021), the KP dataset utilizes a dictionary-based approach to the coding of economic sentiment. Kayser and Peress translated their English-language sentiment dictionaries into five additional languages (French, German, Spanish, Portuguese, and Italian), allowing them to code equivalent measures of economic news tone for multiple countries. The KP dataset contains separate news tone measures concerning coverage of "the economy in general, growth, unemployment and inflation" (p. 12). Our analysis relies solely on the first of these measures. The tone measures are based on coding of the tone (positive or negative) of individual sentence fragments containing terms denoting relevant economic concepts. In turn, these fragment-level tone scores are aggregated by month, such that the monthly tone score is given by the ratio of positive fragments to all positive/negative fragments. This approach normalizes the measure for monthly variation in the volume of economic news.

To the KP dataset, we add measures of growth in pretax and disposable incomes and income shares at different points in the income distribution derived from the World Inequality Database (WID). These measures allow us to replicate in the cross-national sample precisely the same descriptive analyses estimated with US data in Jacobs et al. (2021). We rely exclusively on WID measures for the population of individuals over twenty years of age, assuming income is distributed equally among household members (e.g., for average pretax income of the top 5 percent, the variable name is aptinc992j_p95p100). We are also able to use the KP dataset to search for evidence of the possible mechanisms of class-biased economic news, examining the empirical predictions set out in the preceding section. For measures of GDP growth and the unemployment rate, we rely on the indicators included in the KP dataset, which combine data from the Organization for Economic Cooperation and Development and the International Monetary Fund. In addition, we capture corporate

---

[6] Kayser and Peress' (2021) used keyword searches to identify stories concerning the economy.
[7] For a list of the newspapers included in the KP dataset, see Kayser and Peress (2021, p. 9, Table 1).

performance using a measure of the market capitalization of listed domestic companies as a percentage of GDP, obtained from the World Development Indicators dataset (variable name: mkt_capitalization).

As noted, the KP dataset consists of monthly observations. To align with the analysis in Jacobs et al. (2021), we collapse these data to the quarterly level, taking the mean value for each variable within quarters. For economic variables that we observe only annually (such as income growth for income groups), we use linear interpolation to produce monthly values (prior to collapsing the data to quarters). All income-growth variables record twelve-month growth as a percentage. Income share variables are twelve-month first-differences in the proportion of income captured by a particular group. GDP growth is observed quarterly. Finally, we take first differences by month in the unemployment rate and capture monthly percentage growth in market capitalization (again, collapsing these by quarter in the analysis).

Descriptive Patterns across Countries

We start by asking the descriptive question of whether the economic news differentially captures the changing fortunes of individuals in different income groups. We do so by estimating, in different model specifications, the relationship between news tone and income growth at various points along the income distribution. Because our theoretical logic operates via market dynamics, we focus our analysis on the relationship between news tone and changes in market incomes,[8] but we show toward the end of this subsection that the pattern is remarkably similar when we instead examine changes in disposable income.

Given the spatial and temporal structure of our data, simply pooling the observations and estimating the relationships of interest by OLS would not be appropriate, as this requires implausible assumptions regarding the independence of observations over time and across the panels (i.e., the thirty-two newspapers). Accordingly, throughout this section and the next, we estimate dynamic models of economic tone that incorporate newspaper-specific fixed effects and time trends, quarter-of-year fixed effects, and four lags of the dependent variable. Our goal is to model the "nuisance" variance within our data, in the form of temporal trends and autocorrelations, so that our remaining inferences regarding the associations between news tone and changes in the economy are credible. More precisely, we estimate the following regression model:

$$\Delta Tone_{i,t} = \beta_i + \beta_i^T \cdot Time_t + \sum_{k=1}^{4} \beta^{Tone,k} \cdot Tone_{i,t-k}$$
$$+ \sum_{q=1}^{3} \beta_q^Q \cdot Qtr_t^q + \sum_{g \in G} \beta^g \cdot \delta Inc_t^g + \epsilon_t,$$

[8] The WID pretax income measure includes social insurance (e.g., pension) contributions and benefits.

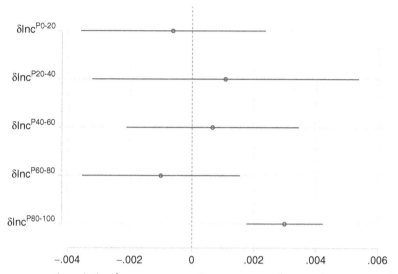

FIGURE 11.4 Association between economic news tone and pretax income growth for
each income quintile, conditional on income growth for all other quintiles
Sources: World Inequality Database; Kayser and Peress (2021).

where $Tone_{i,t}$ is economic news tone for newspaper i at time t, the β_i are newspaper fixed effects, the β_i^T are newspaper-specific time trends, $Time_t$ is a time
counter, Qtr_t^q are quarterly dummies, and G is a set of income quantiles that
varies by model. We also allow a newspaper-specific AR1 process in the errors
and estimate panel-corrected standard errors.[9]

First, dividing each country's population into income quintiles, we ask how
the tone of the economic news relates to income growth for each quintile, conditional on income growth in all of the other quintiles. We display, in Figure
11.4, estimates of these associations across the sixteen countries, revealing
that growth in the top quintile is significantly associated with economic tone.
The estimate implies that, in this cross-national sample, a standard deviation
increase in the average income of the top 20 percent is associated with an
increase in the positivity of economic news of 0.13 standard deviation units.
There is no sign that income growth in any other quintile is associated with
the tone of economic news, as the relevant coefficients cannot be reliably distinguished from zero. The top-20 percent coefficient is also significantly larger
than the first- ($p = 0.02$) and fourth-quintile ($p = 0.02$) coefficients.

We next turn to the association between economic news tone and income
growth within progressively narrower slices of the very top of the income distribution. We include, in separate models, measures for the top 10 percent, 5 percent,
1 percent, and 0.1 percent of income earners. As regards income growth at the

---

[9] In these respects, we follow the same estimation procedure as in Jacobs et al. (2021).

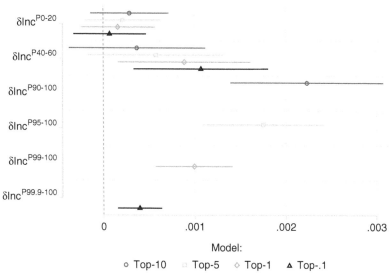

FIGURE 11.5 Association between economic news tone and pretax income growth for top-income groups, controlling for bottom- and middle-income growth
Sources: World Inequality Database; Kayser and Peress (2021).

top, the results, presented in Figure 11.5, suggest that the fortunes of highly afflu-ent subgroups of the population are significantly associated with economic tone in the cross-national sample. A standard deviation increase in income growth among the top 10 percent of earners, for example, is associated with an increase in the positivity of economic tone of 0.11 standard deviations. Equivalent shifts among the top 5 percent, top 1 percent, and top 0.1 percent are associated with increases in economic tone of 0.10, 0.08, and 0.05 standard deviations, respec-tively. The comparison between the top 10 percent and top 0.1 percent in the magnitude of these associations bears emphasis: whereas the top 10 percent group is 100 times the size of the top 0.1 percent group, the magnitude of the former's association with tone is just over double that of the latter. Notwithstanding the sizable correlation between these two income-growth variables ($r = .75$), the results suggest that an outsize share of the association between top 10 percent growth and economic tone reflects the association between tone and a tiny sliver of earners at the very top of the income distribution.

A notable difference between Figure 11.5 and the US results, reported in Jacobs et al. (2021, Figure 11.3), concerns associations between economic tone and income growth in the middle of the distribution. In the United States, there is no sign whatsoever that change in the fortunes of any group below the very top is associated (conditional on income changes at the top) with the positivity of economic news. In the cross-national sample, however, there is evidence that growth in the third quintile is related to economic news sentiment. In models that include the top 1 percent or top 0.1 percent of income earners (diamonds or triangles in Figure 11.5), who have been so central in popular discourse on economic inequality, growth in incomes at the middle is significantly associated with economic tone. Specifically, in the top-1 percent model, a standard deviation increase in growth at the middle of the income distribution is associated with a 0.04 standard deviation increase in tone, while the same increase in the top-0.1 percent model is associated with a tone shift of 0.05 standard deviations. The important substantive implication is that, when we look beyond the United States, there is some evidence that coverage of the economy is, on average, somewhat reflective of the experiences of a broad swath of the population.

Nevertheless, the estimates depicted in Figure 11.5 also imply that there is still a very substantial class bias in economic news in the cross-national sample. For instance, focusing on the top-1 percent model, recall the 0.08 standard deviation shift in tone associated with a standard deviation increase in income growth in this top-income group – an association that is double the estimate for the middle quintile (in the top-1 percent model), even as the latter income group is twenty times larger than the former.

We now evaluate these patterns more formally by constructing a test for the presence of pro-rich bias in the tone of the economic news. This test takes into account the fact that the income groups we are comparing are comprised of different numbers of individuals, with (for instance) the bottom 20 percent being comprised of twenty times more people than the top 1 percent. We define unbiasedness according to the normative principle that every individual's welfare should weigh equally in representations of the nation's welfare. On this "representational equality" principle, the absence of pro-rich bias would require that the correlation between, for instance, bottom-quintile income growth and news tone be twenty times larger than the correlation between top-1 percent income growth and news tone. Under this logic, inferences about biasedness must derive from the ratios of relevant coefficients, rather than the raw coefficients themselves.

On this basis, we estimate models that allow us to assess the degree of descriptive pro-rich bias in news tone. The core specification that we adopt here contains income-growth rates for three income groups: the bottom 20 percent, the top X percent, and the broad middle from the 20th percentile to the lower threshold of the top-X percent group – where we estimate models with $X \in \{10, 5, 1, 0.1\}$ to assess the robustness of the inferences to progressively narrower conceptions of top income.

We separately present results for a comparison of the broad middle to the top (Figure 11.6a) and for a comparison of the bottom to the top (Figure 11.6b). For the former, for each top-income measure, the circle represents the estimated ratio of news tone's association with income growth in the broad middle to news tone's association with income growth for the top-income group. We see that, in Figure 11.6a, the ratio of tone's association with middle-income growth to tone's association with top-income growth is statistically indistinguishable from zero for all but the comparison with top-1 percent income growth. Meanwhile, the diamonds represent the group-size-based normative baseline of unbiasedness for each top-income measure. We do not plot the diamonds for the top-0.1 percent models because these values (799 for the middle-top comparison and 200 for the bottom-top comparison) would be located so far to the right that the x-axis scales would be too large to clearly read off the inferences for the other top-income groups.

To illustrate how one would read this graph, consider the third row in Figure 11.6a, which plots the comparison between the top 1 percent (p99–100) and the income group that lies between the 20th and 99th percentiles (p20–99). The diamond represents the normative baseline for this comparison. If every individual's economic welfare received equal weighting in the news media's depiction of each nation's economic welfare, then the correlation between news tone and income growth for the p20–99 group should be seventy-nine times the size of the correlation between news tone and income growth for the p99–100 group – since the population of the former group is seventy-nine times as large as that of the latter. The plotted circle on this same row represents the *actual* estimated ratio between these two correlations and the 95 percent confidence interval around that estimate for our sixteen countries. As can be seen here, the estimated ratio is a tiny fraction of that normative baseline, indicating that the association between news tone and income growth for the p20–99 group is dramatically smaller than that for tone and income growth of the top 1 percent, once we adjust for the differing sizes of the groups. Figure 11.6b is read in the same way, but with the nonrich comparison group always being the bottom 20 percent, rather than the broad middle.

The core message of Figure 11.6a is that, across all four top-income measures, the estimated ratios are much lower than the normative baseline: in other words, news tone's association with top-income growth is far stronger, relative to that with middle-income growth, than would be expected on the basis of an equal weighting of the welfare of individuals across the income distribution. As the confidence intervals indicate, the inferences in this regard are extremely clear. Figure 11.6b displays, with respect to the bottom-top comparison, a remarkably similar pattern of stark overrepresentation of the welfare of the very rich in the tone of the economic news.[10]

We have so far analyzed tone-income growth relationships for market incomes, but we might wonder whether government intervention changes the picture. To address this question, we undertake precisely the same set of analyses we have presented for pretax incomes, but now substitute measures of growth in disposable income for the pretax indicators. Note that, in doing so, we lose five countries for which disposable income estimates are not available

---

[10] Note that the negative estimate of the ratio of bottom 20 to top 0.1 percent income growth coefficients reflects a (statistically insignificant) negative coefficient on growth at the bottom.

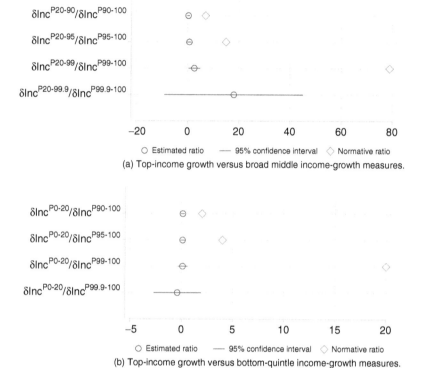

FIGURE 11.6 Estimated coefficient ratios from models predicting economic news tone with pretax income growth for different parts of the income distribution

Notes: Each row in each panel represents a ratio between the news-tone/income-growth correlation for a top-income group to the news-tone/income-growth correlation for a nonrich group. The diamond represents a normative baseline ratio for each comparison, derived from relative population sizes and the principle of equal per capita weighting. The circle (with 95 percent confidence interval) represents, for each comparison, the actual estimated ratio between the two tone-growth correlations. Confidence intervals not apparent where they are smaller than the radius of the dot representing the point estimate.

Sources: World Inequality Database; Kayser and Peress (2021).

(Australia, Canada, Israel, Japan, New Zealand), which together comprise over 40 percent of our observations.

Figure 11.7, which plots associations between news tone and disposable income growth by quintile, yields the same inference as the counterpart figure for pretax incomes: there is a significant positive association between tone and income growth in the top quintile, and only extremely weak evidence of such an association for any other quintile. The estimates indicate that a standard

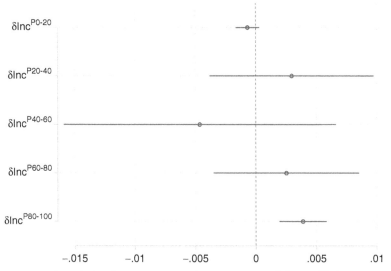

FIGURE 11.7 Association between economic news tone and disposable income growth for each income quintile, conditional on income growth for all other quintiles
Sources: World Inequality Database; Kayser and Peress (2021).

deviation increase in the rate of income growth in the top quintile is associated with a 0.18 standard deviation increase in the tone of economic news.

Figure 11.8 captures relationships between economic tone and narrow slices at the top of the income distribution and is the disposable income counterpart to Figure 11.5. Again, the inferences are largely similar. Economic tone is positively associated with disposable income growth for the top 10 percent, top 5 percent, and top 1 percent of income earners; only among the top 0.1 percent does the association fall from statistical significance. A standard-deviation increase in disposable income growth among the top 10 percent, top 5 percent, and top 1 percent is associated with increases in the positivity of economic tone of 0.15, 0.12, and 0.07 standard deviations, respectively. As in the pretax estimates, tone is also positively associated with income growth in the middle quintile, except in the model including top 10 percent income growth. Depending on the model, a standard deviation increase in the rate of income growth in the middle quintile is associated with economic tone increases of between 0.10 and 0.11 standard deviations.

Finally, Figure 11.9 returns to our formal test for class-biased economic news. Figure 11.9 is exactly parallel to Figure 11.6, but uses disposable income growth instead of pretax income growth. As in Figure 11.6, we are comparing the ratios of growth-tone coefficients for different group pairings against a normative standard of representational equality. By this standard, it will be recalled, coefficient magnitudes should be in proportion to group sizes – that

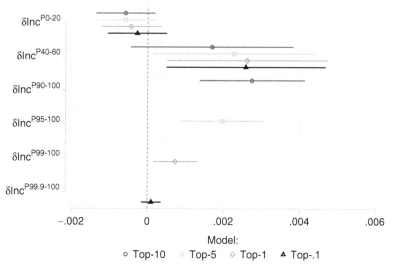

FIGURE 11.8 Association between economic news tone and disposable income growth
for top-income groups, controlling for bottom- and middle-income growth
Sources: World Inequality Database; Kayser and Peress (2021).

is, for instance, the coefficient for income growth in the bottom quintile should
be twenty times that of the top 1 percent (see further discussion earlier). In
each row, the diamond represents the normative baseline ratio of the growth-
tone correlation for the top-income group to the growth-tone correlation for
the middle (11.9a) or bottom (11.9b) income group. So, for instance, we see
that for the comparison of the p20–95 group to the p95–100 group, we would
normatively expect news tone's correlation with the former group's welfare to
be about fifteen times as large as its correlation with the latter group's welfare.
The circle in this row represents the estimated actual ratio between these two
growth-tone correlations. As we can see, the estimated ratio is much smaller
than the normative baseline ratio, indicating that the correlation of news tone
with the welfare of the p20–95 group is in a *per capita* sense (our normative
baseline), dramatically smaller than news tone's correlation with the welfare
of the top 5 percent. Note that we omit comparisons involving the top 0.1
percent: as the coefficients for this group are very imprecisely estimated, the
wide confidence intervals for the corresponding ratios have a distorting effect
on the plot.

   In short, as with the pretax income estimates, the estimated ratios uniformly
diverge from the normative standard of equality. Figure 11.9a shows that the
association between disposable income growth and economic tone is much
stronger – sometimes many times stronger – for top-income groups than for
the broad middle of the income distribution. Figure 11.9b tells a substantively equivalent story for the comparison of top- to bottom-income group

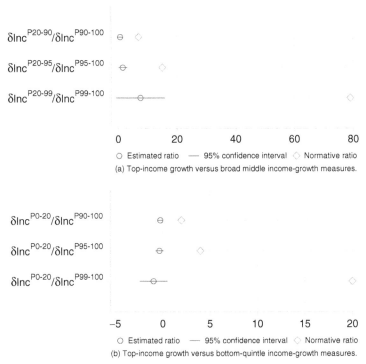

FIGURE 11.9 Estimated coefficient ratios from models predicting economic news tone with disposable income growth for different parts of the income distribution
Notes: Each row in each panel represents a ratio between the news-tone/income-growth correlation for a top-income group to the news-tone/income-growth correlation for a nonrich group. The diamond represents a normative baseline ratio for each comparison, derived from relative population sizes and the principle of equal per capita weighting. The circle (with 95 percent confidence interval) represents, for each comparison, the actual estimated ratio between the two tone-growth correlations. Confidence intervals not apparent where they are smaller than the radius of the dot representing the point estimate.
Sources: World Inequality Database; Kayser and Peress (2021).

coefficients, with the notable qualification that the estimated ratios are actually negative. This pattern reflects the fact that the coefficients for the bottom quintile, while statistically insignificant, are in fact less than zero. In any case, the implication is the same: relative to lower income groups, improvements in the welfare of those at the very top are vastly better reflected in the tone of economic news.

To summarize, our analysis of associations between economic tone and income growth measured at different points in the income distribution reveal a pattern of class-biased economic news across a broad sample of advanced democracies. In Tables 11.A7 and 11.A8 in the Appendix, we show that the comparative results are virtually unaffected by excluding the United States from the analysis. Having said that, there is one notable way in which the United States stands out. Contrary to our earlier US results, we do find some evidence in the cross-national sample of associations between economic tone and income growth below the very top. However, the below-the-top associations are still substantially smaller than those at the top when considered relative to the size of the income groups concerned.

Mechanisms of Class-Biased Economic News in the OECD

We next go looking for evidence of the mechanisms that might explain this normatively troubling descriptive bias in the relationship between economic news tone and distribution. We begin by asking whether and how much of the observed bias can be explained by our central argument: that is, by the media's tendency to cover economic aggregates, which are themselves positively correlated with top-end inequality.

To shed light on this question, we take advantage, as noted earlier, of time-series data on economic aggregates (measures of GDP growth and the unemployment rate) for each country in the KP dataset. To these measures, we add the measure of market capitalization growth obtained from the World Development Indicators. We focus our analysis on the five empirical implications of the covering-the-aggregates argument, outlined earlier. For these tests, we return to using pretax incomes since our proposed mechanism speaks primarily to the relationship between economic aggregates and the market income of the very rich, whether earnings or capital income. We estimate models of the form described earlier, though now we include additional variables – principally, economic aggregates – relevant to our theory.

Estimates for the variables of interest are reported in Table 11.1. We start with a baseline estimate of the correlation between economic news tone and income inequality. If, as we showed in the preceding section, economic news sentiment is relatively more strongly associated with growth in the incomes of the most affluent, then it follows that a change in the share of income captured by the most affluent – here, the top 1 percent of income earners – should be positively associated with economic tone (Prediction 1). The estimates for Model 1 confirm this expectation.

In Models 2 and 3, we consider whether economic aggregates, specifically, GDP growth and change in the unemployment rate, drive the tone of economic news (Prediction 2) and also account, via their correlations with income inequality, for some part of the correlation between inequality and economic tone (Prediction 3). The former expectation is strongly supported in these models: Model 2 shows that GDP growth is positively related to economic tone, while Model 3 indicates that change in the unemployment rate is negatively related to tone. Both coefficients are statistically significant at the 99.9-percent level.

TABLE 11.1 *Mechanisms of class-biased economic news*

	(1)	(2)	(3)	(4)	(5)	(6)
$\Delta IncShare_t^{P99-100}$	0.8329***	0.4735**	0.6666***	0.6137**	0.3052	0.8367***
	(0.2087)	(0.1826)	(0.1891)	(0.2058)	(0.1846)	(0.2086)
δGDP		0.0382***			0.0261***	
		(0.0043)			(0.0038)	
$\Delta Unemp_t$			-0.0738***		-0.0529***	
			(0.0107)		(0.0102)	
$\delta Market\ Cap.$				0.0039***	0.0032***	
				(0.0007)	(0.0006)	
$\Delta IncShare_t^{P99-100}$ ×Ideology						0.0852
						(0.0839)
Constant	0.1463***	0.1429***	0.1563***	0.1186***	0.1284***	0.1466***
	(0.0281)	(0.0260)	(0.0265)	(0.0268)	(0.0245)	(0.0281)
Observations	2061	2061	2061	1947	1947	2061

Standard errors in parentheses. Regressions include quarterly and newspaper-fixed effects, newspaper trends, and 4 lags of economic tone, with panel-corrected standard errors.
*$p < 0.05$, **$p < 0.01$, ***$p < 0.001$

Critically, there is also clear evidence that part of the association between inequality and economic tone reflects correlations between inequality and these two economic aggregates. When GDP growth is controlled for, the association between economic tone and change in the income share of the top 1 percent is sliced by more than two-fifths (Prediction 3). Controlling for change in unemployment has a similar, if more modest, effect: the coefficient on top 1 percent income share change is reduced by one fifth (Prediction 3).

Model 4 addresses the specific role of corporate performance in the covering-the-business-cycle process. We see here that growth in market capitalization is positively related to positive economic tone (Prediction 4). We also see that controlling for this variable reduces the association between economic tone and top 1 percent income share change by more than a quarter (Prediction 5).

Model 5 captures the combined effect of GDP growth, unemployment rate change, and market capitalization growth on the association between economic tone and income inequality. Notably, while the associations between the three growth-related variables shrink in this setup, each variable retains a sizable and statistically significant association with economic tone, which reflects the modest correlations between these variables in the cross-national sample.[11] Most importantly, from the perspective of the covering-the-business-cycle theory, the inclusion of these variables in the same model shrinks the top 1 percent income share change coefficient by almost two-thirds, rendering it statistically insignificant.

Overall, looking across the estimates of Models 1–5, one finds substantial support for the argument that the class bias in economic news across OECD countries reflects journalists' focus on economic aggregates in reporting on economies in which inequality itself is cyclical. Moreover, we show in Table 11.A9 in the Appendix that the results of these mechanism tests are broadly the same when the United States is excluded from the sample.

Last, we leverage Kayser and Peress' coding of the ideological leanings of newspapers to speak to alternative mechanisms. If class-biased economic news reflects the class-biased interests or worldviews of news producers or consumers, then class bias in the tone of economic news should be stronger in those outlets that present a more conservative worldview in general. Model 6 thus adds an interaction between top 1 percent income share change and newspaper ideology. The interaction between inequality and ideology is not statistically significant: the tone of the news in left-wing newspapers is as strongly associated with inequality as is economic news tone in right-wing newspapers. Of course, it is possible to imagine ideological or interest-based mechanisms that might operate for left- as well as right-wing outlets (e.g., even the former are

---

[11] The correlation (r) between GDP growth and unemployment rate change is -.19, whereas the correlations between these variables and market capitalization growth are both less than .04 (in absolute value).

likely to be owned by members of the richest 1 percent and rely on corporate advertising). Yet the lack of any detectable difference should cast at least some doubt on the notion that class biases derive in any straightforward way from media actors' ideological commitments.[12]

CONCLUSION

Our aim in this chapter has been to suggest that there is something worth puzzling over in the relationship between economic news and income distribution in advanced democracies. The analysis that we present here naturally has its limits. In seeking to characterize national media environments, we have drawn on data from only two newspapers per country, and our sample is limited both in the number of countries and the time period covered. Yet we think the evidence in this chapter constitutes at least a prima facie case that economic reporting by leading news outlets in a wide range of advanced democracies aligns relatively poorly with the economic experiences and distributional interests of the nonrich. We hope that other scholars will seek to test this proposition with more data drawn from a wider set of national contexts.

Among the questions that we have not addressed here is what might explain the variation in patterns of class-biased reporting across countries. Table 11.A1 in the Appendix suggests considerable differences in the presence and strength of pro-rich biases in economic news across the OECD contexts in our sample. Some of this variation may be mere "noise," given the small number of available observations for some countries. At the same time, these results may, in fact, understate the variation across the OECD, insofar as Nordic social democracies are not captured in the KP data.

What might explain the cross-national variation in class-biased economic reporting? We suggest a few possibilities in the spirit of hypothesis generation. One conjecture that flows directly, and almost mechanically, from our theoretical argument is that settings in which economic growth and contraction are less strongly (and positively) correlated with top-income shares should see less-biased economic news coverage. We would expect a range of factors – from labor-market rules and institutions to the tax treatment of executive compensation to the degree of financialization of the economy – to condition the link between inequality and the business cycle. Variation in the underlying structure of the political economy should, in turn, generate variation in the pro-rich bias of the economic news. That said, Table 11.A1 does not suggest any straightforward pattern, given the considerable variation across countries typically considered to have broadly similar political economies (e.g., Ireland vs. other liberal countries; Germany and France vs. Austria).

---

[12] This result is consistent with Kayser and Peress's (2021) finding that ideological differences in news coverage of aggregate-level economic phenomena are quite minimal.

We might also imagine variation in the norms and routines that shape the production of news content itself. In characterizing the performance of the economy, journalists might attend more to the distribution of gains and losses in contexts that otherwise make distribution more salient. These might include, for instance, contexts in which inequality is especially high, in which parties on the Left place distributional matters prominently on the agenda, or in which party competition is strongly configured around a distributional dimension of conflict.

We would also emphasize that our analyses by no means settle the question of whether or how the ideology and interests of news producers and consumers shape economic reporting. The news outlets in our sample may represent too little variation in ideological leanings or economic worldviews to pick up the effect of these factors. As we have also noted, a journalistic focus on the business cycle might itself reflect a set of widespread ideological presumptions about the benefits of growth or satisfaction with a set of measures that in fact do a good job of capturing the welfare of the most affluent. Unpacking these possibilities will likely require, in part, the collection of individual-level data tapping media owners' and journalists' economic attitudes and worldviews.

Finally, we point out some complexity in making normative sense of our findings. While periods of economic growth see rising concentrations of income at the top, they also tend to be the periods in which most groups experience absolute income gains. One might, therefore, ask whether it is such a bad thing if the nonrich receive favorable signals about economic performance in periods in which they are gaining in absolute terms, even if they are losing in relative terms. Indeed, news tone has a positive, statistically significant ($p < 0.05$) bivariate relationship (i.e., without controls for other income quintiles) with disposable income growth for all but the first and second income quintiles in the countries in our sample (see Figure 11.A1 in the Appendix). This pattern suggests that the economic news might tend to correctly signal the direction of welfare change for most income groups. This fact, however, does not seem to us to dispose of the normative problem. For one thing, news tone appears to provide no meaningful signal about how the economy has performed for the bottom 20 percent of the income scale; and, more generally, Figure A1 suggests that news tone provides a less-informative signal as we move down the income distribution. More importantly, accepting the signaling of absolute gains as normatively sufficient would commit us to the view that information about distribution is effectively irrelevant for the formation of citizen assessments of economic performance. We see no clear reason to believe that nonrich citizens with full information would be indifferent to the distribution of aggregate gains and losses.[13]

---

[13] Separately, one may wonder if there is necessarily something to be concerned about in our findings if some variant of a "trickle-down" theory of the economy were true. In that case, rising top-income shares today would generate rising incomes for the bottom and middle *tomorrow*.

We also note that these patterns – news tone's positive correlation with both inequality and absolute income gains for middle-income groups – may shed light on the economic and political resilience of advanced capitalist democracies, as examined by Iversen and Soskice (2019). In Iversen and Soskice's view, postwar democracy and advanced capitalism have operated in a symbiotic relationship, as democratic governments have made economic policy choices in response to voter demands for effective economic management, delivering both prosperity and democratic legitimacy. At the same time, as we have shown in Figure 11.1, that growth has in most countries disproportionately benefited the very rich. Our analysis of the informational environment might help explain how incumbents have won support for prosperity-generating policies that exacerbate inequality: as they evaluate governments' economic management, the middle classes receive media signals that track the rise in aggregate prosperity and the absolute gains experienced by their own income groups but are insensitive to the distribution of those gains. Economic reporting that systematically attended to distribution – perhaps applying a "tone penalty" to less-equal allocations – might well heighten the contradictions embedded in advanced capitalist democracy.

Under such a model, lower- and middle-income voters might in principle be well served – i.e., be well informed about future economic outcomes affecting them – by a news media that sends positive signals during periods of rising top-income shares. This model, however, relies on assumptions about the efficacy of trickle-down mechanisms that are generally not empirically well supported (e.g. Andrews et al. 2011; Cingano 2014; Hope and Limberg 2022; Quiggin 2012, Ch. 4; Thewissen 2014).

Deflecting from Racism

Local Talk Radio Conversations about the Murder of George Floyd[*]

Katherine J. Cramer

The contributions to this volume each attempt to understand why advanced capitalist societies are less equal and less redistributive than they were in the 1990s. Our editors point out in their introduction that one set of potential explanations for the general rise in inequality centers on the decisions of elites, and another centers on the attitudes and choices of members of the public.

This chapter focuses on the latter explanation. Why do members of the public not support redistribution when doing so would likely benefit them economically? In the United States, racism is a leading explanation (Alesina and Glaeser 2004; Katznelson, Geiger, and Kryder 1993; Lupu and Pontusson 2011). Racism interrupts the ability of people to feel concern for each other, which support for redistribution requires (Epper, Fehr, and Senn 2020). Instead, people tend to save their concern for those with whom they identify (Fowler and Kam 2007). In the United States, a disproportionate share of low-income earners are people of color. Racism among Whites appears to drive lack of empathy or acknowledgment of the role of racism in economic inequality, which undermines support for more redistribution (Alesina and Glaeser 2004; Elkjær and Iversen, this volume; Knowles et al. 2014; Lupu and Pontusson 2011).

To be clear, it is Whites who are particularly less supportive of redistribution (Alesina and Giuliano 2011; Alesina and La Ferrara 2005), especially

[*] My gratitude to Deb Roy and the Center for Constructive Communication at the MIT Media Lab for use of the RadioSearch archive. Thank you to Hakeem Jefferson, Kennia Coronado, Clint Rooker, participants in the 2021 Midwest Political Science Association Identity Subconference, the editors and authors of this volume, and especially Paul Pierson for comments on earlier versions. Thank you to Kyler Hudson and Kennia Coronado for research assistance. Thank you also to the Natalie C. Holton Chair of Letters & Science at the University of Wisconsin-Madison for funding.

when they perceive the recipients of "welfare" are people of color (Gilens 1999) or when they are living in contexts that suggest they likely perceive that recipients of redistribution are people of color (Luttmer 2001; Poterba 1997). In other words, racism appears to dampen the willingness of Whites to support what Cavaillé calls "redistribution *to*" others (this volume).

The fact that racism prevents redistribution is not news. Political actors in the United States have used racist appeals since the end of slavery to interrupt coalition building between Whites and Blacks that might threaten the fortunes of higher-income Whites (Alesina and Glaeser 2004). But the fact that the relationship between racism and lack of support for redistribution persists suggests we need to know more about how it is reproduced in the current political context.

In recent years, questions about the role of racism in lack of support for redistribution in the United States have arisen frequently with respect to White rural residents. I am drawn to these questions after years of studying what I eventually labeled "rural consciousness," an identification as a rural resident intertwined with a perception of distributive injustice (Cramer 2016; Cramer Walsh 2012). I became aware of this perspective while conducting intensive listening in several dozen communities throughout the state of Wisconsin between 2007 and 2012. In the conversations I witnessed, I heard many White people in smaller communities and rural places expressing a perception that people living outside major metro areas were not getting their fair share of attention, resources, or respect. They said that the decisions that affected their lives were made primarily in cities and communicated out to them with little listening going on to the needs and concerns of people in rural areas. They also perceived that the wealth and the good jobs were primarily in the cities and that their taxpayer dollars were spent primarily on these urban communities, not on communities like their own. Finally, they perceived that the people making the decisions that affected their lives did not respect rural people like themselves.

This perspective tended to coincide with a preference for Republican Party candidates, who in the contemporary era have generally opposed redistribution. Many of the people I listened to perceived that the government was not working for them and therefore were highly skeptical of more government programs. This aversion to government is particularly striking in recent decades, given that rural areas have been particularly slow to recover from the Great Recession of 2007–2008 (Pipa and Geismar 2020; The New Map of Economic Growth and Recovery 2016).

The rural resentment toward urban areas that makes opposition to redistribution seem appropriate has been simmering, if not growing, for decades. Its multifaceted nature facilitates its use as a persuasive tool. The perspectives of resentment I heard in Wisconsin included resentment toward cities, city residents, public employees, liberal elites, Democrats, and people of color. Through this lens, geography represents not just whom the political in-group is, but whom people can trust, and whom they deem deserving. Candidates or politicians priming resentment toward any one of the facets of rural resentment activate negative attitudes toward the other associated groups. Republican Scott Walker rose to power as Wisconsin's governor this way, and Donald Trump used a similar strategy to help win the US presidency.

In the wake of Trump's 2016 victory, Brexit, and other successes for right-wing populist candidates, a key debate has been whether support for these actors is driven by economic or cultural concerns (Inglehart and Norris 2017; Margalit 2019). The understandings that I heard suggest that the driver is not one or the other, but instead the intertwining of the two (Gidron and Hall 2017; Mutz 2018; see also Rooduijn and Burgoon 2017). When people told me they were not receiving their fair share, they were claiming that they deserved more and that others were getting more than they deserved. Such assessments were about economics and culture at the same time. These claims are part of a culture infected with racist notions of what human lives are worth and who works hard (and is therefore deserving) (Soss and Schram 2007). Whether or not people support redistribution rests on their willingness to extend support to others and to see others in the country as members of the same community. In this way, economic concerns cannot be understood independently from cultural concerns in the United States.

In the study that follows, I sought to learn more about how racism in particular is intertwined with economic concerns and interrupts support for redistribution among White residents of rural areas in the United States. Specifically, I sought to listen to the way White residents of rural areas talked about racism and whether and how understandings of economic inequality and redistribution entered. In my earlier fieldwork, the people I listened to seldom talked about racism. For this reason, in this study, I intentionally focused on conversations about racism and listened to the way economics entered.

To do so, I turned to local talk radio shows. Investigating the conversations among hosts and callers on local talk radio shows allowed me to listen to the way people rooted in particular places made sense of politics during the pandemic, when face-to-face fieldwork was not possible. The talk radio audience is extensive,[1] and talk radio is an important source of information among Right-leaning voters in particular in the United States (Dempsey et al. 2021; Mitchell et al. 2021). National talk radio hosts have operated as important opinion leaders within the Republican Party since shortly after the repeal of the Fairness Doctrine in 1987, which made it possible for stations to air

---

[1] In 2019, Nielsen claimed that radio reaches more Americans each week than any other platform, with talk radio as the 2nd most listened-to format (Nielsen Company n.d.). The Pew Research Center reported that 9.6 percent of the US listening audience tuned into news/talk radio between January and November of 2016, and that the online radio audience has grown over time www .pewresearch.org/wp-content/uploads/sites/8/2018/07/State-of-the-News-Media_2017-Archive .pdf; see also (www.statista.com/statistics/822103/share-audience-listening-news-talk-radio/). Berry and Sobieraj (2011) argue the growth of talk radio was driven by deregulation and online listening, not conservative demand.

partisan programming without providing equal time to opposing views (Berry and Sobieraj 2011; see also Bobbitt 2010). Hosts such as Rush Limbaugh have likely been drivers of public opinion and the behavior of party leaders (Hacker and Pierson 2020; Rosenwald 2019).

Local talk radio shows are aired within a particular media market or select region. Many talk radio stations have at least one local show (Bobbitt 2010: Ch. 1). These local shows are important because their content is more likely to tap into placed-based identities and illuminate the relevance of national-level issues for their listeners. Such information increases the chances that people will consider their own socioeconomic circumstances when forming an opinion on it (Chong, Citrin, and Conley 2001) and therefore be more likely to engage in political action (Ozymy 2012).

I focused on shows broadcast out of predominantly White, northern (and primarily Midwestern), and less metropolitan areas in order to focus my attention on the communication among residents comparable to those I had listened to while studying rural resentment. This communication is not necessarily representative of all communication among all conservative Whites, or even among all conservative northern, rural Whites. My intent was to closely observe specific cases of conservatives talking about race and racism to observe whether and how they connect these topics to opposition to redistribution.

Since the focus of my listening was on shows broadcast from places considerably less racially diverse than other rural areas of the country, future work would benefit from listening to similar conversations in other parts of the United States and around the globe, since understandings of race and racism are distinctive in the rural north (Carter et al. 2014).

I focus my analytic listening[2] on local talk show discussions about a particular event that undeniably involved race and racism: the murder of unarmed African-American George Floyd by Derik Chauvin, a White Minneapolis, Minnesota, police officer, and the resulting protests that took place in that city and around the world. Floyd's death on May 25, 2020, was captured on video and lit global protests against racial injustice because of the egregious nature of the way he was killed, with Chauvin kneeling on his neck for over nine minutes while Floyd gasped and pleaded for air.

There was very little explicit connection between racism and redistribution in these conversations. Instead, the shows deflected attention away from race and racism in a variety of ways, preventing much discussion of connections between redistribution or even economics and racism.

Paying attention to situations in which people legitimize turning away from racism is necessary for understanding how racism continues to prevent the United States as well as other countries from pursuing the redistribution that

---

[2] My deep gratitude to Paul Pierson for giving this label to my work. See Cramer (2022; 2023) for extensive explanations of this approach.

would to enable those at the bottom of the income scale to attain a sufficient standard of living in order to thrive. What narratives do people tell that de-emphasize humanitarianism and equality, and instead raise up individualism and aversion to large government (Feldman and Zaller 1992; Hochschild 1981)? What do people tell each other that leads them to perceive the cause of racial inequality is individual initiative rather than systematic disadvantage (see Kam and Burge 2018)?

In what follows, I will discuss when attention to racism arose and will describe and explain how hosts and callers deflected from it and how this prevented consideration of the linkage between racism and redistribution. The results contribute to our understanding of the way US society continues to relegate Blacks to the bottom of the status hierarchy in a way that perpetuates inequality. The active refusal to consider racism casts the problem of inequal-ity as those at the bottom getting more than they deserve, rather than those at the top getting too much, and thereby places responsibility on Blacks for their lack of income, not on broader forces that might be advantaging Whites (see Knowles et al. 2014).

The collective deflection from racism that occurs on these shows perpetuates a view that racism is no longer a factor in the United States. Through this lens, hosts and callers justify their lack of empathy with people of color by treating inequality as the result of individual failings, or as the fault of Democrats, who make it an issue in pursuit of their own political goals.

USING LOCAL TALK RADIO TO LISTEN

To focus on the content of talk radio shows, I used a talk radio data collec-tion tool designed by the Center for Constructive Communication at the MIT Media Lab.[3] This tool, RadioSearch, ingested and automatically transcribed the content of dozens of talk radio stations from around the country for sev-eral years.

I initially focused my listening on a Right-leaning show broadcast out of Duluth, Minnesota, which is located in a rural area of the state in which Floyd was killed. (See Table 12.1 for details on the shows examined.) This was a weekday morning show called "Sound Off with Brad Bennett."[4] Each day, it started with this introduction: "Good morning, Northlanders, and Welcome to Sound Off. For the next 3 hours let your voices be heard about the things that are important to you, the hardworking men and women of the Northland, who pay more than their fair share of taxes." This introduction also announced that host Bennett served as a Marine Corps Sergeant in the Vietnam War, and served three terms on the Duluth School Board.

---

[3] www.ccc.mit.edu/
[4] https://wdsm710.com/shows-sound-off-with-brad-bennett/

TABLE 12.1 *Characteristics of broadcast communities*

Station	Show	Location	City population[1]	2020 Trump vote in county[2]	Percent people of color in city	Percent people of color in county	Median household income in city	Median household income in county
KBUL	Montana Talks	Billings, MT	109,595	60.6%	14.9%	14.1%	$58,394	$61,186
KLIX	Bill Colley Show	Twin Falls, ID	48,951	71.5%	22.5%	21.8%	$50,739	$55,785
KLXX	Joel Heitkamp Show	Fargo, ND	121,889	49.9%	17.3%	15.6%	$52,810	$62,218
KOAN	Eddie Burke Show	Anchorage, AL	293,531	52.8%	42.1%	–	$82,716	–
KZSE	MPR News with Kerri Miller	Rochester, MN	118,924	43.8%	25%	20.9%	$74,527	$80,096
WAOK	Wanda Stokes Show	Atlanta, GA	488,800	26.2%	61.7%	60.4%	$66,657	$61,980
WDSM	Sound Off with Brad Bennett	Duluth, MN	85,195	41.3%	11.7%	9.1%	$55,819	$60,434
WTAQ	John Muir Show	Green Bay, WI	104,565	52.8%	31.3%	19.7%	$49,029	$64,458

[1] Population and race/ethnicity data are from 2019 American Community Survey 5-year estimates. Income data are from ACS 2019 1-year estimates. Percent people of color is defined as percent not identifying as non-Hispanic white alone.

[2] www.usatoday.com/in-depth/graphics/2020/11/10/election-maps-2020-america-county-results-more-voters/6226197002/. For Anchorage, Percent Trump support reported is for entire state since Alaska does not have counties (and information is not provided in the ACS estimates by borough. Anchorage is in Anchorage Borough.). Counties are as follows: Billings, MT, is located in Yellowstone County; Twin Falls, ID, is in Twin Falls County; Fargo, ND, is in Cass County; Rochester, MN, is located in Olmstead County; Atlanta, GA, is located in Fulton County with parts of the city extending into DeKalb County; Duluth, MN, is located in St. Louis County; and Green Bay, WI, is located in Brown County.

My logic of comparison was to focus on this show, then compare the content with shows hosted by White men in other states that were also broadcasting to White, rural, northern, and conservative audiences (Billings, Montana; Twin Falls, Idaho; Anchorage, Alaska; and Green Bay, Wisconsin). I wanted to know what patterns in these understandings were common across White, rural northern communities. I also compared these understandings to those I heard on less conservative shows broadcast to White, rural, and northern communities, in order to illuminate the partisan and ideological nature of the patterns (i.e., a Minnesota Public Radio statewide talk show; a center-left show broadcast out of Fargo, North Dakota, hosted by Joel Heitkamp, the brother of former Democratic US Senator from North Dakota Heidi Heitkamp). Finally, I contrasted these patterns to the way a Black female host targeting an urban, southern, and Black audience (in Atlanta) and her callers talked about George Floyd's death and ensuing protests as a most different comparison case, to help illuminate the distinctiveness of the understandings in the White, rural, and northern communities.

Floyd was killed on May 25, 2020. These shows began discussing his death on the morning of May 28th, after demonstrations turned violent in Minneapolis. I listened to entire broadcasts of the shows on this and the following several days, as well as broadcasts in the preceding months, on the day after the November 3, 2020, presidential election, and on the morning after the January 6, 2021, insurrection at the US Capitol, to deepen my understanding of the contexts of these talk radio on-air communities.

As I listened to a show, I typed transcripts of what was said and noted observations on the tone and voice characteristics of callers. (The RadioSearch tool created machine transcriptions, but they were not sufficiently accurate for my purposes.) I periodically compared transcripts across stations and wrote memos about the patterns that I was noticing. When I completed my listening, I read through the transcripts station by station, starting with WDSM and worked out geographically through the other Right-leaning shows. I then analyzed the transcripts from the contrast shows (from Fargo and Atlanta).

As I read through the transcripts, I examined whether and how conversations about the economy, economic concerns, and economic inequality arose, and looked for the connections people made between economic inequality and race or racism. I recorded these observations in a memo along with excerpts from the transcripts that had led me to these conclusions.

It did not take long to notice that detouring away from race or racism was more prominent than conversations about race or racism. I therefore investigated how people steered each other away from racial and economic inequality and what the conversations suggested about hosts', listeners', and callers' concerns and understandings. Three major characteristics of the connection between race and economic inequality emerged: (1) the avoidance of race and racism, (2) a shifting of the conversation to blame political opponents, and (3) an assertion of values that justified these shifts.

EMPIRICAL FINDINGS

The local talk radio shows I listened to clearly communicate identity with a particular place and the people living there. The stations air these shows in a line-up of nationally syndicated shows, such as The Rush Limbaugh Show, The Sean Hannity Show, The Mark Levin Show, The Savage Nation, and The Mike Gallagher show.[5] The Fox news stations' local talk shows reference, quote, and rebroadcast some of the content from these national shows. Even when the hosts and callers on the local shows talk about national issues, they do so while referencing their local community. The hosts and their producers (who are often a part of the conversation as well) refer to their histories in the community. Hosts greet callers with their first name and place of residence (e.g., "Hello, Sandy from Silver Bay!") The advertisers tend to be local and are sometimes guests on the shows. (The Duluth show regularly welcomed representatives of the Benna Ford car dealership, Chad Walsh from the Dead On Arms shooting range, or "Lady O" from Lady Ocalat's Emporium [a fortune-telling business]).

Regular callers are important parts of the shows' communities (Brownlee and Hilt 1998). The shows celebrate first-time callers on the air and in online descriptions of the broadcasts's content.[6] Callers influence the agenda and how it gets discussed, even when the host pulls in another direction. Such tension is the exception, however. Consensus is the norm, and callers are generally treated warmly, and sometimes even memorialized. On the Duluth show, Bennett and producer Kenny Kalligher made a point of honoring local veterans who had recently died. On one such occasion Bennett recalled a deceased listener, Thomas Fontaine, from "up in Grand Moret [Minnesota]," explaining that he was a Vietnam and Desert Storm veteran who "listened to us all of the time.... He had crazy-glued the dial on his radio so you couldn't move it off of WDSM."[7]

Each of these shows is a community unto itself and exudes a tone of familiarity. For example, when a caller gets dropped, hosts use the airwaves to speak directly to that person. "Mary, you call back. I hit the wrong dol garn button and I will get you on. I promise," the Fargo host said one morning.[8]

As I noted earlier, the talk radio audience is considerable and national-level politicians clearly believe these shows have an important reach.[9] High-profile candidates and their surrogates made appearances on these broadcasts during the 2020 election cycle. The host and the producer of the Duluth show talked throughout the 2020 campaign about getting "the big guy" (Trump) on the

---

[5] This is the lineup in which Bennett's show appears.
[6] For example, Steve from Duluth, January 8, 2021.
[7] January 8, 2021.
[8] May 28, 2020.
[9] See Bobbitt (2010: Ch. 9) for consequences of these local shows. See also Hofstetter and Gianos (1997) on politicians' use of these shows to communicate without journalists' scrutiny.

air and were disappointed when the campaign sent "only" his son Eric Trump instead. Aaron Flint, the host of the Billings, Montana, show, welcomed US Senator Steve Daines onto the air on June 3, the morning after the Montana primary elections. On May 29, John Muir enthusiastically welcomed gun rights proponent and Trump supporter Ted Nugent onto his Green Bay show.[10]

Although the conservative shows are often supporting Republican candidates, they do not simply toe the line, at least in the early stages of an issue. For example, Bennett, the Duluth show host, supported the use of masks early in the pandemic before doing so became a partisan issue. He also occasionally resisted extreme right-wing or conspiratorial comments from his audience. For example, on January 11, 2021, after the insurrection at the US Capitol, he lectured that one of the rioters, the "guy with the horns" was not in fact part of Antifa, the antifascist protest movement, as some callers were alleging. The libertarian host of the Twin Falls station, Bill Colley, likewise admonished a caller for suggesting that the reaction to the storming of the Capitol was overblown. One caller asked, "How many police were injured when Antifa did their riots?" Colley shouted back, "So that makes it OK?! What the hell is wrong with you?!! Because stupid people on the left do it?"

CALLER: No I'm just saying it is being blown out of proportion.
COLLEY: Oh my God, there were people storming through the Capitol, breaking windows!! People are dead!!

These hosts did perpetuate conspiracy theories at times. Even after Bennet lectured that the man in the Viking helmet was not part of Antifa, he went on to argue that "There *are* some real things happening here that are just as bad as some of the stuff that is being made up ... [for example], the attempt to destroy free speech.... In the last few days ... almost every one of the [social media] websites of any kind ... has limited or cut off anything conservative. They have even killed the platform for one of the conservative websites out there [Parler]. Does this sound like China? A little bit!" Also, Colley claimed that the understaffing and underresourcing of security personnel on January 6th might have been intentional to justify a subsequent tightening of security at the Capitol.

Although these shows deflected attention away from racism, the hosts made a point to distance themselves from the labels of racist or White supremacist (see Bonilla-Silva 2018). During the first presidential debate in the 2020 general election, Trump refrained from taking moderator Mike Wallace's invitation to denounce White supremacist groups, telling them instead to "stand back and stand by." The next morning, Bennett defended Trump, arguing that Wallace was wrong to insinuate that Trump had never condemned White supremacists. When Floyd was killed, host Muir in Green Bay argued it was ridiculous to tie Trump and his rhetoric to the actions of the officer who had knelt on his neck.

---

[10] Local talk radio is the source of information most trusted after Fox News for Trump supporters in Wisconsin as of October 2018 (Dempsey et al. 2021, Figure 2).

Trump is not a racist. The overwhelming number of Trump supporters are not racist.... We can't help it if there are isolated individuals or groups who are racist who support the Trump presidency.... The reason that they falsely demonize Trump and Trump supporters is because they don't actually have anything on Trump. Trump, even though they don't want to admit it, has been immensely successful for the United States on countless fronts for 3 plus years now. He has done a great job for all Americans, including African Americans.... This is leftists on the political left trying to control African Americans, politically.

Various hosts and guests talked about the importance of unity and a focus on commonalities over differences.[11] However, this attention to unity was typically a desire for less disruption to the status quo, not a desire to unify through attention to difference – a common strategy among Whites confronting the reality of racism (Cramer Walsh 2012). One broadcast that laid this out plain and clear was Bennett's show on January 8, 2021, after the US Capitol insurrection. Within minutes, he and his producer went from lamenting attention to divisions or subgroups to deriding pictures of interracial marriages on TV.

I am getting so sick and tired of being fed— *spoon fed*— that we all have to intermarry. Every time I watch a commercial on TV I see a white guy married to a black guy or a black woman or a white woman married to a black woman and mixed racial kids. That's not a hundred percent the way the world works, it just doesn't. But it seems that there is an effort to force us to accept that as a way of life, that we are going to all become a grey society or a beige society. Who has made that decision that every couple on TV needs to be biracial?

RECOGNIZING THE INJUSTICE OF FLOYD'S DEATH, THEN A SHIFT AWAY

It was in these contexts, in which the Right-leaning hosts distanced themselves from racism while preferring to deny it exists, that they reacted to Floyd's murder. On each of the Right-leaning shows, the hosts' initial response was a recognition that his death was the result of a horrific crime. "As far as George Floyd, I think it was a very serious crime that was committed against him," Bennett in Duluth said.[12] In Green Bay, Muir was similarly blunt. "Based on what this show has seen to date, regardless of the motive, what happened appears to be totally unacceptable."[13] In Anchorage, a guest on the show was even more direct: "Somebody should have walked up to that cop and shot him right there."

However, even though these hosts recognized the injustice of the killing, they each quickly detoured away from the possibility that the incident was reflective of a broader pattern of racial injustice. Many of the hosts interpreted

[11] For example, Congressman Pete Stauber on WDSM November 2, 2020.
[12] May 28, 2020.
[13] The host of this show uses an unusual third person style (e.g., "This show believes..." rather than "I believe...").

the murder as the case of a "bad apple" law enforcement officer. Even when callers suggested racism might be involved, the hosts turned attention back to the officers' individual behavior. On the Green Bay show, Muir read a text from a listener that "Minneapolis obviously has a culture of hate within the police and it is being reciprocated within the community but I will never understand riots."[14] Muir's response was that Floyd's death was a result of "some terrible apples within the police dept." The next day, caller Jim in Green Bay (who may have sent the text the day before), said,

An issue that is being overlooked ... the argument is that you have a few bad apples ... I agree, but what are the chances that in the entire Minneapolis police department you are going to get 4 or 3 to overlook and 1 to commit the crime? I guarantee that if you hand-picked 3 others they would have done the same thing ... I have relatives who are officers in the Green Bay area so I am very much pro law enforcement. I agree to pretty much everything you said so far, but I just wish people would quit saying it's just a few bad apples. Because I think it's worse in some police departments than we want to admit to and we have to as a society, we have to look at that.

Nevertheless, Muir gave the "bad apple" response. "This show does not want to speculate. We don't know how many bad apples are out there. ...officers that were there they certainly failed. Inexplicable, inexcusable. There certainly are bad apples in that field."

Asserting that the officers involved were just bad apples enabled the hosts to refocus attention on the protestors and discount the possibility that they were reacting to racism. They criticized the violent protests and claimed the protestors did not actually care about Floyd's death. "When I see injustice I don't go out and loot the local Target store. How does that bring you justice in any way?" Colley in Twin Falls asked.[15] In Billings, host Flint had his own string of questions. "*Everybody* is criticizing what [officer Chauvin] did, so why are you burning down police precincts, AutoZones, cars? Why are you spraying a woman in a wheelchair with a fire hydrant? Why are you stealing TVs? That is not protesting, that is rioting and nothing to do with what this cop did."[16] A caller, Herb from Sheboygan Falls, asked Muir on his Green Bay show, "That man murdered that man ... [but] that being said, why with the economy the way it is would you burn down an AutoZone and loot a Target? Their whole message gets distorted and lost."

Herb's comment acknowledged the economic challenges that many people were facing. Such comments were not unusual on these shows. But Herb, like others, did not talk about these economic struggles as shared across racial groups. Instead, he brought up economic concerns as a reason to ridicule the way people in Minneapolis were responding to Floyd's murder.

[14] May 28, 2020.
[15] May 28, 2020.
[16] May 28, 2020.

BLAMING DEMOCRATS

As the days of protests continued, the hosts not only deflected attention away from racism, they deflected blame for the events onto other targets. Occasionally, the hosts suggested that Floyd was intoxicated and therefore to blame for his own death.[17]

More prominently, though, hosts focused on Democrats as the main target of blame. On the Billings, Montana, show, caller Monte in Livingston claimed that Floyd's death was part of a pattern of police shootings in Minneapolis.[18] Host Flint agreed that Chauvin had crossed the line, but then he quickly deflected blame onto Democrats. "Senator [Amy] Klobuchar, Democrat presidential candidate, failed to hold [Chauvin] accountable when she was a prosecutor."

Others deflected blame onto Democratic presidential candidate Joe Biden. Bennett in Duluth said, "You can hear Biden trying to blame this on the Trump administration. What is missing here? Biden has been in office 44 years, Schumer, Pelosi, the lovely Maxine Waters for 48 years, and yet they blame America's problems on President Donald Trump who has been in office for about 3 years."[19]

Another common version of Democrat-blaming was to point out that the riots were happening in cities led by Democrats. On Bennett's show, Sandy from Silver Bay said, "Everyone agreed the officer made the wrong choice. You have a constitutional right to peaceable protest. However, you do not have the right to destroy anything. Now you are breaking the law and need to pay the consequences. Now, Brad [referring to the host], as far as I can see a lot of this is taking place in Democratic states and those with sanctuary cities."[20] Later in the show Bennett brought on the Republican candidate for the Minnesota US Senate seat, Jason Lewis.[21] Lewis asserted, "Look, this is a colossal failure of leadership, and it is no different than their colossal mismanagement of COVID and nursing homes or their mismanagement of the inner cities for decades upon decades. We have had liberals control – left-wing politicians, liberal Democrats – control the most urban areas and now we've reached this breaking point."

The hosts went beyond accusations of negligent leadership. Some of them claimed that Democrats were actually fueling the riots to improve their chances of a Biden win in November. On June 2nd on Bennett's show, caller Todd from Duluth suggested, "Pelosi says she's going to impeach again, and Biden and the Democrats are going to bail the demonstrators out of jail. Looks like

---

[17] Examples of blaming Floyd: Bennett in Duluth on May 29th, June 1st and June 2nd, Colley from Twin Falls on May 28th and June 1st, Burke in Anchorage on May 29th.

[18] May 29, 2020.

[19] May 29, 2020.

[20] May 29, 2020.

[21] Lewis is a former talk radio host whose show went on to national syndication after he appeared regularly on the Rush Limbaugh show. His radio presence launched his successful candidacy for the US House, in which he served 1 term, 2017–2019.

they are funding all of this. Looks like they are going to burn down our cities and destroy our country." Bennett responded with a theory.

If for example I were a conspiracy theorist nut job I would say, "Let's see. We've got the Democrats who have a candidate who probably doesn't have much of a chance of winning against Donald Trump with the economy as robust as it is and with so many people working, how would they possibly be able to kick the stool out from under President Trump? How would they possibly be able to do that?" Well, uh so Joe Biden is raising his hand and saying, "We gotta find a way to destroy the economy! Well how we gonna do that? Well, uh how 'bout we get a pandemic? And we shut the whole country down? Nobody can go to work. Everybody's gonna lose their jobs, they gotta wear masks. Oh! And then on top of that if that isn't good enough if that doesn't kick 'er down enough then how 'bout we have a mass riot and vandalism, we turn Antifa loose and uh destroy oh, I don't know, how about like Minneapolis, how about we destroy 600 buildings in downtown Minneapolis/ St. Paul in about a 3-day period? Burn 'em all down, wreck 'em, destroy 'em? That oughta pretty well kick the economy in the rump, don't ya think?"

Bennett[22] and Flint in Billings[23] talked about an international campaign among liberals to raise money to bail out protesters. They were treating the protests as a coordinated strategy by Democrats to win the presidential election, not as an outcry against racial injustice.

At least one host made an explicit claim that such behavior was part of a long-term strategy to use race to promote socialism. On June 1, host Colley in Twin Falls played a clip of Harvard Professor Cornell West talking with host Anderson Cooper on CNN, and then launched into a narrative that wove together the Democrats, socialism, and race. The clip he played was extensive and included West saying,

I thank God that we have people in the streets. Can you imagine this kind of lynching taking place and people are indifferent?!... You know what's sad about it though, brother, at the deepest level? It looks as if the system cannot reform itself. We have tried Black faces in high places. Too often our Black politicians, professional class, middle class become too accommodated to the capitalist economy, too accommodated to the militarized nation state, too accommodated to the market-driven culture.... And what happens? What happens is we've got a neofascist gangster in the White House who really doesn't care for the most part....[24]

Colley interpreted the clip this way: "So he is talking like a Bolshevik. Look, I can't give you my property. You burned it down, for crying out loud!"[25]

---

[22] June 2, 2020.

[23] June 3, 2020.

[24] www.realclearpolitics.com/video/2020/05/29/cornel_west_america_is_a_failed_social_experiment_ neoliberal_wing_of_democratic_party_must_be_fought.html.

[25] By November, Colley referred to the events over the summer as "classic psyops." "BLM and all that was classic psyops," he said, as a caller claimed, "BLM, Antifa – they are being propelled by foreign agents."

In these commentaries, the hosts were not only deflecting attention away from racism, but deflecting attention away from inequality. Bennet's remarks associated Democrats with both racial unrest and with manufactured economic challenges. Colley discounts Cornel West's system-level critique as socialist. This act of equating Democrats with the protests in response to Floyd's death makes it inappropriate to even consider the relationship of racial injustice to economic concerns.

REVERSE RACISM AND THE REFRAMING OF VICTIMHOOD

The Right-leaning hosts did not completely ignore the issue of racism. However, they did not let it remain the focus of attention for long, except to claim that it is Whites who are the targets of hate. Muir in Green Bay stated matter-of-factly that "BLM is a VERY racist group" whose members "don't actually care about the injustices that have been done to people – they are just there to forward their agenda and personally profit."[26] On Bennett's show, caller Tom from Port Wayne put it this way:

I'm very sad for the country.... Our country is in great peril. It is literally in some places on fire. We have people who were penned up for a long time through this stay-at-home and have lost their minds. They have envy and hatred of the majority of people in this country.... We have never had a moment in which people have such zeal and hatred toward others in the country.[27]

While some of this concern about reverse racism was fear of hatred toward Whites, some of it was anger over a perception that racial minorities were treated better than Whites. This was especially clear on the Flint show in Billings. Elena in Philipsburg complained that nobody rose up in protest "when the government slaughtered the people at Waco or at Ruby Ridge"[28] On June 3, Flint brought up new legislation in New York that was "making it a felony for officials to share illegal immigrant driver data with U.S. customs officials." He took this as a sign of injustice toward law-abiding citizens, presumably Whites. "To me the rioting that is going on in this country is so similar to the illegal alien story where they want to create all these rules and these laws to crack down on the legal and the innocent, us, but then they want to protect people who are acting illegally."

Similar perceptions of injustice and victimhood laced comparisons the hosts drew between the January 6 insurrection and the George Floyd protests. Bennett in Duluth noted that the Minnesota attorney general intended to prosecute any Minnesotans who took part in the insurrection. A caller asked, "But took part

---

[26] May 29, 2020.
[27] June 2, 2020.
[28] May 29, 2020. These are two famous cases of standoffs between federal agents and armed resistors that took place in the early 1990s.

how? Broke windows, or just there? You would want people who did violence. But they didn't do that for the other riots this year." Bennett agreed: "Ok to uphold the rule of law, but let's do it evenly across all political leanings," suggesting a double standard in which liberals taking part in the Floyd protests were not prosecuted although conservatives storming the US Capitol were.

In Twin Falls, Colley voiced similar complaints and drew a connection to a rural versus urban divide. In the days after Floyd's death, he talked about the protests that had erupted in Portland and Seattle. He talked about this as a case of urban lawlessness contrasting with rural common sense. He and a caller joked that people in the nonmetro areas were armed, and would eventually be the last ones standing. A caller said, "Antifa types and these entitled little rich kids showed up in Washington [state], doing it in Tacoma, ran into about 60% of the armed citizens of the town and decided to go back to Seattle to burn it down." Colley responded, "One side has 60 rounds of ammunition, the other doesn't know which bathroom to use [referring to debates over transgender bathrooms]. [laughs] The people who can defend themselves, accurately anyway, are just regular Americans in flyover country, which is why you're not going to see [those protests] happening here."[29]

Hosts and callers framed themselves as victims by claiming their communities were treated unfairly, thereby diverting attention away from racism. Those claims were part of a broader perspective that demographic change was making them the victims of injustice, in which they were not getting their fair share of attention, resources, and respect. One manifestation of this was that these shows occasionally lamented the loss of a whiter time in the United States. Senate candidate Lewis mentioned on Bennett's Duluth show "the same liberal policies that have turned the Twin Cities into something our grandparents wouldn't recognize."[30] Caller Sandy in Silver Bay said, "I look at what is happening right now, this is not the United States" and "On our money it says In God We Trust. Where are you people? You are not trusting God." She, too, was lamenting her image of a past society.[31] Host Bennett conveyed a similar kind of nostalgia when he said, "This has now become a story of how much can we steal, how much can we burn? 'Who's George Floyd? [he said, sarcastically quoting hypothetical protestors.] Let's burn this place … Let's break in and steal everything they got.' Is this Minnesota we're looking at? This looks like Detroit or some other community! It does not look like Minnesota anymore." He read a note from a caller on the air that expressed a similar sentiment: "I am so shameful of the people of this state.… No place deserves this chaos. We are so disheveled in what is happening. So shameful, disgusting. What happened to Minnesota?"[32]

[29] June 1, 2020.
[30] May 29, 2020.
[31] May 29, 2020.
[32] May 29, 2020.

When the hosts gave voice to concerns about their geographic and on-air communities being victims of unequal and unfair treatment, they drew attention away from injustices to people of color, or even injustices, such as economic inequality, that they might have shared with people of color.

MOMENTARY EXPRESSIONS OF EMPATHY OR SOLIDARITY

There *were* moments on these shows during which the hosts and callers expressed empathy with people of color, but they were brief. For example, on May 29th, Bennett at WDSM said,

What do we hear often from low-income minority type people about their housing in certain developments? We hear, "There's—We don't have enough low-income housing. We need more low-income housing. We need better housing, this housing is so old we need better housing." *And I kinda feel for a lot of them many times* [emphasis added]. Until I saw this today. One of the buildings that burned last night that was torched to the ground by one of these supposed people that are concerned about what happened to George Floyd, was a under-construction, affordable housing development that was burned to the ground…. And now what will we hear? "Well, we don't have enough low-income housing. We don't have enough housing for us." You just burned it to the ground!

A few days later Bennett again shifted from empathy, this time using the topic of food deserts. "You know how minorities always say they have a food desert? Well, this Aldi grocery store was extensively looted."[33] And then the next morning, he launched into a similar complaint.

So I think that when we look at the big picture of what is going down here or what has gone down, we have to be very attuned to the fact that a lot of the damage that was created in this community, a lot of the heartbreak, and a lot of the people in the community that are going to suffer now as a way to find food, find clothing because … not only did they lose food stores that were there but a lot of the stores that were damaged were also stores … that they bought clothing at … and it has just become very, very difficult now for some of these areas to get the kinds of support that they need. So when you start sometimes by protesting, you sometimes leave your own communities unprotected, and you sometimes hurt *your own people* by what you do in that community [emphases added].

Sometimes Bennett's language and that of his callers went beyond the use of an ambiguous "you people" to calling people foreigners.[34] This was part of a pattern of othering in which the "them" according to these shows was a vast anti-identity that included urbanites, Democrats, liberals, people of color, and foreigners. They were treated as a general outgroup of un-American residents

---

[33] June 1, 2020.
[34] Minneapolis has a large population of Somali immigrants. "When you have a community that rises up and burns – eventually it is going to cost the taxpayers of that community. That community won't let that remain like a burned-out Mogadishu" (June 15, 2020).

of the United States (Finkel et al. 2020). Caller Don spelled this out from his cell phone on June 8th on Bennett's show. "Defunding the police department is the next step in a liberal experiment that is going to go wrong. Minneapolis is a sanctuary city. We brought in refugees from all different countries, and we've lived under their social liberal rules, and now it has gone bad, and along with the bigger cities, New York, L.A." After a little back and forth with Bennett, he added, "[Floyd] was no saint, and the cop was no saint, but to demonize – to say that there is systemic racism in the Twin Cities, that's a failure of how Minneapolis is run. It has nothing to do – nothing other than a reflection of the policies they continue to do to divide people by. We bring in people you know, they support different laws. Moslems have their view of how they think things should be run, they came from a different country. Instead of adopting our rules, they want to change everything."

COMPARING TO TALK ABOUT FLOYD'S DEATH ON LEFT-LEANING SHOWS

To help illuminate the perspectives I was hearing on these conservative shows, I turn now to content from the three Left-leaning shows. I sought to understand whether the hosts' and callers' comments considered a connection between the economic concerns and racism. Did their conversations around the Floyd murder and ensuing events touch upon economic concerns among Whites and people of color? Did they raise a different kind of connection between racism and economic concerns or inequality?

The show broadcast from Atlanta targeted to Blacks made explicit connections. The host, Wanda Stokes, talked about the riots resulting from Floyd's murder in a way that made it clear she and her audience were well aware that people were angry about the racial and economic injustices experienced by Blacks in Minneapolis and elsewhere. She did not have to explain that people were angry. Instead, she focused on how people should be channeling their anger.[35]

Likewise, the Minnesota Public Radio show broadcast out of Rochester, near Minneapolis, addressed Floyd's murder as part of a pattern of injustice to Black Americans. One morning on MPR, civil rights attorney and leader Nekima Valdez Levy Armstrong was a guest. In contrast to the discussions on Heitkamp's show, Armstrong did not find it necessary to accommodate Right-leaning perspectives. "The system" she said, "is rigged when it comes to justice for African Americans. That has been the case since the system was developed. Cries for justice often fall on deaf ears just like the cries of George Floyd. That is very symbolic of what we go through day in and day out." At one point in the interview, the host said, "There is a tension between the process [for bringing the officers involved to trial] and the need for swift justice."

[35] May 28, 2020.

Armstrong responded, "The tension resides in the minds of white America. For Black Americans it is very easy to look at the video and to know that something unlawful happened." Armstrong also challenged the idea that the rioting was inappropriate.

I don't want any more lives to be lost but the reality is that this comes with the territory of people finally being fed up with the status quo, of no accountability. When it gets to this level of frustration, this combustible, you cannot predict or control the outcome. I'm not sure why people are so surprised that it happened here.... Given the volume of people who were present, people who are so outraged, we can't control what they do as a result of their frustration. We are worried about repairing property damage. We need to be worried about the damage that has been done to communities from one generation to the next for maintaining the status quo and allowing police to kill with impunity. *That* is the real problem.

These two shows, targeted to urban audiences, made clear links between racism and injustice. However, in their broadcasts I analyzed, I did not hear emphasis on the manner in which Whites as well as people of color might benefit from greater redistribution.

I turned to the Fargo, North Dakota, show to listen for such a connection. This show's audience was predominantly White and rural. It airs on an agricultural news station that announces crop prices and weather forecasts throughout the shows and broadcasts ABC News.

The show's political orientation was moderate to Left-leaning. Although host Heitkamp's sister is a former Democratic US Senator and Fargo is more liberal politically than the rest of the state, the station's lineup includes an array of conservative-leaning nationally syndicated talk show hosts.

Some of the conversations on this show resembled those on the conservative shows. For example, the hosts and callers complained that the stay-at-home orders were unfair to relatively rural places like theirs, where the COVID-19 virus had not yet spread. Even on the morning of May 29th, as the news of Floyd's murder was spreading, Heitkamp lamented that attention might be diverted by the murder and protests away from the struggles Fargo and other communities tuning in were having with the impacts of the pandemic. This was despite the fact that many of Heitkamp's listeners were living in Minnesota, the state of Floyd's death, since Fargo is located on the border of Minnesota and North Dakota. On the morning of May 29th, Heitkamp said, "With COVID there is a lot going on. Just understand we are going to be on this Minneapolis story, but lots going on, as this whole COVID thing happens. I hope the governor [of Minnesota] doesn't give all his attention to Minneapolis because in outstate Minnesota the policies the governor has in place are crippling. They are really hard on certain businesses."

Such comments about the competition for attention between more rural communities and urban places were common on his show. On the morning of May 29th, Heitkamp's listeners were also reeling at the time over the death of a White police officer in Grand Forks, North Dakota, who was shot and killed while on duty. Heitkamp lamented that although this was a tremendous loss to their local community, it would never be noticed by the national press. "I brought that up to a national reporter yesterday. Do they even know that we have an officer who died? Do they know what happened?" At times like this, Heitkamp's resentment about the attention that urban areas received resembled that of the conservative hosts.

Heitkamp's commentary was different from that of the more conservative hosts. He urged his listeners to have empathy across prominent divides. He encouraged them to notice that it was possible to mourn the death of a White police officer *and* a Black man killed by an officer. "You can have empathy. You can care and be heartbroken about what happened in Grand Forks and still question what happened in Minneapolis. You can be that person."[36]

Heitkamp also contrasted with the conservative hosts in his direct consideration of race and whiteness. He noted that his audience members likely had little experience with people who were not White. He said that the stations that carry his show in Canada, Minnesota, South Dakota, and North Dakota "don't have a diverse of a culture so they might not know the sheer logistics of the neighborhoods where the riots are taking place."[37] The local weather and sports reporters on his show also talked openly about racism.

Although Heitkamp considered the role of racism and expressed more empathy with the people protesting Floyd's death, his ability to consider the similarities in economic challenges faced by Whites and people of color was constrained by his audience and by his own rural versus urban frame. For example, some of his callers suggested Floyd was partly to blame, but Heitkamp disagreed, in an instructive rather than chastising manner. For example, a caller said, "I just wanted to mention this guy [Chauvin] should be charged with murder, but what if [Floyd] died of a heart attack? We need to wait and see the results of the autopsy. I think you said he clearly murdered the guy." Heitkamp cut the caller short, saying, "I said he clearly caused his death. If I had my arm around your neck and you suffocated would I be charged?"[38] Heitkamp resisted the callers' attempts to move away from the injustice of Floyd's death, but he nevertheless moved quickly to more common ground, such as claims that the rioting was unjustified, or their shared support for police in general. In the days after Floyd's death, Heitkamp regularly commented that the looters and protestors using violence ought to be charged, taking a tough-on-crime stance that resembles the comments on some of the conservative broadcasts.

Some of his audience members seemed to believe he was not doing enough to counteract conservative narratives. On May 29th, he read a text from a listener sent after others on the show had questioned the point of the looting.

[36] May 28, 2020.
[37] May 28, 2020.
[38] May 28, 2020.

"One of you responded, 'They tried peacefully kneeling and you all had problems with that, too'" (referring to the National Football League players' protests during the playing of the national anthem).

However, other audience members questioned the support for the protests that he or others had voiced. Heitkamp relayed one story of such backlash. He explained that while he was broadcasting on the Saturday night after Floyd's death, when protests had turned violent in Fargo (May 30, 2020), a listener had sent him a message. He recalled the message like this: "'I don't care. Those Black' and then using the N word 'should all be shot.' And then he goes on and writes, 'Any of our officers marching with them' and then uses the N word 'should be shot, too'."[39]

In these ways, portions of Heitkamp's audience limited how much he could highlight common cause with people of color. Also, his own resentment toward the attention given to urban concerns constrained any move toward recognition of common cause across racial lines, even when the conversation was focused on economic affairs. On May 29th, one of his guests was a business leader from Morehead, Minnesota, a community just across the Red River from Fargo. They talked about the injustice of Floyd's death, but the emphasis of their conversation was on the perception that the rioting and protests were taking attention away from the serious economic challenges facing small towns in the pandemic and the way the restrictions on opening up businesses, created with urban businesses in mind, were economically devastating. In other words, the show did not draw attention to the ways economic challenges are similar across different social groups and communities, but instead on the competition between rural and urban areas for attention and resources.

Heitkamp may have been encouraging his audience to have more empathy, but he was still in the business of maintaining, if not growing, an audience of listeners. Like the conservative hosts, his commentary and that of the callers and guests he welcomed on, had to resonate with a predominantly White audience. To varying degrees, these shows faced the tragedy of Floyd's death by tapping into a set of widespread values that further inhibited the connection these shows made between racism and economic inequality or other shared economic concerns.

One of the more common values that hosts and callers invoked as they detoured away from racism was accountability. Heitkamp, like the conservative hosts, noted that, yes, the officers involved in Floyd's death needed to be held accountable, but then said the rioters needed to be held accountable as well.

Heitkamp's emphasis on a respect for law and order was common on the conservative shows as well. Immediately after the storming of the US Capitol, many hosts denounced that violence, as they denounced the violent protests

---

[39] June 1, 2020.

against Floyd's death. Bennett in Duluth opened his broadcast the day after the insurrection by saying that yesterday was an "absolute disaster" in Washington, D.C., and laid out his law-and-order conception of good citizenship.

First of all, some of the TV stations tried to portray this as Trump patriots who had gone amuck. Let me just tell you that in my estimation patriots enlist and defend their country. They work hard, they do their best, raise families, good families, help their neighbors, perform civic duties, they grit their teeth and pay their taxes but they do pay. They show up and vote. They compete and whether they win or lose they do both with grace. They do not storm their Capitol over a lost election…. Hopefully they will be arrested and they will be jailed.[40]

Likewise in Twin Falls that same morning, Colley took his listeners to task for thinking that the Capitol Police were traitors. He said he had been watching a video of the officers at the Capitol being stampeded.

Some people were screaming 'traitors!' What did you think they were going to do? March in with you and hold members of Congress hostage?! Some of you are saying they should choose their side. You expect them to lose their jobs in this tough economy? You think they should sacrifice their job but you shouldn't?!… Those Capitol officers, their job is to protect that building and the people inside it. That is their mission.

Although one can imagine how referencing widely shared values could help draw attention to shared concerns, the manner in which hosts talked about them reinforced divides. For example, especially on the conservative shows, discussion of patriotism portrayed real Americans as White Christians. Also, the shows celebrated civic engagement in their communities, but demonized government while doing so. The shows regularly emphasized that local businesses, organizations, and volunteers were the appropriate safety net for their communities, not government. In Duluth, Bennett and Kalligher criticized the enormous bill that the government was running up by sending out pandemic recession stimulus checks. But they applauded the fact that a local grocery store was handing out gift cards to "deserving" people, funded by donations from community members.

The shows conveyed a blatant reverence for capitalism and the free market. For example, on Bennett's show in Duluth on June 1st, caller Don argued that what was going on in Minneapolis and in other cities was the failure of leadership in liberal cities, among Democrats, and the left-wing protestors. "Failure of these people to respect any type of authority. They chastise capitalism. I challenge any of these people if they would like to go to a third world country and ask these people if they would like to be involved in capitalism that supports all these people who can go out and protest."

[40] January 7, 2021.

DISCUSSION AND CONCLUSION

The inability to understand and share the feelings of members of racial out-groups is a part of racism that dampens Whites' support for redistributive policy. The local conservative talk radio shows I listened to for this study suggest that one of the ways this lack of understanding is perpetuated is by denying the existence of racism and by painting those who draw attention to racism as un-American. The hosts and callers justified deflections from the topic of racism while they reaffirmed beliefs in accountability, capitalism, and law and order. Broadcasts of these shows on topics other than Floyd's death conveyed that the communities of these shows were understanding public affairs through a lens that emphasized these values as well as patriotism, Christianity, and aversion to big government. The way they did so conveyed that considerations of either racism or a greater role for the government in the economy (e.g., through redistribution) were anti-American.

The image of the archetypal American conveyed on the conservative shows, and on Heitkamp's show, was that of a hard-working, flag-bearing, God-fearing, rural White male. This undermined empathy with people of color, and reduced the chances of recognizing that a broad swath of Americans are victims of economic inequality and are harmed economically by a lack of redistribution.[41] Associating Democrats with people of color and the ambiguous specter of socialism also made it seem ridiculous to even consider redistribution. These hosts and their callers claimed that Democrats had fostered the violent protests after Floyd's death to push their political goals of "Bolshevism." In this perspective, communities were not getting their fair share because of the lack of Americanness of people of color and their allies.

Notice what this means about the way the aversion to redistribution is intertwined with racism. In this interpretation, it is the Democrats who are using racism to achieve downward redistribution. This is quite the opposite of perceiving that it is the Republicans who are using racism to inhibit empathy to prevent such redistribution from taking place.

Whether or not this understanding is part of an explicit political strategy, this is a notable framing. It is different from what we would expect from a divide-and-conquer strategy, in which attention to the haves versus have-nots is redirected through a frame of makers versus takers. Instead, it would seem to result from an attempt to cast support for redistribution as a threat to the very fabric of the country. It also opens up the possibility for those opposed to redistribution to campaign to people of color and argue that the actors and

---

[41] Notice how consequential perspectives are for the likelihood that people will experience empathy toward others, even when those others are in an outgroup such as immigrants that is currently politically potent (Williamson et al. 2020).

organizations calling themselves allies are more interested in imposing social-ism than in achieving racial justice. In other words, as this perspective gains traction, it creates an opportunity for the Republican Party to win votes among people of color.

Looking closely at the way political commentators like these talk radio hosts treat the possibility of redistribution reinforces what we know about the relationship between race or ethnic difference and support for redistribution more globally: that this relationship varies from country to country and seems to most centrally depend on how the political culture equates the presence of racial or ethnic "others" (e.g., immigrants) with concerns about the viability of social policy (Burgoon 2014). How racism matters for the possibility of redistribution depends on whether and how people use racism in these debates. Some might use racism to stoke fear over the way resources are currently allo-cated (i.e., Brexit). Some might use racism by ironically deflecting away from the topic in a way that prevents recognition of shared economic concerns among people of a wide range of cultural backgrounds.

The fact that the use of racism to prevent redistribution in the United States is a centuries-old story might suggest that this is not likely to change any time soon. But I draw your attention back to one of the Left-leaning contrast shows, the Joel Heitkamp Show, broadcast out of Fargo, North Dakota. There are cur-rently spaces in American political culture in which people are actively strug-gling with the archetype of the true American as a hard-working, flag-bearing, God-fearing, rural, White male, rather than insisting on the defense of this image. It is notable that the shows I investigated, except for the Atlanta show, took place in the North, which has lagged behind the South in coming to terms with the legacies of slavery (Bartels and Cramer 2019). We should pay attention to communication in which people are actively struggling with the notion that real Americans are White Americans, because such moments may be a source of political change. Public opinion scholars have famously taken manifestations of ambivalence as signs of civic incompetence (Converse [1964] 2006). But maybe instead they should be taken as signals from the public that a reckoning of their competing values and commitments is in order (Hochschild 1993, 204–206).

These occasions of ambivalence are also a caution against concluding that the processes of understanding that we witness on these shows are the act of members of the audience adopting the talking points fed to them by the local show hosts, national show hosts, or a shadow set of political elites generat-ing the shows' content. Yes, there is a sharing of arguments in an apparently concerted fashion, particularly among conservative media outlets. But these arguments gain traction because they resonate with the experiences and under-standings of the audience. The expressions of ambivalence are reminders that people are active processors who are guided by elites, but nevertheless have minds of their own.

Heitkamp's discussion of racism took place in a context in which rural consciousness was common. He regularly stated that policies are made with major cities in mind. He reinforced the idea that his listening areas were neglected. The avoidance of racism we hear in these broadcasts is part of a perspective in which it is these nonmetro communities and the people within them who are the victims, not people of color in the cities. Through this lens, people are perceiving that they are not heard enough by policymakers and that those who *are* heard are people of color who are allied with those they believe are in power, wealthy liberal urbanites.

In this way, people justify deflecting attention away from racism and away from the possibility of recognizing the ways in which their struggles are similar to those in larger metropolitan areas. When rural Whites understand economic policy this way, through a zero-sum framework in which listening to people of color comes at the expense of listening to people like themselves, it is not surprising that participants in these shows deflect attention away from racism.

13

Class and Social Policy Representation

Macarena Ares and Silja Häusermann

Class- and income-biases in political representation in advanced democratic systems have been documented in many studies. The interests and preferences of citizens in lower income categories or lower social classes are on average less well represented in democratic politics than the interests and preferences of middle- and upper- (income) class citizens. This finding holds both for representation in terms of political attitudes (Bartels, this volume; Giger et al. 2012; Rosset et al. 2013; Rosset and Stecker 2019), as well as in terms of policy responsiveness, in particular social policies and redistribution (e.g., Elsässer, Hence, and Schäfer 2020; Mathisen et al., this volume; Schakel, Burgoon, and Hakverdian 2020). In terms of implications and consequences, research on class-biased unequal representation has not only documented representation deficits, but also demonstrated detrimental effects of nonrepresentation, for example, in terms of political participation and alienation (Mathisen and Peters, this volume; Offe 2009).

Most of these studies assume that voters are aware of "objective" misrepresentation on these issues. However, given data constraints, this is oftentimes hard to study empirically, and we still have rather limited knowledge about the structure and extent of perceived representation. Rennwald and Pontusson (2021) thus advocate a "subjectivist turn" in the study of unequal representation, in order to better understand the extent, determinants and consequences of grievances caused by misrepresentation. We share their argument that voter perceptions of representation cannot simply be assumed, but rather need to be studied empirically. Moreover, we know little about voters' perception of representation across different subfields of social and distributive policies. Hence, we need to know both: (a) whether citizens feel badly represented by "politicians" and the political system overall, and (b) whether perceptions of misrepresentation are also manifest when inquiring about specific and tangible welfare policy areas on which parties and elites can intervene. Moreover, placing the focus on how voters perceive representation on specific policy logics and fields sheds light on the complexity of these perceptions. There are reasons to believe that different dimensions of representation (on different principles and areas of social policy) are not identical, and that class differences in perceptions of misrepresentation may vary across them, with potentially relevant implications. If citizens in lower social classes or income groups, for example, perceive a lack of representation when it comes to pensions and unemployment (typical social consumption policies), and citizens of higher social and income classes perceive a lack of representation in the areas of education and childcare infrastructure, both groups of voters may be similarly dissatisfied with representation.

In this paper, we leverage newly collected data from the ERC project "welfarepriorities"[1] on voters' social policy priorities, their perception of parties' social policy priorities, as well as their evaluation of overall social policy representation to study these questions. We focus on social policy as a field that is key to the literature on unequal representation. Indeed, this strand of research has always had a tendency to focus – implicitly or explicitly – on fiscal and social policies when assessing representation and congruence; a focus that is reasonable given that the direct distributive outcomes of these policies could redistribute power relations and reinforce or mitigate patterns of unequal representation.

The chapter is structured as follows: In the next section, we explain why studying perceptions of misrepresentation matters, particularly in what concerns specific welfare policies. We develop hypotheses on the class biases in both party and systemic representation along different social policy dimensions. We also put forward different expectations as to how the presence of strong challenger parties on the radical left and/or the radical right can mitigate some of these perceptions of unequal representation across different systems. The subsequent section presents our data and measures. The analysis section studies class as a determinant of perceived representation by voters' preferred party and the system overall on different policy dimensions and across different party-political contexts.

THEORY

Distributive policies, and social policies in particular, have always occupied a special place in the study of unequal representation. Not only is social policy one of the key areas of state expenditures and material redistribution, it is also an area that affects social stratification and thus very directly links to those material inequalities that structure and exacerbate unequal representation. At the same time, however, social policy and redistribution have always

[1] We acknowledge funding from the European Research Council (ERC) Grant "WELFAREPRIORITIES," PI Prof. Silja Häusermann, University of Zurich, Grant n°716075.

been fields for which representation has been difficult to study because despite extensive divergences in material "objective" class interests in this field, actual attitudinal differences are not very large (Ares 2017; Rosset and Stecker 2019). Indeed, a wide range of public opinion surveys show that lower-, middle-, and even upper-class citizens on average tend to support expansive, generous social policies (Elsässer 2018; Garritzmann et al. 2018a; Häusermann et al. 2022), especially when they are asked for their unconstrained preferences. Hence, even though there is evidence of class bias in policy responsiveness, it remains hard to assess unequal representation in this field because of attitudinal convergence on social policy support in mature welfare states.

There is reason to think, however, that this seeming attitudinal convergence masks underlying differences in social policy preferences: a lot of the recent literature has shown that rather than in the level of support, citizens today differ more strongly in the type or field of social policy they prioritize: middle-class support is stronger for policies securing life cycle risks than for policies addressing labor-market risks (Jensen 2012; Rehm 2016); furthermore, while middle-class voters prioritize social investment, such as education and childcare much more strongly than voters in lower occupational and income classes, working-class voters prioritize income protection and social compensation policies, such as pensions or unemployment benefits (Garritzmann et al. 2018; Häusermann et al. 2022). While insiders prioritize employment protection, outsiders prioritize redistribution and employment support (Häusermann, Kurer, and Schwander 2014; Rueda 2005). And while working class and national-conservative voters emphasize the protection of national welfare states from open borders, voters in the upper-middle classes and left-libertarian voters prioritize the integration of immigrants and their inclusion in universal social protection schemes (Enggist and Pinggera 2021; Lefkofridi and Michel 2014). All these conflicts and divergences certainly do occur in a context of overall strong support for welfare states (Pinggera 2021); however, social policy conflict today revolves as much around prioritizing particular social policy fields than around contesting levels of benefits, redistribution, and taxation in general.

This is why, in this contribution, we focus on (unequal) representation in terms of social policy *priorities*: do parties (and politicians more generally) attribute similar or different levels of importance to reforms in different social policy fields as their voters? Do parties/elites set other priorities than voters in general and voters from lower social classes in particular? Recent research has emphasized the importance of extending studies of congruence and responsiveness beyond positional measures to also include accounts of the issues and policies that voters prioritize (Giger and Lefkofridi 2014; Traber et al. 2022). More importantly, we study these questions through the "subjectivist lens" of voter perceptions. Do voters feel generally unrepresented by "politicians" in terms of social policy? How do voters' own priorities compare to the priorities they perceive all parties and their preferred party to have?

Answering these questions is relevant to evaluate the extent of the problem of unequal representation, as well as the expected effectiveness of potential remedies to misrepresentation in terms of policies or parties adapting their positions to voters.

Class and Unequal Social Policy Representation

What are our expectations for citizens' differential subjective perceptions of representation? If subjective perceptions match the abundantly documented patterns of unequal congruence and responsiveness along income (see, among others, Elsässer et al. 2020; Giger et al. 2012; Lupu and Warner 2022a; Rosset et al. 2013), we would expect a class gradient in perceptions of representation: higher social classes should perceive better representation of their policy preferences on the part of political elites, in comparison to citizens in lower social classes. These perceptions could stem both from a class gradient in evaluations of input congruence (how well citizens think their preferences get voted into parliament through elections), as well as of output responsiveness (what decisions elected representatives take on policy). In fact, previous research on class-biased representation (Rennwald and Pontusson 2021) has indicated that middle- and upper-middle class voters feel more congruent with the policy positions of parties and politicians than working-class voters, whenever the preferences of these classes diverge. Rennwald and Pontusson (2021) identify a clear class hierarchy in voters' perceptions of being represented by politicians in their countries.

Alternatively, we can also expect that voters could perceive that their voices are equally heard, irrespective of their social class. Since our sample of cases includes many political systems with proportional representation (PR), from a perspective of input representation, these systems typically allow for a wider variety of points of view and preferences to be represented in legislative bodies (Blais 1991). Given the more diversified partisan supply, it should be more likely that individuals of different social classes find a party that represents their interests. Such increased input representation could mitigate perceptions of unequal representation overall.

Finally, a third competing expectation proposes that subjective evaluations of representation are higher among middle-class respondents due to parties' incentives to mobilize electoral coalitions that include the median voter (Elkjær & Iversen, this volume). Even in PR systems, the process of forming government coalitions can move policy to a moderate compromise that is closer to the demands of the median voter. The centripetal pull during government formation could compensate for centrifugal patterns in electoral competition and bring policy closer in line with the preferences of the middle class (Blais and Bodet 2006).

Hence, we can formulate three competing scenarios about perceptions of representation: lacking differences in these perceptions by social class,

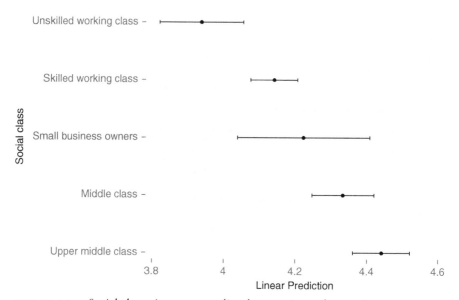

FIGURE 13.1 Social classes' average predicted perceptions of systemic congruence on social policy

Notes: Class as a determinant of perceived systemic congruence. Estimates are based on linear regression models introducing controls for age, sex, trade union membership, and country-FE. The coefficients for all variables are presented in Table 13.A2 in the Appendix.

perceptions of comparatively better representation by the middle classes, and perceptions of comparatively better representation by the upper classes. In terms of differences across institutional systems, the first scenario could be more likely to take place in PR systems due to the greater differentiation of the partisan supply and the accompanying input representation. The second scenario should be more likely in majoritarian systems, but could also emerge in PR systems due to the dynamics generated at the government formation and policymaking stages (Blais & Bodet, 2006).

Figure 13.1 indicates that when voters are inquired specifically about social policies – very much in line with previous research on class-biased subjective representation (Rennwald and Pontusson 2021) – we observe a class gradient in perceptions of systemic congruence (i.e., perceived congruence between "citizens" and "politicians" overall), with these perceptions progressively improving as we move up in the social structure, from the unskilled working class, to the upper-middle class.

Figure 13.1 plots social classes' average evaluation of the extent to which *"political decision-makers share your (the respondent's) views about which reforms in social policy are the most important"* (as measured on a 10-point scale). This figure corroborates one of the central tenets of unequal representation studies: the upper classes are indeed more likely to perceive politicians' (social policy) priorities as congruent with their own. The 0.5-point difference between the upper and unskilled class on this attitude amounts to approximately a fourth of the standard deviation of this variable. This class gradient in perceptions of feeling represented on welfare reform policies is comparable to the findings from Rennwald and Pontusson (2021).

This initial evidence of unequal systemic congruence substantiates the importance of addressing these perceptions in what concerns social policy. However, this general measure could be masking some substantial heterogeneity in perceptions of unequal welfare policy representation for two reasons. First, while this item captures voters' perceptions of congruence on social policy generally (without referring to a specific logic or field), it could be conflating perceived policy misrepresentation with some general systemic dissatisfaction (Easton 1975), which is usually more widespread among lower class citizens (Oesch 2008; Rydgren 2007). Second, there are reasons to expect that perceptions of welfare policy congruence are likely to differ across social policy dimensions. In current welfare politics, the literature distinguishes in particular three areas of social policy reform where such class preferences and class perceptions of representation may diverge consistently and substantively: *social consumption policies, social investment policies and welfare chauvinism*. In these policy fields, voter preferences and party responses may well diverge in different ways.

Social consumption policies refer to those social policies that substitute income in the event of a disruption of employment (e.g., in the case of sickness, accident, unemployment, or old age). They denote the "traditional" passive income transfer policies of the welfare states that were strongly developed in continental Western Europe in the second half of the twentieth century (Esping-Andersen 1999). They may be more or less redistributive in their institutional design (depending on the extent to which they are universal, targeted or insurance-based), but they in general tend to equalize income streams between risk groups that relate to social class. For this reason, and because of the immediacy of redistributive effects, social consumption policies are most strongly prioritized and emphasized by working-class voters (as opposed to middle- and upper-class voters) (Garritzmann et al. 2018; Häusermann et al. 2022). At the same time, the hands of political parties and elites to expand these social consumption policies significantly are rather severely tied by fiscal and political constraints. If anything, elites and governments have generally tried to consolidate (or, in some instances, even retrench) social spending in the main areas of social consumption (e.g., Hemerijck 2012). Hence, we would assume class-specific representation to be particularly biased against working-class interests in the area of social consumption.

By contrast, middle- and upper-class voters tend to attribute a decidedly higher importance to social investment policies than working-class voters (Beramendi et al. 2015; Bremer 2021). Rather than replacing income, social investment policies invest in human capital formation, mobilization, and preservation (Garritzmann et al. 2022), for example, via education policies, early childhood education and care policies, or labor-market reintegration policies. The stronger emphasis of middle- and upper-class voters – as compared to working-class voters – on social investment has been explained by different mechanisms, in particular the oftentimes regressive distributive effects of these policies (Bonoli and Liechti 2018; Pavolini and van Lancker 2018), differences in institutional trust (Jacobs and Matthews 2017; Garritzmann et al. 2018b), and higher levels of universalistic values among the middle class (Beramendi et al. 2015). However, the efforts of parties and governments to actually expand social investment policies across Western Europe have remained rather limited (Garritzmann et al. 2022) because of institutional legacies, fiscal and political constraints. Hence, when it comes to social investment, one might expect class-specific perceived representation to be less biased overall, or even biased more strongly against the preferences of middle- and upper-middle class voters.

Finally, middle- and working-class voters clearly differ in the extent to which they emphasize the importance of excluding migrants from welfare benefits and prioritizing the needs of natives. Policies that either lower benefit levels for migrants, or which extend existing benefits only for natives generally enjoy stronger support among the lower classes across all countries of Western Europe (Degen et al. 2018). The mechanism driving this class divergence is supposed to be either economic (welfare competition, e.g., Manow 2018) or value-based (communitarian as opposed to universalistic values, e.g., Enggist 2019). Given the saliency, electoral importance, and much lower fiscal significance of social policies addressing the needs of immigrants, we would expect parties and elites to be more responsive to the, on average, more immigration-skeptical preferences of the lower middle and working classes. Indeed, related studies have found the class bias in representation to be much weaker when it comes to immigration policies than when it comes to distributive policies (Elsässer 2018). Hence, like social investment, one may expect weaker class bias or even reversed class bias in perceived representation of welfare chauvinism preferences.

Overall, we would thus expect the class bias in perceived party representation to be strongest when it comes to social consumption, because this is the area where strongly expansionist demands among citizens clash with an agenda of fiscal consolidation or even retrenchment among elites. By contrast, we would expect this bias to be weaker when it comes to social investment and welfare benefits for immigrants.

Within the paradigms of social consumption and investment, we can further differentiate different policy fields, such as pensions and unemployment benefits within social consumption, as well as (higher) education, active labor-market policies and childcare services when it comes to social investment. Regarding these fields, we would overall expect subjectively perceived representation biases to be strongest in those policies that are most salient and important to voters. Based on both the risk distribution and political importance (e.g., Rehm 2016; Jensen 2012; Enggist 2019), this would suggest that we expect stronger biases in the areas of pensions, education, and immigrants' benefits than when it comes to unemployment support and childcare services.

Social Policy Congruence by Party Configuration

The observation of unequal, class-biased representation entails the question of context conditions that might mitigate or exacerbate the class bias in perceived (in)congruence. Indeed, a more varied political supply in terms of political parties would seem as one potential factor affecting the extent to which citizens perceive their preferences to be adequately represented or not, particularly at the stage of electoral competition. As previous research has indicated, at the government formation and policymaking stages, centripetal pressure to build majorities via coalitions imply that, even in PR systems, policy could be more responsive to middle-class demands (Blais and Bodet 2006; Elkjær and Iversen, this volume).

The role of nonmainstream parties in diversifying the political supply in terms of representation seems particularly relevant, not only because these parties tend to mobilize voters explicitly with reference to their opposition to the dominant mainstream or government parties (Mair 2013), but also because left and right challenger parties have particular incentives to be responsive to their voters in terms of social policy. In particular, right challenger parties tend to mobilize disproportionally among voters from the working and lower middle classes (Oesch and Rennwald 2018). The electorate of left challenger parties is more heterogeneous in terms of social class, but at the same time, these parties tend to emphasize issues of social justice, egalitarianism, and distribution and should thus be particularly sensitive to representing the specific social policy preferences of their electorate.

We can thus theorize four context configurations in terms of party supply and derive expectations regarding the class bias in representation (Table 13.1).

TABLE 13.1 *Strength of expected class bias in representation of social policy preferences, depending on challenger parties*

	Presence of strong right-wing challenger	Absence of strong right-wing challenger
Presence of strong left-wing challenger	Weak (moderate) class bias	Moderate class bias
Absence of strong left-wing challenger	Moderate class bias	Strong class bias

We expect the strongest class bias in perceived representation in systems where challenger parties are weak, such as majoritarian electoral systems that tend to entail obstacles for challenger party mobilization. In these systems, we would expect, in particular, working-class voters to perceive elite congruence among mainstream parties and hence a larger distance between their priorities and the ones of their preferred party or the party system in general. The absence of challenger parties could deteriorate perceptions of unequal priority representation, since these parties tend to improve salience-based congruence (Giger and Lefkofridi 2014). While we expect challenger parties on the left and right to mitigate some of the class-biased perceptions of representation, this could differ across social policy logics because of the issues these parties emphasize toward voters. Challenger parties on the right mobilize strongly in lower social classes, and they tend to do so, largely, in terms of policies related to immigration and welfare chauvinism (e.g., Hutter and Kriesi 2016; Kriesi et al. 2012), or of consumptive policies (Enggist and Pinggera 2021). Hence, right-wing challenger parties could particularly mitigate class biases on the logics of social consumption and benefits for migrants. Challenger parties on the left, in contrast, have typically mobilized lower-class electorates on an economic platform, have abstained from anti-immigration stances, and have also attempted to mobilize higher-grade classes on investment-oriented policies. Hence, these parties could mitigate class biases on the social consumption and investment dimensions, but not on welfare chauvinism. We expect class biases in representation to be most strongly mitigated in contexts of diversified supply, with strong challengers on both the left and right.

While these expectations are based on the types of social policy priorities typically taken by different party families (and the social groups they mobilize electorally), deviations from these expectations could arise from how the logic of party competition might affect the salience of these topics. While having a diversified supply can increase the range of policy priorities present in the party system (e.g., with a party explicitly advocating for welfare chauvinism), rising contestation and politicization of issues could also fuel perceptions of lack of representation, if not by voters' preferred party, then by the system overall. Following the same example, having strong contestation on the issue of welfare chauvinism both from challenger parties on the left and right might bring further attention to welfare chauvinistic voters about the many parties that do *not* share their position. An expansion in the scope of conflict (Schattschneider 1960) can diversify the policy priorities taken by parties, but also highlight the different opinions held by other parties and voters. This is why we also propose that in highly diversified landscape, with challengers on both the left and right, the mitigation of class biases might be lower than initially expected and still be moderate. We purposely leave this expectation rather open and up for empirical investigation.

DATA AND OPERATIONALIZATION

We use original data from a survey conducted in the context of the ERC project "welfarepriorities." Data were collected in eight Western European countries with 1,500 respondents each in Denmark, Sweden, Germany, the Netherlands, Ireland, the United Kingdom, Italy, and Spain. The questionnaire and sample design were in our hands, while the actual fieldwork was done in cooperation with a professional survey institute (Bilendi) using their online panels. The target population was a country's adult population (>18 years). The total sample counts 12,129 completed interviews that were conducted between October 2018 and January 2019. Different measures were taken in order to increase the survey's representativeness and to ensure high-quality answers. First, we based our sampling strategy on quotas for age, gender, and educational attainment, drawn from national census figures. Age and gender were introduced as crossed quotas, with six age groups (18–25, 26–35, 36–45, 46–55, 56–65, 66 or older) for both female and male respondents. Second, we account for remaining bias from survey response by including poststratification weights adjusting for age, gender, and educational attainment. The full dataset together with some validation tests are presented extensively in a specific working paper (Häusermann et al. 2020).

Measures of Social Policy Representation

The survey includes a wide range of items capturing social policy positions and priorities, as well as a question on systemic congruence and on the respondents' evaluation of party priorities.

There are several different items that enable us to measure social policy priorities. For this chapter, we use *point distribution questions*, in which respondents were asked to allocate 100 points to six policy fields, reflecting the relative importance they attribute to different strategies of welfare state expansion.[2] The six items were presented in a randomized order, so as not to prime the importance given to them. Through this type of question, we can account for the multidimensionality of welfare preferences, while at the same time we pay respect to the constraint that is inherent in the concept of priorities. At the same time, we do not force respondents to prioritize: the point-distribution question does allow for respondents attributing an equal number of points across all fields or reforms (as opposed to a mere *ranking* question of the different fields/reforms). Respondents were asked to allocate points to the six following social policy fields, covering social consumption, social investment,

---

[2] Question wording: "Now imagine that the government had the means to improve benefits in some social policy fields, but not in all of them. You can allocate 100 points. Give more points to those fields in which you consider benefit improvement more important, and fewer points to those areas in which you consider benefit improvement less important."

and welfare chauvinism: Old age pensions, Childcare, University education, Unemployment benefits, Labor-market reintegration services, and Services for social and labor-market integration of immigrants.

This point distribution question was asked to respondents in the first five minutes of the (roughly) twenty- five-minute survey. Most importantly, in the last third of the survey, the respondents were then again confronted with the same type of point-distribution question. However, the question was then asked with regard to their perception of party priorities. Respondents were asked in which of the above areas they think a particular party would prioritize improvements of social benefits.[3] Answer fields were identical as above and again randomized. Each respondent had to complete this task twice, once for his/her own preferred party (i.e., the party they indicated they had voted for in the last national election) and once for an additional, randomly chosen party (among the main parties in the country).[4] Since in this paper, we focus, among other aspects, on "party representation" by the respondents' preferred party, our sample is restricted to respondents who did indicate they had chosen a party in the last national election.

Overall, and across countries and parties, respondents clearly tended to attribute most importance to the expansion of old age pensions, followed by tertiary education and childcare, followed by unemployment benefits and reintegration measures, and – lastly – integration services for immigrants. However, despite roughly similar patterns across countries, there are significant divergences from the country averages cross-sectionally across party electorates and classes (see Häusermann et al. 2022).

We present measures of voters' representation by their preferred party by aggregating the rating of these six specific fields into three different dimensions: social consumption policies (aggregating expansions in the area of pensions and unemployment benefits), social investment policies (childcare, university education, and labor-market reintegration services), and benefits for migrants (services for social and labor-market integration of immigrants). Voters' priorities on each of these dimensions take the average value of the points attributed across the corresponding fields of welfare expansion. We follow the same aggregation strategy to compute the priorities of the different parties on these three policy logics. Measures of parties' priorities on each of these logics are based on the average of points allocated to each of these parties by *all* the available respondents in the sample (i.e., not only their voters). We base

---

[3] Question wording: "In which of the following areas do you think the (party X1) would prioritize improvements of social benefits? You can allocate 100 points. Give more points to those areas in which you think (the party X1) would prioritize improvements and fewer points to those areas where you think (the party X1) would deem improvements less important."

[4] To have a relatively large number of observations of parties' placement, we asked respondents to place only the main parties in the party system. Table 13.A1 in the Appendix includes the list of the parties placed by respondents in each country.

these measures on respondents' average placement of parties and not on the individual placements provided by respondents to avoid risks of endogeneity stemming from voters projecting their own policy stances onto their preferred parties. It is important to notice, however, that parties' average placement by all respondents or by their voters only is similar. To compute the measure of subjective representation by voters' preferred party, we simply subtract the party's placement on each dimension from respondents' self-placement.

On top of measuring subjective representation by respondents' preferred party, we also compute a measure of proximity to the party system in general. This measure allows us to add further detail to the question of how distant individuals perceive the party system to be on the three specific welfare policy logics: consumption, investment, and benefits for migrants. This measure captures the average proximity between a voter and all parties in the system and is calculated by first computing the distance between voters' priorities and those of each party within the system, and second, averaging over these distance measures to arrive to a single measure of subjective system proximity. Both distances (to preferred party and to the party system) are measured on the original 0–100 scale from the point distribution task.

Using such newly developed measures requires evaluations of validity, which we have conducted. First, respondent behavior indicates that they were able and willing to engage with the task at hand: even though they could have eschewed the difficult task of indicating the relative importance for particular policies, fewer than 2 percent of respondents attributed equal point numbers across policy fields. Also, fewer than 6 percent of all respondents attributed 100 points to one field and 0 to all others. We have also conducted extensive analyses to test the internal validity of our items (Ares et al. 2019). Regarding the point distribution question, we used data on people's priorities regarding welfare *retrenchment* (as opposed to expansion) to test if reported preferences are consistent. Our data show that 85 to 90 percent of respondents gave consistent answers, that is, they did *not* simultaneously prioritize retrenchment *and* expansion in the same policy field. Regarding external validity, we find roughly the same "order of priorities" between policy fields as Bremer and Bürgisser (2020), who also study the relative importance of social policies.

Determinants of (Non)representation

Our analyses focus on differences in party and system proximity by social class. We implement a market-based definition of social class based on occupational categories. To operationalize class, we rely on a simplified version of Oesch's (2006) scheme, commonly used in current analyses of postindustrial class conflict (Ares 2020; Häusermann and Kriesi 2015; Oesch and Rennwald 2018). This simplified version of the scheme distinguishes five social classes along Oesch's vertical dimension, which captures marketable skills – that is, how the labor market stratifies life chances. In descending order, the *upper-middle class*

aggregates professionals (including self-employed professionals) and employers with more than ten employees; the *middle class* is constituted of associate
professionals and technicians; the *skilled working class* includes generally and
vocationally skilled employees; the *unskilled working class* includes routine
low and unskilled workers (in manufacturing, service, or clerical jobs); and a
fifth category for *small business owners* aggregates self-employed individuals
without a professional title and employers with fewer than ten employees. All
results referring to the priorities and perceptions of small business owners must
be considered with certain caution since they constitute a small group in the
sample, hence reducing the precision of some estimates. Following many studies
of unequal policy responsiveness, we conduct additional analyses that address
unequal representation by income groups instead of class by assigning respondents to five income quintiles. While these results also report income biases in
social policy representation, they are smaller than inequalities based on social
class. This is in line with a growing number of studies repeatedly showing a
greater explanatory value of class on redistributive and welfare policies.

The first part of the analyses starts by addressing class differences in party
representation on three types of welfare policies (social consumption, social
investment, and benefits for migrants) as well as by each of the policies underlying these logics separately. As explained earlier, for each of these logics and
policies, proximity is measured with respect to respondents' preferred party
and to the system overall. In these models, the outcome variables are distances
in points; hence, the models are estimated as linear regression models including controls for age, sex, trade union membership, and country-fixed effects.
These control variables are included consistently across all models (except for
the analyses by party system type, which do not include country-fixed effects).

The second part of the analyses addresses how the configuration of the partisan supply could mitigate/accentuate class inequalities in perceived congruence.
Since the number of country-level observations is limited to eight, to address
this question, we split the sample into four groups depending on whether challenger left- and/or right-wing alternatives had strong electoral support at the
last national election. We consider electoral support as strong if either the left-
or right-wing challenger block (including one or more parties) receives more
than 10 percent of the vote. Following this classification decision, we observe
four countries in which the left- and right-wing challenger blocks are strong:
Denmark, Germany, the Netherlands, and Sweden. There are two countries
in which we do not observe neither a strong left- nor right-wing challenger:
Ireland and the United Kingdom. In Spain, there is a strong challenger party on
the left only, while in Italy we only find a strong challenger on the right.[5] Given

---

[5] For the time of data collection, in 2018, M5S was clearly a challenger party, but cannot be catego-
rized as left or right. Therefore – and in line with most party family classifications for this time – we
did not classify it in a substantive ideological party family. In particular, the 2018 programme of
M5S was very vague on social policy, while our data focus on very specific social policy preferences.

the reduced number of cases in some of these types of party configuration, we must be cautious in interpreting these results. The figures always indicate the countries on which the models are estimated.

To facilitate the interpretation of the results, they are presented by means of figures displaying average adjusted predictions or average marginal effects. The full models with all control variables are included in Tables 13.A2–13.A5 in the Appendix.

RESULTS

Subjective Social Policy Representation by Preferred Party and Party System

As displayed in Figure 13.1, there are apparent class inequalities in how voters perceive politicians' social policy priorities in relation to theirs, with working-class voters perceiving politicians as less congruent. This raises the question of whether this perception of unequal representation is also manifest when we focus on more specific welfare policies. To address this knowledge gap, the analyses discussed later model subjective representation by (a) voters' preferred party and by (b) the party system, on respondents' social class. Figure 13.2 presents class differences (with respect to the upper-middle class) in how distant voters are from their preferred party and the main parties in the country in terms of their prioritization of different welfare expansion logics: social consumption, social investment, and benefits for the labor-market integration of migrants. Comparing the two different measures – by preferred party and system – allows us to gain some insights about how good/bad representation by voters' preferred party is, in comparison to the system overall. We could think of a context in which most parties in the system provided poor representation to the demands of the working class, but a specific party mobilized the priorities and electoral support of the lower-grade classes. In such a context, we would observe class gradient in terms of systemic representation, but not on party representation. This is not, however, what Figure 13.2 indicates.

Proximity to parties is measured through points distributed to the different areas of benefit expansion, with higher values indicating support for further expansion of benefits in that particular area. Hence, positive party-voter distances indicate that the voter prioritizes expansion to a greater extent than the party (system) does. Correspondingly, negative values indicate that voters prioritize expansion in that area less than parties. In light of the evidence indicating that the working classes tend to prioritize consumption over investment policies, and our expectation that political elites will be more sensitive to investment-oriented expenditure, we should observe a class gradient in subjective proximity to parties. This is, in fact, what Figure 13.2 displays. There are two key findings to take from these analyses. First, social classes differ in how proximate they perceive their preferred party and the party system on the three dimensions of welfare expansion considered. Evaluations of party

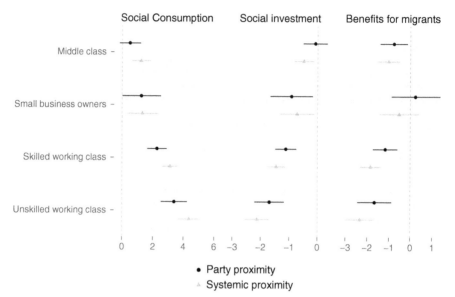

FIGURE 13.2 Social class differences in proximity to preferred party and party system
Notes: Class as a determinant of proximity across party systems (coefficients indicate differences to the upper-middle class). Estimates are based on linear regression models introducing controls for age, sex, trade union membership, and country-FE. The coefficients for all variables are presented in Table 13.A3 in the Appendix.

and systemic representation are better for the upper-middle and middle class than for the working class. On consumption-oriented expansion, the distance to voters' preferred party is 3.4 points greater for the working class than for the upper-middle class. This difference increases to 4.4 points if we focus on systemic proximity instead. A difference of 3–4 points might seem little, but we should assess it relative to the in-sample range. A four-point difference amounts to about 50 percent of the standard deviation of the consumption proximity measure, this effect is larger than other class differences identified on commonly studied preference variables (like preferences on redistribution, gay rights, or environmental issues) (Häusermann et al. 2022).[6]

The class gradient is also manifest in party and systemic representation on the expansion of investment and migrant integration but, in this case, with a negative sign. Again, the priorities of the upper-middle classes appear better represented and, in these fields, the lower-grade classes prioritize expansion

---

[6] In the eighth round of the European Social Survey, attitudinal differences between working- and middle-class voters are between 0.06 and 0.13 standard deviations for "support for unemployed," "gay adoption rights," and "environment," class effects are slightly larger for "EU integration" and "immigration," 0.24 and 0.32 standard deviations, respectively.

to a lesser extent than their preferred party (or the party system) – this is reflected in negative measures of proximity. On social investment policies, the distance to their own party is about 1.7 points larger for the unskilled working class than for the upper-middle class. This difference increases to 2.1 when it is measured with respect to the party system. As we expected, unequal representation is larger on the social consumption dimension. The difference between the upper-middle class and the unskilled working class in the proximity to voters' preferred party is twice as large for social consumption than for investment policies. Hence, it appears that the class bias is lower on the topics of social investment and benefits for migrants, on which the working classes prioritize expansion to a lesser extent than the parties they vote for (and in the system) do.

The second interesting finding stemming from these analyses is that the two measures of class inequalities in subjective representation display a greater similarity than we might have expected. In other words, class differences in perceptions of proximity are similar, whether gauged against respondents' preferred party or the main parties in the system. While distances to own parties are usually smaller, they still display a class gradient, hence showing that class differences in congruence are manifest even when compared against voters' preferred party. We take this as a sign indicating that even voters' preferred party – in a relatively diverse party system, as in most Western European countries – do not eliminate class biases in perceptions of representation. We address to what extent the configuration of the partisan supply can compensate for some of these inequalities in further analyses discussed later.

Additional estimations (included in Table 13.A4 and Figure 13.A1 in the Appendix) address inequalities based on income quintiles instead of social classes. The results portray a similar income gradient in subjective representation. Income differences are smaller than class differences – which is in line with current research highlighting the importance of class for the *type* of welfare expansion prioritized (Häusermann et al. 2022). Moreover, there are no income differences in party or systemic representation concerning the expansion of welfare benefits for migrants, which matches the finding that it is not the poorest voters who tend to support more welfare chauvinistic policies (Bornschier and Kriesi 2013).

Addressing different logics of social policy reform separately returns some interesting divergences. We can disaggregate these analyses further by addressing perceptions of proximity by specific policies. Our initial expectation was that class inequalities should be larger on those policies that are important and salient to a majority of voters – like pensions, education, or immigrants' benefits. On other policy areas, voters' attitudes and priorities are less likely to be strong and well defined. Figure 13.3 displays some interesting class differences across policies. The strongest class gradient appears for two social consumption policies that are largely salient across countries and strongly demanded by lower-class voters: pensions and unemployment

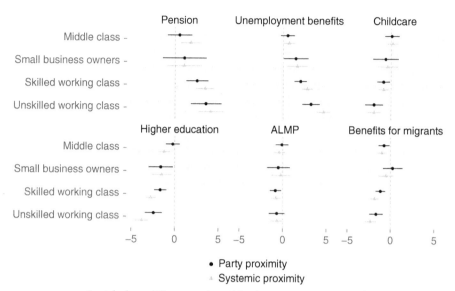

FIGURE 13.3 Social class differences in subjective proximity to preferred party and party system, by social policy area
Notes: Class as a determinant of proximity across party systems (coefficients indicate differences to the upper-middle class). Estimates are based on linear regression models introducing controls for age, sex, trade union membership, and country-FE. The coefficients for all variables are presented in Table 13.A5 in the Appendix.

benefits. As we could derive from the previous figure, class differences are smaller for investment policies, but, moreover, it becomes apparent that unequal distance on this dimension is mostly driven by the prioritization of the expansion of higher education by upper middle-class voters, which is more commonly shared by parties. On childcare and active labor-market policies, we find practically no difference between the distance perceived by upper- or lower-class voters. Hence, across different policies, class differences in perceived party proximity are greater on those policies that are generally more salient to voters.

Evaluations of Party Proximity and Systemic Proximity under Different Party System Configurations

The configuration of the partisan supply, particularly the presence (absence) of strong challenger parties on the left and right of the ideological spectrum, could mitigate (strengthen) some of the class inequalities in perceptions of proximity revealed in Figure 13.2. As shown in Table 13.A2 in the Appendix, a more varied party system could improve input representation by providing a wider range of programmatic supply to voters (e.g., radical Right parties explicitly

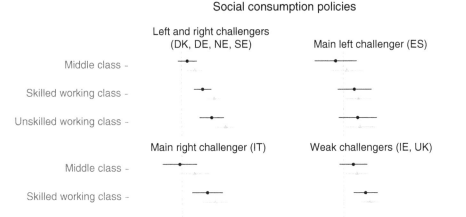

FIGURE 13.4 Social class differences in subjective proximity to preferred party and the party system on social consumption across different party system configurations
Notes: Class as a determinant of proximity across party systems (coefficients indicate differences to the upper-middle class). Estimates are based on linear regression models introducing controls for age, sex, and trade union membership. Average differences for small business owners are not presented because they represent a small group in the sample, with a low number of occurrences when the analyses are disaggregated by party system.

advocating for welfare chauvinistic policies, or radical Left parties promoting consumptive policies) and, moreover, challenger parties have been more successful in mobilizing a working-class support base. This is why we expected class biases in representation to be strongest in systems without strong challenger parties and weakest in systems with left- and right-wing challengers. In systems with strong challenger parties on either the left or right, we expect these class differences to be moderate and to vary depending on the specific social policy logic under consideration.

The four panels in Figures 13.4 to 13.6 present average class differences in proximity to the preferred party and to the system by different configurations of the party system. The analyses draw on data from eight different countries, which are not uniformly distributed across the four types of partisan supply. Specifically, only Spain has a party system with a strong challenger on the left exclusively, while Italy represents the only case with a strong challenger only on the right ideological camp.

Social investment policies

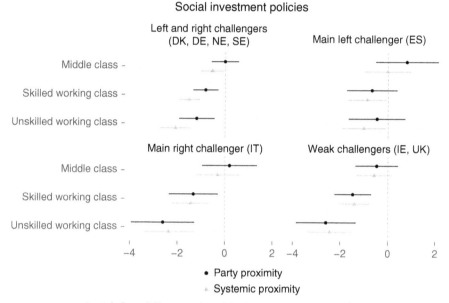

FIGURE 13.5 Social class differences in subjective proximity to preferred party and the party system on social investment across different party system configurations
Notes: Class as a determinant of proximity across party systems (coefficients indicate differences to the upper-middle class). Estimates are based on linear regression models introducing controls for age, sex, and trade union membership. Average differences for small business owners are not presented because they represent a small group in the sample, with a low number of occurrences when the analyses are disaggregated by party system.

The analyses summarized in Figure 13.4 return two interesting results. First, they indicate that, overall, the trends in unequal congruence identified in Figures 13.2 and 13.3 are persistent across most configurations of the partisan supply. Working-class voters perceive their own party and the system as less congruent with their consumption priorities (in comparison to the upper-middle class) in most of the countries under study. Second, there is one case for which there are no apparent class inequalities in terms of consumption priorities: Spain. In this country, in which the partisan supply is characterized by the presence of a strong left-wing challenger (Podemos), but the absence of one on the right, there are no class differences in perceptions of proximity, either by voters' preferred party or the system overall. This could indicate that, in a country in which a strong challenger Left party has pursued a clear antiausterity agenda, working-class demands are better represented. However, if class biases were mitigated by the more diversified party supply in general, this absence of a class gradient should also be manifest in those systems in which we observe both a right- and left-wing challenger. This is not what the top left panel in the figure

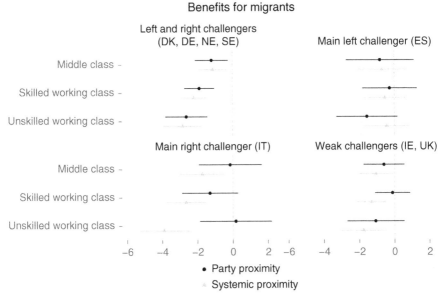

FIGURE 13.6 Social class differences in subjective proximity to preferred party and the party system on benefits for migrants across different party system configurations
Notes: Class as a determinant of proximity across party systems (coefficients indicate differences to the upper-middle class). Estimates are based on linear regression models introducing controls for age, sex, and trade union membership. Average differences for small business owners are not presented because they represent a small group in the sample, with a low number of occurrences when the analyses are disaggregated by party system.

indicates. Moreover, the class inequalities visible under this diversified party supply are not driven by any of the four countries included in this type, but rather consistent across them. Hence, these results do not support our expectation about congruence with the lower-grade classes being improved in contexts of a more diversified partisan supply. Moreover, Figure 13.5 (addressing congruence with social investment priorities) displays a similar pattern. Class differences in perceptions of congruence are rather constant across different party systems with Spain, again, being the exception without a class gradient. Since we only observe one country with a strong challenger exclusively on the left, it is difficult to generalize these results, particularly because Podemos' agenda strongly emphasized antiausterity economic policies – in response to earlier cutbacks on key welfare policies, including pensions, unemployment benefits, or education.

Finally, Figure 13.6 addresses priorities for the expansion of benefits for migrants. On this dimension, there is some substantive variation in the class differences in congruence manifest across different party systems. In countries with no strong right-wing challenger party (irrespective of whether there is a strong left-wing challenger or not), there are no class differences in perceptions of congruence with voters' preferred party or with the system overall. In these contexts, parties are equally congruent with all classes. When a right-wing challenger is present in the party system, we do observe a class gradient in perceptions of proximity. Interestingly, in the case of Italy, in which we do not observe a strong contender on the left, the unskilled working class perceives the party system as more distant from their own priorities but not their preferred party. This could indicate that, presumably, radical-right voters perceive their party as congruent with their demands. We have to be cautious, however, in this interpretation, since it is based on a single country observation. In this case, the absence of a class gradient in countries without a right-wing challenger runs against our initial expectation that these parties could channel the welfare chauvinistic demands of the lower classes. However, we can also interpret this absence of class differences along the same interpretation provided for the analyses by policy fields by referring to salience. In countries like Spain, Ireland, and the United Kingdom, immigration has been a less salient topic until more recently. On policies that are less salient to voters (of different class location), it is less surprising to find no class gradient in perceptions of congruence. Overall, the different results do not lend support to the expectation that a diversified partisan supply mitigates class biases in perceived proximity, mostly because we do observe such biases in party systems with challenger parties on both the right and the left. However, the patterns observed for Spain on the logics of consumption and investment, and in Italy on welfare chauvinism seem to indicate that parties could mitigate some of these inequalities.

CONCLUSION

This chapter set out to address a shortcoming in existing literature which, in spite of profusely documenting the lower policy responsiveness to the interests of lower-income citizens, paid relatively little attention – with some exceptions (e.g., Rennwald and Pontusson 2021) – to how citizens perceive opinion congruence. We did this by focusing on an area that is particularly relevant to redress material and political inequalities: welfare policy. Leveraging new data on voters' and parties' social policy priorities, this chapter has shown that there is a class gradient underlying voters' perceptions of representation. Lower-grade classes generally report worse perceptions of congruence between politicians' social policy priorities and their own. Moreover, these class differences are manifest not only when enquiring about social policy in general, but also when voters have to explicitly state parties' and their own positioning on specific and concrete social policies. The detailed nature of the data allowed us to gauge voters' assessment of party and systemic representation on three welfare policy logics and six policy fields. Overall, the analyses report a class gradient in the proximity that voters' report to their own party and to the party system in general. Upper-middle class voters perceive parties' priorities as closer to their own.

The analyses also revealed some interesting differentiation in the size of class inequalities across welfare policies. Representation (by own party and the system) is more class-biased on those policies that the literature has identified as more salient to voters and to the working class in particular. We find a stronger class gradient in proximity on social consumption policies, in comparison to social investment or welfare chauvinism. Class differences are particularly strong for the expansion of pensions, unemployment benefits, and tertiary education, while they are negligible for childcare and active labor-market policies.

As discussed by Bartels in this volume, by focusing on average differences in the placement of different social classes and political parties on social policy, our analyses do not explore the dispersion of preferences within social classes. In other words, lower average representation of the working classes' preferences could mask different levels of representation within this class, if variance in preferences among workers is high. In additional analyses (not shown), we study, precisely, the dispersion of social policy preferences by social class. Our results indicate that there are no substantive differences in the variance of these preferences across groups: on consumption, investment, and welfare chauvinistic policies, the difference in variance between the upper and lower class is of 2 points at most.

These results indicate that it might be hard to redress some of these inequalities in congruence. The lower-grade classes prioritize further expansion in those policy areas that represent a bigger portion of social spending (most notably, pensions). It appears very unlikely that parties' policy platforms will adopt a strongly expansionary pension agenda, moving the system's position closer to the working class demands. Moreover, voters' own preferred parties do not seem to fully mitigate perceptions of unequal representation either. Even if distance to preferred party is usually smaller than to the system, it still displays a class gradient. Our expectations about the lower classes possibly being better represented on the issue of investment and, especially, welfare chauvinism are also partly disconfirmed by the analyses. We expected the upper classes to be less well represented on these logics because these groups desire further expansion on investment, which parties could be limited in delivering due to tight budget constraints and because parties might have been more responsive to welfare chauvinistic trends. However, also on these two logics, the higher-grade classes perceive better representation, even if to a lower extent than on the consumption logic. Faced with important demographic and socioeconomic transformations, worse perceptions of congruence might hinder the possibilities for governments to introduce welfare reforms. Responsiveness plays an important role in building a "reservoir of goodwill" on which governments can capitalize to survive difficult periods of more "responsible" but less-responsive decisions (Linde and Peters 2020). The absence of such a reservoir might undermine the capability for parties to make hard choices.

While our analyses allow us to focus, in depth, on a specific and relevant area – social policy – conclusions about the implications of this unequal representation for satisfaction with government and democracy more generally would require a more encompassing focus that also includes other policy areas. Voters could prioritize minimizing distance to parties on other issues not included in our analyses, which would indicate that they perceived these other issues as more salient for the vote choice. In such a case, when voters do not choose the party that is closest to them on the question of welfare reform (or when minimizing this distance is not the only consideration), we might expect class differences in incongruences with one's preferred party to be less consequential. Additional analyses suggest that voters indeed tend to elect parties that are close to them on social policies, but also that this is not the only consideration, since some of them do vote for parties that are not minimizing distances on this issue. For about 25 percent of respondents, there would indeed be another party (different to the one they voted for) significantly closer to them (10 or more points closer on the 100-point scale). However, there are no apparent class differences in whether voters select the party that is closest to them on social policy.

In a last step of the analyses, we took into consideration whether the configuration of the partisan supply could moderate some of the class inequalities identified in the first step of the analyses. While we expected the class gradient to be mitigated under an expanded political supply with challenger parties on the left *and* right of the ideological spectrum, this is not what the evidence indicates. In fact, class biases in representation are rather robust across contexts, especially in what concerns consumption and investment policies. The only manifest exception is the Spanish case, for which we do not find class differences in perceived representation. We are, however, cautious to attribute this merely to the presence of a strong radical left challenger because class biases are also apparent in countries in which both left and right challengers exist. Moreover, the Spanish case alone, with a left-wing challenger characterized by emphasizing a strong anti-austerity agenda, may be quite particular. Welfare chauvinism is the only logic for which we observe stronger variation across party configurations. These differences, however, point to issue salience as a potentially conditioning factor. Class biases on welfare chauvinism appear to be smaller in countries in which the salience of the immigration issue is lower. The class gradient is also more moderate on social policies that are typically less salient to the public, like childcare or active labor-market policies. Hence, while strong challenger parties mitigate class biases in some cases (in Spain, or on benefits for migrants in Italy), the relative salience of different issues – affected by an expansion of conflict with the presence of strong challengers on both ends of the ideological spectrum – in turn, rather seems to heighten class biases. Further analyses might attempt to adjudicate between these factors by addressing cases that vary on the two dimensions. Despite the complex context-effects conditioning class biases, however, the main finding of our analysis is the consistent existence of class biases in representation across different areas of the welfare state and social policy.

Bibliography

Abrams, Leah R., Mikko Myrskylä, and Neil K. Mehta. 2021. "The Growing Rural–Urban Divide in US Life Expectancy: Contribution of Cardiovascular Disease and Other Major Causes of Death." *International Journal of Epidemiology* 50(6): 1970–78.

Acemoglu, Daron, and James A. Robinson. 2006. *Economic Origins of Dictatorship and Democracy*. New York: Cambridge University Press.

Achen, Christopher H. 1977. "Measuring Representation: Perils of the Correlation Coefficient." *American Journal of Political Science* 21(4): 805–15.

Achen, Christopher H. 1978. "Measuring Representation." *American Journal of Political Science* 22(3): 475–510.

Achen, Christopher H. 1985. "Proxy Variables and Incorrect Signs on Regression Coefficients." *Political Methodology* 11(3/4): 299–316.

Adams, James, and Lawrence Ezrow. 2009. "Who Do Europeans Parties Represent? How Western European Parties Represent the Policy Preferences of Opinion Leaders." *Journal of Politics* 71(1): 206–23.

Adolph, Christopher. 2013. *Bankers, Bureaucrats, and Central Bank Politics: The Myth of Neutrality*. New York: Cambridge University Press.

Aghion, Philippe, Eve Caroli, and Cecilia García-Peñalosa. 1999. "Inequality and Economic Growth: The Perspective of the New Growth Theories." *Journal of Economic Literature* 37(4): 1615–60.

Albaugh, Quinn M. 2020. "Do Voters Discriminate against Working-Class Candidates? Evidence from Fifty Years of Self-Reported Candidate Occupations." Unpublished Manuscript.

Alesina, Alberto, and George-Marios Angeletos. 2005. "Fairness and Redistribution." *American Economic Review* 95(4): 960–80.

Alesina, Alberto, and Paola Giuliano. 2011. "Preferences for Redistribution." In *Handbook of Social Economics*, Vol. 1, eds. Jess Benhabib, Alberto Bisin, and Matthew O. Jackson, 93–131. San Diego: Elsevier.

Alesina, Alberto, and Edward L. Glaeser. 2004. *Fighting Poverty in the US and Europe: A World of Difference*. New York: Oxford University Press.

Alesina, Alberto, and Eliana La Ferrara. 2005. "Preferences for Redistribution in the Land of Opportunities." *Journal of Public Economics* 89(5–6): 897–931.

Alesina, Alberto, Armando Miano, and Stefanie Stantcheva. 2018. "Immigration and Redistribution." NBER Working Paper 24733.

Alexiadou, Despina. 2020. "Revolving-Door Politics and Income Inequality: A Study on the Role of Finance Ministers in Europe." Unpublished manuscript.

Alexiadou, Despina. 2022. "Cabinet Ministers and Inequality." *European Journal of Political Research* 61(2): 326–50.

Allan, James, and Lyle Scruggs. 2004. "Political Partisanship and Welfare State Reform in Advanced Industrial Societies." *American Journal of Political Science* 48(3): 496–512.

Alvarado, Facundo, Anthony B. Atkinson, Thomas Blanchet, Lucas Chancel, Luis Bauluz, Matthew Fisher-Post, Ignacio Flores, Bertrand Garbinti, Jonathan Goupille-Lebret, Clara Martínez-Toledano, Marc Morgan, Theresa Neef, Thomas Piketty, Anne-Sophie Robilliard, Emmanuel Saez, Li Yang, and Gabriel Zucman. 2020. "Distributional National Accounts Guidelines Methods and Concepts Used in the World Inequality Database." World Inequality Lab, https://wid.world/ (Accessed May 3, 2021).

Amat, Francesc, and Pablo Beramendi. 2020. "Democracy under High Inequality: Capacity, Spending, and Participation." *Journal of Politics* 82(3): 859–78.

Anderson, Christopher J., and Pablo Beramendi. 2008. "Income, Inequality, and Electoral Participation." In *Democracy, Inequality, and Representation: A Comparative Perspective*, eds. Christopher J. Anderson and Pablo Beramendi, 278–311. New York: Russell Sage Foundation.

Andrews, Dan, Christopher Jencks, and Andrew Leigh. 2011. "Do Rising Top Incomes Lift All Boats?" *The B.E. Journal of Economic Analysis & Policy* 11(1): 1–45.

Ansell, Ben W., and Jane Gingrich. 2022. "Concentration and Commodification: The Political Economy of Post-Industrialism in America and Beyond." In *The American Political Economy: Politics, Markets, and Power*, eds. Jacob S. Hacker, Alexander Hertel-Fernandez, Paul Pierson, and Kathleen Thelen, 375–406. New York: Cambridge University Press.

Ansolabehere, Stephen, John M. de Figueiredo, and James M. Snyder. 2003. "Why Is There So Little Money in U.S. Politics?" *Journal of Economic Perspectives* 17(1): 105–30.

Ansolabehere, Stephen, Jonathan Rodden, and James M. Snyder. 2008. "The Strength of Issues: Using Multiple Measures to Gauge Preference Stability, Ideological Constraint, and Issue Voting." *American Political Science Review* 102(2): 215–32.

Ansolabehere, Stephen, James M. Snyder, and Micky Tripathi. 2002. "Are PAC Contributions and Lobbying Linked? New Evidence from the 1995 Lobby Disclosure Act." *Business and Politics* 4(2): 131–55.

Anzia, Sarah F. 2022. *Local Interests: Politics, Policy, and Interest Groups in US City Governments*. Chicago: University of Chicago Press.

Anzia, Sarah F., and Christopher Berry. 2011. "The Jackie (and Jill) Robinson Effect: Why Do Congresswomen Outperform Congressmen?" *American Journal of Political Science* 55(3): 478–93.

Ares, Macarena. 2017. "Class Voting in Post-industrial Economies: A Comparative and Longitudinal Approach." Ph.D. Dissertation, European University Institute.

Ares, Macarena. 2020. "Changing Classes, Changing Preferences: How Social Class Mobility Affects Economic Preferences." *West European Politics* 43(6): 1211–37.

Ares, Macarena, and Mathilde van Ditmars. 2020. "Who Continues to Vote for the Left? Social Class of Origin, Intergenerational Mobility and Party Choice in Western Europe." Unpublished manuscript.

Ares, Macarena, Matthias Enggist M., Silja Häusermann, and Michael Pinggera. 2019. "Attitudinal Constraint in Welfare Priorities: Political Interest and Welfare Publics." Paper prepared for the Annual Conference of the European Political Science Association, Belfast.

Ares, Macarena, Matthias Enggist, Silja Häusermann, and Michael Pinggera. 2020. "Attitudinal Constraint in Social Policy Preferences." Unpublished manuscript.

Armingeon, Klaus, Sarah Engler, Lucas Leemann, and David Weisstanner. 2023. "Comparative Political Dataset 1960–2021." University of Zürich, Leuphana University Lueneburg and University of Lucerne.

Armingeon, Klaus, Virginia Wenger, Fiona Wiedemeier, Christian Isler, Laura Knöpfel, David Weisstanner, and Sarah Engler. 2018. *Comparative Political Data Set 1960–2016*. Bern: Institute of Political Science, University of Bern.

Arnesen, Sveinung, and Yvette Peters. 2018. "The Legitimacy of Representation: How Descriptive, Formal, and Responsiveness Representation Affect the Acceptability of Political Decisions." *Comparative Political Studies* 51(7): 868–99.

Arrese, Ángel. 2018. "Austerity Policies in the European Press: A Divided Europe?" In *The Media and Austerity: Comparative Perspectives*, eds. Laura Basu, Steve Schifferes, and Sophie Knowles, 113–27. London: Routledge.

Artiles, Miriam, Lukas Kleine-Rueschkamp, and Gianmarco León-Ciliotta. 2021. "Accountability, Political Capture and Selection Into Politics: Evidence from Peruvian Municipalities." *Review of Economics and Statistics* 103(2): 397–411.

Austen-Smith, David, and John R. Wright. 1994. "Counteractive Lobbying." *American Journal of Political Science* 38(1): 25–44.

Axelrod, Robert. 1980. "More Effective Choice in the Prisoner's Dilemma." *Journal of Conflict Resolution* 24(3): 379–403.

Aylott, Nicholas. 2003. "After the Divorce: Social Democrats and Trade Unions in Sweden." *Party Politics* 9(3): 369–90.

Bailard, Catie Snow. 2016. "Corporate Ownership and News Bias Revisited: Newspaper Coverage of the Supreme Court's Citizens United Ruling." *Political Communication* 33(4): 583–604.

Baldassarri, Delia, and Andrew Gelman. 2008. "Partisans without Constraint: Political Polarization and Trends in American Public Opinion." *American Journal of Sociology* 114(2): 408–46.

Baldwin, Peter. 1990. *The Politics of Social Solidarity: Class Bases of the European Welfare State 1875–1975*. New York: Cambridge University Press.

Baltrunaite, Audinga, Piera Bello, Alessandra Casarico, and Paola Profeta. 2014. "Gender Quotas and the Quality of Politicians." *Journal of Public Economics* 118: 62–74.

Barber, James Alden, Jr. 1970. *Social Mobility and Voting Behavior*. Chicago: Rand McNally and Company.

Barber, Michael J. 2016. "Representing the Preferences of Donors, Partisans, and Voters in the US Senate." *Public Opinion Quarterly* 80(S1): 225–49.

Barnes, Lucy, and Timothy Hicks. 2018. "Making Austerity Popular: The Media and Mass Attitudes toward Fiscal Policy." *American Journal of Political Science* 62(2): 340–54.

Barnes, Tiffany, and Gregory W. Saxton. 2019. "Working-Class Legislators and Perceptions of Representation in Latin America." *Political Research Quarterly* 72(4): 910–28.

Barr, Nicholas. 2001. *The Welfare State as Piggy Bank: Information, Risk, Uncertainty, and the Role of the State.* New York: Oxford University Press.

Barr, Nicholas. 2012. *Economics of the Welfare State,* 5th ed. New York: Oxford University Press.

Bartels, Larry M. 1985. "Power and Influence as a Covariance Structure." *Political Methodology* 11(1/2): 49–69.

Bartels, Larry M. 1990. "Public Opinion and Political Interests." Paper presented at the annual meeting of the Midwest Political Science Association, Chicago.

Bartels, Larry M. 1996a. "Pooling Disparate Observations." *American Journal of Political Science* 40(3): 905–42.

Bartels, Larry M. 1996b. "Public Opinion and Political Interests." Unpublished manuscript.

Bartels, Larry M. 2003. "Democracy with Attitudes." In *Electoral Democracy*, eds. Michael MacKuen and George Rabinowitz, 48–82. Ann Arbor: University of Michigan Press.

Bartels, Larry M. 2008. *Unequal Democracy: The Political Economy of the New Gilded Age.* Princeton: Princeton University Press.

Bartels, Larry M. 2012. "The Muddled Majority." *Boston Review*, July 1.

Bartels, Larry M. 2016. *Unequal Democracy: The Political Economy of the New Gilded Age,* 2nd ed. Princeton: Princeton University Press.

Bartels, Larry M. 2017. "Political Inequality in Affluent Democracies: The Social Welfare Deficit." Unpublished manuscript.

Bartels, Larry M., and Katherine J. Cramer. 2019. "The Struggle(s)for Equality: Civil Rights, Women's Rights, and Political Change." Unpublished manuscript.

Bashir, Omar S. 2015. "Testing Inferences about American Politics: A Review of the 'Oligarchy' Result." *Research and Politics* 2(4): 1–7.

Baumard, Nicolas. 2016. *The Origins of Fairness: How Evolution Explains Our Moral Nature.* New York: Oxford University Press.

Baumgartner, Frank R., Jeffrey M. Berry, Marie Hojnacki, David C. Kimball, and Beth L. Leech. 2009. *Lobbying and Policy Change: Who Wins, Who Loses, and Why.* Chicago: Chicago University Press.

Bawn, Kathleen, Martin Cohen, David Karol, Seth Masket, Hans Noel, and John Zaller. 2012. "A Theory of Political Parties: Groups, Policy Demands and Nominations in American Politics." *Perspectives on Politics* 10(3): 571–97.

Becher, Michael. 2016. "Endogenous Credible Commitment and Party Competition over Redistribution Under Alternative Electoral Institutions." *American Journal of Political Science* 60(3): 768–82.

Becher, Michael, and Irene Menendez. 2019. "Electoral Reform and Trade-offs in Representation." *American Political Science Review* 113(3): 694–709.

Becher, Michael, and Daniel Stegmueller. 2021. "Reducing Unequal Representation: The Impact of Labor Unions on Legislative Responsiveness in the U.S. Congress." *Perspectives on Politics* 19(1): 92–109.

Becher, Michael, Daniel Stegmueller, and Konstantin Kaeppner. 2018. "Local Union Organization and Law Making in the US Congress." *Journal of Politics* 80(2): 539–54.

Beckers, Kathleen, Stefaan Walgrave, Hanna Valerie Wolf, Kenza Lamot, and Peter Van Aelst. 2021. "Right-Wing Bias in Journalists' Perceptions of Public Opinion." *Journalism Practice* 15(2): 243–58.

Belchior, Ana Maria. 2014. "Explaining MPs' Perceptions of Voters' Positions in a Party-Mediated Representation System: Evidence from the Portuguese Case." *Party Politics* 20(3): 403–15.

Bell, Carole V., and Robert M. Entman. 2011. "The Media's Role in America's Exceptional Politics of Inequality: Framing the Bush Tax Cuts of 2001 and 2003." *International Journal of Press/Politics* 16(4): 548–72.

Bénabou, Roland, and Jean Tirole. 2006. "Belief in a Just World and Redistributive Politics." *Quarterly Journal of Economics* 121(2): 699–746.

Bénabou, Roland, and Jean Tirole. 2016. "Mindful Economics: The Production, Consumption, and Value of Beliefs." *Journal of Economic Perspectives* 30(3): 141–64.

Bensel, Richard F. 1984. *Sectionalism and American Political Development, 1880–1980*. Madison: University of Wisconsin Press.

Beramendi, Pablo. 2012. *The Political Geography of Inequality: Regions and Redistribution*. New York: Cambridge University Press.

Beramendi, Pablo, Silja Häusermann, Herbert Kitschelt, and Hanspeter Kriesi, eds. 2015. *The Politics of Advanced Capitalism*. New York: Cambridge University Press.

Bernardi, Fabrizio, and Macarena Ares. 2017. "Education as the (Not So) Great Equalizer: New Evidence Based on a Parental Fixed Effect Analysis for Spain." Unpublished manuscript.

Bernauer, Julian, Nathalie Giger, and Jan Rosset. 2015. "Mind the Gap: Do Proportional Electoral Systems Foster a More Equal Representation of Women and Men, Poor and Rich?" *International Political Science Review* 36(1): 78–98.

Berry, Jeffrey M., and Sarah Sobieraj. 2011. "Understanding the Rise of Talk Radio." *PS: Political Science and Politics* 44(4): 762–67.

Besley, Timothy. 2006. *Principled Agents: Motivation and Incentives in Politics*. Oxford: Oxford University Press.

Besley, Timothy, Jose G. Montalvo, and Marta Reynal-Querol. 2011. "Do Educated Leaders Matter?" *The Economic Journal* 121(554): 205–27.

Best, Heinrich. 2007. "New Challenges, New Elites? Changes in the Recruitment and Career Patterns of European Representative Elites." *Comparative Sociology* 6(1–2): 85–113.

Best, Heinrich, and Maurizio Cotta, eds. 2000. *Parliamentary Representatives in Europe 1848–2000: Legislative Recruitment and Careers in Eleven European Countries*. New York: Oxford University Press.

Bhalotra, Sonia, and Irma Clots-Figueras. 2014. "Health and the Political Agency of Women." *American Economic Journal: Economic Policy* 6(2): 164–97.

Bhatti, Yosef, and Robert S. Erikson. 2011. "How Poorly Are the Poor Represented in the U.S. Senate?" In *Who Gets Represented?*, eds. K. Enns Peter and Christopher Wlezien, 223–46. New York: Russell Sage Foundation.

Binmore, Ken G. 1994. *Game Theory and the Social Contract: Just Playing*, Vol. 2. Cambridge: Massachusetts Institute of Technology Press.

Bjørklund, Tor. 1992. "Sentrum-Periferi Dimensjonen." In *Politikk mellom økonomi og kultur*, ed. Bernt Hagtvet, 339–64. Oslo: Ad Notam Gyldendal.

Blais, André, and Marc André Bodet. 2006. "Does Proportional Representation Foster Closer Congruence Between Citizens and Policy Makers?" *Comparative Political Studies* 39(10): 1243–62.

Blanchet, Thomas, Lucas Chancel, and Amory Gethin. 2022. "Why Is Europe More Equal Than the United States?" *American Economic Journal: Applied Economics* 14(4): 480–518.

Blanes Vidal, Jordi, Mirko Draca, and Christian Fons-Rosen. 2012. "Revolving Door Lobbyists." *American Economic Review* 102(7): 3731–48.

Blinder, Alan S. 1973. "Wage Discrimination: Reduced Form and Structural Estimates." *Journal of Human Resources* 8(4): 436–55.

Block, Fred. 1977. "The Ruling Class Does Not Rule: Notes on the Marxist Theory of the State." *Socialist Revolution* 7(3): 6–28.

Blood, Deborah J., and Peter C. B. Phillips. 1995. "Recession Headline News, Consumer Sentiment, the State of the Economy and Presidential Popularity: A Time Series Analysis 1989–1993." *International Journal of Public Opinion Research* 7(1): 2–22.

Boadway, Robin, and Michael Keen. 2000. "Redistribution." In *Handbook of Income Distribution*, eds. Anthony Atkinson and François Bourguignon, 679–789. San Diego: Elsevier.

Bobbitt, Randy. 2010. *Us against Them: The Political Culture of Talk Radio*. Lanham, MD: Lexington Books.

De Boef, Suzanna De, and Paul M. Kellstedt. 2004. "The Political (and Economic) Origins of Consumer Confidence." *American Journal of Political Science* 48(4): 633–49.

Bonica, Adam. 2020. "Why Are There So Many Lawyers in Congress?" *Legislative Studies Quarterly* 45(2): 253–89.

Bonilla-Silva, Eduardo. 2018. *Racism without Racists: Color-Blind Racism and the Persistence of Racial Inequality in America*, 5th ed. Lanham: Rowman & Littlefield.

Bonoli, Giuliano, and Fabienne Liechti. 2018. "Good Intentions and Matthew Effects: Access Biases in Participation in Active Labour Market Policies." *Journal of European Public Policy* 25(6): 894–911.

Bornschier, Simon, and Hanspeter Kriesi. 2013. The Populist Right, the Working Class, and the Changing Face of Class Politics. In *Class Politics and the Radical Right*, ed. Jens Rydgren, 10–29. New York: Routledge.

Borwein, Sophie. 2021. "Do Ministers' Occupational and Social Class Backgrounds Influence Social Spending?" *Politics, Groups, and Identities* 10(4): 558–80.

Bovens, Mark, and Anchrit Wille. 2017. *Diploma Democracy: The Rise of Political Meritocracy*. New York: Oxford University Press.

Bowman, Jarron. 2020. "Do the Affluent Override Average Americans? Measuring Policy Disagreement and Unequal Influence." *Social Science Quarterly* 101(3): 1018–37.

Boydstun, Amber E., Benjamin Highton, and Suzanna Linn. 2018. "Assessing the Relationship between Economic News Coverage and Mass Economic Attitudes." *Political Research Quarterly* 71(4): 989–1000.

Brady, Henry E. 1985. "The Perils of Survey Research: Interpersonally Incomparable Responses." *Political Methodology* 11(3–4): 269–91.

Brady, Henry E., Sidney Verba, and Kay Lehmann Schlozman. 1995. "Beyond SES: A Resource Model of Political Participation." *American Political Science Review* 89(2): 271–94.

Branham, J. Alexander, Stuart N. Soroka, and Christopher Wlezien. 2017. "When Do the Rich Win?" *Political Science Quarterly* 132(1): 43–62.

Bratton, Kathleen, and Leonard P. Ray. 2002. "Descriptive Representation, Policy Outcomes, and Municipal Day-Care Coverage in Norway." *American Journal of Political Science* 46(2): 428–37.

Bremer, Björn. 2021. "Public Preferences Towards Social Investment: Comparing Patterns of Support Across Three Continents." In *The World Politics of Social Investment, Volume I: Welfare States in the Knowledge Economy*, eds. Garritzmann L. Julian, Silja Häusermann, and Bruno Palier. New York: Oxford University Press.

Bremer, Björn, and Reto Bürgisser. 2020. "Public Opinion on Welfare State Recalibration in Times of Austerity: Evidence from Survey Experiments." *SocArXiv*.

Broockman, David E., and Christopher Skovron. 2018. "Bias in Perceptions of Public Opinion among Political Elites." *American Political Science Review* 112(3): 542–63.

Brooks, Clem, and Jeff Manza. 2007. *Why Welfare States Persist: The Importance of Public Opinion in Democracies*. Chicago: University of Chicago Press.

Brownlee, Jodeane F., and Michael L. Hilt. 1998. "A Comparison of Two Omaha Radio Talk Shows: Local vs. National Issues." *Feedback* 39(2): 8–16.

Brunner, Eric, Stephen L. Ross, and Washington Ebonya. 2013. "Does Less Income Mean Less Representation?" *American Economic Journal: Economic Policy* 5(2): 53–76.

Bueno, Natália S., and Thad Dunning. 2017. "Race, Resources, and Representation: Evidence from Brazilian Politicians." *World Politics* 69(2): 327–65.

Burden, Barry. 2007. *Personal Roots of Representation*. Princeton: Princeton University Press.

Burgoon, Brian. 2014. "Immigration, Integration and Support for Redistribution in Europe." *World Politics* 66(3): 365–405.

Burgoon, Brian, Jonas Pontusson, Noam Lupu, and Wouter Schakel. 2022. "Understanding Unequal Representation." *European Journal of Political Research* 61(2): 297–303.

Busemeyer, Marius R., and Torben Iversen. 2020. "The Welfare State with Private Alternatives: The Transformation of Popular Support for Social Insurance." *Journal of Politics* 82(2): 671–86.

Butler, Daniel M. 2014. *Representing the Advantaged: How Politicians Reinforce Inequality*. New York: Cambridge University Press.

Butler, Daniel M., and Adam M. Dynes. 2016. "How Politicians Discount the Opinions of Constituents with Whom They Disagree." *American Journal of Political Science* 60(4): 975–89.

Butler, Daniel M., and David W. Nickerson. 2011. "Can Learning Constituency Opinion Affect How Legislators Vote? Results from a Field Experiment." *Quarterly Journal of Political Science* 6(1): 55–83.

Cagé, Julia. 2020. *The Price of Democracy: How Money Shapes Politics and What to Do about It*. Cambridge: Harvard University Press.

Call, Andrew C., Scott A. Emett, Eldar Maksymov, and Nathan Y. Sharp. 2018. "Meet the Press: Survey Evidence on Financial Journalists as Information Intermediaries." Unpublished manuscript.

Calonico, Sebastian, Matias Cattaneo, and Rocio Titiunik. 2014a. "Robust Data-driven Inference in the Regression-Discontinuity Design." *Stata Journal* 14(4): 909–46.

Calonico, Sebastian, Matias Cattaneo, and Rocio Titiunik. 2014b. "Robust Nonparametric Confidence Intervals for Regression-Discontinuity Designs." *Econometrica* 82(6): 2295–326.

Calonico, Sebastian, Matias Cattaneo, and Rocio Titiunik. 2015. "Optimal Data-Driven Regression Discontinuity Plots." *Journal of the American Statistical Association* 110(512): 1753–69.

Calzada, Ines, and Eloisa Del Pino. 2008. "Perceived Efficacy and Citizens' Attitudes Toward Welfare State Reform." *International Review of Administrative Sciences* 74(4): 555–74.

Campante, Filipe R. 2011. "Redistribution in a Model of Voting and Campaign Contributions." *Journal of Public Economics* 95 (7–8): 646–56.

Campbell, Rosie, and Philip Cowley. 2014. "Rich Man, Poor Man, Politician Man: Wealth Effects in a Candidate Biography Survey Experiment." *British Journal of Politics and International Relations* 16(1): 56–74.

Campos, Nauro F., and Franceso Giovannoni. 2017. "Political Institutions, Lobbying and Corruption." *Journal of Institutional Economics* 13(4): 917–39.

Canes-Wrone, Brandice, Michael C. Herron, and Kenneth W. Shotts. 2001. "Leadership and Pandering: A Theory of Executive Policymaking." *American Journal of Political Science* 45(3): 532–50.

Cappelen, Alexander W., James Konow, Erik Ø. Sørensen, and Bertil Tungodden. 2013. "Just Luck: An Experimental Study of Risk-Taking and Fairness." *American Economic Review* 103(4): 1398–413.

Caraley, Demetrios. 1992. "Washington Abandons the Cities." *Political Science Quarterly* 107(1): 1–30.

Carnes, Nicholas. 2012. "Does the Numerical Underrepresentation of the Working Class in Congress Matter?" *Legislative Studies Quarterly* 37(1): 5–34.

Carnes, Nicholas. 2013. *White-Collar Government: The Hidden Role of Class in Economic Policy Making*. Chicago: University of Chicago Press.

Carnes, Nicholas. 2015. "Does the Descriptive Representation of the Working Class 'Crowd Out' Women and Minorities (And Vice Versa)? Evidence from the Local Elections in America Project." *Politics, Groups, and Identities* 3(2): 350–65.

Carnes, Nicholas. 2016. "Why Are There So Few Working-Class People in Political Office? Evidence from State Legislatures." *Politics, Groups, and Identities* 4(1): 84–109.

Carnes, Nicholas. 2018. *The Cash Ceiling: Why Only the Rich Run for Office – And What We Can Do About It*. Princeton: Princeton University Press.

Carnes, Nicholas. 2020. "Has Research on Working-Class Politicians Excluded Women? A Response to Barnes, Beall, and Holman." Unpublished manuscript.

Carnes, Nicholas, and Eric Hansen. 2016. "Does Paying Politicians More Promote Economic Diversity in Legislatures?" *American Political Science Review* 110(4): 699–716.

Carnes, Nicholas, and Noam Lupu. 2015. "Rethinking the Comparative Perspective on Class and Representation: Evidence from Latin America." *American Journal of Political Science* 59(1): 1–18.

Carnes, Nicholas, and Noam Lupu. 2016a. "Do Voters Dislike Working-Class Candidates? Voter Biases and the Descriptive Underrepresentation of the Working Class." *American Political Science Review* 110(4): 832–44.

Carnes, Nicholas, and Noam Lupu. 2016b. "What Good Is a College Degree? Education and Leader Quality Reconsidered." *Journal of Politics* 78(1): 35–49.

Carnes, Nicholas, and Noam Lupu. 2023a. "Are There Social Class Gaps in Nascent Political Ambition? Survey Evidence from the Americas." Unpublished manuscript.

Carnes, Nicholas, and Noam Lupu. 2023b. "The Economic Backgrounds of Politicians." *Annual Review of Political Science* 26: 253–70.

Carnes, Nicholas, Miriam Golden, Noam Lupu, Eugenia Nazrullaeva, and Stephane Wolton. 2021. "Global Legislator Database," https://doi.org/10.7910/DVN/U1ZNVT, Harvard Dataverse, V1.

Carranza, Rafael, Marc Morgan, and Brian Nolan. 2022. "Top Income Adjustments and Inequality: An Investigation of the EU-SILC." *Review of Income and Wealth*.

Carter, J. Scott, Mamadi Corra, Shannon K. Carter, and Rachel McCroskey. 2014. "The Impact of Place? A Reassessment of the Importance of the South in Affecting Beliefs about Racial Inequality." *Social Science Journal* 51(1): 12–20.

Case, Anne and Angus Deaton. 2020. *Deaths of Despair and the Future of Capitalism*. Princeton, NJ: Princeton University Press.

Cavaillé, Charlotte. 2023. *Fair Enough: Demand for Redistribution in the Age of Inequality*. New York: Cambridge University Press.

Cavaillé, Charlotte, and Kris-Stella Trump. 2015. "The Two Facets of Social Policy Preferences." *Journal of Politics* 77(1): 146–60.

Chattopadhay, Raghabendra, and Esther Duflo. 2004. "Women as Policy Makers: Evidence from an India-Wide Randomized Policy Experiment." *Econometrica* 72(5): 1409–44.

Chinn, Menzie D., and Hiro Ito. 2006. "What Matters for Financial Development? Capital Controls, Institutions, and Interactions." *Journal of Development Economics* 81(1): 163–92.

Chinn, Menzie D., and Hiro Ito. 2008. "A New Measure of Financial Openness." *Journal of Comparative Policy Analysis* 10(3): 309–22.

Chong, Dennis, Jack Citrin, and Patricia Conley. 2001. "When Self-Interest Matters." *Political Psychology* 22(3): 541–70.

Christiano, Thomas. 2008. *The Constitution of Equality: Democratic Authority and Its Limits*. New York: Oxford University Press.

Cingano, Federico. 2014. "Trends in Income Inequality and Its Impact on Economic Growth." OECD Social, Employment, and Migration Working Papers. Paris: OECD.

Comparative Candidate Survey. 2016. Comparative Candidates Survey Module I – 2005–2013 [Dataset – cumulative file]. Distributed by FORS, Lausanne, 2020.

Comparative Candidate Survey. 2020. Comparative Candidates Survey Module II – 2013–2019 [Dataset – cumulative file]. Distributed by FORS, Lausanne, 2020.

Condon, Meghan and Amber Wichovsky. 2020. "Inequality in the Social Mind: Social Comparison and Support for Redistribution." *Journal of Politics* 82(1): 149–161.

Congleton, Roger, and Yongjing Zhang. 2013. "Is It All About Competence? The Human Capital of US Presidents and Economic Performance." *Constitutional Political Economy* 24(2): 108–24.

Converse, Philip E. 1964. "The Nature of Belief Systems in Mass Publics." In *Ideology and Discontent*, ed. David E. Apter, 206–61. Glencoe: Free Press.

Converse, Philip E. 2006. "The Nature of Belief Systems in Mass Publics (1964)." *Critical Review* 18(1–3): 1–74.

Coppedge, Michael, John Gerring, Carl Henrik Knutsen, Staffan I. Lindberg, Jan Teorell, David Altman, Michael Bernhard, Agnes Cornell, M. Steven Fish, Lisa Gastaldi, Haakon Gjerløw, Adam Glynn, Allen Hicken, Anna Lührmann, Seraphine F. Maerz, Kyle L. Marquardt, Kelly McMann, Valeriya Mechkova, Pamela Paxton, Daniel Pemstein, Johannes von Römer, Brigitte Seim, Rachel Sigman, Svend-Erik Skaaning, Jeffrey Staton, Aksel Sundtröm, Eitan Tzelgov, Luca Uberti, Yi-ting Wang, Tore Wig, and Daniel Ziblatt. 2021. "V-Dem Codebook v11." Varieties of Democracy (V-Dem) Project.

Cornejo, Marcela, Carolina Rocha, Diego Castro, Micaela Varela, Jorge Manzi, Roberto González, Gloria Jiménez-Moya, Héctor Carvacho, Belén Álvarez, Daniel Valdenegro, Manuel Cheyre, and Andrew G. Livingstone. 2021. "The Intergenerational Transmission of Participation in Collective Action: The Role of Conversation and Political Practices in the Family." *British Journal of Social Psychology* 60(1): 29–49.

Cornes, Richard, and Roger Hartley. 2005. "Asymmetric Contests with General Technologies." *Economic Theory* 26(4): 923–46.

Costello, Anna B., and Jason W. Osborne. 2005. "Best Practices in Exploratory Factor Analysis: Four Recommendations for Getting the Most from Your Analysis." *Practical Assessment Research and Evaluation* 10.

Cramer, Katherine J. 2016. *The Politics of Resentment: Rural Consciousness in Wisconsin and the Rise of Scott Walker*. Chicago: University of Chicago Press.

Cramer, Katherine J. 2022. "The Qualitative Study of Public Opinion." In *Handbook on Politics and Public Opinion*, ed. Thomas J. Rudolph, pp. 41–53. Northampton: Edward Elgar.

Cramer, Katherine J. 2023. "Interviewing Ordinary People." In *Doing Qualitative Methods: From Research Design to Publication*, eds. Jennifer Cyr and Sara Goodman. New York: Oxford University Press.

Cramer Walsh, Katherine. 2012. "Putting Inequality in Its Place: Rural Consciousness and the Power of Perspective." *American Political Science Review* 106(3): 517–32.

Curto-Grau, Marta, Albert Sole-Olle, and Pilar Sorribas-Navarro. 2018. "Does Electoral Competition Curb Party Favoritism?" *American Economic Journal: Applied Economics* 10(4): 378–407.

Cutler, David M., Lawrence F. Katz, David Card, and Robert E. Hall. 1991. "Macroeconomic Performance and the Disadvantaged." *Brookings Papers on Economic Activity* 1991(2): 1–74.

Dahl, Robert A. 1957. "The Concept of Power." *Behavioral Science* 2(3): 201–15.

Dahl, Robert A. 1961. *Who Governs? Democracy and Power in an American City*. New Haven: Yale University Press.

Dahl, Robert A. 1971. *Polyarchy: Participation and Opposition*. New Haven: Yale University Press.

Dahl, Robert A. 1989. *Democracy and Its Critics*. New Haven: Yale University Press.

Dahl, Robert A. 2006. *On Political Equality*. New Haven: Yale University Press.

Dal Bo, Ernesto, and Frederico Finan. 2018. "Progress and Perspectives in the Study of Political Selection." *Annual Review of Economics* 10: 541–75.

Dal Bó, Ernesto, Frederico Finan, Olle Folke, Torsten Persson, and Johanna Rickne. 2017. "Who Becomes A Politician?" *Quarterly Journal of Economics* 132(4): 1877–914.

Dallinger, Ursula. 2022. "On the Ambivalence of Preferences for Income Redistribution: A Research Note." *Journal of European Social Policy* 32(2): 225–36.

Dalton, Russell J. 2017. *The Participation Gap: Social Status and Political Inequality*. New York: Oxford University Press.

Davis, Aeron. 2002. *Public Relations Democracy: Politics, Public Relations and the Mass Media in Britain*. Manchester: Manchester University Press.

Davis, Aeron. 2018. "Whose Economy, Whose News?" In *The Media and Austerity: Comparative Perspectives*, eds. Laura Basu, Steve Schiffres, and Sophie Knowles, 157–70. London: Routledge.

Degen, Daniel, Theresa Kuhn, and Joroen van der Waal. 2018. "Granting Immigrants Access to Social Benefits? How Self-Interest Influences Support for Welfare State Restrictiveness." *Journal of European Social Policy* 29(2): 148–65.

Dempsey, Sadie, Jiyoun Suk, Katherine J. Cramer, Lewis A. Friedland, Michael W. Wagner, and Dhavan V. Shah. 2021. "Understanding Trump Supporters' News Use: Beyond the Fox News Bubble." *The Forum* 18(3): 319–46.

Demsas, Jerusalem. 2021. "60 Percent of Likely Voters Say They're in Favor of Public Housing. So Why Isn't There More of It?" Vox.

DiMaggio, Anthony R. 2017. *The Politics of Persuasion: Economic Policy and Media Bias in the Modern Era.* New York: SUNY Press.

Dow, Jay K. 2009. "Gender Differences in Political Knowledge: Distinguishing Characteristics-Based and Returns-Based Differences." *Political Behavior* 31(1): 117–36.

Downs, Anthony. 1957. *An Economic Theory of Democracy.* New York: Harper.

Dreher, Axel, Michael Lamla, Sarah Lein, and Frank Somogyi. 2009. "The Impact of Political Leaders' Profession and Education on Reforms." *Journal of Comparative Economics* 37(1): 169–93.

Duch, Raymond M., and Randolph T. Stevenson. 2008. *The Economic Vote: How Political and Economic Institutions Condition Election Results.* New York: Cambridge University Press.

Easton, David. 1975. "A Re-Assessment of the Concept of Political Support." *British Journal of Political Science* 5(4): 435–57.

Einstein, Katherine Levine, David M. Glick, and Maxwell Palmer. 2020. *Neighborhood Defenders.* New York: Cambridge University Press.

Elkjær, Mads Andreas. 2020. "What Drives Unequal Policy Responsiveness? Assessing the Role of Informational Asymmetries in Economic Policy-Making." *Comparative Political Studies* 53(14): 2213–45.

Elkjær, Mads Andreas, and Torben Iversen. 2020. "The Political Representation of Economic Interests: Subversion of Democracy or Middle-Class Supremacy?" *World Politics* 72(2): 254–90.

Elkjær, Mads Andreas, and Torben Iversen. 2023. "The Democratic State and Redistribution: Whose Interests Are Served?" *American Political Science Review* 117(2): 391–406.

Elkjær, Mads A. and Michael B. Klitgaard. 2021. "Economic Inequality and Political Responsiveness: A Systematic Review." *Perspectives on Politics,* first view.

Ellis, Christopher. 2017. *Putting Inequality in Context: Class, Public Opinion, and Representation in the United States.* Ann Arbor: University of Michigan Press.

Elsässer, Lea. 2018. *Wessen Stimme zählt? Soziale und politische Ungleichheit in Deutschland.* Frankfurt: Campus Verlag.

Elsässer, Lea, Svenja Hense, and Armin Schäfer. 2017. "Dem Deutschen Volke'? Die Ungleiche Responsivität des Bundestags." *Zeitschrift Für Politikwissenschaft* 27(2): 161–80.

Elsässer, Lea, Svenja Hense, and Armin Schäfer. 2018. "Government of the People, by the Elite, for the Rich: Unequal Responsiveness in an Unlikely Case." Unpublished manuscript.

Elsässer, Lea, Svenje Hense, and Armin Schäfer. 2021. "Not Just Money: Unequal Responsiveness in Egalitarian Democracies." *Journal of European Public Policy* 28(12): 1890–908.

Emmenegger, Patrick, Silja Häusermann, Bruno Palier, and Martin Seeleib-Kaiser, eds. 2011. *The Age of Dualization: Structures, Policies*. New York: Oxford University Press.

Enggist, Matthias. 2019. "Welfare Chauvinism – Who Cares? Evidence on Priorities and the Importance the Public Attributes to Expanding or Retrenching Welfare Entitlements of Immigrants." Unpublished manuscript.

Enggist, Matthias, and Michael Pinggera. 2021. "Radical Right Parties and Their Welfare State Stances – Not So Blurry After All?" *West European Politics* 45(1): 102–28.

Enns, Peter K. 2015. "Relative Policy Support and Coincidental Representation." *Perspectives on Politics* 13(4): 1053–64.

Epper, Thomas, Ernst Fehr, and Julien Senn. 2020. "Other-Regarding Preferences and Redistributive Politics." Unpublished manuscript.

Erikson, Robert. 2015. "Income Inequality and Policy Responsiveness." *Annual Review of Political Science* 18: 11–29.

Erikson, Robert, and John H. Goldthorpe. 1992. *The Constant Flux: A Study of Class Mobility in Industrial Countries*. New York: Oxford University Press.

Esaiasson, Peter, and Sören Holmberg. 1996. *Representation from Above: Members of Parliament and Representative Democracy in Sweden*. Aldershot: Dartmouth Publishing Company.

Esping-Andersen, Gøsta. 1985. *Politics Against Markets: The Social Democratic Road to Power*. Princeton: Princeton University Press.

Esping-Andersen, Gøsta. 1990. *The Three Worlds of Welfare Capitalism*. Princeton: Princeton University Press.

Esping-Andersen, Gøsta. 1999. *Social Foundations of Postindustrial Economies*. New York: Oxford University Press.

Evans, Geoffrey, Anthony Heath, and Mansur Lalljee. 1996. "Measuring Left-Right and Libertarian-Authoritarian Values in the British Electorate." *British Journal of Sociology* 47(1): 93–112.

Feigenbaum, James, Alex Hertel-Fernandez, and Vanessa Williamson. 2018. "From the Bargaining Table to the Ballot Box: Political Effects of Right to Work Laws." NBER Working Paper 24259.

Feldman, Stanley, and John Zaller. 1992. "The Political Culture of Ambivalence: Ideological Responses to the Welfare State." *American Journal of Political Science* 36(1): 268–307.

Feldstein, Martin. 1995. "The Effects of Marginal Tax Rates on Taxable Income: A Panel Study of the 1986 Tax Reform Act." *Journal of Political Economy* 103(3): 551–72.

Feldstein, Martin. 1999. "Tax Avoidance and the Deadweight Loss of the Income Tax." *Review of Economics and Statistics* 81(4): 674–80.

Fenno, Richard F. 1977. U.S. "House Members in Their Constituencies: An Exploration." *American Political Science Review* 71(3): 883–917.

Ferreira, Fernando, and Joseph Gyourko. 2009. "Do Political Parties Matter? Evidence from US Cities." *Quarterly Journal of Economics* 124(1): 399–422.

Figueiredo, John M. de, and Brian Kelleher Richter. 2014. "Advancing the Empirical Research on Lobbying." *Annual Review of Political Science* 17(1): 163–85.

Finkel, Eli J., Christopher A. Bail, Mina Cikara, Peter H. Ditto, Shanto Iyengar, Samara Klar, Lilliana Mason, Mary C. McGrath, Brendan Nyhan, David G. Rand, Linda J. Skitka, Joshua A. Tucker, Jay J. Van Bavel, Cynthia S. Wang, and James N. Druckman. 2020. "Political Sectarianism in America." *Science* 370(6516): 533–36.

Finseeras, Henning. 2008. "Immigration and Preferences for Redistribution: An Empirical Analysis of European Survey Data." *Comparative European Politics* 6(4): 407–431.

Fiorina, Morris P. 1981. *Retrospective Voting in American National Elections*. New Haven: Yale University Press.

Flavin, Patrick. 2012. "Income Inequality and Policy Representation in the American States." *American Politics Research* 40(1): 29–59.

Flavin, Patrick. 2015a. "Campaign Finance Laws, Policy Outcomes, and Political Equality in the American States." *Political Research Quarterly* 68(1): 77–88.

Flavin, Patrick. 2015b. "Lobbying Regulations and Political Equality in the American States." *American Politics Research* 43(2): 304–26.

Flavin, Patrick. 2018. "Labor Union Strength and the Equality of Political Representation." *British Journal of Political Science* 48(4): 1075–91.

Folke, Olle. 2014. "Shades of Brown and Green: Party Effects in Proportional Election Systems." *Journal of the European Economic Association* 12(5): 1361–95.

Fong, Christina. 2001. "Social Preferences, Self-Interest, and the Demand for Redistribution." *Journal of Public Economics* 82(2): 225–46.

Fong, Christina M., Samuel Bowles, and Herbert Gintis. 2006. "Strong Reciprocity and the Welfare State." In *Handbook of the Economics of Giving, Altruism and Reciprocity*, Vol. 2, eds. Serge-Christophe Kolm and Jean Mercier Ythier, 1439–64. San Diego: Elsevier.

Fong, Christina M., and Panu Poutvaara. 2019. "Redistributive Politics with Target-Specific Beliefs." Unpublished manuscript.

Fowler, James H., and Cindy D. Kam. 2007. "Beyond the Self: Social Identity, Altruism, and Political Participation." *Journal of Politics* 69(3): 813–27.

Fox, Richard L., and Jennifer L. Lawless. 2005. "To Run or Not to Run for Office: Explaining Nascent Political Ambition." *American Journal of Political Science* 49(3): 642–59.

Fox, Richard L., and Jennifer L. Lawless. 2014. "Uncovering the Origins of the Gender Gap in Political Ambition." *American Political Science Review* 108(3): 499–519.

Freier, Ronny, and Sebastian Thomasius. 2015. "Voters Prefer More Qualified Mayors, But Does It matter for Public Finances? Evidence for Germany." *International Tax and Public Finance* 23(5): 875–910.

Fuhrmann, Matthew. 2020. "When Do Leaders Free-Ride? Business Experience and Contributions to Collective Defense." *American Journal of Political Science* 64(2): 416–31.

Gagliarducci, Stefano, and Tommaso Nannicini. 2013. "Do Better Paid Politicians Perform Better? Disentangling Incentives from Selection." *Journal of the European Economic Association* 11(2): 369–98.

Galasso, Vincenzo, and Tommaso Nannicini. 2011. "Competing on Good Politicians." *American Political Science Review* 105(01): 79–99.

Gallego, Aina. 2010. "Understanding Unequal Turnout: Education and Voting in Comparative Perspective." *Electoral Studies* 29(2): 239–48.

Gallego, Aina. 2015. *Unequal Political Participation Worldwide*. New York: Cambridge University Press.

Gans, Herbert J. 2004. *Deciding What's News: A Study of CBS Evening News, NBC Nightly News, Newsweek, and Time*. Evanston: Northwestern University Press.

Garfinkel, Irwin, Lee Rainwater, and Timothy M. Smeeding. 2006. "A Re-Examination of Welfare States and Inequality in Rich Nations: How In-kind Transfers and Indirect Taxes Change the Story." *Journal of Policy Analysis and Management* 25(4): 897–919.

Garrett, Geoffrey. 1998. "Global Markets and National Politics: Collision Course or Virtuous Circle?" *International Organization* 52(4): 787–824.

Garritzmann, Julian L., Marius R. Busemeyer, and Erik Neimanns. 2018a. "Public Demand for Social Investment: New Supporting Coalitions for Welfare State Reform in Western Europe?" *Journal of European Public Policy* 25(6): 844–61.

Garritzmann, Julian L., Marius R. Busemeyer, and Erik Neimanns. 2018b. "Trust, Public Opinion, and Welfare State Reform." Unpublished manuscript.

Garritzmann, Julian L., Silja Häusermann, and Bruno Palier, eds. 2022. *The World Politics of Social Investment, Volume I: Welfare States in the Knowledge Economy.* New York: Oxford University Press.

Garz, Marcel, and Gregory J. Martin. 2021. "Media Influence on Vote Choices: Unemployment News and Incumbents' Electoral Prospects." *American Journal of Political Science* 65(2): 278–93.

Gaventa, John. 1980. *Power and Powerlessness: Quiescence and Rebellion in an Appalachian Valley.* Urbana: University of Illinois.

Gaxie, Daniel, and Laurent Godmer. 2007. "Cultural Capital and Political Selection: Educational Backgrounds of Parliamentarians." In *Democratic Representation in Europe: Diversity, Change, and Convergence*, eds. Mauricio Cotta and Heinrich Best, 106–35. Oxford: Oxford University Press.

Gentzkow, Matthew, and Jesse Shapiro. 2010. "What Drives Media Slant? Evidence From U.S. Daily Newspapers." *Econometrica* 78(1): 35–71.

Gerber, Elisabeth, and Daniel Hopkins. 2011. "When Mayors Matter: Estimating the Impact of Mayoral Partisanship on City Policy." *American Journal of Political Science* 55(2): 326–39.

Gerring, John, Erzen Oncel, Kevin Morrison, and Daniel Pemstein. 2019. "Who Rules the World? A Portrait of the Global Leadership Class." *Perspectives on Politics* 17(4): 1079–97.

Gidron, Noam, and Peter A. Hall. 2017. "The Politics of Social Status: Economic and Cultural Roots of the Populist Right." *British Journal of Sociology* 68(S1): S57–S84.

Giger, Nathalie, and Davy-Kim Lascombes. 2019. "Growing Income Inequality, Growing Legitimacy: A Longitudinal Approach to Perceptions of Inequality." Unequal Democracies Working Paper no. 11, University of Geneva.

Giger, Nathalie, and Zoe Lefkofridi. 2014. "Salience-Based Congruence between Parties and their Voters: The Swiss Case." *Swiss Political Science Review* 20(2): 287–304.

Giger, Nathalie, Jan Rosset, and Julian Bernauer. 2012. "The Poor Political Representation of the Poor in a Comparative Perspective." *Representation* 48(1): 47–61.

Gilens, Martin. 1999. *Why Americans Hate Welfare: Race, Media, and the Politics of Antipoverty Policy.* Chicago: University of Chicago Press.

Gilens, Martin. 2005. Inequality and Democratic Responsiveness. *Public Opinion Quarterly* 69(5): 778–96.

Gilens, Martin. 2009. "Preference Gaps and Inequality in Representation." *PS: Political Science & Politics* 42(2): 335–41.

Gilens, Martin. 2012. *Affluence and Influence: Economic Inequality and Political Power in America.* Princeton: Princeton University Press.

Gilens, Martin. 2015a. "Descriptive Representation, Money, and Political Inequality in the United States." *Swiss Political Science Review* 21(2): 222–8.

Gilens, Martin. 2015b. "The Insufficiency of 'Democracy by Coincidence': A Response to Peter K. Enns." *Perspectives on Politics* 13(4): 1065–71.

Gilens, Martin. 2016. "Simulating Representation: The Devil's in the Detail." *Research and Politics* 3(2): 1–3.

Gilens, Martin, and Craig Hertzman. 2000. "Corporate Ownership and News Bias: Newspaper Coverage of the 1996 Telecommunications Act." *Journal of Politics* 62(2): 369–86.

Gilens, Martin, and Benjamin I. Page. 2014. "Testing Theories of American Politics: Elites, Interest Groups, and Average Citizens." *Perspectives on Politics* 12(3): 564–81.

Gilens, Martin, and Benjamin I. Page. 2016. "Critics Argued with Our Analysis of US Political Inequality. Here Are 5 Ways They're Wrong." *Washington Post.*

Gimpel, James G., Nathan Lovin, Bryant Moy, and Andrew Reeves. 2020. "The Urban–Rural Gulf in American Political Behavior." *Political Behavior* 42(4): 1343–68.

Gimpelson, Vladimir, and Daniel Treisman. 2018. "Misperceiving Inequality." *Economics & Politics* 30: 27–54.

Gingrich, Jane, and Silja Häusermann. 2015. "The Decline of the Working-Class Vote, the Reconfiguration of the Welfare Support Coalition and Consequences for the Welfare State." *Journal of European Social Policy* 25(1): 50–75.

Gintis, Herbert, Samuel Bowles, Robert T. Boyd, and Ernst Fehr, eds. 2005. *Moral Sentiments and Material Interests: The Foundations of Cooperation in Economic Life.* Cambridge: Massachusetts Institute of Technology Press.

Glaeser, Edward L. 2011. *The Triumph of the City.* New York: MacMillan.

Gohlmann, Silja, and Roland Vaubel. 2007. "The Educational and Occupational Background of Central Bankers and Its Effect on Inflation: An Empirical Analysis." *European Economic Review* 51(4): 925–41.

Goidel, Kirby, Stephen Procopio, Dek Terrell, and H. Denis Wu. 2010. "Sources of Economic News and Economic Expectations." *American Politics Research* 38(4): 759–77.

Golder, Matt, and Jacek Stramski. 2010. "Ideological Congruence and Electoral Institutions." *American Journal of Political Science* 54(1): 90–106.

Goldin, Claudia, and Lawrence F. Katz. 2009. "The Race between Education and Technology: The Evolution of US Educational Wage Differentials, 1890 to 2005." NBER Working Paper 12984.

Gomila, Robin. 2021. "Logistic or Linear? Estimating Causal Effects of Experimental Treatments on Binary Outcomes Using Regression Analysis." *Journal of Experimental Psychology: General* 150(4): 700–9.

Gonthier, Frederic. 2017. "Parallel Publics? Support for Income Redistribution in Times of Economic Crisis." *European Journal of Political Research* 56(1): 92–114.

Goos, Maarten, and Alan Manning. 2007. "Lousy and Lovely Jobs: The Rising Polarization of Work in Britain." *Review of Economics and Statistics* 89(1): 118–33.

Goubin, Silke and Staffan Kumlin. 2022. "Political Trust and Policy Demand in Changing Welfare States: Building Normative Support and Easing Reform Acceptance?" *European Sociological Review* 38(4): 590–604.

Graham, Jesse, Jonathan Haidt, and Brian A Nosek. 2009. "Liberals and Conservatives Rely on Different Sets of Moral Foundations." *Journal of Personality and Social Psychology* 96(5): 1029–46.

Greve, Bent. 2020. *Austerity, Retrenchment and the Welfare State.* Cheltenham: Edward Elgar.

Griffin, John D., and Brian Newman. 2005. "Are Voters Better Represented?" *Journal of Politics* 67(4): 1206–27.

Griffin, John D., and Brian Newman. 2013. "Voting Power, Policy Representation, and Disparities in Voting's Rewards." *Journal of Politics* 75(1): 52–64.

Griffin, John D., Brian Newman, and Patrick Buhr. 2019. "Class War in the Voting Booth: Bias Against High-Income Congressional Candidates." *Legislative Studies Quarterly* 45(1): 131–45.

Grisold, Andrea, and Paschal Preston. 2020. *Economic Inequality and News Media: Discourse, Power, and Redistribution.* New York: Oxford University Press.

Groseclose, Tim, and Jeffrey Milyo. 2005. "A Measure of Media Bias." *Quarterly Journal of Economics* 120(4): 1191–237.

Grossman, Gene M., and Elhanan Helpman. 2001. *Special Interest Politics.* Cambridge: Massachusetts Institute of Technology Press.

Gruber, Jon, and Emmanuel Saez. 2002. "The Elasticity of Taxable Income: Evidence and Implications." *Journal of Public Economics* 84(1): 1–32.

Grumbach, Jacob M. 2015. "Does the American Dream Matter for Members of Congress? Social-Class Backgrounds and Roll-Call Votes." *Political Research Quarterly* 68(2): 306–23.

Grumbach, Jacob M., Jacob S. Hacker, and Paul Pierson. 2022. "The Political Economy of Red States." In *The American Political Economy: Politics, Markets, and Power*, eds. S. Hacker Jacob, Alexander Hertel-Fernandez, Paul Pierson, and Kathleen Thelen. New York: Cambridge University Press.

Guardino, Matt. 2019. *Framing Inequality: News Media, Public Opinion, and the Neoliberal Turn in U.S. Public Policy.* New York: Oxford University Press.

Gulzar, Saad. 2021. "Who Enters Politics and Why?" *Annual Review of Political Science* 24: 253–75.

Ha, Shang E., and Richard R. Lau. 2015. "Personality Traits and Correct Voting." *American Politics Research* 43(6): 975–98.

Hacker, Jacob S., and Paul Pierson. 2010. "Winner-Take-All Politics: Public Policy, Political Organization, and the Precipitous Rise of Top Incomes in the United States." *Politics & Society* 38(2): 152–204.

Hacker, Jacob S, and Paul Pierson. 2011. *Winner-Take-All Politics: How Washington Made the Rich Richer – And Turned Its Back on the Middle Class.* New York: Simon & Schuster.

Hacker, Jacob S., and Paul Pierson. 2020. *Let Them Eat Tweets: How the Right Rules in an Age of Extreme Inequality.* New York: Liveright Publishing Corporation.

Hacker, Jacob S., Amelia Malpas, Paul Pierson, and Sam Zacher. 2023. "Bridging the Blue Divide: The Democrats' New Metro Coalition and the Unexpected Prominence of Redistribution," Unpublished Manuscript.

Hacker, Jacob S., Paul Pierson, and Kathleen Thelen. 2015. "Drift and Conversion: Hidden Faces of Institutional Change." In *Advances in Comparative-Historical Analysis*, eds. James Mahoney and Kathleen Thelen, 180–208. New York: Cambridge University Press.

Hacker, Jacob S., Philipp Rehm, and Mark Schlesinger. 2013. "The Insecure American: Economic Experiences, Financial Worries, and Policy Attitudes." *Perspectives on Politics* 11(1): 23–49.

Haidt, Jonathan. 2012. *The Righteous Mind: Why Good People are Divided by Politics and Religion*. New York: Pantheon.

Hainmueller, Jens, and Michael Hiscox. 2006. "Learning to Love Globalization: Education and Individual Attitudes Toward International Trade." *International Organization* 60(2): 469–98.

Hakhverdian, Armen. 2015. "Does It Matter that Most Representatives Are Higher Educated?" *Swiss Political Science Review* 21(2): 237–45.

Hall, Andrew B. 2015. "What Happens When Extremists Win Primaries?" *American Political Science Review* 109(1): 18–42.

Hall, Peter A. 2006. "Systematic Process Analysis: When and How to Use It." *European Management Review* 3(1): 24–31.

Hall, Richard L., and Alan V. Deardorff. 2006. "Lobbying as Legislative Subsidy." *American Political Science Review* 100(1): 69–84.

Han, Sung Min, and Kangwook Han. 2021. "Political Leaders, Economic Hardship, and Redistribution in Democracies: Impact of Political Leaders on Welfare Policy." *Political Studies* 69(4): 921–43.

Hansen, Eric, Nicholas Carnes, and Virginia Grey. 2019. "What Happens When Insurers Make the Insurance Laws? State Legislative Agendas and the Occupational Makeup of Government." *State Politics and Policy Quarterly* 19(2): 155–79.

Harper, John. 2021. "Small Number of States Dominate Defense Spending," National Defense, February 25.

Harsanyi, John C. 1962. "Measurement of Social Power, Opportunity Costs, and the Theory of Two-Person Bargaining Games." *Behavioral Science* 7(1): 67–80.

Hart Research Associates. 2019. "National Housing Online Survey," February-March.

Hartley, Thomas, and Bruce Russett. 1992. "Public Opinion and the Common Defense: Who Governs Military Spending in the United States?" *American Political Science Review* 86(4): 905–15.

Häusermann, Silja, Macarena Ares, Matthias Enggist, and Michael Pinggera. 2020. "Mass Public Attitudes on Social Policy Priorities and Reforms in Western Europe: WELFAREPRIORITIES Dataset 2020." Welfarepriorities Working Paper 1/20.

Häusermann, Silja, Achim Kemmerling, and David Rueda. 2020. "How Labor Market Inequality Transforms Mass Politics." *Political Science Research and Methods* 8(2): 344–55.

Häusermann, Silja, and Hanspeter Kriesi. 2015. "What Do Voters Want? Dimensions and Configurations in Individual-level Preferences and Party Choice." In *The Politics of Advanced Capitalism*, eds. Pablo Beramendi, Silja Häusermann, Herbert Kitschelt, and Hanspeter Kriesi, 202–30. Cambridge: Cambridge University Press.

Häusermann, Silja, Thomas Kurer, and Hanna Schwander. 2014. "High-skilled Outsiders? Labor Market Vulnerability, Education and Welfare State Preferences." *Socio-Economic Review* 13(2): 235–58.

Häusermann, Silja, Thomas Kurer, and Hanna Schwander. 2016. "Sharing the Risk? Households, Labor Market Vulnerability, and Social Policy Preferences in Western Europe." *Journal of Politics* 78(4): 1045–60.

Häusermann, Silja, Michael Pinggera, Matthias Enggist, and Macarena Ares. 2022. "Class and Social Policy in The Knowledge Economy." *European Journal of Political Research* 61(2): 462–84.

Hayes, Thomas. 2013. "Responsiveness in an Era of Inequality: The Case of the US Senate." *Political Research Quarterly* 66(3): 585–99.

Heath, Oliver. 2015. "Policy Representation, Social Representation, and Class Voting in Britain." *British Journal of Political Science* 45(1): 173–93.

Heckman, James, and Tim Kautz. 2012. "Hard Evidence on Soft Skills." *Labour Economics* 19(4): 451–64.

Hedlund, Ronald D, and H. Paul Friesema. 1972. "Representatives' Perceptions of Constituency Opinion." *Journal of Politics* 34(3): 730–52.

Hemerijck, Anton. 2013. *Changing Welfare States*. New York: Oxford University Press.

Hemingway, Alexander. 2020. "The Unequal Descriptive and Substantive Representation of Class." Ph.D. Dissertation, University of British Columbia.

Hemingway, Alexander. 2022. "Does Class Shape Legislators' Approach to Inequality and Economic Policy? A Comparative View." *Government and Opposition* 57(1): 84–107.

Henrich, Joseph, Robert Boyd, Samuel Bowles, Colin Camerer, Ernst Fehr, Herbert Gintis, and Richard McElreath. 2001. "In Search of Homo Economicus: Behavioral Experiments in 15 Small-Scale Societies." *American Economic Review* 91(2): 73–78.

Herman, Edward S., and Noam Chomsky. 1994. *Manufacturing Consent: The Political Economy of the Mass Media*. London: Vintage Books.

Hertel-Fernandez, Alexander. 2018. *Politics at Work: How Companies Turn Their Workers into Lobbyists*. New York: Oxford University Press.

Hertel-Fernandez, Alexander. 2019. *State Capture: How Conservative Activists, Big Businesses, and Wealthy Donors Reshaped the American States – and the Nation*. New York: Oxford University Press.

Hertel-Fernandez, Alexander, Matto Mildenberger, and Leah Stokes. 2019. "Legislative Staffers and Representation in Congress." *American Political Science Review* 113(2): 1–18.

Hibbs, Douglas A. 1987. *The Political Economy of Industrial Democracies*. Cambridge: Harvard University Press.

Hicks, Timothy, Alan M. Jacobs, and J. Scott Matthews. 2016. "Inequality and Electoral Accountability: Class-Biased Economic Voting in Comparative Perspective." *Journal of Politics* 78(4): 1076–93.

Hill, Seth J., and Gregory A. Huber. 2019. "On the Meaning of Survey Reports of Roll-call 'Votes'." *American Journal of Political Science* 63(3): 611–25.

Hochschild, Jennifer. 1981. *What's Fair? American Beliefs about Distributive Justice*. Cambridge: Harvard University Press.

Hochschild, Jennifer. 1993. "Disjunction and Ambivalence in Americans' Political Outlooks." In *Reconsidering the Democratic Public*, eds. E. Marcus George and Russell Hanson, 187–210. State College: Pennsylvania State University Press.

Hofstetter, C. Richard, and Christopher L. Gianos. 1997. "Political Talk Radio: Actions Speak Louder than Words." *Journal of Broadcasting & Electronic Media* 41(4): 501–15.

Hollanders, David, and Rens Vliegenthart. 2011. "The Influence of Negative Newspaper Coverage on Consumer Confidence: The Dutch Case." *Journal of Economic Psychology* 32(3): 367–73.

Hope, David, and Julian Limberg. 2022. "The Economic Consequences of Major Tax Cuts for the Rich." *Socio-Economic Review* 20(2): 539–59.

Hopkins, David A. 2017. *Red Fighting Blue: How Geography and Electoral Rules Polarize American Politics*. New York: Cambridge University Press.

Hsieh, Chang-Tai, and Enrico Moretti. 2019. "Housing Constraints and Spatial Misallocation." *American Economic Journal* 11(2): 1–39.

Høyer, Anne. 2015. "Party-Union Ties: 60 Years of Decline?" M.A. Thesis, University of Oslo.

Hoyt, Crystal L., and Brenten H. DeShields. 2021. "How Social-Class Background Influences Perceptions of Political Leaders." *Political Psychology* 42(2): 239–63.

Huber, Evelyne, and John D. Stephens. 2001. *Development and Crisis of the Welfare State: Parties and Policies in Global Markets.* Chicago: University of Chicago Press.

Hutter, Swen, Edgar Grande and Hanspeter Kriesi. 2016. *Politicizing Europe: Integration and Mass Politics.* New York: Cambridge University Press.

Hvidberg, Kristoffer B, Claus Kreiner and Stefanie Stantcheva. 2020. "*Social Position and Fairness Views.*" National Bureau of Economic Research.

Iammarino, Simona, and Philip McCann. 2013. *Multinationals and Economic Geography: Location, Technology, and Innovation.* Cheltenham: Edward Elgar.

Imai, Kosuke, Luke Keele, Dustin Tingley, and Teppei Yamamoto. 2011. "Unpacking the Black Box of Causality: Learning about Causal Mechanisms from Experimental and Observational Studies." *American Political Science Review* 105(4): 765–89.

Imai, Kosuke, Luke Keele, and Teppei Yamamoto. 2010. "Identification, Inference and Sensitivity Analysis for Causal Mediation Effects." *Statistical Science* 25(1): 51–71.

Inglehart, Ronald, and Pippa Norris. 2017. "Trump and the Populist Authoritarian Parties: The Silent Revolution in Reverse." *Perspectives on Politics* 15(2): 443–54.

International Labor Organization. 2020a. "Employment by Sex and Occupation." https://tinyurl.com/khzhmswx (Accessed May 3, 2021).

International Labor Organization. 2020b. "Statistics on Union Membership." https://ilostat.ilo.org/topics/union-membership/ (Accessed May 3, 2021).

Iversen, Torben, and David Soskice. 2001. "An Asset Theory of Social Policy Preferences." *American Political Science Review* 95(4): 875–93.

Iversen, Torben, and David Soskice. 2006. "Electoral Institutions and the Politics of Coalitions: Why Some Democracies Redistribute More Than Others." *American Political Science Review* 100(2): 165–81.

Iversen, Torben, and David Soskice. 2009. "Distribution and Redistribution: The Shadow of the Nineteenth Century." *World Politics* 61(3): 438–86.

Iversen, Torben, and David Soskice. 2019. *Democracy and Prosperity: Reinventing Capitalism through a Turbulent Century.* Princeton: Princeton University Press.

Iversen, Torben, and John D. Stephens. 2008. "Partisan Politics, the Welfare State, and Three Worlds of Human Capital Formation." *Comparative Political Studies* 41(4–5): 600–37.

Jacobs, Lawrence, and Benjamin I. Page. 2005. "Who Influences US Foreign Policy?" *American Political Science Review* 99(1): 107–23.

Jacobs, Alan M., and J. Scott Matthews. 2017. "Policy Attitudes in Institutional Context: Rules, Uncertainty, and the Mass Politics of Public Investment." *American Journal of Political Science* 61(1): 194–207.

Jacobs, Alan M., J. Scott Matthews, Timothy Hicks, and Eric Merkley. 2021. "Whose News? Class-Biased Economic Reporting in the United States." *American Political Science Review* 115(3): 1016–33.

Jæger, Mads Meier. 2006. "Welfare Regimes and Attitudes Towards Redistribution: The Regime Hypothesis Revisited." *European Sociological Review* 22(2): 157–70.

Jaeger, Mads Meier. 2009. "United but Divided: Welfare Regimes and The Level and Variance in Public Support for Redistribution." *European Sociological Review* 25(6): 723–37.

Jann, Ben. 2008. "The Blinder–Oaxaca Decomposition for Linear Regression Models." *The Stata Journal* 8(4): 453–79.

Jensen, Casten. 2012. "Labor Market- Versus Life Course-Related Social Policies: Understanding Cross-Program Differences." *Journal of European Public Policy* 19(2): 275–91.

Jones, Benjamin, and Benjamin Olken. 2005. "Do Leaders Matter? National Leadership and Growth Since World War II." *Quarterly Journal of Economics* 120(3): 835–64.

Joosten, Max. 2022. "Who Influences Whom? Inequality in the Mutual Responsiveness Between Voters and Elites." Unequal Democracies Working Paper no. 35, University of Geneva.

Joshi, Devin K. 2015. "The Inclusion of Excluded Majorities in South Asian Parliaments: Women, Youth, and the Working Class." *Journal of Asian and African Studies* 50(2): 223–38.

Kalla, Joshua L., and David E. Broockman. 2016a. "Campaign Contributions Facilitate Access to Congressional Officials: A Randomized Field Experiment." *American Journal of Political Science* 60(3): 545–58.

Kalla, Joshua L., and David E. Broockman. 2016b. "Congressional Officials Grant Access to Individuals Because They Have Contributed to Campaigns: A Randomized Field Experiment." *American Journal of Political Science* 60: 545–58.

Kallis, Giorgos, and Luis Diaz-Serrano. 2021. "Are Political Leaders with Professional Background in Business Bad for Climate Mitigation?" Unpublished manuscript.

Kam, Cindy D., and Camille D. Burge. 2018. "Uncovering Reactions to the Racial Resentment Scale across the Racial Divide." *Journal of Politics* 80(1): 314–20.

Kasara, Kimuli, and Pavithra Suryanarayan. 2015. "When Do the Rich Vote Less Than the Poor and Why? Explaining Turnout Inequality across the World." *American Journal of Political Science* 59(3): 613–27.

Katznelson, Ira. 2013. *Fear Itself: The New Deal and the Origins of Our Time*. New York: W.W. Norton & Company.

Katznelson, Ira, Kim Geiger, and Daniel Kryder. 1993. "Limiting Liberalism: The Southern Veto in Congress." *Political Science Quarterly* 108(2): 283–306.

Kayser, Mark A., and Michael Peress. 2021. "Does the Media Cover the Economy Accurately? An Analysis of Sixteen Developed Democracies." *Quarterly Journal of Political Science* 16(1): 1–33.

Kayser, Mark A., and Christopher Wlezien. 2011. "Performance Pressure: Patterns of Partisanship and the Economic Vote." *European Journal of Political Research* 50(3): 365–94.

Kelly, Nathan, Jana Morgan, Chris Witko, and Peter Enns. 2019. "Buying Words: How Campaign Donations Influence the Congressional Economic Agenda." Unpublished manuscript.

Kendall, Diana Elizabeth. 2011. *Framing Class: Media Representations of Wealth and Poverty in America*, 2nd ed. Lanham: Rowman & Littlefield.

Kenworthy, Lane. 2009. "The Effect of Public Opinion on Social Policy Generosity." *Socio-Economic Review* 7(4): 727–40.

Kenworthy, Lane, and Leslie McCall. 2007. "Inequality, Public Opinion and Redistribution." *Socio-Economic Review* 6(1): 35–68.

Kenworthy, Lane, and Jonas Pontusson. 2005. "Rising Inequality and the Politics of Redistribution in Affluent Countries." *Perspectives on Politics* 3(3): 449–71.

Kevins, Anthony. 2021. "Race, Class, or Both? Responses to Candidate Characteristics in Canada, the UK, and the US." *Politics, Groups, and Identities* 9(4): 699–720.

Kim, In Song, Jan Stuckatz, and Lukas Wolters. 2020. "Strategic and Sequential Links Between Campaign Donations and Lobbying." MIT Political Science Department Research Paper No. 2021-2.

Kinder, Donald R., and Nathan P. Kalmoe. 2017. *Neither Liberal nor Conservative: Ideological Innocence in the American Public.* Chicago: University of Chicago Press.

Kingdon, John W. 1989. *Congressmen's Voting Decisions*, 3rd ed. Ann Arbor: University of Michigan Press.

Kirkland, Patricia. 2021. "Business Owners and Executives as Politicians: The Effect on Public Policy." *Journal of Politics* 83($): 1652–68.

Kitschelt, Herbert. 1994. *The Transformation of European Social Democracy.* New York: Cambridge University Press.

Kitschelt, Herbert. 2000. "Linkages between Citizens and Politicians in Democratic Polities." *Comparative Political Studies* 33(6): 845–79.

Kitschelt, Herbert, and Philipp Rehm. 2014. "Occupations as a Site of Political Preference Formation." *Comparative Political Studies* 47(12): 1670–706.

Kittilson, Miki Caul, and Leslie Schwindt-Bayer. 2010. "Engaging Citizens: The Role of Power-Sharing Institutions." *Journal of Politics* 72(4): 990–1002.

Kluegel, James R., Csepeli, György, Kolosi, Tamás, Örkény, Antal, and Neményi, Mária. 2011. "Accounting for the Rich and the Poor: Existential Justice in Comparative Perspective." In *Social Justice and Political Change: Public Opinion in Capitalist and Post-Communist States*, eds. James R. Kluegel, David S. Mason and Bernd Wegener, 179–208. New York: De Gruyter.

Knowles, Eric D., Brian S. Lowery, Rosalind M. Chow, and Miguel M. Unzueta. 2014. "Deny, Distance, or Dismantle? How White Americans Manage a Privileged Identity." *Perspectives on Psychological Science* 9(6): 594–604.

Knowles, Sophie. 2018. "Financial Journalists, the Financial Crisis and the 'Crisis' in Journalism." In *The Media and Austerity: Comparative Perspectives*, eds. Laura Basu, Steve Schifferes, and Sophie Knowles, 183–95. London: Routledge.

Knowles, Sophie, Gail Phillips, and Johan Lidberg. 2017. "Reporting the Global Financial Crisis: A Longitudinal Tri-Nation Study of Mainstream Financial Journalism." *Journalism Studies* 18(3): 322–40.

Kolodny, Niko. 2023. *The Pecking Order: Social Hierarchy as a Philosophical Problem.* Cambridge: Harvard University Press.

Kollmeyer, Christopher J. 2004. "Corporate Interests: How the News Media Portray the Economy." *Social Problems* 51(3): 432–52.

Konow, James. 2003. "Which Is the Fairest One of All? A Positive Analysis of Justice Theories." *Journal of Economic Literature* 41(4): 1188–239.

Korpi, Walter. 1983. *The Democratic Class Struggle.* London: Routledge.

Korpi, Walter, and Joakim Palme. 1998. "The Paradox of Redistribution and the Strategy of Equality: Welfare State Institutions, Inequality and Poverty in the Western Countries." *American Sociological Review* 63(5): 661–87.

Korpi, Walter, and Joakim Palme. 2003. "New Politics and Class Politics in the Context of Austerity and Globalization: Welfare State Regress in 18 Countries, 1975–95." *American Political Science Review* 97(3): 425–46.

Kostelka, Filip, André Blais, and Elisabeth Gidengil. 2019. "Has The Gender Gap in Voter Turnout Really Disappeared?" *West European Politics* 42(3): 437–63.

Kriesi, Hanspeter, Edgar Grande, Martin Dolezal, Marc Helbling, Dominic Höglinger, Swen Hutter, and Bruno Wüest. 2012. *Political Conflict in Western Europe*. New York: Cambridge University Press.

Kriesi, Hanspeter, Edgar Grande, Romain Lachat, Martin Dolezal, Siomon Bornschier, and Timotheos Frey. 2006. "Globalization and the Transformation of the National Political Space: Six European Countries Compared." *European Journal of Political Research* 45(6): 921–56.

Krimmel, Katherine, and Kelly Rader. 2021. "Racial Unfairness and Fiscal Politics." *American Politics Research* 49(2): 143–56.

Kurer, Thomas. 2020. "The Declining Middle: Occupational Change, Social Status, and the Populist Right." *Comparative Political Studies* 53(10–11): 1798–835.

Kuziemko, Ilyana, Michael I. Norton, Emmanuel Saez, and Stefanie Stantcheva. 2013. "How Elastic Are Preferences for Redistribution? Evidence from Randomized Survey Experiments." NBER Working Paper 18865.

Kwon, Hyeok Yong, and Jonas Pontusson. 2010. "Globalization, Labour Power and Partisan Politics Revisited." *Socio-Economic Review* 8(2): 251–81.

Lahoti, Rahul, and Soham Sahoo. 2020. "Are Educated Leaders Good for Education? Evidence from India." *Journal of Economic Behavior & Organization* 176: 42–62.

Lamont, Michèle. 2002. *The Dignity of Working Men: Morality and the Boundaries of Race, Class, and Immigration*. Cambridge: Harvard University Press.

Langton, Kenneth P. 1969. *Political Socialization*. New York: Oxford University Press.

Larcinese, Valentino. 2007. "Voting over Redistribution and the Size of the Welfare State: The Role of Turnout." *Political Studies* 55(3): 568–85.

Larcinese, Valentino, Riccardo Puglisi, and James M. Snyder. 2011. "Partisan Bias in Economic News: Evidence on the Agenda-Setting Behavior of U.S. Newspapers." *Journal of Public Economics* 95(9–10): 1178–89.

Lawless, Jennifer L., and Richard L. Fox. 2005. *It Takes a Candidate: Why Women Don't Run for Office*. New York: Cambridge University Press.

Lax, Jeffrey, Justin Phillips, and Adam Zelizer. 2019. "The Party or the Purse? Unequal Representation in the US Senate." *American Political Science Review* 113(4): 917–940.

Lee, Sang Yoon, and Ananth Seshadri. 2019. "On the Intergenerational Transmission of Economic Status." *Journal of Political Economy* 127(2): 855–921.

Lee, David S., Enrico Moretti, and Matthew J. Butler. 2004. "Do Voters Affect or Elect Policies? Evidence from the U. S. House." *Quarterly Journal of Economics* 119(3): 807–59.

Le Galès, Patrick, and Paul Pierson. 2019. "'Superstar Cities' and the generation of durable inequality." *Daedalus* 148(3): 46–72.

Lefkofridi, Zoe, and Elie Michel. 2014. *Exclusive Solidarity? Radical Right Parties and the Welfare State*. Rochester: Social Science Research Network.

Leighley, Jan E., and Jennifer Oser. 2018. "Representation in an Era of Political and Economic Inequality: How and When Citizen Engagement Matters." *Perspectives on Politics* 16(2): 328–44.

Lenz, Gabriel S. 2012. *Follow the Leader? How Voters Respond to Politicians' Policies and Performance*. Chicago: University of Chicago Press.

Levey, Noam M. 2017. "Trump Voters Would Be Among the Biggest Losers in Republicans' Obamacare Replacement Plan." *Los Angeles Times*, March 12.

Levi, Margaret. 1991. *Consent, Dissent, and Patriotism*. New York: Cambridge University Press.

Lewis-Beck, Michael. 1988. *Economics and Elections: The Major Western Democracies*. Ann Arbor: University of Michigan Press.

Lijphart, Arend. 1997. "Unequal Participation: Democracy's Unresolved Dilemma." *American Political Science Review* 91(1): 1–14.

Limberg, Julian. 2020. "What's Fair? Preferences for Tax Progressivity in the Wake of the Financial Crisis." *Journal of Public Policy* 40(2): 171–93.

Lin, Ken-Hou, and Donald Tomaskovic-Devey. 2013. "Financialization and US Income Inequality, 1970–2008." *American Journal of Sociology* 118(5): 1284–329.

Linde, Jonas, and Yvette Peters. 2020. "Responsiveness, Support, and Responsibility: How Democratic Responsiveness Facilitates Responsible Government." *Party Politics* 26(3): 291–304.

Lindert, Peter. 2004. *Growing Public: Social Spending and Economic Growth Since the Eighteenth Century*. New York: Cambridge University Press.

Lloren, Anouk, Jan Rosset, and Reto Wüest. 2015. "Descriptive and Substantive Representation of Poor Citizens in Switzerland." *Swiss Political Science Review* 21(2): 254–60.

Lovenduski, Joni. 2016. "The Supply and Demand Model of Candidate Selection: Some Reflections." *Government and Opposition* 51(3): 513–28.

Lovenduski, Joni, and Pippa Norris. 1994. "Labour and the Unions: After the Brighton Conference." *Government and Opposition* 29(2): 201–17.

Lukes, Steven. 1974. *Power: A Radical View*. London: Macmillan Education UK.

Lupu, Noam, and Jonas Pontusson. 2011. "The Structure of Inequality and the Politics of Redistribution." *American Political Science Review* 105(2): 316–36.

Lupu, Noam, and Alejandro Tirado Castro. 2023. "Unequal Policy Responsiveness in Spain." *Socio-Economic Review*.

Lupu, Noam, and Zach Warner. 2017. "Mass-Elite Congruence and Representation in Argentina." In Alfredo Joignant, Mauricio Morales, and Claudio Fuentes, eds., *Malaise in Representation in Latin American Countries: Chile, Argentina, Uruguay*. New York: Palgrave Macmillan.

Lupu, Noam, and Zach Warner. 2022a. "Affluence and Congruence: Unequal Representation Around the World." *Journal of Politics* 84(1): 276–90.

Lupu, Noam, and Zach Warner. 2022b. "Why Are the Affluent Better Represented around the World?" *European Journal of Political Research* 61(1): 67–85.

Luttmer, Erzo F. P. 2001. "Group Loyalty and the Taste for Redistribution." *Journal of Political Economy* 109(3): 500–28.

Macdonald, David. 2020. "Trust in Government and the American Public's Responsiveness to Rising Inequality." *Political Research Quarterly* 73(4): 790–804.

Mair, Peter. 2013. *Ruling the Void: The Hollowing of Western Democracy*. London: Verso.

Manow, Philip. 2018. *Die Politische Ökonomie des Populismus*. Berlin: Suhrkamp.

Manrique-Vallier, Daniel. 2012. "A Mixed-Membership Approach to the Assessment of Political Ideology from Survey Responses." Unpublished manuscript.

Mansbridge, Jane. 2003. "Rethinking Representation." *American Political Science Review* 97(4): 515–28.

Manwaring, Rob, and Josh Holloway. 2022. "A New Wave of Social Democracy? Policy Change across the Social Democratic Party Family, 1970s–2010s." *Government and Opposition* 57(1): 171–91.

Manza, Jeff, and Clem Brooks. 2008. "Class and Politics." In *Social Class: How Does It Work?*, eds. Annette Lareau and Dalton Conley. New York: Russell Sage Foundation.

Marble, William, and Clayton Nall. 2020. "Where Self-Interest Trumps Ideology: Liberal Homeowners and Local Opposition to Housing Development." *Journal of Politics* 83(4): 1747–63.

Mares, Isabela. 2003. *The Politics of Social Risk: Business and Welfare State Development*. New York: Cambridge University Press.

Margalit, Yotam. 2019. "Economic Insecurity and the Causes of Populism, Reconsidered." *Journal of Economic Perspectives* 33(4): 152–70.

Marquis, Lionel, and Jan Rosset. 2021. "Explanations of Poverty and Demand for Social Policy." Unequal Democracies Working Paper no. 23, University of Geneva.

Martin, Paul S., and Michele P. Claibourn. 2013. "Citizen Participation and Congressional Responsiveness: New Evidence that Participation Matters." *Legislative Studies Quarterly* 38(1): 59–81.

Martinez-Bravo, Monica. 2017. "The Local Political Economy Effects of School Construction in Indonesia." *American Economic Journal: Applied Economics* 9(2): 256–89.

Mathisen, Ruben B. 2023. "Affluence and Influence in a Social Democracy." *American Political Science Review* 117(2): 751–58.

Matsunaga, Masaki. 2010. "How to Factor-Analyze Your Data Right: Dos, Don'ts, and How- To's." *International Journal of Psychological Research* 3(1): 97–110.

Matthews, Austin S., and Yann P. Kerevel. 2022. "The Nomination and Electoral Competitiveness of Working Class Candidates in Germany." *German Politics* 31(3): 459–75.

Matthews, J. Scott. 2019. "Issue Priming Revisited: Susceptible Voters and Detectable Effects." *British Journal of Political Science* 49(2): 513–31.

Mayhew, David R. 1974. *Congress: The Electoral Connection*. New Haven: Yale University Press.

McCall, Leslie, and Lane Kenworthy. 2009. "Americans' Social Policy Preferences in the Era of Rising Inequality." *Perspectives on Politics* 7(3): 459–84.

McCarty, Nolan, Keith T. Poole, and Howard Rosenthal. 2006. *Polarized America*. Cambridge: Massachusetts Institute of Technology Press.

McDonald, Michael D., and Ian Budge. 2005. *Elections, Parties, Democracy*. New York: Oxford University Press.

Meltzer, Allan H, and Scott F. Richard. 1981. "A Rational Theory of Government." *Journal of Political Economy* 89(5): 914–27.

Mendelberg, Tali, Katherine McCabe, and Adam Thal. 2017. "College Socialization and the Economic Views of Affluent Americans." *American Journal of Political Science* 61(3): 606–23.

Mill, John Stuart. 1977[1861]. *The Collected Works of John Stuart Mill*. Edited by John M. Robson. Vol. XIX: Essays on Politics and Society Part II. Considerations on Representative Government. London: Routledge.

Miller, Warren E., and Donald E. Stokes. 1963. "Constituency Influence in Congress." *American Political Science Review* 57(1): 45–56.

Mirrlees, James A., 1971. "An Exploration in the Theory of Optimal Income Taxation." *Review of Economic Studies* 38(2): 175–208.

Mitchell, Amy, Mark Jurkowitz, Baxter J. Oliphant, and Elisa Shearer. 2021. "How Americans Navigated the News in 2020: A Tumultuous Year in Review." Pew Research Center.

Moe, Terry M. 2005. "Power and Political Institutions." *Perspectives on Politics* 3(2): 215–33.

Moene, Karl Ove, and Michael Wallerstein. 2001. "Inequality, Social Insurance, and Redistribution." *American Political Science Review* 95(4): 859–74.

Monroe, Alan D. 1979. "Consistency between Public Preferences and National Policy Decisions." *American Politics Quarterly* 7(1): 3–19.

Moretti, Enrico. 2013. *The New Geography of Jobs*. New York: Mariner Books.

Mudge, Stephanie. 2018. *Leftism Reinvented*. Cambridge: Harvard University Press.

Munger, Michael C., and Melvin J. Hinich. 1994. *Ideology and the Theory of Political Choice*. Ann Arbor: University of Michigan Press.

Muro, Mark, Eli Byerly-Duke, Yang You, and Robert Maxim. 2020. *Biden Voting Counties Equal 70% of America's Economy*. Washington, DC: Brookings.

Mutz, Diana C. 1992. "Mass Media and the Depoliticization of Personal Experience." *American Journal of Political Science* 36(2): 483–508.

Mutz, Diana C. 2018. "Status Threat, Not Economic Hardship, Explains the 2016 Presidential Vote." *Proceedings of the National Academy of Sciences* 115(19): E4330–39.

Müller, Jan-Werner. 2021. *Democracy Rules*. New York: Farrar, Straus and Giroux.

Nadeau, Richard, Richard G. Niemi, and Timothy Amato. 1999. "Elite Economic Forecasts, Economic News, Mass Economic Judgments, and Presidential Approval." *Journal of Politics* 61(1): 109–35.

Nagel, Jack H. 1975. *The Descriptive Analysis of Power*. New Haven: Yale University Press.

Naoi, Megumi. 2020. "Survey Experiments in International Political Economy: What We (Don't) Know About the Backlash Against Globalization." *Annual Review of Political Science* 23: 333–56.

Neundorf, Anja, Kaat Smets, and Gema M. García-Albacete. 2013. "Homemade Citizens: The Development of Political Interest During Adolescence and Young Adulthood." *Acta Politica* 48(1): 92–116.

Newman, Benjamin. 2013. "My Poor Friend: Financial Distress in One's Social Network, the Perceived Power of the Rich, and Support for Redistribution." *Journal of Politics* 76(1): 126–38.

Nielsen Company. *Audio Today 2019: How American Listens.*

Niemanns, Erik. 2023. "Welfare States, Media Ownership and Attitudes towards Redistribution," *European Journal of Public Policy* 30(2): 234–53.

Nolan, Brian, Max Roser, and Stefan Thewissen. 2018. "Median Household Income and GDP." In *Generating Prosperity for Working Families in Affluent Countries*, ed. Brian Nolan. New York: Oxford University Press

Norris, Pippa, and Joni Lovenduski. 1995. *Political Recruitment: Gender, Race and Class in the British Parliament*. New York: Cambridge University Press.

Nyhan, Brendan. 2012. "Does the US Media Have a Liberal Bias?: A Discussion of Tim Groseclose's Left Turn: How Liberal Media Bias Distorts the American Mind." *Perspectives on Politics* 10(3): 767–71.

Oaxaca, Ronald. 1973. Male-Female Wage Differentials in Urban Labor Markets. *International Economic Review* 14(3): 693–709.

OECD. 2011. *Divided We Stand: Why Inequality Keeps Rising.*

Oesch, Daniel. 2006. *Redrawing the Class Map: Stratification and Institutions in Britain, Germany, Sweden and Switzerland.* New York: Palgrave MacMillan.

Oesch, Daniel. 2013. *Occupational Change in Europe: How Technology and Education Transform the Job Structure.* New York: Oxford University Press.

Oesch, Daniel, and Line Rennwald. 2018. "Electoral Competition in Europe's New Tripolar Political Space: Class Voting for the Left, Centre-Right and Radical Right." *European Journal of Political Research* 57(4): 783–807.

Offe, Claus. 2009. "Participatory Inequality in the Austerity State: A Supply-Side Approach." In *Politics in the Age of Austerity*, eds. W. Streeck and A. Schäfer. Wiley Blackwell.

Ogorzalek, Thomas K. 2018. *The Cities on the Hill: How Urban Institutions Transformed National Politics.* New York: Oxford University Press.

O'Grady, Tom. 2019. "Careerists versus Coal-Miners: Welfare Reforms and the Substantive Representation of Social Groups in the British Labour Party." *Comparative Political Studies* 52(4): 544–78.

Olson, Mancur. 1965. *The Logic of Collective Action.* Cambridge: Harvard University Press.

Open Secrets. 2021. "Defense: Summary." www.opensecrets.org/industries/indus .php?ind=D&cycle=All (Accessed September 21, 2021).

Osberg, Lars, and Timothy Smeeding. 2006. "'Fair' Inequality? Attitudes Toward Pay Differentials: The United States in Comparative Perspective." *American Sociological Review* 71(3): 450–73.

Ostrom, Elinor. 1998. "A Behavioral Approach to the Rational Choice Theory of Collective Action: Presidential Address, American Political Science Association, 1997." *American Political Science Review* 92(1): 1–22.

Ostrom, Elinor and James Walker. 2003. *Trust and Reciprocity: Interdisciplinary Lessons for Experimental Research.* New York: Russell Sage Foundation.

Ozymy, Joshua. 2012. "The Poverty of Participation: Self-Interest, Student Loans, and Student Activism." *Political Behavior* 34(1): 103–16.

Pande, Rohini. 2003. "Can Mandated Political Representation Increase Policy Influence for Disadvantaged Minorities? Theory and Evidence from India." *The American Economic Review* 93(4): 1132–51.

Page, Lionel and Daniel Goldstein. 2016. "Subjective Beliefs About the Income Distribution and Preferences for Redistribution." *Social Choice and Welfare* 47(1): 25–61

Page, Benjamin I., and Robert Y. Shapiro. 1992. *The Rational Public: Fifty Years of Trends in Americans' Policy Preferences.* Chicago: Chicago University Press.

Page, Benjamin I., Larry M. Bartels, and Jason Seawright. 2013. "Democracy and the Policy Preferences of Wealthy Americans." *Perspectives on Politics* 11(1): 51–73.

Page, Benjamin I., Jason Seawright, and Matthew J. Lacombe. 2019. *Billionaires and Stealth Politics.* Chicago: University of Chicago Press.

Park, Alison, Elizabeth Clery, John Curtice, Miranda Phillips, and David Utting. 2012. *British Social Attitudes 29.* London: NatCen Social Research.

Parker, Jonathan, and Annette Vissing-Jorgensen. 2010. "The Increase in Income Cyclicality of High-Income Households and Its Relation to the Rise in Top Income Shares." NBER Working Paper 16577.

Pavolini, Emmanuele, and Wim Van Lancker. 2018. "The Matthew Effect in Childcare Use: A Matter of Policies or Preferences?" *Journal of European Public Policy* 25(6): 878–93.

Pearl, Judea. 2001. "Direct and Indirect Effects." Proceedings of the Seventeenth Conference on Uncertainty in Artificial Intelligence, San Francisco, CA: 411–20.

Pearl, Judea. 2009. *Causality*. New York: Cambridge University Press.

Pereira, Miguel. 2021. "Understanding and Reducing Biases in Elite Beliefs about the Electorate." *American Political Science Review* 115(4): 1308–24.

Persson, Mikael. 2021. "From Opinion to Policy: Links between Citizens, Representatives and Policy Change." *Electoral Studies* 74.

Persson, Mikael. 2023. "Who Got What They Wanted? Investigating the Role of Institutional Agenda Setting, Costly Policies, and Status Quo Bias as Explanations to Income Based Unequal Responsiveness." *Journal of European Public Policy*.

Peters, Yvette, and Sander J. Ensink. 2015. "Differential Responsiveness in Europe: The Effects of Preference Difference and Electoral Participation." *West European Politics* 38(3): 577–600.

Petersen, Michael Bang. 2012. "Social Welfare as Small-Scale Help: Evolutionary Psychology and the Deservingness Heuristic." *American Journal of Political Science* 56(1):1–16.

Petersen, Michael Bang, Daniel Sznycer, Leda Cosmides, and John Tooby. 2012. "Who Deserves Help? Evolutionary Psychology, Social Emotions, and Public Opinion About Welfare." *Political Psychology* 33(3): 395–418.

Petrova, Maria. 2008. "Inequality and Media Capture." *Journal of Public Economics* 92(1–2): 183–212.

Pettersson-Lidbom, Per. 2008. "Do Parties Matter for Economic Outcomes? A Regression-Discontinuity Approach." *Journal of the European Economic Association* 6(5): 1037–56.

Pierson, Paul. 1993. "When Effect Becomes Cause: Policy Feedback and Political Change." *World Politics* 45(4): 595–628.

Pierson, Paul. 1996. "The New Politics of the Welfare State." *World Politics* 48(2): 143–79.

Pierson, Paul. 2000. "Increasing Returns, Path Dependence, and the Study of Politics." *American Political Science Review* 94(2): 254–67.

Pierson, Paul. 2016. "Power in Historical Institutionalism." In *The Oxford Handbook of Historical Institutionalism*, eds. Orfeo Fioretos, Tulia Faletti, and Adam Sheingate, 124–41. New York: Oxford University Press.

Pierson, Paul, and Eric Schickler. 2020. "Madison's Constitution Under Stress: A Developmental Analysis of Political Polarization." *Annual Review of Political Science* 23: 37–58.

Piketty, Thomas. 2014. *Capital in the Twenty-First Century*. Cambridge: Harvard University Press.

Piketty, Thomas, and Emmanuel Saez. 2014. "Inequality in the Long Run." *Science* 344(6186): 838–43.

Piketty, Thomas, Emmanuel Saez, and Gabriel Zucman. 2018. "Distributional National Accounts: Methods and Estimates for the United States." *Quarterly Journal of Economics* 133(2): 553–609.

Pilotti, Andrea. 2015. "The Historical Changes and Continuities of Swiss Parliamentary Recruitment." *Swiss Political Science Review* 21(2): 246–53.

Pinggera, Michael. 2021. "Congruent with Whom? Parties' Issue Emphases and Voter Preferences in Welfare Politics." *Journal of European Public Policy* 28(12): 1973–92.

Pipa, Tony, and Natalie Geismar. 2020. *Reimagining Rural Policy: Organizing Federal Assistance to Maximize Rural Prosperity*. Washington, DC: Brookings.

Pitkin, Hanna Fenichel. 1967. *The Concept of Representation*. Berkeley: University of California Press.

Pitkin, Hanna Fenichel. 1969. "The Concept of Representation." In *Representation*, ed. Hanna Pitkin, pp. 1–23. New York: Atherton.

Pontusson, Jonas. 2005. *Inequality and Prosperity: Social Europe vs. Liberal America*. Ithaca: Cornell University Press.

Pontusson, Jonas. 2015. "Introduction to the Debate: Does Descriptive Misrepresentation by Income and Class Matter?" *Swiss Political Science Review* 21(2): 207–12.

Pontusson, Jonas, and David Weisstanner. 2018. "Macroeconomic Conditions, Inequality Shocks and the Politics of Redistribution, 1990–2013." *Journal of European Public Policy* 25(1): 31–58.

Poterba, James M. 1997. "Demographic Structure and the Political Economy of Public Education." *Journal of Policy Analysis and Management* 16(1): 48–66.

Powell, G. Bingham, Jr. 2019. *Ideological Representation Achieved and Astray: Elections, Institutions, and the Breakdown of Ideological Congruence in Parliamentary Democracies*. New York: Cambridge University Press.

Powell, Richard J., Jesse T. Clark, and Matthew P. Dube. 2020. "Partisan Gerrymandering, Clustering, or Both? A New Approach to a Persistent Question." *Election Law Journal* 19(1): 79–100.

Przeworski, Adam, and John Sprague. 1988. *Paper Stones: A History of Electoral Socialism*. Chicago: University of Chicago Press.

Quiggin, John. 2012. *Zombie Economics*. Princeton: Princeton University Press.

Rahman, K. Sabeel, and Kathleen Thelen. 2019. "The Rise of the Platform Business Model and the Transformation of Twenty-First-Century Capitalism." *Politics and Society* 47(2): 177–204.

Ram, Rati. 2021. "Income Convergence across the U.S. States: Further Evidence from New Recent Data." *Journal of Economics and Finance* 45(2): 372–80.

Rehfeld, Andrew. 2009. "Representation Rethought: On Trustees, Delegates, and Gyroscopes in the Study of Political Representation and Democracy." *American Political Science Review* 103(2): 214–30.

Rehm, Philipp. 2009. "Risks and Redistribution an Individual-level Analysis." *Comparative Political Studies* 42(7): 855–81.

Rehm, Philipp. 2011. "Social Policy by Popular Demand." *World Politics* 63(2): 271–99.

Rehm, Philipp. 2016. *Risk Inequality and Welfare States*. New York: Cambridge University Press.

Rennwald, Line, and Jonas Pontusson. 2021. "Social Class, Union Power and Perceptions of Political Voice: Liberal Democracies, 1974–2016." Unequal Democracies Working Paper 22, University of Geneva.

Rennwald, Line, and Jonas Pontusson. 2022. "Class Gaps in Perceptions of Political Voice: Liberal Democracies 1974–2016." *West European Politics* 45(6): 1334–60.

Rhodes, Jesse H., and Brian F. Schaffner. 2017. "Testing Models of Unequal Representation: Democratic Populists and Republican Oligarchs?" *Quarterly Journal of Political Science* 12(2): 185–204.

Rigby, Elizabeth, and Gerald C. Wright. 2011. "Whose Statehouse Democracy? Policy Responsiveness to Poor versus Rich Constituents in Poor versus Rich States." In *Who Gets Represented?*, eds. Peter Enns and Christopher Wlezien, 189–222. New York: Russell Sage Foundation.

Rigby, Elizabeth, and Gerald C. Wright. 2013. "Political Parties and Representation of the Poor in the American States." *American Journal of Political Science* 57(3): 552–65.

Rodden, Jonathan A. 2019. *Why Cities Lose: The Deep Roots of The Urban-Rural Political Divide*. New York: Basic Books.

Rodrik, Dani. 1997. *Has Globalization Gone Too Far?* Washington, DC: Institute for International Economics.

Rodrik, Dani. 2011. *The Globalization Paradox: Democracy and the Future of the World Economy*. New York: W.W. Norton & Company.

Rodrik, Dani. 2018. "Populism and The Economics of Globalization." *Journal of International Business Policy* 1(1): 12–33.

Rogowski, Ronald, and Mark Andreas Kayser. 2002. "Majoritarian Electoral Systems and Consumer Power: Price-Level Evidence from the OECD Countries." *American Journal of Political Science* 46(3): 526–39.

Rokkan, Stein. 1966. "Norway: Numerical Democracy and Corporate Pluralism." In *Political Oppositions in Western Democracies*, ed. Robert Dahl, 70–116. New Haven: Yale University Press.

Rooduijn, Matthijs, and Brian Burgoon. 2017. "The Paradox of Well-Being: Do Unfavorable Socioeconomic and Sociocultural Contexts Deepen or Dampen Radical Left and Right Voting among the Less Well-Off?" *Comparative Political Studies* 51(13): 1720–53.

Rosenwald, Brian. 2019. *Talk Radio's America: How an Industry Took over a Political Party That Took Over the United States*. Cambridge: Harvard University Press.

Rosset, Jan, and Anna Spohie Kurella. 2021. "The Electoral Roots of Unequal Representation: A Spatial Modelling Approach to Party Systems and Voting in Western Europe." *European Journal of Political Research* 60(4): 785–806.

Rosset, Jan, and Christian Stecker. 2019. "How Well Are Citizens Represented by their Governments? Issue Congruence and Inequality in Europe." *European Political Science Review* 11(2): 145–60.

Rosset, Jan, Nathalie Giger, and Julian Bernauer. 2013. "More Money, Fewer Problems? Cross-Level Effects of Economic Deprivation on Political Representation." *West European Politics* 36(4): 817–35.

Rosset, Jan, Jonas Pontusson, and Jérémie Poltier. 2023. "Redistributive Policy Preferences and Government Responsiveness in a Dynamic Perspective: Western Europe 2008–19." Unequal Democracies Working Paper No. 41. University of Geneva.

Roth, Christopher, Sonja Settele, and Johannes Wohlfart. 2020. "Risk Exposure and Acquisition of Macroeconomic Information." Unpublished manuscript.

Roth, Christopher, Sonja Settele, and Johannes Wohlfahrt. 2022. "Risk Exposure and Acquisition of Macroeconomic Information." *American Economic Review: Insights* 4(1): 34–53.

Rothman, Stanley, and S. Robert Lichter. 1985. "Personality, Ideology and World View: A Comparison of Media and Business Elites." *British Journal of Political Science* 15(1): 29–49.

Rothstein, Bo. 1998. *Just Institutions Matter: The Moral and Political Logic of the Universal Welfare State*. New York: Cambridge University Press.

Rueda, David. 2005. "Insider-Outsider Politics in Industrialized Democracies: The Challenge to Social Democratic Parties." *American Political Science Review* 99(1): 61–74.

Rueda, David. 2007. *Social Democracy Inside Out*. New York: Oxford University Press.

Rueda, David, and Daniel Stegmueller. 2019. *Who Wants What?: Redistribution Preferences in Comparative Perspective*. New York: Cambridge University Press.

Rugman, Alan. 2012. *The End of Globalization*. New York: Random House.

Rydgren, Jens. 2007. "The Sociology of the Radical Right." *Annual Review of Sociology* 33: 241–62.

Sabl, Andrew. 2015. "The Two Cultures of Democratic Theory: Responsiveness, Democratic Quality, and the Empirical-Normative Divide." *Perspectives on Politics* 13(2): 345–65.

Sadin, Meredith. 2012. "Campaigning with Class: The Effect of Social Class on Voter Evaluations." Unpublished manuscript.

Saez, Emmanuel, Joel Slemrod, and Seth H. Giertz. 2012. "The Elasticity of Taxable Income with Respect to Marginal Tax Rates: A Critical Review." *Journal of Economic Literature* 50(1): 3–50.

Saint-Paul, Gilles. 1999. "Toward a Theory of Labor Market Institutions." UPF Economics and Business Working Paper 433.

Sanders, Elizabeth. 1999. *Roots of Reform: Farmers, Workers, and the American State, 1877–1917*. Chicago: University of Chicago Press.

Schakel, Wouter. 2021. "Unequal Policy Responsiveness in the Netherlands." *Socio-Economic Review* 19(1): 37–57.

Schakel, Wouter, and Brian Burgoon. 2022. "The Party Road to Representation: Unequal Responsiveness in Party Platforms." *European Journal of Political Research* 61(2): 304–25.

Schakel, Wouter, and Daphne Van Der Pas. 2021. "Degrees of influence: Educational Inequality in Policy Representation." *European Journal of Political Research* 60(2): 418–37.

Schakel, Wouter, Brian Burgoon, and Armen Hakverdian. 2020. "Real but Unequal Representation in Welfare State Reform." *Politics and Society* 48(1): 131–63.

Schattschneider, E. E. 1960. *The Semisovereign People*. New York: Holt, Rinhart and Winston.

Scheve, Kenneth, and David Stasavage. 2016. *Taxing the Rich: A History of Fiscal Fairness in the United States and Europe*. Princeton: Princeton University Press.

Schickler, Eric. 2016. *Racial Realignment: The Transformation of American Liberalism, 1932–1965*. Princeton: Princeton University Press.

Schifferes, Steve, and Sophie Knowles. 2018. "The UK News Media and Austerity." In *The Media and Austerity: Comparative Perspectives*, eds. Laura Basu, Steve Schifferes, and Sophie Knowles, 15–29. London: Routledge.

Schlozman, Kay Lehman, Sidney Verba, and Henry E. Brady. 2012. *The Unheavenly Chorus: Unequal Political Voice and the Broken Promise of American Democracy*. Princeton, NJ: Princeton University Press.

Scholars for Reform. 2021. "Open Letter on the History, Impact, and Future of the Filibuster." May 4.

Schröder, Martin, and Florian Vietze. 2015. "Mediendebatten Über Soziale Ungleichheit, Armut Und Soziale Gerechtigkeit Seit 1946 Und Wie Sie Mit Einkommensungleichheit Zusammenhängen/Media Debates about Social Inequality, Poverty and Social Justice since 1946 and How They Are Connected to Income." *Zeitschrift für Soziologie* 44(1): 42–62.

Schwindt-Bayer, Leslie A., and William Mishler. 2005. "An Integrated Model of Women's Representation." *Journal of Politics* 67(2): 407–28.

Seelkopf, Laura and Hanna Lierse. 2016. "Taxation and Inequality: How Tax Competition Has Changed the Redistributive Capacity of Nation States in the OECD." In *Welfare State Transformations and Inequality in OECD Countries*, eds. Melike Wulfgramm, Tonia Bieber and Stephan Leibfried, 89–109. London: Palgrave Macmillan.

Sevenans, Julie, Awenig Marié, Karolin Soontjens, Stefaan Walgrave, Christian Breunig, and Rens Vliegenthart. 2020. "Inequality in Politicians' Perceptions of Public Opinion." Unpublished manuscript.

Sides, John, Michael Tesler, and Lynn Vavreck. 2018. *Identity Crisis: The 2016 Presidential Campaign and the Battle for the Meaning of America*. Princeton, NJ: Princeton University Press.

Simon, Herbert A. 1953. "Notes on the Observation and Measurement of Political Power." *Journal of Politics* 15(4): 500–16.

Skitka, Linda J., and Philip E. Tetlock. 1993. "Providing Public Assistance: Cognitive and Motivational Processes Underlying Liberal and Conservative Policy Preferences." *Journal of Personality and Social Psychology* 65(6):1205.

Smets, Kaat, and Carolien van Ham. 2013. "The Embarrassment of Riches? A Meta-Analysis of Individual-Level Research on Voter Turnout." *Electoral Studies* 32(2): 344–359.

Sojourner, Aaron. 2013. "Do Unions Promote Electoral Office Holding? Evidence from Correlates of State Legislatures' Occupational Shares." *Industrial & Labor Relations Review* 66(2): 467–86.

Solt, Frederick. 2008. "Economic Inequality and Democratic Political Engagement." *American Journal of Political Science* 52(1): 48–60.

Soroka, Stuart N. 2006. "Good News and Bad News: Asymmetric Responses to Economic Information." *Journal of Politics* 68(2): 372–85.

Soroka, Stuart N. 2012. "The Gatekeeping Function: Distributions of Information in Media and the Real World." *Journal of Politics* 74(2): 514–28.

Soroka, Stuart N., and Christopher Wlezien. 2008. "On the Limits to Inequality in Representation." *PS: Political Science & Politics* 41(2): 319–27.

Soroka, Stuart N., and Christopher Wlezien. 2010. *Degrees of Democracy: Politics, Public Opinion, and Policy*. New York: Cambridge University Press.

Soroka, Stuart N., Dominik A. Stecula, and Christopher Wlezien. 2015. "It's (Change in) the (Future) Economy, Stupid: Economic Indicators, the Media, and Public Opinion. Supplementary Information." *American Journal of Political Science* 59(2): 457–74.

Soskice, David. 2022. "The United States as Radical Innovation Driver: The Politics of Declining Dominance?" In *The American Political Economy: Politics, Markets, and Power*, eds. S. Hacker Jacob, Alexander Hertel-Fernandez, Paul Pierson, and Kathleen Thelen. New York: Cambridge University Press.

Soss, Joe, and Sanford E. Schram. 2007. "A Public Transformed? Welfare Reform as Policy Feedback." *American Political Science Review* 101(1): 111–27.

Stacy, Darrian. 2021. "Wealth and Political Inequality in the U.S. Congress." Ph.D. Dissertation, Vanderbilt University.

Stepan, Alfred, and Juan J. Linz. 2011. "Comparative Perspectives on Inequality and the Quality of Democracy in the United States." *Perspectives on Politics* 9(4): 841–56.

Storper, Michael. 1997. *The Regional World: Territorial Development in a Global Economy*. New York: Guilford Press.

Storper, Michael. 2013. *Keys to the City: How Economics, Institutions, Social Interaction, and Politics Shape Development*. Princeton: Princeton University Press.

Streeck, Wolfgang. 2011. "The Crisis of Democratic Capitalism." *New Left Review* 71: 5–29.

Streeck, Wolfgang. 2016. *How Will Capitalism End? Essays on a Failing System*. London: Verso.

Svallfors, Stefan. 2012. "Welfare Attitudes in Context." In *Contested Welfare States: Welfare Attitudes in Europe and Beyond*, ed. Stefan Svallfors, 222–40. Stanford: Stanford University Press.

Svallfors, Stefan. 2016. "Who Loves the Swedish Welfare State? Attitude Trends 1980–2010." In *The Oxford Handbook of Swedish Politics*, ed. Jon Pierre, 22–36. New York: Oxford University Press.

Swank, Duane. 2016. "Taxing Choices: International Competition, Domestic Institutions and the Transformation of Corporate Tax Policy." *Journal of European Public Policy* 23(4): 571–603.

Swenson, Peter. 2002. *Capitalists Against Markets*. New York: Oxford University Press.

Swers, Michele L. 2005. "Connecting Descriptive and Substantive Representation: An Analysis of Sex Differences in Cosponsorship Activity." *Legislative Studies Quarterly* 30(3): 407–33.

Szakonyi, David. 2021. "Private Sector Policy Making: Business Background and Politicians' Behavior in Office." *Journal of Politics* 83(1): 260–76.

Sznycer, Daniel, Maria Florencia Lopez Seal, Aaron Sell, Julian Lim, Roni Porat, Shaul Shalvi, Eran Halperin, Leda Cosmides, and John Tooby. 2017. "Support for Redistribution Is Shaped by Compassion, Envy, and Self-Interest, but Not a Taste for Fairness." *Proceedings of the National Academy of Sciences* 114(31): 8420–25.

Tarditi, Valeria, and Davide Vittori. 2021. "We Are Different': Do Anti-Establishment Parties Promote Distinctive Elites? An Analysis of the Spanish Case." *Representation* 57(1): 21–39.

Tesler, Michael. 2015. "Priming Predispositions and Changing Policy Positions: An Account of When Mass Opinion Is Primed or Changed." *American Journal of Political Science* 59(4): 806–24.

Tesler, Michael. 2016. *Post-Racial or Most-Racial? Race and Politics in the Obama Era*. Chicago: University of Chicago Press.

The New Map of Economic Growth and Recovery. 2016. Economic Innovation Group. https://eig.org/wp-content/uploads/2016/05/recoverygrowthreport.pdf.

Thewissen, Stefan. 2014. "Is It the Income Distribution or Redistribution That Affects Growth?" *Socio-Economic Review* 12(3): 545–71.

Thomas, Richard. 2018. "The Economic Recovery on TV News." In *The Media and Austerity: Comparative Perspectives*, eds. Laura Basu, Steve Schifferes, and Sophie Knowles, 63–79. London: Routledge.

Thomsen, Danielle M. 2017. *Opting Out of Congress: Partisan Polarization and the Decline of Moderate Candidates*. New York: Cambridge University Press.

Thomsen, Danielle M. 2019. "Book Review: The Cash Ceiling." *Perspectives on Politics* 17(2): 576–7.

Tingley, Dustin, Teppei Yamamoto, Kentaro Hirose, Luke Keele, and Kosuke Imai. 2014. "Mediation: R Package for Causal Mediation Analysis." *Journal of Statistical Software* 59(5): 1–38.

Tomasello, Michael. 2016. *A Natural History of Human Morality*. Cambridge: Harvard University Press.

Traber, Denise, Miriam Hänni, Nathalie Giger, and Christian Breunig. 2022. "Social Status, Political Priorities and Unequal Representation." *European Journal of Political Research* 61(2): 351–73.

Trounstine, Jessica. 2018. *Segregation by Design: Local Politics and Inequality in American Cities*. New York: Cambridge University Press.

Trump, Kris-Stella, and Ariel White. 2018. "Does Inequality Beget Inequality? Experimental Tests of the Prediction that Inequality Increases System Justification Motivation." *Journal of Experimental Political Science* 5(3): 206–16.

Tullock, Gordon. 1980. "Efficient Rent Seeking." In *Toward a Theory of the Rent-Seeking Society*, eds. James M. Buchanan, Robert D. Tollison, and Gordon Tullock, 97–112. College Station: Texas A&M University Press.

Verba, Sidney, and Norman H. Nie. 1972. *Participation in America: Political Democracy and Social Equality*. Chicago: University of Chicago Press.

Verba, Sidney, Norman H. Nie, and Jae-o Kim. 1978. *Participation and Political Equality: A Seven-Nation Comparison*. New York: Cambridge University Press.

Verba, Sidney, Kay Lehman Schlozman, and Henry E. Brady. 1995. *Voice and Equality: Civic Voluntarism in American Politics*. Cambridge: Harvard University Press.

Verbist, Gerlinde, Michael F. Förster, and Maria Vaalavuo. 2012. "The Impact of Publicly Provided Services on the Distribution of Resources: Review of New Results and Methods." OECD Social, Employment and Migration Working Papers No. 130.

Vivyan, Nick, Markus Wagner, Konstantin Glinitzer, and Jakob-Moritz Eberl. 2020. "Do Humble Beginnings Help? How Politician Class Roots Shape Voter Evaluations." *Electoral Studies* 63.

Vogel, Steven K. 2018. *Marketcraft: How Governments Make Markets Work*. New York: Oxford University Press.

Volkens, Andrea, Tobias Burst, Werner Krause, Pola Lehmann, Theres Matthieß, Nicolas Merz, Sven Regel, Bernhard Weßels, and Lisa Zehnter. 2020. The Manifesto Project. Version 2020b. Berlin: Wissenschaftszentrum Berlin für Sozialforschung (WZB). https://doi.org/10.25522/manifesto.mpds.2020b (Accessed May 3, 2021).

Volscho, Thomas W., and Nathan J. Kelly. 2012. "The Rise of the Super-Rich: Power Resources, Taxes, Financial Markets, and the Dynamics of the Top 1 Percent, 1949 to 2008." *American Sociological Review* 77(5): 679–99.

Wagner, Manuel. 2021. "Unequal Responsiveness and Direct Democracy: The Case of Switzerland." University of Geneva: Unequal Democracies Working Paper No. 26

Walzer, Michael. 1983. *Spheres of Justice: A Defense of Pluralism and Equality*. New York: Basic Books.

Warburton, Eve, Burhanuddin Muhtadi, Edward Aspinall, and Diego Fossati. 2021. "When Does Class Matter? Unequal Representation in Indonesian Legislatures." *Third World Quarterly* 42(6): 1252–75.

Weaver, David H., Lars Willnat, and G. Cleveland Wilhoit. 2019. "The American Journalist in the Digital Age: Another Look at U.S. News People." *Journalism and Mass Communication Quarterly* 96(1): 101–30.

Weber, Till. 2020. "Discreet Inequality: How Party Agendas Embrace Privileged Interests." *Comparative Political Studies* 53(10–11): 1767–97.

Weir, Margaret, Harold Wolman, and Todd Swanstrom. 2005. "The Calculus of Coalitions: Cities, Suburbs, and the Metropolitan Agenda." *Urban Affairs Review* 40(6): 730–60.

Weissberg, Robert. 1978. "Collective vs. Dyadic Representation in Congress." *American Political Science Review* 72(2): 535–547.

Whitely, Paul F., and Patrick Seyd. 1996. "Rationality and Party Activism: Encompassing Tests of Alternative Models of Political Participation." *European Journal of Political Research* 29(2): 215–34.

Wilensky, Harold L. 1975. *The Welfare State and Equality*. Berkeley: University of California Press.

Wilensky, Harold L., Gregory M. Luebbert, Susan Reed Hahn, and Adrienne M. Jamieson. 1985. *Comparative Social Policy: Theories, Methods, Findings*. Vol. 62.

Williamson, Scott, Claire L. Adida, Adeline Lo, Melina R. Platas, Lauren Prather, and Seth H. Werfel. 2021. "Family Matters: How Immigrant Histories Can Promote Inclusion." *American Political Science Review*: 115(2): 686–93.

Winship, Christopher, and Bruce Western. 2016. "Multicollinearity and Model Misspecification." *Sociological Science* 3: 627–49.

Witko, Christopher, Jana Morgan, Nathan Kelly, and Peter Enns. 2021. *Hijacking the Agenda: Economic Power and Political Influence*. New York: Russell Sage Foundation.

Wlezien, Christopher. 2017. "Public Opinion and Policy Representation: On Conceptualization, Measurement, and Interpretation." *Policy Studies Journal* 45(4): 561–82.

Wlezien, Christopher, and Stuart N. Soroka. 2011. "Inequality in Policy Responsiveness?" In *Who Gets Represented?*, eds. Peter K. Enns and Christopher Wlezien, 285–310. New York: Russell Sage Foundation.

Wren-Lewis, S. 2018. "'Mediamacro': Why the News Media Ignores Economic Experts." In *The Media and Austerity Comparative Perspectives*, eds. Laura Basu, Steve Schifferes, and Sophie Knowles, 170–82. London: Routledge.

Wüest, Reto, and Jonas Pontusson. 2018. "Descriptive Misrepresentation by Social Class: Do Voter Preferences Matter?" Unpublished manuscript.

Young, Kevin A., Tarun Banerjee, and Michael Schwartz. 2018. "Capital Strikes as a Corporate Political Strategy: The Structural Power of Business in the Obama Era." *Politics & Society* 46(1): 3–28.

Zechmeister, Elizabeth. 2006. "What's Left and Who's Right? A Q-method Study of Individual and Contextual Influences on the Meaning of Ideological Labels." *Political Behavior* 28(2): 151–73.

Index

Printed in the USA
CPSIA information can be obtained
at www.ICGtesting.com
LVHW020715181223
766606LV00008B/788

9 781009 428644